EVERYDAY DEMOCRACY

Everyday Democracy

CIVIL SOCIETY, YOUTH, AND THE STRUGGLE AGAINST
AUTHORITARIAN CULTURE IN CHINA

Anthony J. Spires

Columbia University Press
New York

Columbia University Press
Publishers Since 1893
New York   Chichester, West Sussex
cup.columbia.edu

Library of Congress Cataloging-in-Publication Data
Names: Spires, Anthony J., 1970– author.
Title: Everyday democracy : civil society, youth, and the struggle against
authoritarian culture in China / Anthony J. Spires.
Description: New York : Columbia University Press, 2024. |
Includes bibliographical references and index.
Identifiers: LCCN 2024020927 | ISBN 9780231211505 (hardback) |
ISBN 9780231211512 (trade paperback) | ISBN 9780231558945 (ebook)
Subjects: LCSH: Civil society—China. | Youth—Political activity—China. |
Authoritarianism—China. | Democratization—China. | Social
institutions—Political aspects—China. | Organizational
behavior—Political aspects—China. | Political culture—China.
Classification: LCC JQ1516 .S866 2024 | DDC 306.20951—dc23/eng/20240807
LC record available at https://lccn.loc.gov/2024020927

Cover design: Noah Arlow
Cover image: Shutterstock

CONTENTS

Acknowledgments   vii

PART I
OVERVIEW AND BACKGROUND

Introduction   3

Chapter One
Democracy in China: A Century of Debate   16

PART II
THE AUTHORITARIAN STATUS QUO

Chapter Two
Civil Society Under Hegemonic Authoritarianism   31

Chapter Three
Struggling to Come Together as Equals   64

PART III
YOUTH-LED VOLUNTARY ASSOCIATIONS AS CRUCIBLES
OF A DEMOCRATIC COUNTERHEGEMONY

Chapter Four
Rejecting Formalism: Alternative Narratives of Volunteering   95

Chapter Five
Equality as Culture and Practice   114

Chapter Six
Handling Differences of Opinion and Building Consensus   130

Chapter Seven
Nurturing the Skills and Habits of Democracy   153

Chapter Eight
(S)Electing Leaders   188

Chapter Nine
Selecting Newcomers and Screening for Common Values   217

PART IV
CONCLUSION AND IMPLICATIONS

Conclusion
Implications for Democratic Development in China and Beyond   233

APPENDIX: SOME REFLECTIONS ON FIELDWORK,
RE-PRESENTATION, AND ETHICS   251

NOTES   261

REFERENCES   283

INDEX   297

ACKNOWLEDGMENTS

A book almost two decades in the making owes a debt of gratitude to many people. I first thank the civil society participants in China whose trust and openness with me were foundational to my efforts here. I hope one day I can acknowledge them more openly and convey the depth of gratitude I feel for their generosity.

The writing of this book began as a chapter in my doctoral dissertation at Yale University. I thank my adviser, Deborah Davis, for her patient guidance and encouragement throughout my ten years at Yale and beyond.

This research was funded in part by a South China Program Research Grant from the Hong Kong Institute of Asia-Pacific Studies at the Chinese University of Hong Kong. Over the years, some of the book's main ideas were presented at workshops, meetings, and invited talks at the American Sociological Association, Rennes 2 University, Hong Kong University, L'École des hautes études en sciences sociales (EHESS), the Public Intellectuals Program of the National Committee on U.S.-China Relations, the Indiana University East Asian Studies Center, the University of California–Santa Barbara, the International Society for Third-Sector Research Asia Pacific 2019 Conference, and the Ruhr University Bochum. The feedback I received from colleagues and friends at these events was invaluable, helping to shape the final work and clarify my ideas.

I benefited tremendously from a month-long academic writing residency hosted by the Rockefeller Foundation's Bellagio Center on the shores of Lake

Como, Italy. It was during this period in 2013 that I was first able to sit down and begin to process the sheer volume of data I had collected to that point. The collegiality of my fellow residents during that month was unparalleled, and I remain grateful for the convivial conversations, questions, and feedback on my work during our time together. I completed the full manuscript for this book on the shores of Taiwan's Sun-Moon Lake, listening to the cicadas singing their summer song and drinking the finest teas in the world. I am grateful to my Taiwanese in-laws for so graciously looking after me and my family during those final weeks of writing.

I thank Kai Erikson, Ron Eyerman, John Nguyet Erni, Ling-Yun Tang, Kin-man Chan, Eli Friedman, and my colleagues at the Chinese University of Hong Kong's Center for Civil Society Studies and its later incarnation, the Center for Social Innovation Studies. The encouragement and interest from Markiana Chau, my former student, colleague, and (still) friend kept me energized and optimistic even when the weight of the work ahead seemed overwhelming. Philippe Schmitter, Matthew Baggetta, Ann Swidler, Ming-Chi Chen, Chris Rhomberg, Bin Xu, Rachel Stern, Weijun Lai, Tom Gold, and several anonymous reviewers for Columbia University Press gave generously of their time as well as insightful comments and constructive questions on various articulations of the arguments that appear in this book. I remain humbled that Eric Schwartz, at Columbia University Press, approached me with interest in the manuscript, and I am grateful for the excellent guidance and advice he offered throughout the publication process. All mistakes and errors are obviously my own.

I thank my partner, Reiser Yu, for his endurance of this work over the years, and his indulgence of my random excited outbursts about new thoughts or connections I frequently made when working through my data. And, finally, I thank our child Riley, whose toddlerhood was punctuated by my periodic disappearances as I hid myself away somewhere quiet to finish this book. I hope that one day you'll appreciate and understand what I was doing, and why.

PART I

Overview and Background

INTRODUCTION

Within a society where virtually all major social institutions—from schools to workplaces to government—are stitched together with the heavy threads of authoritarian rule, can civil society associations still be expected to serve as large free schools of democracy?

In daily life, few people in China, as perhaps in most strong authoritarian states, have the opportunity to experience anything approaching democratic organizational culture. The educational, political, and business institutions that envelop and shape people's lives are typically hierarchical and often autocratic, with one "leader" above others at each level of administration. Top-down norms permeate most organizational settings in such a context, and even grassroots nongovernmental organizations (NGOs) founded by people who advocate for democratic political reforms are not immune to the entrenched assumptions and practices of authoritarianism. Although hierarchy, of course, is not unique to China, China today has few of the bottom-up voluntary associations, religious congregations, self-help groups, community sports leagues, and other relatively egalitarian organizational forms that can counterbalance hierarchical tendencies and that are commonplace features of broader social life in democratic societies.

Many previous studies of civil society in authoritarian regimes have focused on the relationship between the state and civil society organizations, asking how civil society might press the state for change or form an effective opposition or revolutionary force. Although these are clearly important questions, in this book I shift the scholarly lens to look at the ways authoritarianism shapes the possibilities for democratic culture to emerge and develop. I trace how participants in Chinese civil society groups struggle to articulate and pursue an alternative social vision despite the political sensitivities and risks that often surround their activities. For some, this vision is inchoate and seemingly just beyond their grasp. Others have a much sharper view of what they are doing and what they aim to achieve. Regardless of where they fall on this spectrum, civil society participants across a range of organizational forms share common democratic yearnings and face the same daunting obstacles in their efforts to push back against the authoritarian norms and practices of mainstream society.

A great deal of the interest in Chinese civil society over the past thirty years has been premised on the idea that extraparty associations may usher in a new era of democracy in China. Inspired by the revolutions in Eastern and Central Europe of the 1980s and 1990s and the role civil society groups played there, scholars have sought to discover what a nascent civil society might mean for a rapidly changing China. Beginning in the 1990s, an initial focus on government-organized nongovernmental organizations (GONGOs) has given way in recent years to research on relatively independent NGOs, with an eye toward understanding these groups' relationships with the Chinese state.[1] The generally shared motivation behind this wave of research is quite straightforward: new groups of people coming together around common interests may be able to influence government officials and government policy in a realm relevant to their concerns. Given the long-dominant role of the Chinese state in so many areas of life, this focus on state-society relations is well warranted. The same is true for studies of other authoritarian and semi-authoritarian states.

Yet civil society's significance is not limited to how professionalized NGOs advocate for particular interests or how social service delivery NGOs—government backed or otherwise—interact with the state. Scholars of the United States and other societies, following in the tradition of Alexis de Tocqueville, have long argued that bottom-up voluntary associations are among the fundamental building blocks of democracy, in part because they can help teach the skills and habits necessary for actively engaged democratic citizenship.[2] In this book, I look at a range of groups—GONGOs, professionalized NGOs, and voluntary associations—to understand the influence of mainstream authoritarian norms and practices on their internal organizational culture. As Richard Madsen has suggested, in looking at civil society groups in China, "perhaps the only way of assessing the significance of such groups would [be] from the inside—from a perspective that could have gained insight not simply into the quantity of their material resources but the quality of the moral commitments that gave them their vision and strength."[3]

Empirically, this book is a study of China, but my broader goal is to suggest ways in which authoritarianism as a political ordering affects the possibility for civil society in similar contexts. To this end, I suggest that we consider China as the exemplar of the twenty-first-century authoritarian state, not only because it encompasses almost one-fifth of the world's population but also because in recent decades it has emerged as a global economic powerhouse capable of harnessing and applying the most advanced surveillance and control technologies available to any government. At seventy-five years and counting since the establishment of the People's Republic of China (PRC) in 1949, the Chinese Communist Party (CCP) has in recent years also retightened its control over the economy, education, and society more broadly, despite an earlier period of economic reform beginning in 1979 that many observers assumed and hoped would lead to political liberalization and democracy.

In this book, I make several arguments. First, the proliferation of non-profit organizations in the United States since the 1960s, and NGOs globally since the end of the Cold War, has led many students of civil society, but particularly those looking at China, to elide the distinction between NGOs and voluntary associations. Much of the underlying motivation for interest in NGOs in any authoritarian state is based on the understanding that they can provide for interest group representation and therefore amplify the voices of the disadvantaged or the discontented. Their presence and activities are believed to help build pressure on authoritarian states and, eventually, to promote political change in the direction of democracy.[4] I also look at groups that call themselves NGOs, but I shine a brighter light on groups that more closely approximate ideal-typical Tocquevillian voluntary associations. I argue that it is within these sorts of groups, not professionalized NGOs, that we are most likely to find the emergence of a democratic culture, without which any future democratic political institutions are unlikely to survive. In doing so, I draw attention to the other major way civil society is thought to promote democratization—that is, through the inculcation of the values, skills, and habits of a democratic citizenry. In studies of China, and in studies of other authoritarian regimes, this culture-building potential of civil society has been generally neglected.

Second, the dominant organizational culture inherent to most associational life in China is hierarchical and autocratic. Drawing on descriptions of life inside government agencies, GONGOs, professionalized NGOs, and typical university-based student organizations, I argue that we should consider China as an example—and perhaps the exemplar—of an "authoritarian society." At the same time, inspired by late twentieth-century adaptations of Gramsci's concept of hegemony, I argue that this authoritarian organizational culture constitutes a form of hegemony that permeates Chinese associational life.

Third, drawing a sharp contrast with mainstream organizational norms, I show how bottom-up, youth-led voluntary associations are leading the way in constructing a counterhegemony that nurtures and brings to life a range of democratic values, like equality and mutual respect. By experimenting and seeking to translate their ideals and values into practice, participants in these groups are actively contesting the mainstream, authoritarian power relations that assume and perpetuate inequality.

In making these arguments, I suggest that civil society organizations in an authoritarian state are birthing rooms rather than classrooms of democracy, spaces in which still birth is as possible as live birth.[5] Yet despite the fragility implied by this metaphor, the bulk of the analysis weighs against the many doubts people often express about the ability for a democratic culture to take root in China—from popstars like Jackie Chan, who has said that Chinese people need to be "controlled,"[6] to scholars like the late Lucien Pye, whose work suggests that authoritarianism is a seemingly inbuilt and inescapable cultural trait inherent to Chinese civilization.[7] Despite the CCP's recent turn against "dangerous" ideologies from "the West," the democratic ideals and practices described in this book have taken root in fertile soil.

Focusing on the internal organizational cultures that animate and shape civil society organizations from within, I take inspiration from the work of scholars like Kathleen Blee, who lays out the "intellectual work of activism" as "interpreting the world, developing a shared ideology, and shaping frames that will translate the particular problems of an aggrieved group into universal conditions appealing to a broader public."[8] Although some research on Chinese civil society has managed to look at the third question—navigating appeals to the general public that simultaneously are acceptable to the state[9]—my interest lies with the first two aspects of this intellectual work, namely the ways activists interpret the world and develop a shared vision of how things could be different.

One of the appeals of Blee's articulation of "activism" is that it is broad enough to encompass activities and processes undertaken across any range of societies. Of course, although the study of civil society in democracies can help us begin to consider the potential of activist organizations in China, many practices that hold broadly true across democratic societies are banned outright or are deeply constrained under the social and political realities of authoritarian regimes. These include the accountability of politicians subject to electoral pressure, media that are free to report on corruption and that can be used by civil society to promote alternative views of societal problems, the right to association without fear of repression, and numerous other practices.

The obvious magnitude of these systemic differences has perhaps pushed researchers of authoritarian systems away from some of the enduring questions that have animated studies of democracies. I have found little extant literature that investigates how or whether civil society in authoritarian states might build the kind of democratic culture and habits that scholars from Tocqueville onward have seen as essential to a functioning democracy. Perhaps the general assumption has been that civil society in authoritarian regimes is unable to inculcate democratic values (for a multitude of reasons) or, alternatively, that the question of democratic culture building should be relegated to a post-transition era when the authoritarian state has been overturned and democratic institutions have been formally established.

Yet China today, like other authoritarian and semi-authoritarian states, has a range of groups and individuals who are actively contributing to a diverse and dynamic civil society. In this book, I look at a variety of civil society actors working across multiple issue domains. I draw on data collected over a thirteen-year period in China, analyzing microlevel practices of hierarchy, autocracy, and the stifling of dissent within civil society organizations to develop a distinctly sociological definition of "hegemonic authoritarianism." I identify in the process a widespread but nascent democratic counterhegemonic discourse that holds common across a variety of civil society forms, including GONGOs, professionalized NGOs, and voluntary associations. Most broadly, the Gramscian perspective I propose and elaborate in this book highlights the ways in which civil society serves as a space for culture making, a space in which the cultural hegemony of dominant society is produced *and* conflicts with ground-up counterhegemonies. I suggest that when the Communist Party deploys ideals of freedom, equality, and democracy in the story it tells itself and its people about the goals of Chinese socialism, it is simultaneously encouraging youth to embrace a value system antithetical to authoritarian rule and planting the seeds of its own destruction.

In the remainder of this introduction, I briefly discuss the kinds of data I use to make my arguments and walk readers through the book's organization, offering summaries of each of the subsequent chapters.

DATA AND METHODOLOGY

This research draws on fieldwork conducted in stages over a period of roughly thirteen years, from 2005 through 2017. During that time, I engaged in hundreds of hours of participant observation in numerous gatherings that brought together a diverse array of civil society participants. I joined training programs focused on professionalization of the NGO sector that included participants from both GONGOs and grassroots groups. I volunteered as a conference organizer and a regular participant in two grassroots NGOs, one a professionalized NGO and the other a volunteer-based association. I occasionally acted as a translator and facilitator at meetings that included international NGOs, GONGOs, and grassroots NGO staff and volunteers, academics, philanthropists, and Chinese and foreign government officials. These groups' work ran the gamut from women's rights to environmental protection, labor rights, HIV/AIDS, children's welfare, autism, rural education, and other social issues. Although the majority of my long-term exposure was to groups based in southern China, I also met with groups in or from most other areas of the country. The topics and issues I investigated included government relations, funding and finances, management issues, media relations, and other concerns. As such, this book is one part of a larger research agenda on civil society in China.

Based on initial introductions to local civil society actors by scholars in southern China, the first period of intensive fieldwork ran for about fifteen months between 2005 and 2007, with some follow-up work continuing into 2009. During the initial fieldwork period, in addition to participant observation, I also conducted interviews with 101 people, more than half of whom I interviewed at least twice. These included participants in more than thirty grassroots NGOs as well as GONGO staff, government officials, and a handful of representatives of foreign-based NGOs and foundations. Another twenty people regularly joined the participant-observation activities I took part in. Although I did not formally interview them, informal chats with these people certainly informed my understandings of the dynamics at play.

Having identified in the first period the organizational culture issues dealt with in this book, the second period of fieldwork included targeted interviews with another eighty people, including sixty participants of two youth-led volunteer-based groups. This work was conducted between 2012 and 2013, with some follow-up interviews in later years. To preserve confidentiality, I call these groups "Together" and "Bridges." Volunteers in Together work in rural villages across southern China, repairing dilapidated housing, providing basic medical care, and pursuing "social rehabilitation" by working to combat discrimination against the (mostly elderly) people who were isolated from mainstream society decades ago because they had contracted an infectious disease. Bridges volunteers work in rural schools to enhance the education of local students by emphasizing, for example, art, music, English, and other curricula not normally featured in poorer villages where educational resources are especially limited. Both groups are distinctive in that their activities are almost entirely organized by volunteers and led by youth. Most of the interviewees from Together and Bridges were introduced to me by the paid staff or the founders of the groups. They were, on average, in their early to mid-twenties when I spoke to them. Most of them were from working-class backgrounds, including many from rural areas or smaller cities scattered around southern China. This is not a random sample of either group but rather one of convenience. Having said that, both groups' staff accommodated my request for introductions to a diverse group of volunteers with respect to their role and length of experience in the organizations and their gender. In addition to a period of focused interviews on the topic of organizational culture, I also closely followed both Bridges and Together from 2005 to 2015, joining some activities as a participant and engaging in many small-group conversations about their work and development.

Because my research with Bridges and Together forms a large part of the basis of this book, especially part III, here I offer a bit more detail about their background and origins. Although Bridges and Together draw from the same pool of volunteers—university students—and are both based in southern China, they have virtually no crossover in their actual participants. Nonetheless, they have many things in common. Both groups employ a bare-bones staff composed of three to five former volunteers working for little or no pay. Their boards are composed primarily of former volunteers, and both groups have experimented greatly with various staff roles, governance structures, and funding models since their founding (circa 2001, in both cases). Since their founding, both groups have received some financial assistance from Chinese domestic companies and individuals, with occasional funds from Hong Kong and foundations based in one or two other countries. Neither group has been able to employ a trained accountant consistently, and overall expenses have mostly been covered personally by the volunteers through odd jobs, on-campus charity bazaars, and other small-scale fundraising activities. Although both groups rely mostly on volunteers from universities in southern China, they maintain off-campus offices and are independent of any one university. Both legally registered their main offices as nonprofit organizations (*minban feiqiye*, or private noncommercial enterprises) around 2013, after years of lobbying by supporters in academia, business, and even government. Both groups do have an organizational center, but I focus on what takes place in the smaller groups that actually undertake the vast majority of the organizations' work. The center is arguably more responsible for setting the tone of the groups' culture; facilitating the sharing of experiences among the smaller, more local groups; and, where possible, fundraising and handling government relations to keep the groups afloat. Bigger issues are discussed at an annual members' meeting, but generally these are not decision-making events. Rather, the focus of these gatherings—typically organized by the center with representatives from various branches—is on reviewing the previous year's activities, providing a platform to share experiences, and discussing each smaller group's plans for the coming year or months.

Within the larger pool of interviewees—including within Bridges and Together—a number of people were quite adept at deep self-reflection. Some individuals—typically but not always those with long-term experience in civil society groups—became key interlocutors and research partners whose insight greatly advanced the project's intellectual goals. Periodically presenting them with my tentative analyses or describing the puzzles underlying the study helped check or correct interpretations of earlier data, generating insight that either confirmed or challenged me to rethink conclusions reached up to that point. Although all the interactions described here were essential in producing this final text, these key interlocutors were invaluable sources of insight, helping sharpen my analytical focus and increasing my confidence in my interpretations. Virtually all the interviews and conversations described here were held in Chinese, and all translations are my own.

ORGANIZATION OF THE BOOK

This book is organized into four parts. Part I provides the context for the broader underlying questions and arguments motivating book. Following this introduction, chapter 1 provides readers with some background to the long-standing history of scholarly debate about democracy in China. With the advent of economic reforms under Deng Xiaoping in 1979, many people inside and outside China had high hopes that political reforms to the CCP's one-party rule would soon follow. Although those hopes have not been borne out, democracy is not a new idea in China. Since the late nineteenth century, Chinese people have been debating democracy's benefits, drawbacks, purposes, and suitability for China. Chapter 1 briefly surveys the thinking, scholarship, and debates about political change and the prospects for democratization. In keeping with the broader emphasis of the book, I introduce arguments and evidence across a variety of social science approaches to set the backdrop for my discussions of what democratic culture means in Chinese civil society.

Part II introduces readers to what I call "The Authoritarian Status Quo" in Chinese organizational life broadly and civil society specifically. Chapter 2 addresses how a long-standing ruling party (the CCP, in this case) can be so successful at penetrating and molding social life that authoritarian organizational norms and practices become pervasive features of the everyday exercise of authority, even within civil society. Borrowing insight from Tocqueville and Gramsci, I analyze microlevel practices of hierarchy, autocracy, and the stifling of dissent within civil society organizations. Developing a distinctively sociological definition of "hegemonic authoritarianism" that builds on Gramsci, I argue that the exercise of power within Chinese civil society mirrors practices at work in the larger political system, suppressing democratic yearnings that, nonetheless, persist in a nascent counterhegemony. I further suggest that authoritarian norms and practices make up the dominant organizational culture in China and should be understood as the constitutive backbone of an authoritarian society.

Chapter 3 asks the question, "How can a group of people who hold divergent opinions and viewpoints come together as equals and achieve a consensus on the best course of action or view of a particular problem?" For many Chinese civil society participants, effective communication (*goutong*) is not simply a give-and-take exchange of information but implies, rather, a search for consensus and mutual understanding. In this chapter, I show

how entrenched practices of interaction predicated on autocracy, hierarchy, and the suppression of dissent make communicating as equals an almost impossible task. I first highlight troubles in *listening*, a skill that is deeply linked to power relations in a group yet seldom discussed in studies of this sort. The bulk of the chapter is then dedicated to exploring the connections between inequality and communication in civil society organizations. I do this through three case studies—meetings and activities in which attempts to articulate one's opinions, to be heard by others, and to reach a consensus were undermined by a lack of experience in nonhierarchical settings. These three diverse settings—a meeting of environmentalists, an early gathering of Together, and a labor NGO educational activity—bring to life the tug-of-war taking place between authoritarian organizational norms and nascent democratic values and practices.

Part III comprises the bulk of this book and focuses squarely on the ways in which participants in Bridges and Together have worked to build democratic organizational cultures despite the weighty influences of the larger society. Chapter 4 focuses on how these young volunteers have rejected the norms and practices of government-directed volunteering and constructed their own narratives about what it means to volunteer. It begins by showing how over the past twenty-odd years, volunteering has developed as a new field for government control and regulation of an emergent civil society. This chapter then contrasts the experiences of young volunteers—mostly university students and recent graduates—in Together and Bridges with the officially approved student organizations of normal university life. I argue that the instrumental organization of volunteers characterizes the party-state's efforts to funnel youthful enthusiasm and compassion into particular political projects and officially prescribed goals. Unhappy with the formalistic nature of these activities, youth engaging in bottom-up volunteer initiatives articulate other priorities, including a strong desire for meaningful, personal engagement that state-led programs and typical university student organizations are largely unable to provide.

Chapter 5 introduces readers to the ways in which Bridges and Together volunteers talk and think about equality, a value that is fundamental to democratic practice in both everyday life and larger political settings. I argue that equality is a central and conscious concern in the organizational cultures of both groups and highlight how they weave the pursuit of equality into their internal organizational practices. Intimately linked with the concept of equality are questions of hierarchy and leadership, both of which I also discuss in separate sections. As equality appears throughout this book as an ideal that informs multiple kinds of practices, I also use this chapter to fill in the cultural backdrop that will clarify why certain decisions have been made and how particular democratic structures and practices have emerged.

One of the fundamental problems confronting any scholar of social and political order concerns the question of how differences among people are resolved. Having argued in chapter 5 that participants in Bridges and Together place a strong emphasis on equality and aim to avoid hierarchical organizational practices, in chapter 6, I examine how differences of opinion are handled in the absence of any clear or overriding authority. Relatedly, I examine what leadership looks like in a group in which no one individual is granted the authority to make binding decisions on the group. This chapter wraps up by analyzing questions about conflict resolution, revealing in the process how participants in these organizations give life to their democratic values as they work to build consensus and cooperate as an association of equals.

Scholars of democratic societies have long argued that participation in voluntary associations provides opportunities to develop a broad range of skills, habits, and dispositions that support democratic culture and democratic political practice. Chapter 7 examines how grassroots voluntary associations can generate democratic skills and habits despite the overwhelmingly authoritarian organizational culture that dominates mainstream Chinese society. This chapter features an account of the lessons volunteers in Bridges and Together believe have been imparted by their experiences and the implications that their self-described "transformations" hold for broader understandings of the development of democratic culture. It further considers the values that underpin their organizational practices and suggests that these practices and democratic values are both interwoven and mutually reinforcing, reconfirming but also expanding Tocqueville's insight into the importance of voluntary association for democratic culture.

Chapter 8 deals explicitly with questions of leadership and authority, focusing primarily on Together and Bridges but, more fundamentally, shedding light on how civil society participants view the role of leaders and how changing ideas of leadership inform their struggles to shed mainstream authoritarian practices. The chapter begins with an introduction to the kind of formalistic elections that students in China are most likely to encounter in on-campus organizations and then contrasts these with the experimentation pursued by Bridges and Together, while highlighting the latter's novelty in the Chinese context. It further draws attention to a number of tensions and choices faced by both groups as they consider how to best distribute organizational authority and responsibility, including learning how to balance accumulated experience with a commitment to welcoming and nurturing new ideas as well as how to weigh the pros and cons of elections over the traditional appointment systems inherited from mainstream society. The chapter concludes with an account of one professionalized NGO's innovative experiment in holding elections for its leadership.

Given the overwhelming strength of authoritarian norms in mainstream society, chapter 9 takes up the question of cultural survival, analyzing how Bridges and Together select and screen newcomers for common values. Each year, Bridges and Together both attract far more new applicants than they are able to absorb. Rather than agreeing to exponentially grow their volunteer numbers and risk losing their sense of common purpose and shared values, they are highly selective when choosing newcomers. Selectivity helps ensure that the groups' activities meet their self-imposed high standards and also protects the culture of the organizations from the potentially destructive influence of newcomers who are steeped in the norms of mainstream authoritarian organizations. This chapter reveals how their choices are largely driven by their commitment to a culture of openness and mutual respect. Although participants acknowledge the risk of selecting people too much like themselves, the criteria used are designed not to avoid ideas current members might disagree with, but rather to ensure open attitudes, humility, and tolerance of different ideas.

Part IV is composed of a single concluding chapter in which I consider the implications of the study for the development of democratic culture in China and under conditions of authoritarianism more generally. I do so by looking first at the prospects for Bridges and Together volunteers to take their values and practices into their work lives and other social spaces. Then I return to the bigger impact of the authoritarian society and its implications for democratic change in China. I conclude by looking at the broader discussion of civil society and democratic development with which the book opened and positing how the concepts derived from this study of China can be used to deepen our understanding of other authoritarian regimes.

For several years now I have felt deeply the irony of being an American writing about democracy and authoritarianism in China while democratic norms and practices in my native country—and the world more broadly—have been treated with increasing disdain and disregard by politicians, political parties, and many forms of social and traditional media. Their erosion and the regression into authoritarianism obvious in many countries reveal the antithesis of the kinds of democratic values and practices I discuss in this book. Yet, in some ways, this study of democratic culture under conditions of authoritarianism—as fantastical as the possibility may appear at first glance— offers lessons not just for understanding authoritarianism but also for revaluing democratic values and norms within long-standing democracies. Perhaps it is in the contestation of authoritarian norms and practices, and the attendant articulation of democratic ideals, that we can learn the most about the power of democracy as universal human aspiration and a vehicle to deliver human freedoms. This was a possibility I first began to see when living in Taiwan from 1992 to 1997, just as it was emerging from the grip of Chiang Kai-shek's authoritarian regime, feeling its way toward democratic elections, a free and open media, and the opportunities for progress on human rights made possible by the veritable explosion of social movements during that time. Living in Taiwan during the 1990s surely motivated my continuing interest in how democracies come alive in both institutions and in people's lived experience, and it inevitably informed the ways I interpreted what I observed while conducting the research presented here. A short appendix offers additional reflections on the fieldwork, analysis, and ethical considerations that went into developing this book.

Chapter One

DEMOCRACY IN CHINA

A Century of Debate

Authoritarian thought has dominated China's political culture for thousands of years.

—SUZANNE OGDEN, *INKLINGS OF DEMOCRACY IN CHINA*

With the advent of economic reforms under Deng Xiaoping in 1979, many people inside and outside China had high hopes that political reforms to the Chinese Communist Party's (CCP's) one-party rule would soon follow. Yet even in the 1980s, democracy was not a new idea in China. Since the late nineteenth century, Chinese people have been debating about democracy's benefits, drawbacks, purposes, and suitability for China. The most influential of these early intellectuals was perhaps Guangdong-born Liang Qichao. A child prodigy trained in the Confucian classics, Liang was critical of the failings of China's imperial system and the Confucian ideology that underpinned it. In the late nineteenth and early twentieth centuries, Liang's writings were widely influential in China. His proposals for reforming China into a constitutional monarchy, however, were considered too radical by the Empress Dowager Cixi, and just before the turn of the century, Liang fled to Japan rather than be captured by Qing authorities. Ultimately, his essays and arguments about modernization helped lay the political groundwork for the overthrow of the Qing Dynasty and the 1911 Republican Revolution.

During this heady time of expansive social and political change, Liang and his Cantonese compatriots Sun Yat-sen (the father of modern China) and Kang Youwei were inspirational voices pushing for the construction of an original national narrative in China, cultivating a sense of "Chinese-ness" that would eventually help lead to the creation of China as a modern nation-state.

More important, perhaps, their investigations of foreign political models, in particular, democracy, introduced the very terms of great debates over how a "modern" China should develop. Their frustration at seeing China carved up—at least along its coastal trading ports—by European colonial powers inspired them and their contemporaries to ask how a once-great civilization could be brought to such subservient status so quickly.[1] As Andrew Nathan writes in his tome on the subject, *Chinese Democracy*, "Liang's explorations of Western thought focused on a central conundrum: that the countries of the world that were powerful were also democratic."[2]

Liang's initial attraction to democracy quickly turned to disillusionment, however, on a trip to the United States in 1903. Dismayed at the corruption he observed in New York City politics and unimpressed with President Roosevelt after a meeting in the White House, Liang concluded that "the republican form of government is not as good as constitutional monarchy, which has fewer flaws and functions more efficiently."[3] Critical of what he saw as character flaws in the Chinese immigrant population of San Francisco, Liang left the United States convinced that Chinese people were not ready for democracy: "Were we now to resort to rule by this majority, it would be the same as committing national suicide . . . In a word, the Chinese people must for now accept authoritarian rule; they cannot enjoy freedom."[4]

This disillusionment led Liang to conclude that an "enlightened despotism" was necessary for China to rebuild itself as a strong and unified nation. The need for a singular, strong leader was clearly demonstrated, in his view, because "groups of activists have been unable to organize a solidly based association; or if one does get formed, it disbands almost as soon as it gathers. Someone's recent remark is most apt: 'They can neither organize an association of more than three people nor maintain a party for over a year.' Can people like this create a state that will survive in this world of fierce competition?"[5]

Liang Qichao was not the only Chinese scholar-activist of the early twentieth century to lament the decline of Chinese power and to see traditional culture as a key weakness holding the country back. The New Culture movement of the mid-1910s to the 1920s congealed around the writings of a group of intellectuals who rejected key precepts of Confucianism and led a charge to embrace science and democracy. The author Hu Shi, a graduate of Cornell University and Columbia University who later became the Republic of China's ambassador to the United States, was a fiercely influential advocate of increasing literacy by writing in the vernacular (*baihua*)—the way many people actually spoke—instead of the stilted formal style of classical

Chinese, a monumental change in the way people accessed knowledge. Another literary luminary of the time, Lu Xun, is perhaps most famous for his "The True Story of Ah Q," in which the peasant protagonist exemplifies the small-mindedness, self-deceit, and brutality that Lu thought typified Chinese behavior of the time. Controversial but extremely popular among readers, Lu Xun's calls to rid Chinese culture of its so-called backwardness enriched the fervent debate about what exactly China needed to do to become a modern nation.

Contemporary Chinese academics continue to debate and discuss China's progress toward democracy, sometimes in a very public way. In 1998, two prominent intellectuals, Mao Yushi and Fang Jue, circulated powerful essays promoting, in Mao's case, the virtues of liberal democracy for China and, in Fang's case, advocating deep structural and institutional change to build a democratic China.[6] Professor Yu Keping, well-known in academic and official circles for his support of "good governance" and civil society, has been making the case for many years that China is moving toward democratic practices at local levels. Highlighting successful innovations in transparency, rule of law, and accountability, for example, Yu argues that China is tracking well toward a more democratic system—even if, as his critics point out, he is not openly calling for universal suffrage, elections, and the other aspects of democratic practice that most political scientists regard as essential to democracy.[7]

Despite bold calls by members of the intelligentsia for democratization and the positive steps China has made, at least in the eyes of Yu and others, the perceptions of Chinese cultural inadequacies and the need for strong autocratic leadership have persisted throughout the past century. This belief is not held only by political elites; even contemporary pop culture icons have espoused such thinking. Most famously, kung fu movie star Jackie Chan, born and raised in Hong Kong, proclaimed while attending a gathering of global business interests in China in 2009 that "Chinese people must be controlled." His comments were widely derided in Chinese-language media but apparently were met with applause by other attendees at the invite-only annual event.[8]

Alongside the continuous questioning of Chinese people's fitness for democracy, by most accounts, China's first attempt at democratic government did not fare well. The establishment of the Republic of China in 1911 led not to radical democratic transformation but rather to a collapse into warlordism and intense civil strife. More than a decade of public debate and discussion among leading intellectuals had resulted in little more than naked power struggles and a continuation of traditional hierarchical norms. As Suzanne Ogden describes it:

> By 1915, the national parliament had become a tool of the warlords, not a representative body for the Chinese people. It was devoid of political power. Constitutions were made and unmade, and the "people's rights" were ignored. Few efforts were made to propagate the ideas of democracy among the vast Chinese population, and the people remained unaware that they were supposed to consent to their government. Isolated amid a culture and society not predisposed by tradition to democratic forms, democratic political institutions collapsed. The idea of representative government was not powerful enough to cause officials or the common people to abandon their culture-bound, hierarchical patterns of thinking about power or to exercise their rights as individuals.[9]

In the ensuing decades and indeed through the end of the twentieth century, attempts at institutionalizing democracy in China would seemingly come to naught. As Andrew Nathan writes, all efforts to establish functioning electoral systems and promote political liberalization during the Republican period and after the founding of the People's Republic of China (PRC) in 1949 failed miserably: "Elections were corrupt, parliaments were factionalized, the free press was irresponsible, political groups were unprincipled. Political actors outside these institutions refused to accept the outcomes of elections, did not obey laws passed by legislatures, and did not respect the legal freedoms of the free press or the organizational rights of legally constituted organizations. At base, the failure of democracy consisted in a failure of democratic institutions to acquire authority, or in Samuel Huntington's phrase, to become institutionalized."[10]

Still, throughout the twentieth century, recurring social movements led by youth, intellectuals, and workers called for greater political accountability on the part of the government, if not full-fledged democracy. Protests have come and gone, however, without moving the needle on structural political reform much at all. Attempts at democratic practice in China in the 1980s—such as the much-vaunted village-level elections that were authorized in 1987—have proven unable to shift the locus of legitimacy and effective power from the CCP to the people. As Thomas Bernstein argues, "even when village elections work well, the power of elected village committees is limited because they necessarily function within an authoritarian political environment that is not structured to respond to the demands of constituents. Solutions to problems of the greatest concern that face rural China are largely beyond the capacity of village committees to solve."[11] The larger political environment, that is, is not vulnerable to change motivated by this lowest-level effort at democratic practice. Despite occasional signals from the top that elections might one day be expanded, over the past few decades political reform has happened only at the margins, in what John James Kennedy and Dan Chen[12] call "delimited innovations" that avoid any suggestion of change at the national or provincial levels. Voting in rural areas and in urban residents committees is generally viewed as a rite, not a "right."[13] For CCP members in particular, voting is understood as a duty to demonstrate one's fealty to the regime,[14] not as an opportunity to express one's preferences from a slate of freely competing candidates nor a chance to nurture a deeper democratic culture.[15]

Liang Qichao's concern that Chinese society was not yet ready to support a democratic political system has been a recurring refrain in elite Chinese discussions of democracy and has been used to justify delayed political reforms since the founding of the PRC. Considering the possibility of expanding elections above the level of rural villages, Bernstein writes that the CCP leadership believes that "democracy understood as competitive elections is something for which the country is not ready and will not be ready for another generation or two."[16]

Yet the question of readiness is not so easily settled, couched as it often is in terms of Chinese culture and its presumed authoritarian foundations. Although democracy in the PRC has been hobbled by repression and continuing refrains of Liang's thesis, since the 1990s Taiwan's successful transition from an authoritarian state to a vibrant democracy has challenged the notion that Chinese culture is somehow incompatible with democratic values and practice.[17] Linda Chao and Ramon H. Myers argue, for example, that a particular strand of Chinese political culture in Taiwan was a key factor in this transition, a belief system that emphasized "tolerance and magnanimity toward political opponents and a willingness to engage them in dialogue, resolve differences, and achieve consensus."[18] More recently, Yun-han Chu has argued that Taiwan's experience could both inspire and provide a model for democratization in China:

Taiwan-based political, economic, and social actors are potentially powerful catalysts for democratic change in China. Taiwan's transformative power lies not just in its experience with economic modernization, social pluralism, and democratic development, but also in its "Chinese-ness." The people of Taiwan in their daily lives have preserved and practiced Chinese social customs; dietary habits; conceptions about the body and health; notions of life, death, fate, and the supernatural; and family-based ethics. The elements of modernity embodied in the Taiwanese model are inspirational, while the island's shared linguistic and cultural heritage with China makes Taiwan's way of life relevant, comprehensible, and accessible.[19]

Despite a lack of institutional change in the PRC, Chinese leaders have frequently emphasized elements of a harmony-seeking political culture akin—at least rhetorically—to what Chao and Myers saw at work in Taiwan. Mao's emphasis on "democratic centralism" called for "discussion of an issue within the party (or among the people) followed by unified implementation of whatever decision was reached at the top. 'The mass line' involved gathering information from the masses before making a decision, then persuading the masses to accept the decision."[20] Although this consultative approach has democratic elements, in practice it has not meant free and open elections nor universal suffrage. Yet Chinese leaders from Mao onward continue to refer to democracy as a goal—or an already existing feature—of the Chinese state. Former president Hu Jintao, in a 2006 speech, assured his audience at Yale University that China valued human dignity and was moving steadily toward a broader democracy. In his words:

The Chinese civilization has always given prominence to the people and respect for people's dignity and value. . . . We will vigorously promote social and economic development, protect people's freedom, democracy and human rights according to law, achieve social fairness and justice and enable the 1.3 billion Chinese people to live a happy life. . . . Today, China is endeavoring to build a harmonious society. It is a society of democracy and rule of law, fairness and justice, integrity, fraternity, vitality, stability, order and harmony between man and nature. It is a society where there is unity between the material and the spirit, democracy and rule of law, fairness and efficiency, and vitality and order.[21]

Despite such seemingly democratic aspirations, the CCP has not been willing to loosen its control over the political system or tolerate any challenge to its rule. Just two years after Hu's speech, the Charter 08 movement was launched by a number of prominent intellectuals in China, criticizing continuing human rights restrictions and calling for constitutional reform and political liberalization. Continuing a long pattern of coercion and repression of democracy advocates and so-called troublemakers, many authors and signatories of the charter were interrogated by the police or jailed for their efforts, most famously Liu Xiaobo, the Nobel Peace Prize laureate who languished in a Chinese prison until his death in 2017.[22] In the years since, activists of all stripes have been detained, disappeared, or in other ways deterred from public pursuit of democratic claims on the state.[23]

POST-1989 DEBATES ABOUT DEMOCRACY AND CIVIL SOCIETY

Over the past thirty years, democracy and civil society in China have become deeply intertwined areas of intense scholarly interest. The very first issue of the *Journal of Democracy* (published in 1990) featured an article by Thomas Gold, a sociologist at the University of California, Berkeley, entitled, "Tiananmen and Beyond: The Resurgence of Civil Society in China." Writing just one year after the tumultuous and ultimately tragic protest movement in Beijing's Tiananmen Square, Gold paints a vivid portrait of both Mao-era suppression of civil society and Deng's gradual relaxation of economic controls. It was the latter, he notes, that led to a flowering of multiple worker-led and student-led demonstrations, including Beijing's Democracy Wall movement (1978), pro-democracy student demonstrations in Hefei and Shanghai (1986), unrest in Tibet (1987), and the 1989 protests that swept across many of China's major cities. Between the mid-1970s and 1989, protestors' collective demands included redress for abuses stretching back to the 1950s, a clampdown on corruption, curbs on inflation, and support for freedom of the press. Summing up these dramatic and visible signs of popular discontent, Gold says:

> All these doings point to the resurgence of Chinese civil society, flourishing in the fertile soil of autonomous economic activity. The reaction of the CCP old guard, much like that of its Polish comrades in 1981, grew not only out of its Leninist inability to admit the legitimacy of any independent group or action, but out of its Confucian contempt for youth and change as well. The policy of economic fang [liberalization] was at the heart of the trouble, but since shutting down the open economy would be too costly, the only alternative was to wage war against autonomous activities in other sectors of Chinese society.[24]

Gold's strong conclusion about the import of economic liberalization and these protest movements presaged three decades of renewed academic and popular inquiries asking, in one way or another, "What are the prospects for civil society development and democratization in China?" But the relationship among the economy, civil society, and democratization is not simply linear. As discussed more in chapter 2, in open societies, civil society organizations can also be quite undemocratic internally, and their effect on politics within the larger society can be more polarizing than integrative. Even in the youth-led movement of 1989—often remembered as a democratic movement—elite university students were seemingly unable to recognize the value of incorporating workers into the movement or to innovate past the factionalism that Liang Qichao had observed in San Francisco some eighty-five years earlier. In her analysis of the 1989 Tiananmen movement, Ogden argues that:

> the student leaders themselves were anything but democratic in their words, actions, and organization. Their organization mimicked that of the Party—understandably, since that was the only organizational style they knew. They were hierarchical in decision making, demanded obedience, and treated each other according to rank within the movement. The top leaders were dictatorial and secretive, and many of the students who participated in the protests of 1989 subsequently accused them of abuse of authority, factionalism, and corruption. Perhaps most telling, the students refused to cooperate with the workers in the 1989 demonstrations and had little interest in workers' demands for better pay and working conditions. The students had no intention of granting leadership rights to the workers, and they never adopted the idea of "one person, one vote" as a goal. Their goal was greater individual freedom for themselves, not democratization.[25]

Since the brutal repression that ended the 1989 protests, there has been a recurring scholarly conversation about civil society and political liberalization in China. In 1993, for example, the journal *Modern China* brought together historians and social scientists to explore the applicability of the civil society concept and the significance of emergent nongovernmental organizations (NGOs) for social and political life.[26] Following that, numerous academic articles and books have continued the effort to assess the potential of what appears to be a rapidly growing Chinese civil society.[27] The majority of these works have dealt with the question of government-organized nongovernmental organizations (GONGOs) and their potential (or lack thereof) for autonomy as well as their influence on the Chinese state.

More recent works have begun to explore the situation of grassroots NGOs, including questions about advocacy, ties to global civil society, and domestic and foreign funding.[28]

In virtually all of this scholarship, the Chinese state looms large, either in the foreground as a key agent driving NGO behavior or in the background as an ever-present factor shaping the space and possibilities for civil society actors. Given the CCP's continued wariness of groups organizing outside its control, and its continued willingness to engage in repression, it is understandable that state–civil society relations have been the predominant framing for most research. Yet despite the outpouring of interest in activists and organizations, little if any of this growing body of literature has considered the democratic skills-building potential of civil society organizations.

Recalling Tocqueville's interest in the democratic "habits of the heart" that he believed U.S. associations nurtured,[29] and the flowering of neo-Tocquevillian scholarship in the late twentieth century, questions of whether or how Chinese civil society might nurture a democratic culture deserve considered exploration. It would be easy to discount the possibility of democratic culture having space to grow in China, particularly given the objective constraints of authoritarian politics and the CCP's fear of losing control. As Ogden's observation makes clear, moreover, the "only organizational style" protestors in 1989 knew was one characterized by authoritarian principles, norms, and behaviors. Although this organizational culture persists—a phenomenon I tackle in chapter 2—newer developments in Chinese civil society have allowed for an alternative, democratic organizational model to emerge.

DEMOCRATIC CULTURE, NOT "POLITICAL CULTURE"

My interest in the organizational cultures of Chinese civil society is unusual in current approaches to studying civil society in authoritarian states, but it may appear to some readers close in nature to debates about Chinese political participation and political culture. Most prominent in recent literature is perhaps the work of the late political scientist Tianjian Shi. Shi's groundbreaking survey of political participation in Beijing, based on data collected in 1988 and early 1989, analyzed ways in which Beijing residents pursued political redress for problems in their work units or daily life and how they sought to use limited election opportunities for personal gain.[30] His work showed that rather than breeding apathy and indifference, politics in a communist country can involve active participation by citizens who use whatever means is at their disposal to pursue their individual and family interests. Geared toward maximizing personal welfare, this kind of political participation—which Shi defines even more narrowly as "efforts of people to influence their rulers"—is not the focus of my research.[31]

My focus is on what also might mistakenly be equated with "political culture" as it has been used in the political science literature. A concept popularized in the United States by Gabriel Almond in the 1950s and taken up by many others afterward, political culture has been applied in China in varying ways.[32] Lucian Pye's work on Chinese culture, arguably the most influential in this approach to understanding Chinese politics, advocated a psychoanalytical perspective in defining traditional Chinese culture as characterized by hierarchy, paternalism, and obedience to authority figures.[33] From imperial China through to the Republican era and into the Communist period, Pye believed these cultural attributes persisted, in part driven by what he saw as slow-changing family norms in which paternalism and authoritarianism were reproduced despite rapid transformations in social and economic realities.[34] My arguments do not deny the import or persistence of these sorts of cultural norms, but I suggest that under the CCP they have gained new structural support while simultaneously being fundamentally contradicted and challenged by the demands of modernity and the impacts of globalization. That is, these ways of approaching authority and its exercise are not so deeply imbued in Chinese society that they are unchallengeable or unchangeable, especially by a younger generation.

Tianjian Shi also employed the concept of political culture in several surveys in mainland China and in Taiwan. Despite surveying the more psychological usages of the term "culture," as Pye did, Shi's work generally operationalized the concept as a mixture of attitudes toward authority and politically relevant behavior. In analyzing a 1993 nationwide survey in China, for example, Shi discusses the frequency of respondents' newspaper reading, talking with others about political issues and national affairs, questions about whether they expect to be treated fairly by government officials, perceptions of hierarchy in the family and government, and support for political and economic reform.[35] Several aspects of Shi's findings and arguments support the lines of analysis I develop further in this book. In keeping with the general thrust of modernization theory, Shi's finding that "the higher the respondents' education, the more likely they are to support political reform"[36] suggests that the young people active in Chinese civil society today would be more predisposed to democratic processes, values, and reforms. In analyzing his 1988–1989 survey data—even after the violent repression of the Tiananmen movement—Shi writes that "influenced by ideas of liberty and democracy, the younger generation in China gives higher priority to self-expression and independence. As its basic value orientation and value priorities are fundamentally different from those of older people, the younger generation is unlikely to accept traditional social norms and the existing rules of the game in society."[37]

In a 1993 article, Andrew Nathan and Tianjian Shi expanded the study of political culture with their analysis of a nationwide statistically representative survey conducted in 1990. With an eye to cross-national comparisons, they modeled their survey in part on the approach taken thirty years earlier in *The Civic Culture*, a survey of five democratic nations conducted in 1959–1960 by Gabriel Almond and Sidney Verba.[38] In a first-of-its-kind survey, they sought to explore three questions about political culture in China: "do citizens perceive the government as salient to their lives . . . do people believe that they have the capability to understand and engage in politics . . . [and] to what extent are citizens prepared to be tolerant of those who hold different political beliefs?"[39] Their overall conclusion on these three points is clear:

> Nothing in our data supports the theory that Chinese political culture is an absolute bar to democracy. When compared to residents of some of the most stable, long-established democracies in the world, the Chinese population scored lower on the variables we looked at, but not so low as to justify the conclusion that democracy is out of reach. In general, as theory predicts, the more urban and educated sectors showed more democratic attitudes, supporting expectations derived from modernization theory that China's culture will move closer to the patterns characteristic of democratic countries as the economy grows. Once in place, a democratic regime could speed the pace of cultural change by actively inculcating the popular attitudes it needs to survive.[40]

In their analysis, they make the case that "while some of the attitudes associated with democracy are less prevalent in China than in some other countries, Chinese political culture today is neither especially traditional nor especially totalitarian."[41] Their analysis finds resonance in work by Baogang He, who, after surveying similar literature about the antidemocratic elements of Chinese culture, builds an argument leading to the conclusion that "the assumption that China's culture does not meet the cultural conditions suited to democracy is partially wrong, because there is indeed an emerging democratic culture in China."[42] To justify his guarded optimism,

He discusses not only the earliest advocates of democracy from the May Fourth movement but also a bevy of activist intellectuals active in the 1980s, as well as the potential for China's increased openness to the world and economic exchange to reinvigorate ideas of basic rights and freedoms that are conducive to a democratic system.

In short, existing scholarship provides ample reason to expect that authoritarianism in China would be hard to root out. Yet there is also grounded evidence and reasonable arguments to support the development of democratic political culture as a viable path forward for Chinese politics.

The distinction I would draw between the kinds of "political culture" described by Shi, Nathan, and others is that democracy is not simply relevant for politics writ large. It is not simply in the realm of institutions—like legislatures and judicial systems—where culture comes into play. As theorists from Gramsci to Foucault have argued, culture itself is a realm of power and contestation in which battles for legitimacy and domination are played out. In the organizational lives of civil society actors in China, national-level politics is not the most immediate way in which democratic culture matters. As I show in the following chapters, rather, it is in the day-to-day experiences of authority and (in)equality that democracy begins to take meaning. Although this kind of "everyday democracy" can certainly affect expectations and aspirations for larger political life, it needs to be analyzed with an eye toward its own distinctiveness. Doing so reveals much about the nature of power and the possibility of broader change despite the constraints of authoritarianism.

CONCLUSION

In contrast to much of the Chinese intelligentsia's debates in the early twentieth century or in the 1980s, the ground-level discussions featured in this book are not focused on democracy's utility for bringing about economic modernization, strengthening the country, or pursuing institutional political reform. They also are not predominately concerned with how culture is understood in the realm of formal politics. Rather, the contemporary discussions about democracy that I highlight in this book are about how today's civil society actors are striving—sometimes succeeding, sometimes failing—to develop a culture of equality, respect, and dignity that would form part of the basis of a broader democratic culture.

The approach I take in this book is a divergence from the standard political sociology accounts of civil society in China (including much of my own work). It crosses boundaries between that subfield of the discipline, organizational sociology, and cultural sociology. It runs in parallel with Bin Xu's[43] work on the "culture of democracy" and the small but growing literature on cultural sociology in and of China, including Xu's *The Politics of Compassion: The Sichuan Earthquake and Civic Engagement* (2017) and earlier works by sociologists, including Richard Madsen, Craig Calhoun, and Guobin Yang.[44] Readers will find that my interest here is in what Xu (2022) calls "culture in interaction." His definition is useful, as it encompasses the kinds of phenomena that form the basis for this study, namely:

> norms of interactions, including conventions, rules, and expectations concerning appropriate ways in which individuals and groups engage in interactions in specific situations . . . they are mostly the meaning-making processes between individuals rather than of individuals; in other words, the analytical unit in this perspective is the interaction between at least two people, in a small group, and often at the meso level. This conception is deeply rooted in the rich tradition of microsociology and pragmatism, which focuses on individual actors' definition of situation, projection of self-images, interaction order, group culture, and forming and reforming norms at the microlevel.[45]

The microlevel interactions I focus on in this book reveal how democratic discourse—whether because of the processes of (post-)modernity or globalization and world culture—has taken root in the popular imagination in China and pushed the understanding of democracy beyond politics writ large. China's tremendous economic growth over the past forty years, uneven though it may be, has created a generation of young people who, unlike their forebears a century ago, have no need to see China as a "weak" nation. Constructing their own version of democratic norms and practices is within their reach and need not be postponed because of concerns about economic strength (although that is not the only source of democratic confidence). As I show more directly in part III of this book, what is significantly different today from earlier democratic movements and debates, and from the high-level public opinions offered by Chinese elites to the CCP leadership, is the emergence at the grassroots level of small-group habits and practices that make up the everyday building blocks of democratic culture. In part II, however, I first introduce the inheritance of authoritarian norms and practices that civil society participants struggle to overcome as they craft a new, counterhegemonic worldview and an attendant set of practices and interaction norms.

PART II

The Authoritarian Status Quo

Chapter Two

CIVIL SOCIETY UNDER HEGEMONIC
AUTHORITARIANISM

Within a society where virtually all major social institutions—from schools to workplaces to government—are stitched together with the heavy threads of authoritarian rule, can civil society associations still be expected to serve as large free schools of democracy? The search to answer this question underpins the research that has resulted in this book, a sociological study of civil society and democratic culture building in China, the world's largest authoritarian state.

In this chapter, I show how a long-standing ruling party can be so successful at penetrating and molding social life that authoritarian organizational norms and practices become pervasive features of the everyday exercise of authority, even within civil society. I begin by considering two related literatures. First, I discuss Tocquevillian perspectives on civil society associations and explicate various views on how civil society may serve to promote democracy in authoritarian states. I suggest that most studies of civil society in authoritarian states to date have focused on state-society relations, despite democratic culture building comprising a key aspect of both Alexis de Tocqueville's original analyses and a substantial body of literature on the topic. I then introduce a Gramscian perspective, highlighting the ways in which civil society can be analyzed as a space in which the hegemony of the dominant group in society is produced and is contested by bottom-up counterhegemonies. Drawing on data collected from a range of Chinese civil society groups, I analyze micro-level practices of hierarchy, autocracy, and the stifling of dissent within civil society organizations to develop a distinctly sociological definition of "hege-monic authoritarianism," identifying in the process a nascent democratic counterhegemonic discourse.

I begin by considering the application of Tocquevillian and Gramscian perspectives to civil society in authoritarian regimes. I then introduce the specific case of China, discussing the recent rise of civil society and non-governmental organizations (NGOs) and the widespread process of social-ization into authoritarian norms and practices. From there, I turn to the empirical data on the internal organizational cultures of civil society groups, discussing the ways in which hierarchy, autocracy, and the stifling of dissent at the micro level are both widespread and reflect political practices at work in the larger system.

FROM TOCQUEVILLE TO GRAMSCI:
CIVIL SOCIETY, DEMOCRACY, AND AUTHORITARIANISM

The Contributions of Civil Society to Democracy and Democratization

Inspired by Alexis de Tocqueville's nineteenth-century tour de force, *Democracy in America*, many social scientists have long argued for the crucial role of civil society in establishing and maintaining democracy.[1] Fascinated by (and also fearful of) the American experiment with democracy,[2] Tocqueville attributed the strength of democracy in the United States to the self-governing character of American society. "Americans combine," he observed, "to give fetes, build churches, distribute books, and send missionaries to the antipo-des. Hospitals, prisons, and schools take shape in that way . . . In every case, at the head of any new undertaking, where in France you would find the government or in England some territorial magnate, in the United States you are sure to find an association."[3] Rather than turn to government to solve communal problems, he suggested, Americans generally look to one another for help: "if some obstacle blocks the public road halting the circu-lation of traffic, the neighbors at once form a deliberative body; this impro-vised assembly produces an executive authority which remedies the trouble before anyone has thought of the possibility of some previously constituted authority beyond that of those concerned."[4]

Often drawing implicitly or explicitly on Tocqueville, contemporary social scientists have adapted and extended his insight to analyze the links between associational life and the prospects for democratization in authoritarian regimes. In much of that scholarship, research has typically focused on the ability (or failure) of civil society to gather and amplify the demands of different interest groups and then to challenge and democratize the state. Such studies evince a commonly held view that "especially in political contexts of tyranny or deep injustice, the central contributions of associations have been to check illegitimate political power, to offer resistance, and to check official power."[5] Research in this vein often depicts civil society as "an autonomous sphere of social power within which citizens can pressure authoritarians for change, protect themselves from tyranny, and democratize from below."[6] In Muthiah Alagappa's broad review of the literature: "Civil society is viewed as a supporting structure to democratize the state. Associational life is thought to provide the social infrastructure for liberal democracy, supply the means to limit, resist, and curb the excesses of the state and market, present alternatives when they fail, facilitate service delivery at the local level, assist in conflict management, deepen democracy (by cultivating civic virtues, establishing democratic norms, and spreading democracy to more domains of life), offer a voice to disadvantaged groups, and promote economic development."[7]

Such a laundry list of the virtues and power of civil society has helped shape and motivate a global research agenda, leading scholars in places without longstanding democratic traditions or in backsliding new democracies to query how civil society may combat or democratize authoritarian regimes. The intellectual and political appeal of this approach can be seen in contemporary studies of countries on almost every continent, from Algeria and Saudi Arabia[8] and Uganda and Kazakhstan[9] to Iran,[10] Thailand,[11] China,[12] and Russia.[13] This focus on civil society's interactions with the state is not limited to only those optimistic about civil society's democratizing effects[14] but also in scholarship that cautions against assuming civil society necessarily serves democratic functions, like Edward Aspinall's study of political polarization in Indonesia or Sheri Berman's study of Weimar Germany.[15]

Working within a framework of state-society relations, studies like these have been invaluable for making sense of the ways in which authoritarian states incorporate, repress, or are sometimes transformed by civil society.[16] Another key facet of Tocqueville's insight—the democratic culture-building functions of civil society—has received little attention in research on authoritarian states, despite its central place in Tocqueville's original analyses and a substantial body of subsequent literature on the ways in which participation in civil society may serve to socialize people into democratic citizenship.[17]

Tocquevillian Perspectives on Associations and Democratic Culture

Extant social theory generally holds that civil society associations are productive of democracy in two ways. First, as exemplified in much literature on civil society in authoritarian regimes (and in democracies), civil society can provide for interest-group representation. For example, people with HIV can band together to demand better public health policies or petition that lower-cost treatment be made available to people with HIV, amplifying their voices to policymakers. The second way in which civil society is thought to bolster democracy comes from Tocqueville's observation that Americans learn the skill and habits of democracy by coming together as equals around common causes.

Tocqueville attributed the equality evident in American associations—and American society more generally—to the equality of origins of Americans. In his view, because the United States never had a formal aristocracy, its people had only ever known equality, and, therefore, when they came together (in civil society) they viewed one another as equals and worked to set aside narrow personal interests in favor of the larger interests of their community. Although clearly Tocqueville's analysis downplayed the many forms of inequality present in the United States in the 1830s, his argument continues to influence contemporary scholars who agree that it is within the organizations of civil society that Americans learn how to be democratic.

Within this body of literature, Pamela Paxton has argued that "voluntary associations provide a training ground for new political leaders, help members practice compromise and learn tolerance, and stimulate individual participation in politics."[18] In the same vein, Larry Diamond has articulated a strong form of the "habits of democracy" requirement to assess the contribution of an association to democracy: "An organization may be able to represent group interests, check the power of the state, and perform many other democratic functions even if it is not internally democratic. But if, in its own patterns of governance, it perpetuates norms that penalize dissent, exalt the leader over the group, and cloak the exercise of power, one thing it will not do is build a culture of democracy. If civil society organizations are to function as 'large free schools' for democracy . . . they must function democratically in their internal processes."[19]

Other scholars, including Theda Skocpol, Joshua Cohen, Joel Rogers, Robert Putnam, Robert Leonardi, and Rafaella Nanetti[20] echo Diamond's thinking in arguing, as Archon Fung puts it, that "associations conducive to democracy themselves have forms that are consistent with democratic principles."[21] Ultimately, such scholarship suggests, associations can develop democratic habits in their members only inasmuch as their internal practices evidence democratic values. In turn, internally democratic cultures are necessary for associations in civil society to contribute to a democratic politics in the larger political sphere.

It is to the process of "civic socialization," as elucidated by Archon Fung, that this book speaks most directly. In his sweeping review of the literature, Fung observes that:

> Of the hypothesized effects of associations on democracy, the category that has received the most contemporary attention has concerned how associations affect the attitudes, skills, and behaviors of individuals in ways that benefit democracy. One version of this view focuses upon the attitudes and dispositions of citizens. In this view, secondary associations inculcate civic virtues in their members. Such virtues include attention to the public good, habits of cooperation, toleration, respect for others, respect for the rule of law, willingness to participate in public life, self-confidence, and efficacy . . . To the extent that individuals possess these values, democracy itself becomes more robust, fair, and effective in myriad ways.[22]

To be sure, even in studies of well-established democracies, the potential of civil society to instill democratic skills has been a key area of contestation, with some work lamenting a perceived decline in sociability and a shift away from face-to-face associational interactions.[23] In surveying U.S. associational life, for example, Theda Skocpol worries about the late twentieth-century trend toward professionalization and "memberless" organizations. In her assessment, these new associations, which are typically "managed from the top with few opportunities for member leverage from below," ultimately deprive average citizens of the chance to engage in the most basic experiences of U.S. democracy.[24] Others have argued that the internal cultures of civil society organizations need not necessarily foster democratic norms or behaviors. Civil society, observes Alagappa, "is populated by diverse formal and informal organizations with widely varying structures, resources, purposes, and methods. Not all civil society organizations have the purpose, potential, or consequence of advancing democracy."[25]

Indeed, the broader sociological literature on cultures of democratic communication arguably gives little reason to assume that democratic culture—at least one that has implications for a democratic politics—is a clear product of all civil society organizations. Empirical sociological work on the intersections of democratic culture and communication in civil society groups in the United States, despite being the original source of Tocqueville's inspiration, raises strong doubts as to whether American civil society is up to the task of supporting, preserving, and reproducing a democratic politics. In contrast to the ideal-typical Tocquevillian images of people coming together as equals to work towards common goals, learning and practicing the skills and habits of democracy, a number of scholars looking at the political implications of small group norms and voluntary associations in the United States have revealed dynamics of exclusion, a learned political apathy, and racial and class bias that would leave advocates of participatory democratic norms dismayed if not outright disillusioned.[26]

The nature of debate about associations in democracies and associations in authoritarian states is, by definition and necessity, different. Many assumptions that hold broadly true across democratic societies—such as accountability of politicians subject to electoral pressure; media that are free to report on corruption and that civil society can use to promote alternative views on societal problems; and the right to association without fear of repression—are not characteristic of social and political life under authoritarian regimes. The concerns with social inequalities and the harm they likely do to public democratic discourse and decision-making—which are rightfully and importantly topics of scholarly discussion in the United States and other democratic countries—are rendered almost irrelevant in China's one-party authoritarian state, where public discussion and the state's interactions with civil society are highly constrained, at best.

More pointedly, unspoken in Fung's summarization of the literature is that most studies of the internal dynamics and impacts of civil society have been concerned with the socializing effects of associations *in democracies*. Far fewer scholars have sought to investigate the internal cultures of associations in authoritarian regimes.

In the section that follows, I supplement this work on Tocqueville with another theoretical perspective that is essential as a lens for understanding the political implications of civil society organizations under authoritarian regimes: Antonio Gramsci's concept of hegemony.

A Gramscian Perspective on Civil Society Under Authoritarianism

When Tocqueville was trying to understand the success of democracy in the United States, he placed central emphasis on the democratic habits and "mores"[27] that he believed Americans exhibited. Rather than geography or good laws, he argued, it was the "habits, opinions, usages, and beliefs" of Americans that helped them "maintain a democratic republic."[28] "I am convinced," he writes, "that the luckiest of geographical circumstances and the best of laws cannot maintain a constitution in despite of mores, whereas the latter can turn even the most unfavorable circumstances and the worst laws to advantage. The importance of mores is a universal truth to which study and experience continually bring us back."[29]

Tocqueville's emphasis on mores and habits can be seen as presaging the concerns of the widely influential Italian communist, Antonio Gramsci. One of Gramsci's key political concerns was to understand how the liberal-bourgeois class took and maintained control of state power in the industrialized nations of Western Europe. Writing in the 1920s and 1930s, Gramsci contrasted his native Italy and other European states with the newly formed Soviet Union, concluding that the associations comprising civil society were a prime battleground for contesting visions of social and political legitimacy. The control that the dominant economic class exerted in the realm of society, he argued, was more subtle than explicit, based largely on consent rather than simply on coercion, and geared toward reproducing the worldview of the dominant class. By legitimizing their domination over the working classes through cultural means, defining the order they established as natural, the ruling classes in European society had cultivated a pervasive hegemony that made their domination seem almost inevitable. The organizations of civil society were, in Gramsci's analysis, simultaneously the conveyors of this hegemony and the sites of its production. In contrast to optimistic neo-Tocquevillian assessments of the democratizing potential of civil society, Gramsci saw the state as including both political and civil society. We should, then, perhaps not be surprised to see civil society organizations practicing and reproducing norms favorable to the state, especially a strong authoritarian state. Whereas much ink has been spilled describing the coercion exercised by authoritarian regimes toward civil society groups, here I explore how an authoritarian state's preferred norms and practices actually work within civil society to suppress the emergence of democratic alternatives.

For Gramsci, the distinction commonly drawn between the state and civil society was arguably a false one. Rather than seeing the state *and* society, Gramsci suggests we should more properly seek to uncover and recognize the state *in* society. His critique of a book by Daniel Halévey makes clear this interfolding of the lines between the official bodies and actions of the state and the hegemony produced within civil society: "For Halévey, 'State' is the representative apparatus; and he discovers that the most important events of French history . . . have not been due to initiatives by political organisms deriving from universal suffrage, but to those either of private organisms (capitalist firms, General Staff, etc.) or of great civil servants unknown to the country at large, etc. But what does that signify if not that by 'State' should be understood not only the apparatus of government, but also the 'private' apparatus of 'hegemony' or civil society?"[30]

Although Gramsci nowhere gives a single clear definition of "hegemony," in another passage, he writes that the production of hegemony is a state project: "the State is the entire complex of practical and theoretical activities with which the ruling class not only justifies and maintains its dominance, but manages to win the active consent of those over whom it rules."[31] Gramsci's innovative concept of hegemony, as Stuart Hall observes, forces us to rethink "the moral, cultural, and intellectual dimensions of power, on its double articulation in state and in civil society, on the inter-play between authority, leadership, domination, and the 'education of consent,'" leaving us with "an enlarged conception of power, and its molecular operations, its investment on many different sites."[32]

In the pages that follow, I suggest that we may consider the tensions apparent within civil society in an authoritarian state between a hierarchical, autocratic culture and a more bottom-up, democratic yearning as a contest between the ruling power's hegemony and a nascent counterhegemony. Such a reading, although not directly referencing a contest between two class-based groups, is in line with other extensions of Gramscian thought.[33] Ernesto Laclau and Chantal Mouffe, for example, argued eloquently for how the social movements that swept through Europe and North America in the 1960s and 1970s should be understood as non-class-based contestations of hegemony:

These new political subjects: women, students, young people, racial, sexual, and regional minorities, as well as the various anti-institutional and ecological struggles, not only cannot be located at the level of relations of production . . .;

on top of this, they define their objectives in a radically different way. Their enemy is not defined by its function of exploitation, but by wielding a certain power. And this power, too, does not derive from a place in the relations of production, but is the outcome of a form of organization characteristic of the present society. This society is indeed capitalist, but this is not its only characteristic; it is sexist and patriarchal as well, not to mention racist.[34]

Such "popular democratic struggles," Roger Simon emphasizes, "have their own specific qualities and cannot be reduced to the class struggle although they are related to it in various ways."[35] Laclau and Mouffe argue that the traditional Marxist relegation of political struggles to a subordinate position vis-à-vis the economism of history had blinded socialist theorists and the socialist movement to other, non-class-based forms of oppression. Their analysis points to hegemony as a practice of politics, writing that Gramsci "does not confine the primacy of the political to revolutionary conjunctures, but makes it the articulatory principle of every social institution, including periods of stability."[36]

In an exemplary application of a non-class-based understanding of hegemony generated at around the same time as Laclau and Mouffe's writing, the concept of "hegemonic masculinity" developed by gender scholar R. W. Connell and colleagues[37] drew direct inspiration from Gramscian perspectives on domination and struggle. Their formulation identifies hegemonic masculinity as "the pattern of practice (i.e., things done, not just a set of role expectations or an identity) that allowed men's dominance over women to continue."[38] While describing a particular expression of masculinity as "hegemonic," Connell follows Gramsci in arguing that hegemony "does not mean total cultural dominance, the obliteration of alternatives. It means ascendancy achieved within a balance of forces, that is, a state of play. Other patterns and groups are subordinated rather than eliminated."[39] This novel perspective on hegemony demonstrates the pliability of Gramsci's concept to address deeply entrenched forms and practices of domination that do not have an obvious or solely economic character.

As Connell suggests, to paint Gramsci's picture of civil society as rigid, stagnant, or impenetrable to forces of revolution would be inaccurate. As much scholarship from the past several decades has emphasized, he also saw civil society as a site of contestation in which the dominated classes could construct and articulate a counterhegemony, based on their experiences and worldviews, to challenge the status quo vision of legitimate social and political order. Although Gramsci had in mind a working-class counterhegemony that might lead to socialist revolution, Stuart Hall has applied this same principle to argue that counterhegemony could help make sense of the surprisingly successful ascendancy of Thatcherism in the United Kingdom. Hall viewed the United Kingdom in the decades between World War II and the mid-1970s as a time of broad social agreement in which people took for granted the existence of the welfare state. Thatcherism, Hall argues, "was a project to engage, to contest, *that* project, and, wherever possible, to dismantle it, and to put something *new* in place. It entered the political field in an historic contest, not just for power, but for popular authority, for hegemony."[40] "By studying this 'counter-hegemony' at work," Hall observes, one can begin "to understand what a 'hegemonic political project' might be like."[41]

These extensions of Gramsci offer a guide for understanding the nature and operation of hegemony within civil society under authoritarianism. In the pages that follow, I propose we consider an authoritarian political party, the Chinese Communist Party (CCP), as the progenitor and beneficiary of a particular sort of hegemony. Through its tight control over institutions like education, the courts, mass organizations (e.g., the All-China Federation of Trade Unions and the Communist Youth League), business, and religious groups, the party continuously works to embed its political expectations—including its organizational norms and practices—into all realms of associational life, reinforcing its legitimacy and right to rule.[42] Using interviews and participant observation data that focus on the internal organizational culture of Chinese civil society organizations, and by investigating the kinds of "pattern of practice" that reinforce standing power relations, we can see the contours of a broad hegemonic authoritarianism begin to take form.

In contrast to the ways in which the political science literature has adopted the term "hegemonic" as a descriptor for a form of hybrid political system with limited elections[43] and the ways that Theodor Adorno and his colleagues[44] have used "authoritarian" to describe certain personality traits and political preferences, I propose a distinctively sociological definition of "hegemonic authoritarianism" that builds on insight from Gramsci and his analysis of civil society. This conceptualization emphasizes the overarching institutionalized norms and practices that structure and shape the organizational lives of people living under an authoritarian state. It allows us to see how authoritarian regimes can generate a particular model of exercising authority that permeates virtually all aspects of associational and organizational life. Once entrenched, this pattern of practice becomes a taken-for-granted way of experiencing and exercising power that works to suppress democratic alternatives, even within civil society.

The Authoritarian Society

In trying to anticipate democratic challenges to authoritarian regimes, observers often look to dissidents and organizational actions like public protests for signs of impending change. In the former Soviet Union and its satellites, the emergence of individual dissidents, like Andrei Sakharov in Russia and Václav Havel in Czechoslovakia, demonstrated that the human spirit does yearn for something beyond compulsory rule following and that the human imagination persists in dreams of freedom even within the overwhelmingly narrow confines of totalitarianism. Although China today is, arguably, *merely* authoritarian and not totalitarian,[45] the same kinds of yearnings are articulated by individual activists and are palpable in civil society organizations. Deploying the advantages of advanced surveillance technology, China's mature authoritarian state is able to identify and remove from society—or at least the public eye—influential individuals who challenge its political and cultural hegemony.[46] China provides many such examples, from Nobel Prize winner and democracy advocate Liu Xiaobo to people less well-known outside the country, like Xu Zhiyong, a Peking University law graduate who became an outspoken rights activist before being imprisoned in 2014. Of course, authoritarian states are generally wary of people organizing outside of state control, typically seeking to repress, coopt, or occasionally even tolerate civil society groups as long as political change is not on the agenda.[47]

As important as dissidents and civil society organizations may be for nurturing, inspiring, and leading democratic change, the obstacles they face are not simply repressive state officials or legal prohibitions. The social norms and practices that support authoritarianism can be so deeply ingrained across multiple social arenas that they work not only to ensure the regular functioning of the authoritarian state but also as a means for producing and reproducing an authoritarian society. As I will argue, although Chinese civil society participants often imagine NGOs as more participatory, democratic spaces in which their voices will matter, their hopes and aspirations are frequently dashed by the reality of life inside their groups. Comparing their experiences inside civil society groups to other organizational settings reveals the depth and pervasiveness of the authoritarian practices they chafe against.

More broadly, authoritarianism is commonly studied as a repressive form of political arrangement that maintains power in the hands of a particular leader or group,[48] whereas democracy is characterized as a set of political structures and processes as well as a cultural or societal system that is perceived to support those structures and processes.[49] In the study of democracy, it is the merging of the two—institutions and structures on one hand, and cultural systems on the other—that allows analysts to discuss democratic societies virtually interchangeably with democratic political systems. In contrast, analyses of authoritarianism focus predominantly on formal political structures or repressive state actions, with some occasional references to (political) history or cultural influences writ large.

Marlies Glasius, in a recent critique of the political science literature on authoritarianism, argues that we should distinguish between authoritarian practices that suppress accountability and "illiberal practices," defining the latter as "patterned and organized infringements of individual autonomy and dignity."[50] At over seventy years in control and counting, mature authoritarian states like China's, however, show us how these two aspects of authoritarian rule can intimately align to create an "authoritarian society." The resultant hegemonic authoritarianism, systematically produced and reproduced through a mixture of coercion and consent, emerges from the combination of the brute force of the state with the illiberal practices of power that are nurtured and embedded in the society's broader organizational life. As the data I present below suggest, in an authoritarian society, the lack of freedoms in the larger political sphere is mirrored at the microlevel arenas of social life, subtly but consistently reinforcing the status quo. In line with other scholarship on authoritarian resilience,[51] these dynamics require us to consider authoritarian society not as an aberration from an assumed modern democratic orthodoxy but as a stable social and political system capable of sustaining itself much further into the future.

CIVIL SOCIETY AND THE INTRODUCTION OF NGOS TO CHINA

Since the end of the Cold War in the early 1990s, international philanthropic organizations and the democracy-promotion arms of democratic governments have given a resource-rich boost to the "NGO-ization" of social concerns around the globe. Monies for and ideas about best practices have flowed from largely international sources to some of the world's most troubled spots, including for issues like education, health care, and labor rights but also for the development of NGOs.[52] The 1995 United Nations Conference on Women in Beijing is widely credited with introducing the term NGO to China, as hosting rights obliged the People's Republic of China (PRC) government to hold an NGO forum alongside the official gathering of United Nations (UN) state delegations. During the leadup to the conference, China's first few grassroots NGOs were just beginning to emerge around environmental concerns and women's rights, and the government was establishing new government-organized NGOs (GONGOs) to address the growing needs of an increasingly complex society. Having been influenced directly or indirectly by the Women's Conference, in the 1990s and early 2000s many new citizen-initiated groups embraced the label NGO, and others adopted the descriptor "grassroots," as both terms highlighted their nongovernmental origins and sometimes helped them win favor from foreign donors. The Women's NGO Forum and subsequent international training programs and exchanges depicted a professionalized NGO "world" that attracted Chinese idealists and visionary social activists. Indeed, many of China's grassroots NGOs were launched by charismatic individuals who articulated compelling visions for addressing wrongs, helping people in need, and pursuing other goals that promised to have an impact on Chinese society for the better.

After an initial debate in the early 1990s as to whether China ever had or could have something akin to civil society,[53] scholarship on the topic sought to make sense of the state's support for GONGOs and, more recently, its treatment of emerging grassroots civil society organizations. Over the past three decades, the number of officially registered NGOs in China has grown tremendously, from less than five thousand in 1988 to more than nine hundred thousand in 2021.[54] Although most observers believe the vast majority of these to be GONGOs, since the turn of the century, there has also been rapid growth in grassroots NGOs in any number of fields, from HIV/AIDS to environmental protection to labor rights.[55] Research has taken up a rich variety of topics, including how civil society groups engage in policy advocacy, how political concerns and the legal framework for associations afford or restrict opportunities for groups to form and grow, philanthropy by China's newly wealthy economic elites, and participation in government-directed volunteer efforts.[56] Like the broader literature on civil society in authoritarian states, however, most of this has been carried out under the general framing of state-society relations, seeking to understand how organizations are influenced by or interact with state actors.

Defining Civil Society

Whether in democracies, authoritarian states, or transnationally, a consensus on the definitions of civil society and NGOs has proven elusive.[57] In authoritarian states, the debate has often centered around whether GONGOs should be considered a part of civil society. Erica Frantz, for example, describes GONGOs as "essentially fake civil society organizations staffed by regime allies,"[58] whereas scholarship on GONGOs in China has argued that questions of autonomy from the state are not so black and white.[59] Another important distinction in the field more generally is between NGOs and voluntary associations. Although voluntary associations may be NGOs, not all NGOs are voluntary associations. Many NGOs are composed predominantly of paid staff engaged in professional advocacy or social service delivery work. This distinction is crucial for considerations of democracy because voluntary associations are the civil society form most typically viewed as inculcating the skills and habits of democracy. What might be a coming together of equals in a voluntary group, easily becomes, in a professionalized NGO, a relationship between employer—the organization, the founder, or the "boss"—and employee. Many professionalized NGOs also take on the pyramidal structure of a business, with a leader at the top—in China, this is typically the NGO's founder—and others beneath them at various levels. This process of bureaucratization and professionalization is familiar to social scientists who study any number of organizational realms, but in the NGO field, its potentially depoliticizing effects and impacts on social change movements have been identified and critiqued around the globe, from Armenia to South Africa and Bangladesh to Palestine.[60]

In terms of their internal dynamics and cultures, GONGOs and professionalized NGOs in China have much more in common with each other than with Tocquevillian ideal-typical voluntary associations. Both are generally dominated by a leader at the top and, once they reach a certain scale, are staffed by paid professionals arranged in layers of hierarchy who wield varying degrees of authority over the group's agenda and its actual work. Professionalized NGOs and even some GONGOs do attract and utilize volunteers, but seldom do volunteers participate in their day-to-day decisions, much less in steering the direction of the group as a whole.

In this chapter, I depart from recent scholarship on China that maintains and interrogates the divide between GONGOs, NGOs, and voluntary associations. Although some distinctions do feature in my analysis, grouping these three into the catchall term "civil society organizations" allows us to see more clearly what they share—a common inheritance of authoritarian norms and practices and the propensity to serve as sites for the reproduction and contestation of hegemonic authoritarianism.

Socialization Into Authoritarian Culture

Before examining the organizational cultures experienced by civil society participants, it is instructive to consider the patterns of power that shape daily life in other realms of association. As many readings of Gramsci suggest, education is a particularly useful institution to begin to see how hegemony works, and here I argue it is especially revealing of how hegemonic authoritarianism works. In China, like most countries today, school is arguably the first and most impactful public institution that a person consciously encounters, shaping one's understanding of the social world writ large. Schools are structured by the same sorts of power relations and hierarchies of decision-making that would be identifiable to almost anyone educated in the modern era. Young pupils are typically at the bottom of any chain of authority, and their behaviors are carefully supervised and regulated by teachers. Teachers, in turn, are supervised by department heads and, above them, a principal. In China's one-party system, however, teachers and even the principal fall under the authority of a Communist Party secretary. Party secretaries are charged with ensuring the overall politically "correct" functioning of schools, from primary grades on up through university. In short, schools in China provide not only educational basics but also serve as sites of deliberate training to shape Chinese citizens into political subjects of an authoritarian regime. This first site of contact with the realities of hegemonic authoritarianism provides a lasting education in the political structuring of society, one that will be reinforced in other settings as people progress into adulthood.

Although small children may be only vaguely aware of the larger power dynamics that structure their schools, they experience hierarchical authority relations at the microlevel from an early age. Starting in primary school, each Chinese classroom typically has a class leader, a fellow student selected for each classroom, out of as many as fifty students. Some teachers allow elections for class leaders, but they are often chosen by teachers with an eye toward those students who are most well-behaved or those with the highest grades. Several other lower-level "student cadre" positions collectively teach students about political organization and political life. Even when student leaders are elected, teachers have "the power to both recommend and to block the election of a certain student."[61] As student cadres, class leaders help teachers keep order in the classroom, keep tabs on misbehaving classmates outside of school hours, and are authorized to deduct points from individual students or small groups for various infractions.[62] In such a system, children have early and direct experience with upper-level peers of the same age exercising authority over them in a formal setting. They normally also understand that these class leaders are, in turn, subject to the control of adult teachers and still others above them.[63] As anthropologist Mette Hansen argues, "the cadre system remains one of the most significant tools for training students to govern themselves and their peers and adapt to and internalize hierarchical structures. It is a political tool and a technology of discipline in the Foucauldian sense."[64] Universities continue the institutionalization of hierarchy among peers by mandating standardized, formal leadership roles in school-approved student clubs, student unions, academic departments, and various organizations sponsored by the Communist Youth League.[65]

Beyond schools, private businesses and government agencies in China are typically organized in a top-down fashion, and workers across many fields have very clear understandings of their relationship to those above (*shangmian*) and those below (*xiamian*). Business owners, or bosses (*laoban*), are often seen as being in charge of everyone and everything, dictating to employees on matters both big and small. Despite the CCP's early propagation of the egalitarian term comrade (*tongzhi*), an expansive, standardized hierarchy divides civil servants into twenty-seven different ranks, with up to fourteen different grades within each rank.[66] Titles of government officials, as well, convey the exact rank someone occupies, with desk head (*chuzhang*) below office head (*zhuren*) and division deputy (*fu sizhang*) beneath division head (*sizhang*). In everyday life, to avoid offending by pointing out a superior's still-subordinate-to-someone status, lower-ranked people often dispense with the deputy title when directly addressing a higher-ranked deputy, so that, for example, a vice minister (*fu buzhang*) is addressed as minister (*buzhang*), at least when not in the presence of the higher-ranking actual minister. This face-giving practice inflates the importance of the deputy and allows the subordinate to avoid demeaning the superior by pointing out his or her deputy status. Such wordplay performances highlight and solidify the hierarchy that structures many organizations.

Although formal hierarchical structures are familiar to observers of democratic societies, in an authoritarian state they have far-reaching impacts on people's objective power status and their subjective sense of dignity. Yet such a situation is not without its discontents. Many people active in Chinese civil society resent and resist such top-down status quo power relations and the daily indignities they entail. Nonetheless, as the bulk of the data suggests, even leaders of grassroots NGOs, like their nonactivist peers in China, have grown up in an authoritarian state and thus often end up reproducing many of the authoritarian practices that some of them, rhetorically at least, would like to see dismantled.

Deepening Contradictions:
The Evolution of Civil Society–State Relations in China

The culture of authoritarianism presented in this analysis should not be misconstrued as a static one, although I do argue it is hegemonic in the Gramscian sense. It is, rather, the increasingly obvious outcome of decades-long contestations between the governability an increasingly powerful authoritarian state desires and the democratic visions of bottom-up civil actors. Central to this struggle has been the rising role of the individual and the increasing embrace of rights by both the state and the people. Not surprisingly, many of the Chinese state's actions with regards to civil society have sown the seeds of discontent and contestation by the very people it seeks to govern.

The wide-sweeping market reforms initiated in 1979 by the late Deng Xiaoping drastically transformed China's economy, and in the process, opened society up to new ideas and expectations about political responsiveness and individual autonomy. Moving from a centrally planned economy—in which jobs were assigned by those above—to one in which private entrepreneurship and innovation were increasingly encouraged and rewarded created an economic system that privileged individual initiative. For many people, this radically new way of pursuing financial security encouraged them to imagine other ways in which they could take more control over their own lives and prospects, including through political reform. Indeed, the turmoil of the 1989 student-led protest movement in Tiananmen Square—which saw protests not just in Beijing but in cities nationwide—came about in part because of the increasingly free flow of ideas and expectations that political reform would accompany or follow economic reforms. Liberal intellectuals, university students, and even some top party officials in the mid- to late-1980s were openly discussing what democracy, civil society, and elections in China might look like if the party were to loosen its reins on political power. The violent suppression of protestors in June 1989 quickly put an end to such public conversations, but many of the questions and ideas that began circulating during that period persisted in quieter corners and smaller, less public circles of friends.

China's oldest environmental NGO, Friends of Nature, was founded in 1994 with the explicit permission of the central government Ministry of Civil Affairs. Global civil society also played an obvious role in stimulating the emergence of grassroots groups. Leading up to and following the 1995 UN Conference on Women, numerous women's rights NGOs emerged to press for social and policy change on a variety of fronts. The Global Fund, with its requirements for community involvement in the distribution of donor monies to help fight HIV-AIDS, facilitated the growth of numerous health-focused groups and gave LGBT groups at least limited political cover in their community-building efforts. After Tiananmen, the government, recognizing its inability to see into societal problems the way that members of local communities could, officially encouraged the formation of volunteer organizations in major Chinese cities.[67] Such policy innovations offered the state a means to uncover simmering social problems before they boiled over but also gave individual volunteers the chance to exercise their judgement to determine what problems deserved attention and to devise solutions to address them. This combination of state-led volunteering efforts and bottom-up civil society initiatives, beginning in the 1990s, continued through the early 2000s with the arrival of the seemingly civil society–friendly Hu-Wen administration in 2002.

At the same time, as economic reform deepened in the 1980s through the early 2000s, there was a marked rise in expressions of individualism.[68] These changes were widespread and dramatic, with people increasingly free to choose their occupation, casting off rigid restrictions on internal migration to take up jobs in cities where work was newly available, purchasing (and choosing decorations for) their apartments as opposed to living in assigned housing, traveling and studying abroad, sharing personal views and experiences on the internet, establishing and promoting nonstate media platforms, embracing the state-legitimated language of rights and pressing their grievances against particular government actors, and a host of other actions aimed at pursuing or expressing individual desires, dreams, and aspirations.

For much of the Hu-Wen administration, the increasing individuation of Chinese life writ large was accompanied by a semiofficial sanctioning of China's emergent civil society groups, which had begun to take off in larger numbers just as Hu ascended to power and the internet allowed more people to connect virtually and in person.[69] An increasing rights awareness among the general population led to a number of high-profile legal victories by rights protection (*weiquan*) lawyers that received positive nationwide media attention. Hu's slogan of building a "harmonious society" initially seemed expansive enough to encompass civil society groups and critical voices from the legal profession (and other fields) who sought to press for legal, political, and social reforms. Yet what now appears as an almost golden age for civil society during the Hu era came to a quick close as he headed out of office, setting the stage for a broader crackdown by Xi Jinping's administration from 2012 onward.

On the eve of Xi's ascension to power, the Hu-Wen government had already begun regretting the relatively loose rein it had given to civil society groups. Others have documented the changes occurring during this period, including the suppression and crackdown on civil society and rights protection lawyers.[70] Hand in hand with repression, however, has also come a more subtle form of control over the sector. Realizing that its capacity to control at the microlevel has its limits, the party has in the past decade begun to employ less coercive measures to shift the focus and energies of civil society actors in China. Through mechanisms, such as a newly introduced Charity Law and a new INGO Law, the party has publicly declared what sorts of fields are open to civil society involvement—helping needy children, for example—and which are verboten—anything that can be construed as vaguely political—from both domestic NGOs and international actors.[71] At the same time, while erecting barriers to support from more liberal—and thus suspicious—international donors and INGOs,[72] the state has begun to offer government funds to properly registered groups. Crucially, the state's purchasing of services program is competition based, inhibiting cooperation across groups and adding an additional layer of screening to ensure that only organizations working for state goals can gain access to the large amounts of funding the state controls and the political security and legitimacy conferred by a state seal of approval.[73] Yet even this newly developed state effort is not a wholly monolithic top-down enterprise, as at least one study of government procurement in China has found that NGOs providing services through state contracts sometimes also find room to engage successfully in advocacy.[74]

Hegemonic authoritarianism has been constructed through multiple means. Building on a presumed Chinese tradition of patriarchal control—as some of my interviewees referenced—is one method. Modeling hierarchy and autocracy early in the educational system is another. Inserting itself into civil society through procurement of services has given the state yet another way to remind civil society actors who is in charge—both of the funding that most groups need, and of the agendas that they are allowed to pursue without fear of repression. Finally, the state conveys through various channels—including the Charity Law, for example—the desirability of (a narrow imagination of) professionalization and bureaucratic structures within civil society organizations, packaging them as imperatives of modernity and in line with the political norms of China as a whole.

The party's promoting of rhetorical democracy while using multiple means to insinuate its preferred organization of authority into the realm of civil society has set the stage for a multifaceted contest of ideas that cannot be quickly or neatly resolved. To be sure, the spate of recent repressive actions taken by authorities could make this back-and-forth between the state and civil society look as if the state is winning a Manichean battle between good and evil. A longer-term view, however, reveals a more nuanced picture, one in which the democratic yearnings of civil society actors are nurtured by many of the party-state's own actions over decades of policy shifts.

DEMOCRATIC YEARNINGS

In research conducted across more than a decade, the democratic yearnings of civil society participants came through as a consistent and recurring theme regardless of organizational type or field of activity. Even though most people offered no clear articulation of democracy, NGOs were often talked about as an idealized space where equality should be valued, a place where multiple voices should be free to speak and are meant to be heard, and a place where individuals could use their personal skills to make a difference in society. There was, moreover, a sense that NGOs, in particular, were somehow supposed to be different from the authoritarian organizations people experienced in other realms of life. As one young volunteer put it, "The term itself, 'nongovernmental', should mean it's somehow different from the way the government does things, right?"

Such imaginings of NGOs and civil society probably have multiple origins. For a slightly older generation, one can argue that Marxism introduced the idea of equality to China, and that over the past seven decades—and despite many episodes of political violence—the notion of equality has taken root in local soil, at least as an ideal. For some in a younger generation—especially those active in bottom-up volunteer-based groups—in the past decade and more the party's own claiming and propagation of democracy (*minzhu*), freedom (*ziyou*), and equality (*pingdeng*) as "core socialist values"[75] has given these ideals an assumed Chinese-ness. As one university-age volunteer explained as she reflected on her earlier naivete, "We grow up reading this stuff about democracy and equality in our textbooks and think they're a part of Chinese values."

Although my research covered groups around the country, it is not by accident that the two youth-led voluntary groups that perhaps best represent the emergence of a democratic counterhegemony have grown (up) in southern China. For the participants in these particular groups—including university-age students through to people in their early forties now—proximity to Hong Kong, globalization, and an upward trajectory of material prosperity since the 1980s are other factors leading to their identification with these "core socialist values." At the same time, the CCP's embrace of the market economy since 1978 has created an ideological vacuum in which democratic principles are attractive to some young people, offering a kind of idealized morality and belief system that allows them to pursue meaningful lives. Importantly, the absence of nationwide political repression during their lives—many are too young to have understood the 1989 Tiananmen protests or were born afterward—has allowed this youngest generation of Chinese youth the freedom to be politically naïve, at least for some period of time.

Some participants in Chinese civil society, especially those involved for a longer period of time, are deeply engaged in exploring the meaning of democracy. Although "What is democracy?" is perhaps the strictest translation of the question a few respondents raised—*shenma jiaozuo minzhu?*—in the context of their experiences within civil society, the actual meaning of the question is perhaps better rendered with multiple inferences as: "What does it mean *to be* democratic? How does a person, or an organization, *be* democratic? How does one put democratic values and virtues into practice?" Reflections on these questions were offered throughout my fieldwork, even when people did not explicitly use the term "democracy"—a loaded and sometimes controversial word in any context but particularly so in an authoritarian state.

Rather than discuss "democracy" per se, participants in GONGOs and professionalized NGOs often articulated their idealized view of civil society by drawing a contrast with the undemocratic realities of the organizations where they worked or, for younger volunteers, with the "normal" university clubs they had also joined. A conversation early in my fieldwork with a staff member of a labor rights organization crystallized for me a problem many would later describe in other settings. This middle-aged former factory worker confided in me about the suppression of differing opinions in her organization and the reticence of her colleagues to challenge decisions taken by the group's leadership, even when they disagreed. Her view exemplified the desires and frustrations voiced by many of my respondents:

> People in NGOs, even though they're in NGOs, don't have a real sense of equality (*pingdeng de xintai*). The people above think "I'm better, I'm better at analyzing things, I'm clearer on things" and the people below think "I should obey (*fucong*), because I'm below." But I think this is exactly where there should be the biggest difference between NGOs on the one hand and businesses and government agencies on the other. I also feel equality ought to be the biggest advantage of NGOs over government agencies and businesses.
>
> But it doesn't work that way so often. Like you have a PhD, so what you say counts more than what some lower-level person thinks. Even if that lower-level person is right, and you're saying the same thing, people are more inclined to believe you when you say it, because you have a PhD.

Her emphasis on equality and her sense of what *should* separate NGOs from other realms of organizational life was common to many civil society participants. At another professionalized NGO where several staff members had left recently, one current staff member attributed their departure to their dashed expectations about the democratic potential of the group:

> Most of the people who left recently did so because their contracts were up, sure, but a main reason for most of them was that they had objections to the way things were run. Not towards [the leader] personally per se, but towards the style of the entire organization. Some of them said that they were drawn to NGOs because they expected it would be something different, or that when they visited other NGOs they were very impressed with the way everyone

discusses issues and problems as equals. But here the boss (*laoda*) makes all the decisions.

Before coming here, I thought NGO people would all be idealistic, like me. But then I got here and realized that the reality is not actually like that. Most people on staff look at this as a job, a career, not an ideal they're devoting their life to working at, trying to make become a reality. Their motivation doesn't necessarily come from their heart . . . This is very different than what I expected before I came here.

Indeed, less than a year after this conversation, it was largely her own disillusionment that drove her to resign from her position.

THE FAULT LINES OF A CONTESTED HEGEMONY

The sorts of democratic yearnings recounted above were often cited as both motivations to participation and as reasons for disillusionment with life inside Chinese civil society organizations. In part III, I dig deeper into these topics. In the next sections of this chapter, however, I analyze three key themes—hierarchy, autocratic leadership, and the stifling of dissent—as the larger fault lines along which hegemonic authoritarianism is contested within Chinese civil society. Although these three phenomena are analytically distinct, in practice they typically are experienced as intertwined and mutually reinforcing.

Hierarchy

As I have suggested, in the broader society a top-down (*zishang erxia*) structure of decision-making and exercising power is considered the norm. Reflecting on his previous government job, one worker in a professionalized NGO matter-of-factly asserted that "Chinese people are used to a top-down style. They send documents downwards (*fa wenjian xia lai*), and you just take them, implement your part, then pass them down to those below you with orders telling them what to do. You have to make no decision—that has already been done by those above. It was like this where I worked before, at that national government office."

Indeed, the language of hierarchy permeates virtually every realm of Chinese organizational life, whether in government, schools, business, or civil society. So deeply ingrained is the distinction between "those above" and "those below" that many see this mode of exercising and organizing power not only as normalized but also as almost natural and inevitable.

In talking about a government-run volunteer association where one social work graduate student interned, he had no other way to describe the association's purposes and functions but to default to a series of above-below distinctions. His depiction shows not only how GONGOs are expected to operate in service of government goals but also how the language of hierarchy is seemingly inescapable when analyzing the exercise of authority in this sphere:[76] "Below every community, there are street committees. Below every street committee, there are neighborhood committees. The volunteer association is under the district's Communist Youth League. . . . In most [government-organized] volunteer associations, the association assigns you work, then you go do it. Before we [social work students] started working with them, they only met each other at formal meetings, but those were organized by those above."

Another social work student with experience interning in GONGOs was even more critical of what she saw as the failings of government-directed volunteering for "social service" purposes:

> Most volunteer associations are top-down. They have thousands of people on their registers, but very few of them are individual registrations. The volunteer associations prefer to get volunteers from government agencies or businesses, because that way they can get hundreds of people on their registration roll at once.
>
> I went with people one time to visit the elderly in a nursing home. . . . All the volunteers were from a company. They were organized by the local [government-organized] volunteer association and that company. They took gifts, like fruit and other things, to give to the old people and then took a picture as they were giving them the stuff. . . . I talked to some of the old people there and found that they didn't ask for any of these things. They said that people often come in large groups to give them things—often things they don't even need. And they don't talk with them or anything! They just hand them something and have their picture taken. . . .
>
> Later I asked the leader of the company group and learned that many of them were unhappy about having to go do this. I talked to some of [the employees], too, and they said it was like they were just going to fulfill some assignment given down to them by those above.

In these examples, the top-down organization of "service" activities flows from government agencies to semi-government organs (GONGOs) to private sector business activities, where staff were fulfilling "some assignment given down to them by those above."

In the youth-led, volunteer-based groups I studied, contestation of the hierarchy common to mainstream organizations was fierce. The avoidance of hierarchy in these groups was a priority in their recruitment and orientation for new volunteers, and participants in university-based club branches proudly noted their differences from "normal" student groups: "We're unlike normal student clubs where there's that stupid 'those above' and 'those below.' All the four years I've been in it, all we've ever had is a 'person in charge' for each different activity. Everyone puts their ideas out for consideration. There isn't some 'plan' or anything like that, where hierarchical distinctions come into play. Besides, [the larger off-campus group] has always emphasized equality, so in our club we emphasize equality, too. We're extremely sensitive to those [typical] sorts of status distinctions."

Many volunteers gave as an example of their commitment to equality the widespread custom of *not* making distinctions based on age differences among volunteers. As one explained:

When we meet each other, we don't have to call out "elder brother" or "elder sister" or "junior sister." We just call the other person's name. This feels so much closer. It's a feeling I got when I first joined, and I agree with this custom. Because when you call out "elder brother" or "elder sister," it feels like there's a gulf between people. It's true, though, that that is our actual [hierarchical] relationship, and that the elder ones do have more experience than us junior volunteers. But we don't emphasize that [hierarchical distinction], so that our sense of equality is strong, just like you're interacting with your own brothers and sisters.

Although space for these bottom-up voluntary associations is shrinking due to the state's promotion of government-directed volunteering and increasingly strict regulation and repression,[77] their resistances to mainstream norms and practices bring into greater clarity the exercise of power common across all types of civil society organizations and the larger system in which they are embedded. More generally, of course, rankings of all sorts exist in most societies, and hierarchy is not unique to authoritarianism. But it is the ways that authoritarian hierarchies produce affronts to individual dignity—the "illiberal practices" that Marlies Glasius describes[78]—that makes hierarchy distinctive as a tool and feature of nondemocratic rule.

In the next section, I discuss how the phenomenon of the *laoda*—a typically autocratic leader or boss—contributes to the frustrations expressed by NGO participants and also reflects the entrenched authoritarian norms of mainstream society.

Autocracy

As with other aspects of the internal culture of Chinese civil society groups, the autocratic leadership system found in China's larger political system serves as a model for what one finds within many Chinese NGOs. Although since 1949 the party has had some weaker leaders who made some concessions to others in the party elite, in an article analyzing the reconcentration of power in the hands of China's current president, political scientist Joseph Fewsmith writes that a recent party directive demands the top leadership work towards: "upholding general secretary Xi Jinping as the core of the center and upholding the authority and centralized unity of the leadership. In other words, the work of the whole Party must revolve around Xi Jinping. If it is possible to codify personalistic leadership, this document does it."[79] Whether it be Mao Zedong, Deng Xiaoping, or Xi Jinping, the model of the (almost) all-powerful leader at the top is well-known and reproduced across all manner of Chinese institutions.

Although no civil society groups have such explicitly codified personal leaderships as that party directive stipulates for Xi Jinping, in most groups the role of the top leader is clearly undisputed. Indeed, in virtually all the professionalized NGOs and GONGOs I studied, people often follow the custom whereby the term *laoda* (literally, old big) is used to describe the person with the greatest authority. In general, the term implies a clear hierarchical relationship and refers to a central figure (the *laoda*) who often employs an autocratic leadership style.

GONGOs, in particular, are an ideal place to observe autocracy at work, as they usually have little need to aspire to democratic practices or emphasize democratic values in their public rhetoric. Although autocratic *laoda* can be found in almost any organization without regard to gender, at one GONGO dedicated to women's issues, it is predictable—albeit ironic—that the male *laoda* dominates. As one senior (female) staff member described it: "If we have a meeting that lasts two hours, our laoda talks for an hour and 20 minutes. He asks for our thoughts, but nobody says anything. Then we figure in about 10 minutes of break time. . . . In the remaining 30 minutes it's just free talk, people chatting with each other. If laoda picks up on something he finds interesting, he'll take the topic and run with it, using up the remaining time. Our meetings are all about laoda telling us what to do or what he thinks."

Although there are exceptions, the domineering attitude of NGO leaders is a refrain repeated across GONGOs and professionalized NGOs of all stripes. The typical *laoda* is often described as unwilling to listen to the views of others and also prone to use a demeaning tone when addressing "those below": "Sometimes he's so rude, I can't stand it. The other staff really dislike it, too. . . . Sometimes I feel like saying 'I'm not your child!' He thinks that because he's the leader (*lingdao*) he can snap his fingers and you're supposed to come running over."

This style of leadership was common even in grassroots NGOs, regardless of a particular leader's own expressed normative commitments to respect and dignity and the more democratic-sounding goals of the organization. In separate interviews with members of a small team within a professionalized grassroots NGO, the team's leader was viewed with a mixture of respect, fear, and resentment. As one staff member described it:

He shouts at people a lot. He doesn't think about what he has said, though, and he doesn't realize it hurts people to be talked to that way. In this team of four people, there are four hearts (*sigeren you sigexin*) [i.e., the members of the "team" are quite divided.] When people give suggestions, he always replies to them with a really bad attitude to say "No!" . . . You can say "no," but don't get angry and yell at people. . . . He tends to be really explosive! . . . In the [work site], his skills are really good, but he doesn't communicate well. It's always, "You do this! I'll do this." There's no discussion, no choice given to anyone. The tone of voice he uses is like he's barking orders at people.

Again, the speaker's desire to participate and to have voice—"there's no discussion, no choice given to anyone"—reflects a common desire for a more democratic, idealized NGO space where each person matters and their opinion is considered. As another staff member put it, the *laoda* "just tells people to do things without any discussion. If you don't do it, he gets angry and yells. I just can't stand that. I think people need more respect."

As I saw in a number of NGO settings, however, the team's *laoda* himself often holds a very different view. In a self-assessment offered during a formal interview with a visiting foreign "NGO expert," the *laoda* of the small group mentioned previously proclaimed: "We get along really well here. . . . We use participatory management here to run things. I get an extra 100 yuan per month for being the leader here, but it's really only a token amount. I've never seen myself as a leader in that sense. . . . Everyone here participates as equals in the management of the work."

Borrowing the phrase "participatory management" from the foreign-originated training workshops he had attended, and averring that "we get along really well here" were, to me, indications that this small group head had learned what a visiting "expert" would be pleased to hear, whether or not he believed this to be an accurate assessment.[80]

Many civil society staff use the leaders of government offices or businesses where they previously worked as measuring sticks against which they contrast and compare their current *laoda*. In numerous conversations, an unwillingness to explain one's actions and to accept others' opinions was seen as connected to the larger political realities of China and identified as "government-style" arrogance: "He has a government official air about him (*dangguan de weidao*). . . . I think no one on his team will tell him if they disagree with him. But if they don't tell him, he won't know, right?"

A senior staff member at a labor rights NGO described their internal organizational culture as similar to the business where she had worked before: "We're more like a company here. We all do what the boss says (*women dou ting tade*), because it's like he's the authority. . . . In our monthly meetings, he delivers the report on what we did over the past month and talks about the next month's plan. He does all the talking. . . . Even if he asks people for input or opinions, nobody says anything, even if they have something to say."

The deep dissatisfaction with autocratic leadership expressed in many NGOs was, nonetheless, sometimes intertwined with a wistful desire for a benevolent, paternal leadership figure. After writing her frustrations with her *laoda* into her monthly work summary, one NGO worker found his response both disappointing and disillusioning:

> His initial reaction was very defensive, and he was very aggressive, like he was out to get revenge on me, telling me it was my problem and I had to figure it out if I was ever going to be a competent professional. . . . It was awful. I felt like he had negated all I had done. Later I went to talk to him, and he apologized.

But I think he was apologizing for blowing up at me, not for failing to help me deal with the problem. . . . After this I haven't felt like trying to communicate with him. Now I know he's just a person. As strong and as charismatic as he may be, he's just a person.

Several years after this conversation, the same staff member had resigned herself to the situation, accepting the limitations of the *laoda* and also seeing her position at the NGO as "more like a regular job." The reality that the *laoda* would not or could not provide her with the kind of benevolent leadership she had hoped for had settled in, and she no longer imagined the NGO or the people in it as something substantially different from other workplaces.

The Stifling of Dissent and Obstacles to Consensus Building

Chinese civil society participants frequently recounted the stifling of dissent by domineering leaders who criticized or disregarded objections and suggestions with which they disagreed. This suppression of views, in turn, drove staff and volunteers away and also stymied efforts to build consensus around goals, action plans, and myriad other things civil society organizations had to do. At a GONGO with limited space for dissenting views, one staff member offered a bitterly sarcastic assessment of the problem: "Nobody on staff here has differences of opinions with the leader. . . . They all feel like 'This has nothing to do with me', and 'I'll do it as you said, but, if it goes bad, you're the one that will be held responsible.'"

To "not have" differences of opinion, in this case, meant only not being willing to voice dissenting views. Her comments also reveal how staff members with no voice can refuse to take responsibility for a leader's bad ideas. In such an environment, developing and implementing common goals with buy-in from others is nearly impossible, and, in this case, the organization seemed to be under the total control of the leader.

Although keen to contribute to his organization, a staff member in a professionalized NGO acknowledged the *laoda*'s strong technical skills but was frustrated by his inability to listen to others: "Laoda's strength is in his skills—he knows what he's doing. But his weakness is that he doesn't think sometimes. . . . He's too subjective, and he can't accept others' opinions. They don't even offer them anymore, I think, because he yells at them and just says 'No, that won't work' without giving any explanation."

Although the stifling of dissent was typically blamed on a group's leader, a number of people also attributed it to a more general socialization process within Chinese society, suggesting that "those below" had learned to suppress their own voices. In their analysis, fear of the repercussions of unauthorized self-expression in the larger social and political world translated into a reluctance to speak out even within civil society organizations.

At one NGO plagued by high staff turnover, such voluntary suppression of one's voice was considered to be a key problem limiting the group's potential. As one recent university graduate working there saw it:

> I think the biggest problem here is communication. . . . But it's not a structural problem, I think. It's more of a psychological (*xintai*) problem. Chinese people have lots of reservations about offering their opinions or objections to things in a group of people like this. In government agencies I think it's much worse, but it's a problem here, too. . . . Many people fear that others above them may not be able to accept different opinions, and so they either remain silent or say to themselves, "It's my problem, I should try to change myself before I say anything." But even when they can't change themselves, they still won't say anything. They just keep silent.

In her view, the failure of people to speak up when they felt wronged (or felt they had a better idea or disagreed) ultimately left them disillusioned and caused them to leave. Yet when people are driven away from civil society organizations—either by their own "failure" to speak up or by the actions of others—there is no coming together, much less a coming together of equals, and no opportunity to learn and practice consensus building or collective decision-making.

In another grassroots NGO where the *laoda* would sometimes ask for input from "those below," many staff had nonetheless left in frustration at the consequences of speaking up. As one described it: "If you speak up, *laoda* doesn't accept your ideas, then he says you're bad in some way. So, in these circumstances who will dare to speak up? I think that this type of situation is really common in China. You just simply cannot bring up objections (*ni genben jiu buneng tichu yijian*)."

At its most fundamental level, communication in the sense of information exchange requires at least one party to be listening. And although the voluntary suppression of one's voice can be a problem, inside some Chinese civil society groups, other people—not just laoda—are more interested in expressing their views than in listening to others. Frustrated by the inability of some groups to reach a consensus, one person who had engaged in NGO work for several years drew a bright arrow between the larger political realities and what he saw occurring in some newly established volunteer-based groups:

> Many people join these groups—most people I think—because they think it gives them a space to be heard. But in meetings they just sit around, everyone competing with everyone else to have their voice heard. We discuss things over and over again, but no resolution ever gets made, because that's not really what they want out of it. It's fundamentally a problem with the larger environment in China, I think. In China people have no space to voice their thoughts, they have no right to speak their minds (*fayan de quanli*). So, when they discover there's some place they can do it, they get fanatical about joining in meetings because it provides them a space where they can say what they want.

CONCLUSION

In a long-standing authoritarian state like China's, strong autocratic leadership, hierarchical structures, and the stifling of dissent within civil society organizations mirror the exercise of power in the larger political sphere, reflecting a distinctly sociological kind of hegemonic authoritarianism. The autocratic leadership style depicted here has historical precedents stretching back decades, at least. Comments made to Dick Madsen by urban youth hoping to reshape rural cadres into "democratic" leaders during the Cultural Revolution presage, almost to the word, what people told me about NGO leaders today: " 'Cadres never speak to you softly, say, 'Do you mind doing this today?' . . . They always yell at you: 'You do this, you do that!' "[81] Joel Andreas, in his 2019 study of workplace democracy during the Mao era heyday of "industrial citizenship," found similar dynamics at work through the testimony of his interviewees. The undemocratic workplace experiences Andreas documents in Mao-era factories resonate with the accounts of typical organizational dynamics related by civil society participants several decades later. One worker recounting his unwillingness to participate in factory-level committees in the 1960s, for example, explained that "the so-called staff and workers' representatives couldn't really express the workers' opinions; they couldn't really raise complaints to the higher levels. They didn't dare say what they really thought; they just said what the leaders wanted to hear."[82] A key difference between Andreas's study and this one, however, lies in the distinction between what he and others see as workplace "citizenship" and what I suggest is best understood as "membership" in voluntary associations. In Mao's China—and well into the early 1990s, at least—urban factory workers had no effective way to "exit" their workplace arrangements. Their jobs offered, for most, cradle-to-grave "memberships" that proffered a set of rights—including housing and medical care—that could not be easily obtained, if at all, outside the state-controlled system. Voluntary associations, by contrast, are much more vulnerable to "exit" by their members (volunteers). These distinctions have meaningful theoretical and practical implications for volunteer-based civil society groups, including, in this study, the need for such groups to deliver on their promises of a more democratic, participatory space.

As participants within civil society attest, their experiences of authority (and its abuses) inside most civil society organizations are not dissimilar to what they know from schools and from working in businesses or government. Rather than finding civil society as a sphere of distinctly democratic practices and ideals, many experience it as reproducing the same norms and practices of mainstream authoritarian society. Yet, as Gramsci would lead us to expect, the exercise of power in this way also rubs up roughly against a nascent counterhegemony, one that seeks a more democratic way of collaborating, acknowledging each individual's dignity and allowing participants to work together as equals.

That participants in GONGOs, professionalized grassroots NGOs, and even university student organizations working across diverse fields of activity share common complaints about authoritarian practices indicates the breadth and depth of the dominant hegemony and the nascent counterhegemony. As recounted earlier, we should not expect groups that are internally undemocratic to nurture democratic culture or practices. Yet—and crucially—in democratic societies, democratic norms and practices are culturally (and politically) available resources that actors can activate and mobilize to push back against authoritarian encroachment in associational life. By contrast, the model of civil society that the Chinese state allows and promotes works to reinforce authoritarian structures and practices rather than challenge them. The state's antipathy to self-directed voluntary association and the attendant democratic skills and practices that might otherwise develop in them further constrain the possibility for challenge.

Nonetheless, as I show in part III, there are exceptional spaces in which alternative visions of democratic associational life are being articulated and pursued with the optimism that (perhaps) only youth allows. Before turning to the experiments with democratic culture that are taking place inside these unusual groups, in the next chapter I show how the heavy threads of authoritarianism that tie together associational life in China can become chains under which civil society participants struggle to engage as equals.

Chapter Three

STRUGGLING TO COME TOGETHER
AS EQUALS

When Tocqueville departed France for his tour of the young United States in 1831, he took with him the question of how a mass society of equals could function and survive as a political entity without collapsing under the weight of extreme individualism. The European tradition of aristocracy, he reasoned, had constructed in France and elsewhere an elite leadership group with a sense of noblesse-oblige, an obligation to govern for the welfare of the masses and the interests of the larger country. As a group, they were well-educated and distanced enough from the toils of everyday survival to serve as both moral exemplars for the masses and far-thinking leaders whose behavior could, and should, stretch far beyond their own self-interest. In short, they were rich enough to think about more important things than just "getting by," and they should take that obligation as a privilege and a unique responsibility to their fellow human beings.

In the United States, he worried that Americans' equality and pursuit of naked self-interest would lead them to become social recluses, content to look after only their own narrow interests of home and family, without regard for the needs of the larger community, much less the nation. Without a leading group of aristocrats, he wondered, would not the U.S. experiment in democracy likely fail, as each person would naturally focus first on their own welfare and expect others to do the same? In this kind of society, where everyone is equal, would not each person also be paralyzed to act in coordination with others, as there might be no individual benefit in doing so?

Despite the powerful logic of extreme individualism Tocqueville's journey began with, his actual observations led him to a different conclusion about democracy in the United States. He came to believe that the natural equality Americans felt had led them, paradoxically, to come together voluntarily in all sorts of associations, for a hundred and one different purposes. Recognizing the value of strength in numbers, he surmised, they could see the benefit of working with others to achieve goals that, in other places, people had traditionally demanded be pursued by government or kings.

This chapter focuses on a key way in which the notion of equality is expressed in the ways people interact with each other when pursuing (presumably) common goals. As recounted in chapter 2, the Tocquevillian literature linking voluntary associations to well-functioning democracies routinely stresses the cultural norms, practices, and skills developed inside associations. Communication skills, in particular, are considered especially relevant for participating fully in a democracy. Knowing one's own preferences, being able to articulate those in small group conversations, in public gatherings (e.g., town hall meetings), and in writing (e.g., to one's elected representative) have been identified as fundamental political skills for a democratic people.

As Tocqueville's analysis of American associations implies, even at the much smaller yet daily level of interaction within an organization where one works or volunteers, such skills are also crucial to working effectively toward collective goals. This is certainly the case for many nongovernmental organizations (NGOs) and voluntary associations in China, as elsewhere. Yet the context of authoritarianism distinguishes China from the societies in which most research on voluntary association has been conducted. In an authoritarian state, open communication, whether formal or informal, carries certain hazards. In the larger political sphere, where dissent is risky if not dangerous, average people are hard-pressed to articulate a difference of opinion without fear of retribution. At the smaller organizational level, and even within civil society, as I argued in chapter 2, disagreeing openly with "those above," in particular, is challenging.

I did not begin research for this book with an explicit interest in communication. It emerged, rather, as a a result of fieldwork. Beyond the suppression of dissent, which I earlier suggested is one of the key features of hegemonic authoritarianism as enacted within civil society, the problem of communication became a recurring issue in interviews and observations inside Chinese civil society organizations. My focus here hearkens back to Tocqueville's observations on equality. Problems of communication reflect a challenge common to every society, but particularly to democratic societies in which collective decision-making is meant to be the norm: How can a group of people who hold divergent opinions and viewpoints come together as equals and achieve a consensus on the best course of action or view of a particular problem? Answering this question is no simple matter, even for societies with long democratic traditions. The answer was not obvious to any of the Chinese groups I studied, either. What I documented in daily fieldnotes was not a "solution" that some group had struck upon by accident or by design, but rather it was a continuing conversation about the democratic values and practices that *should* differentiate civil society from the ways things normally worked. In part III, I show how consensus building is an ongoing enterprise within voluntary associations committed to equality. In this chapter, however, I first show how entrenched practices of interaction predicated on autocracy, hierarchy, and the suppression of dissent make communicating as equals an *almost* impossible task within much of Chinese civil society.

This chapter begins with an exploration of local understandings of "communication," highlighting how for many Chinese civil society participants, effective communication (*goutong*) is not simply a give-and-take exchange of information but implies, instead, a search for consensus and mutual understanding. A common assertion in scholarly literature holds that one important communication skill honed within civil society groups is the ability to articulate one's views. That notion is evident in this chapter, too. Here, however, I draw on fieldwork and interviews to also highlight troubles in *listening*, a skill that is deeply linked to power relations in a group yet seldom discussed in studies of this sort. After considering the importance of listening, the remaining bulk of this chapter is dedicated to exploring the connections between inequality and communication in voluntary associational settings. I do this through three case studies—meetings and activities in which attempts to articulate one's opinions and to be heard by others were undermined by a lack of experience in nonhierarchical organizations. Most broadly, I argue, these three diverse settings—a meeting of environmentalists, an early gathering of a youth-based volunteer group, and a labor NGO educational activity—offer insight into the tug-of-war taking place between authoritarian organizational norms and nascent democratic values and practices.

THE CHALLENGES OF COMMUNICATING

People in NGOs frequently complained to me about poor communication (*goutong*) in their organization, yet, as I came to understand, by communication people often mean more than simply an exchange of information. The Chinese term *goutong* is composed of two characters meaning "ditch, channel, or trench" and "to pass through." Although it is most commonly translated as communication, a Chinese-English dictionary published as recently as 1989 provides the definition as "link up," with "the new railways that link up the southern provinces" as a main example of usage.[1] In contrast, the contemporary English use of communication understands the term most commonly as "an act or instance of transmitting" or "a process by which information is exchanged between individuals."[2] In contemporary Chinese usage, *goutong* has also taken on this latter meaning, but it still implies a harmonizing of interests, metaphorically akin to how waters feed from one channel into another to form one larger, continuous flow.

Having always translated the term *goutong* as communication, after hearing the problem mentioned in vastly different contexts, in the course of my fieldwork I had to revise my understanding of the term. Depending on the speaker and the circumstances, communication could imply a need for compassion, for listening (which is, of course, understood as half of communication in the common English-language usage of the term), for affirmation, for respect, or for some combination of these things. People who said that communication was bad in their organization often in the same breath expressed feeling personally wounded or unsupported by others in their organization. Or they felt that because of internal hierarchies and personal conflicts of interest, there were no open channels through which they could express themselves to others, and they were frustrated when conflicts went unresolved or unaddressed. Through many conversations and observations, I came to realize that all these very *affective* understandings were fundamental to the way people used communication in talking about their lives inside different civil society groups. At the same time, when the term was invoked as a problem, it also implied a subtle recognition of contested views and stubborn disagreements.

In one professionalized NGO with Hong Kong ties, for example, a lack of transparency and power inequalities between Hong Kong–based organizers and mainlander staff had created bad blood within the group. As one mainland staff member saw it in 2006, such problems were due in large part to communication difficulties: "The communication between us mainland staff and the Hong Kong staff is not too open (*tanbai*). . . . There is, after all, still a big gulf between us." The "gulf" here refers in part to the vastly different worldviews and experiences of the well-educated Hong Kong activists who governed the organization and the local mainland staff, many of whom were former factory workers with little formal education. In addition to these class and background differences, it also refers to the unequal power relations between the mainlanders who did the frontline work and the Hong Kong leaders who directed them.

Another part-time volunteer at this same organization also employed communication as a frame for discussing key problems in the organization. She had recently graduated from a university (in mainland China) and used that experience as her point of reference:

At university, the administrativeness (*xingzhengxing*) is very strong. You do the work that is assigned to you, but that's it. In NGOs it's [supposed to be] different, because your work is intimately connected to other people's work, and if you do it badly you affect other people. . . . But from what I saw last year, it seems that they don't handle that situation very well. I felt their relationships were too complicated. . . . At [this NGO], there were complicated[3] relationships between the mainland staff and the Hong Kong staff, between the staff and the volunteers, and even between the mainland staff themselves. . . . They didn't communicate (*goutong*) well. . . . They had too many disagreements (*shifei tai duo*)—even one of the staff there admitted this to me. . . . And at the end of the year several of their mainland staff left. Some of them even had four or five years' experience there.

The director from Hong Kong took all the power in her hands. . . . One of the older [mainland] staff—in her forties, I would guess—told me that it wasn't always that way. They used to rotate decision-making authority, but it changed. She said she didn't know why it changed . . . And, another thing, their executive committee has absolute decision-making authority. But they've never sat down with all the staff to explain the decisions they make. So often the staff are confused about why they're supposed to be doing certain things.

In her view, the inequalities and dissatisfaction she observed were intimately connected to poor *goutong* within the NGO. Had *goutong* been
handled better, the staff might have been less "confused about why they're
supposed to be doing certain things." It might also have helped to avoid
the "many disagreements" that compelled experienced staff members
to leave.

Indeed, when the term *goutong* is invoked, the speaker may be bringing
together into one expression several distinct issues. Regardless of the specific
problems involved, people often portrayed *goutong* as a tool for consensus
building and an approach to achieve a harmonizing of interests—key
concerns for action in any collective undertaking. But harmonizing interests
is not such a simple task, as interests are often embedded in and reflective
of unequal power relations. That is, while the meaning of *goutong* can be
neutral, or affectively desirable, its invocation also frequently exposes real
power imbalances.

Listening Problems

While recognizing the affective and normative dimensions generally implicit
in the use of *goutong*, in professionalized NGOs and government-organized
nongovernmental organizations (GONGOs) sometimes even the more
mundane meaning of information transmission was also difficult to achieve.
In agenda setting or planning meetings of various sorts, it became clear that
the failure to simply listen to others carefully and respectfully often emerged
as a tangible challenge to cooperation.

Communication in the sense of information exchange requires at least
one party to be listening. Yet inside some Chinese NGOs, one sees people
who are more interested in expressing their views and emotions than in listening to those of others. Given the suppression of free speech and association in China and the top-down authority structures people experience
in their daily lives at school or work, it may be understandable that many
people are more eager to talk than to listen. Yet without someone listening,
simple action—not to mention full cooperation between people with divergent views—is greatly constrained.

Of the many people who mentioned listening as an obstacle to effective
communication, one person who had engaged in NGO work for several
years expressed his frustrations with this problem particularly passionately.
He was also one of the few people who spontaneously introduced the word

"democracy" into our conversation, drawing a clear link between democracy and the complexity of *goutong*:

> My experience working with volunteer-based organizations in China is that they can be very democratic—that's their strength. But they can also be very inefficient. The upside, the democratic upside, cannot be denied, but I don't think people get what democracy is. As I understand it, democracy is supposed to involve different interests (*liyi*), but the problem, at least in the group I was a member of, is that many people doing these groups have no personal interest involved. . . .
>
> As I understand it, democracy is supposed to be about groups of people with similar interests coming together to promote their interest, combining their personal interest with other people's personal interest so that you can have a larger influence. But the volunteer groups in China today are populated by idealists, not people with their own personal interests. In China, I think almost everyone in NGOs are idealists. But I think the key to democracy is about compromise—when one group or person has to back down in order to achieve the best result for everyone. But compromise isn't a word idealists understand. So, nobody in most volunteer-based NGOs knows about compromise, either. They all just want to make their voice heard and beat out everyone else. They always want to win, to beat others (*hen yao qiang de*).
>
> This wasn't only at the group I was in. I also spent a week at [a volunteer-based, education-focused NGO]. I sat in on two of their meetings then, and it was exactly the same—no one listening to anyone! At one of them, they spent 1.5 hours debating toilet cleaning—whether teachers should have to clean the toilets!
>
> I can give you another example—my own brother. When I explained to him about the organization I was joining, he said he wanted to join, too, that it sounded great. I asked him why, and he said, "Well, I'd be happy to pay the 100 yuan annual fee, or whatever it is, just to have a place to go and speak my mind!" That's what most people's motivation is for joining these groups, I think—or at least that's what they want to get out of it.

His experiences were not uncommon. In other settings, I saw and heard similar tales of NGO participants who "always want to win" and expressions of dismay at how that prevented a group from taking any action. I also participated in hours-long meetings over issues as seemingly small as toilet cleaning.

STRUGGLING WITH DEMOCRATIC PRACTICE: THREE CASES

To be "democratic," no matter how strongly desired, is neither simple nor straightforward. Most broadly, the previous comments offer perspectives on the challenges of developing an internally democratic organizational culture while living within a larger authoritarian state where dissension is neither welcomed nor well tolerated. In this section, I offer case examples to paint a more vivid picture of how autocracy, hierarchy, and poor communication are simultaneously enacted and challenged inside Chinese civil society. In these examples, I present observations and dialogue from my own participation in three different events: a meeting of environmentalists; a gathering of student members of Together, which eventually proved critical to the group's future direction; and a labor law education activity. At each of these events, I was already familiar with several of the participants because of prior activities and interactions.

Case 1: When Everyone Is Used to Being *Laoda*

In early 2005, at a meeting called together by a Hong Kong–based environmental group, about a dozen mainlanders, a half-dozen Hong Kong people, myself, and one staff member from a European international NGO (INGO) gathered together on a Guangdong university campus to talk about the possibility of introducing organic farming and the concept of "buying local" to area residents. The mainlanders in attendance were, in general, all elites—successful business owners, midlevel government officials, medical professionals, and the like. I had met many of them at previous gatherings and knew them to be eager environmentalists with a shared goal of addressing some of the area's most urgent pollution problems. At this time in Guangdong, however, there were no fully operational grassroots environmental NGOs other than university groups with virtually no off-campus activities. At this Saturday meeting, there was this loose network of environmentalists but no clear organization and no clear leader.

During the question-and-answer session that followed an initial slide presentation, people began asking detailed technical questions, like how organic and inorganic materials are kept separate during the composting process, what makes something organic or inorganic, and whether food grown on polluted soil can be called organic.

These were reasonable questions, I thought. But the way people went about the discussion felt frustrating to me and to others, as it quickly and repeatedly devolved into chaotic, unending discussion. Several of the mainland men started talking loudly and, at the same time, asking questions and giving their opinions in definitive ways that left nothing open for discussion. The Hong Kong organizer who was trying to lead the discussion was clearly in a difficult position. When the discussion had devolved into a cacophony of (male) voices, and it was clear that nothing could be understood, she smiled and laughed uncomfortably several times.

Throughout the day-long meeting (which included lunch and dinner), the discussion broke down into a noisy exchange of competing voices over and over, each time prompting the organizer to say, variously, "There are lots of good ideas and important questions coming out now. Let's try to take them one by one, OK? . . . Let's try to calm down now, OK? Let me list these ideas out here [on the whiteboard] one by one, OK? . . . Let's let one person at a time speak, OK? Let's list your questions out and then we can address them each more deeply, OK?" This scene was repeated at least three times during the nine-hour day, with between seven and nine mainland men speaking each time. Only once was a mainland woman also talking. None of the people from Hong Kong spoke in this "out-of-turn" way.

During the first devolution of the discussion, it occurred to me that in the absence of real civil society organizations, many Chinese people have had very little opportunity to interact as equals in a group discussion format. During the subsequent devolutions, with between seven and nine men all speaking at the same time, it was clear that the men were dominating. They seemed to be more concerned about making sure they were being heard than in listening to anyone else. Like the people I would interview later who complained about poor communication among NGO participants, as I wrote up my field notes later that night, my reflections on the day were noticeably affective:

> Today wasn't only frustrating but also saddening. These people came here, ostensibly, at least, because they're interested and concerned about agriculture, health, and the environment. But if they're interacting this way how can they ever act together towards a common goal? If they can't respect one another enough to even listen carefully and give everyone a chance to speak, I can't imagine that they could ever set up the kind of cooperative group that the HK people talked about today. Other observers might have faulted the HK

leader for not controlling the situation better, but I think she tried everything she could—explaining, entreating, cajoling, repeating herself. She was eventually successful at getting the men to quiet down, but I think she found it as frustrating as I did.

In the afternoon, after a video presentation about a (male) Hong Kong farmer, questions were directed to him and were asked in a one-by-one fashion, not everyone talking at once. I wondered: Was this a gender thing? Or was it simply that people were more respectful because they were clear that he was the authority, and this was their chance to talk to him?

Yet the gender dynamic at play was not so clear. Only two mainland women were present, and one very eager woman in her thirties talked quite a bit throughout the day about education and "the need to recognize the spirit within all things." The Hong Kong organizer was very patient with her, but she spoke often and got off topic at least three times during the day. A couple of people sitting beside me noticed and actually chatted about it while she was still talking, saying that she has no experience farming (although they did not either, they later admitted). At lunch, she and I sat next to one another, and she brought up the morning's discussion session on her own, apologizing to me and the others at our table, saying that she still had a lot to learn about how to talk and how to share her ideas. She said she had studied management and had previously placed a lot of importance on material things and money, but that for the past couple of years, she has been trying to push that all away. She said that she eventually wanted to share her ideas with others, but for now she was still developing her views on life. In her case, she not only had been successful as a business leader—and, therefore, accustomed to being in charge—but also was now undergoing an almost religious conversion to a new set of "values" and was eager to both enact these in her new life and share them with others.

After this experience, I was initially curious whether this was a one-off event; how much I should read into the seeming gender-inflected dynamics; and whether gender, age, and class would be fault lines along which a cooperation-conflict divide would emerge. I wondered if I might discover a different dynamic in women-dominated or youth-dominated groups. But, as I will argue, subsequent in-depth interviews and observations in other settings suggested that none of these possibilities, although reasonable, were obviously the case. Indeed, a few of the organizations in which respondents complained of communication problems and inequality were operated and governed wholly or almost wholly by women. Although a more gender-focused research agenda is in order, for this and many other reasons, the bulk of my data suggest that problems of listening and consensus building are evident in organizations of any gender composition.[4]

Whether a younger cohort of activists is more likely to develop the communication and other consensus-building skills necessary in a democracy is also an open and reasonable question. To be sure, however, even youth-based groups are not immune to the traditions and norms of the larger society. In the example that follows, the dynamics of a Together meeting demonstrate that the tension between authoritarian practices and democratic ideals is just as real for youth-based groups as it is for other civil society organizations.

Case 2: Protecting Nascent Democratic Practice in the Face of Bureaucratic Encroachment

At one Together meeting in April 2006, many of the themes of contention came into play. On this particular day, two dozen young people—most current university students but also including a few recent graduates and myself—gathered to discuss whether the various university groups in City A would be formally linked through a joint agreement. The nature of student groups in any country can be fickle, as the matriculation and graduation cycle produces a constant flow into and out of organizations. In the case of Together, each year, students from new universities want to join their village activities, which invigorates but also complicates the operations of the group. At this meeting, representatives from seven area schools met to discuss an organizational charter that had been drafted six months prior by a previous group of representatives. In the interim period, some of the original drafters had graduated and were not present, although some of the attendees were from universities that had only recently discovered Together and had yet to participate in any actual activities. The meeting was an all-day event, lasting 12.5 hours (including meals, which we paid for ourselves) and extending into the early hours of the next morning for me and several others who stayed behind.

Although somewhat less chaotic than other planning and agenda-setting meetings I had attended, this day was typical in the variety of viewpoints expressed, problems with listening to others, debate over the "ideal" nature of the organization, and differences over the desirability of top-down versus consensus decision-making. In this case, these differences correlated strongly with the attendees' past involvement with the organization.

My official role as a notetaker, and the majority of attendees' commitment to speaking in turn, allowed me to record in some detail the day's
conversations. Here I present a segment of these discussions, with each
speaker identified by sex (M = male; F = female) and a number. The head
count varied, as some people came in late, but at one point in midmorning
and then again in midafternoon, there were thirteen women out of a total
of twenty-three attendees.

F1 (female 1), a senior Together volunteer, was the predetermined chair
for the meeting. She opened the day by asking how we should proceed
with the day's meeting, but specifically how we should talk about the draft
charter that had been circulated earlier. After about five minutes of discussion, F1 proposed the following choices: (1) Each school has one representative to present that school's opinion on the entire draft charter; or (2) each
article in the draft charter would be taken one by one, with every school's
representative speaking directly to that issue. After another five minutes to
explain these choices, in which people voiced their opinion of the pros and
cons or explained why they favored one over the other, it was put to a vote.
The result was that we would begin with an overview—each school's representative would give their consensus view on the entire draft.

We began with a presentation by M1 (male 1) of the views of the group
at University A. He was a law student, and he jumped into the details of the
draft charter with gusto, starting with:

The first article, line eight, and the seventh article, lines one and two, are
not clear. . . . They also seem to constrain our freedom to act, they seem
quite restrictive. . . . And the fifth article, line four—the ideas are unclear,
and the language isn't so suitable. It's very colloquial . . . In the first article,
line eight, what does it mean when you write "The City A Committee can
organize camps under 'the principles' established by Together"? And what
are the qualifications for being a committee member? It's not clear to us. . . .
The eighth article isn't necessary, we think. . . . The sixth article—who will
implement these things? Is there a way to requalify for committee membership after being kicked out? What about the following year's selection of
committee members? And, too, the responsibilities of the committee members are not clear.

This was, of course, a *lot* of points to make at one time, and people were
audibly and visibly exasperated at the breadth and detail of the questions.

At the same time, however, as the discussion began, it was clear that most people felt these were valid concerns.

M2, an experienced member from University A, added to M1's presentation with the following:

> After discussing it among our group, we feel that the charter needs to be more flexible. Does it need to be so specific, like requiring two people to attend from each school? . . . Can't the charter be broader in scope and direction? Like the City A Committee's purpose (*dingwei*), mission, and structure—all that needs to be explained better. Plus, we need to include our ideals (*linian*), our values (*jiazhiguan*) . . . It seems to me that we're trending toward becoming a "management" (*guanli*) organization, which differs from our original intention. Do we want to be a platform (*pingtai*) or a management organization? And, if the latter, how do we ensure the implementation of these regulations? We need to talk about this, or else we'll end up like last year, with no effectiveness. We also need to develop a consensus. . . . I think we need to create a small group to talk about the charter.

Most people present seemed to understand that asking whether the proposed citywide committee should be a "platform" for exchange or a "management organization" was about the tension between acting in an open, horizontal, democratic fashion versus a top-down, controlling fashion. M2 soon answered his own question, favoring a structure that would allow all member groups to retain a high degree of autonomy but still reap the benefits of cooperation.

Who has the authority to set the agenda, to make decisions, and how much input newcomers should have were recurring themes as the day progressed:

F2: How about we talk about the overall structure of this, the charter?
M3: Umm, because more than half the people here today weren't in on the early discussions, talking about it now is a problem. Can we focus now on specific problems?

Grappling with these fundamental questions of democratic decision-making revealed there were no easy answers. Other attendees were focused on whether such a charter was even necessary if it risked cutting off new ideas and potentialities too soon:

M2: I think we don't need a charter, because we're not an NGO. We're just a group of students that's only been operating for two years. Won't being so specific now affect our healthy development? Won't it constrain us too much?

Given these concerns, how and even whether to proceed with the discussion became a topic of much concern:

F3 (a law student): I think we can talk about principles now and create a group to talk about the specifics.
M3: I have a different opinion. Last year we had practical problems that emerged as we went about doing our work. This committee was set up to help address those. And second, what things can we decide in our own school organizations and what needs to be approved by the City A Committee?
F4: If we don't talk about the charter now, when will we do it? To postpone it until later, if the same problem of so many opinions occurs, what will we do?
F1: Who agrees with discussing the specifics, and who wants to discuss the general direction of the organization? Let's have a vote.

After some clarification questions about the choices, people on each side raised their hands. The group voted 13–7 in support of "general direction." But it did not proceed without resistance.

M4: Hang on, won't this push us into this afternoon and take time away from the discussions of our specific village project plans?

F1 and others suggested that we finish talking about the overall direction in the morning and keep the afternoon agenda as it stood. By an audible consensus of "yes" and "that's right," it was so decided. M2, who favored more autonomy for each member organization, spoke up again about the ideal purpose of the proposed citywide committee:

M2: I think we should be a platform (*pingtai*), not a management organization (*guanli jigou*). By platform, I mean a platform for information exchange and coordination (*xietiao*). Like, we could create a website for the City A Committee, including past work camp information, an introduction to the organization, etc. Just for information. For program coordination (*xiangmu xietiao*), I think we can do it as in the past—whoever is willing to organize a work camp, we will support with opinions and suggestions (*yijian he jianyi*).

For example, if one group wants to do it, we'll give them all the practical suggestions we can.

This direction was favored by F1, who was concerned that the proposed charter would be too top-down, and so she opened it up for more discussion:

F1: I think we're trending toward a *guanli* organization, but I'd like to hear other people's opinions.

F4: Well, why was City A Committee created? Because different schools were already cooperating. Cross-school cooperation and international cooperation—these were the realities. But as for the right to decide where to do camps, I mean, there's no need to specify who has the right to make that decision, and no need to make the City A Committee a management organization.

M2: A volunteer organization's purpose is to be an expression of the volunteer spirit. . . . If we specify rights and rules, I think we'll just look like other organizations. We'll lose the meaning of volunteering.

F1: M3's point was to make camps better, which is the same as M2's. In my opinion, there's no need to create rules just for the sake of having rules. . . . I prefer to have a more inclusive (*baorongxin bijiao da*) and more free (*bijiao ziyou*) organization.

M3: I think M2's talking about an organization in the first stage of development. I'm talking about the second stage of development, because we have already run into some problems.

Indeed, at this stage of Together's development, it was already operating projects involving hundreds of volunteers spread across several cities and in multiple provinces. Yet the notion of a "stage" necessitating a certain development trajectory was not supported by everyone. M2, in particular, agreed that "stages" were to be expected, but insisted on preserving the values that Together had been promoting, especially that of freedom and respecting others' rights to act of their own accord:

M2: I think every organization has different stages, depending on the type of organization it is. Like a business and a volunteer organization, they're different by nature, so they go through different stages. . . . So, my question is—will we help anyone who wants to organize a work camp? For example, I've got a friend who comes to me and says he'd like to organize a work camp. Will we support him or not? Because, in theory *anyone* can organize a work camp. We don't have the right to prevent them from doing so.

Supporting others to launch activities and providing resources to facilitate that, however, are different, as F1 noted:

F1: Together also has some right to say "yes" or "no," because they provide material resources. The last time we had lots of controversy, that's still unresolved, about how to allocate representatives to the City A Committee, how many representatives will each school get, that sort of thing.

A long-time volunteer (who would later join the full-time staff) spoke up at this point to steer the discussion back to the underlying principles of Together:

F5: The point of establishing the City A Committee was to create a platform. Before, the City A Committee was the first regional committee of Together, and the most active one. . . . I think our problems emerged because when the old representatives left they didn't pass on everything to the new people. So now how to resolve these problems? I think the City A Committee should be a platform, not an organization that constrains people (*yueshu renjia*) or manages others (*guanli renjia*). It should be an organization that provides resources to others. Although Together is giving resources, we're a volunteer organization, so Together has no right to say "You must go here to have a camp" or "You cannot go here." We simply won't do that.

F6: Why do we always have to discuss this? On the website it's clear that Together is only a network (*lianxi wangluo*).

M3: But it isn't written in black and white, so people don't know that Together is only a network.

F6: It is, but like F5 said, the information hasn't been passed on from old people to new ones.

F1: So we have a consensus now, right?

It seemed F1 was anxious to move on to another topic now, as she said this in a final, authoritative voice. But she was not to have the final word.

M2: Hang on. Without a vote, how do we know we have a consensus?

F1: All the people have spoken have agreed that we should be a platform, and if the people who haven't spoken haven't spoken it's because they either don't disagree or don't know enough to have a firm opinion yet because they're so new to the organization.

This conversation led to M2 inviting me to interject, "I want to hear what Anthony has to say. . . . Anthony, can you share your thoughts with us?" My response was generic, as I felt in no way qualified to settle a dispute over how to settle a dispute. I ultimately gave what I thought even at the time was a terribly unuseful reply, along the lines of "What you're going through is quite common to many organizations, whether in China or in the United States." I also suggested that it was important to any type of organization, especially to an alliance of this sort, to come to a consensus on fundamentals like shared values and shared purpose.

Indeed, as the conversation unfolded it became clear that recognizing when a consensus has been formed is not always simple, but it is a crucial skill in small-group interactions. What issues need votes? What issues are just "understood" to be not deserving of or necessary to debate further? Frustrations with this challenge boiled up soon, voiced by M5, a newcomer from a university club that had yet to be initiated into the basic principles and practices of Together:

M5: This is very inefficient. Why not have all the people with divergent opinions (*yijian*) talk together and come to a consensus, then talk about it at our next big meeting?

F3: But I think creating a consensus is more important than efficiency.

This last comment by F3 met with an audible chorus of "Yes" and "That's right." Nonetheless, M5 was not ready to concede:

M5: We already have a consensus about the organization as a platform, right?

F5: But a consensus is developed through discussion.

F1: Let's talk about specifics.

M2: [Our Together branch] ran into this problem, and so we divided ourselves into an information group, a finance group, etc. . . . I think we can do the same for City A Committee—how many job responsibilities (*zhineng*) do we have or need, and who will do what?

Not ready to impose a strict format on others, however, M3 suggested that "Last time we had a consensus on this, but because everyone's school is different, it may not work the same for each group."

M3 concurred, adding that even when "job responsibilities" are specified, in practice, it was impossible for anyone to enforce a particular set of demands: "We've had a problem with people not showing up for meetings to vote on things. Sometimes not even half the people come, so then how can you have a binding vote?"

As part of a budding voluntary association with no preexisting authority structure in place, the conversation between M2, M5, and M3 revealed a perhaps universal dilemma of how to get people to commit fully to actions and to actively uphold the group's mission and vision. In the absence of any points system like that present in most Youth League–supervised university clubs, they were scratching their heads to come up with suitable answers.[5]

When the discussion turned to how to assign responsibilities, F4 suggested a tighter and more explicit personnel structure would help keep things moving along "properly" and allow for the kind of hierarchical supervision (*jiandu*) that is common to most university student organizations:

F4: I think committee members have another job responsibility, which is that of oversight (*jiandu*), to make sure internally and externally their organization is doing things properly.
M3: Must it be a specific person, or does everyone have that responsibility?
F4: I think it should be a specific person, because if everyone is charged with doing it, then maybe no one will do it, because they'll all be expecting someone else to do it.

But F4 was also open to suggestions:

M3: I think every committee member can do it, because if they do, I think you can discover problems earlier and resolve them earlier.
M1: I agree with M3.
F4: OK, yeah, I see your point. So, let it be everyone's responsibility.

In the end, the idea of shared responsibility—based on deeply held shared values—won over F4. As M3 noted, there may also be an efficiency boost in such a system, as "you can discover problems earlier and resolve them earlier" without having to rely on someone "above" to take action or make a decision. Not everyone present was willing to take such a leap of faith with their fellow volunteers, however. As with M5 earlier, another new member from an uninitiated school, F6, felt more comfortable with the top-down model she knew well from other organizations:

F6: Student organizations are very efficient in their decision-making, because they have a clear authority structure. The leader (*lingdao*) can make people do things, so you need a leader to be efficient, even in a volunteer organization. If a committee member focuses on one job, his efficiency can be greater.[6]

Notably, no one audibly countered her view. I took it as the typical top-down view and noticed that those who I would expect to hold differing opinions just held their tongue. No one voiced support for her either, however, and the whole suggestion just fell flat. This "cold treatment" seemed to work when people wanted to avoid open disagreement or as a way of muting the person's point.

During a break later on, I talked with M1 on the balcony about F6's comments on efficiency. He was very blunt and emotional, saying, "I'm extremely opposed to that crap they do at school, because it's very forced! If you do what they want you to do, you get rewarded, like with extra points on your moral education grade or nicer comments on your senior thesis."

Attempting to re-engage F6 in a more productive fashion than just ignoring her, M2 asked her, "What do you all, your school, want to get from the City A Committee?"

Her reply would indicate, again, how little she understood the culture of Together: "We want information, based on your experiences, and suggestions. Those are very valuable. . . . I think whether a camp can open should be decided by the City A Committee."

The notion of creating an outside committee to decide what member clubs would do, however, ran counter to the principles of equality and mutual respect that, at this point, were already core to Together's development. Among the experienced members, the collective sense was that in principle *anyone* could work in the villages. The possibility that a "rogue" group could act in the name of Together was occasionally raised as a matter of concern, but in general, the urge to control lost out to the group's shared commitment to freedom of action.

On this particular day, the top-down structures and practices advocated by F6 created an opportunity for M3 to explain Together's core values to her and other newcomers. Later on, the more-experienced M3 turned the day's conversation—and the entire direction of the organization, ultimately—by saying, "I have another role to propose that the City A Committee play. I think we can do trainings for new committee members."

M3's suggestion highlighted the contrasting perspectives of new and old members and reflected a pivotal moment in Together's development, similar to what Kathleen Blee found in studies of newly formed activist groups in Philadelphia. At critical "turning points," Blee notes, some possibilities become closed off while other pathways are fixed.[7] This moment in Together's development set the stage for its future direction, one in which the platform of a coordination center—rather than a central headquarters or head office—would offer a series of trainings to Together branches across southern China.

Although the top-down norms, structures, and practices of typical university clubs were familiar to everyone in the room, in suggesting that the proposed citywide committee could serve mostly a training purpose—rather than a governing purpose—Together began positioning itself as standing in clear contrast to the normal groups that these young people would encounter not only at university but also in other off-campus NGOs as well as in their workplaces after graduation.

M3's patience in this conversation was an intentional demonstration of his conviction that the group had a duty to bring others along into the older members' way of thinking, rather than simply imposing a set of practices without explanation as to their rationale. At this stage, in 2006, other experienced Together members also felt an obligation to teach newcomers about the group's principles (*linian*), using explicit terms like "dignity" and "equality" and "freedom." Their reasoning was that more experienced members had a deeper understanding of elderly villagers' plight, and they wanted to ensure that when newcomers went to the villages, everyone would treat the villagers and their fellow volunteers with respect.

This day's conversation about what the proposed citywide committee should do wrapped up when F1 followed up on M3's suggestion of focusing on trainings. Still, although a consensus had emerged about the avoidance of a top-down structure, there was a collective concern with striking a balance between training people with the tools and practices that had been developed at Together up to that point and remaining open to new ideas and newcomers:

F5: We have to be careful not to make committee members the implementers of everything, but rather responsible for mobilizing volunteers in each of the various schools. Otherwise, we could inhibit the proactiveness of volunteers, and we don't want that.

M2: Too specific a division of labor can become very formulaic, and communication (*goutong*) can suffer.

M3: In dividing up duties on the committee, can we break through the school distinctions and go with individuals, let people choose what they do according to their own interests?

A chorus of "Sure!" and "Yeah!" settled that question. But it led to other puzzles:

M2: But one problem comes up with that. Like with the information group, don't we need at least one person at each school to make sure that information is shared? [Again, a chorus of "yeah," and "sure" arose from the group.] And also, every school needs to tell us what they need for training—like some schools have lots of new people, and we need to know how many people those are.

F7 (an experienced Together member): "But for training, we already know when it's necessary. If lots of new students come in, they won't have the principles (*linian*) they need, so they'll need training.

The emphasis on training newcomers in the principles (*linian*) underlying Together activities was broadly shared. The experienced Together volunteers present implicitly (and, in interviews with me, explicitly) understood that democratic values, such as equality, dignity, participation, and openness, had to be actively nurtured to counter the top-down norms found in typical student experiences. They were always confident that these had appeal, however, even for newcomers like F6 who voiced initial preferences for "clearer" authority structures. Nonetheless, the practices of "normal" groups would not be so easily dismissed, as newcomer F8's comments revealed:

F8: I just joined Together. I think that having fewer people on the committee will increase the efficiency.

Although this search for efficiency was a common refrain among the uninitiated, it was often countered subtly with appeals to openness, as the more experienced F5 and F1 did next:

F5: I still think it's important that committee members' most important role is to serve to mobilize other people.

F1: I agree with F5 on this being the case.

In the many hours it took the group to arrive at this point, we all felt pretty exhausted, like we had been bombarded with a whirlwind of opinions (as some readers may feel by now). The debate was part of an ongoing discussion over what the motivating ideals of the group should be and how they should be put into action. Time and time again, those members of the group who sought to actively construct a more democratic norm asserted the existence of a set of special principles (*linian*) that distinguished Together from the top-down management organizations of the larger society (including, of course, normal student groups at universities).

Yet how exactly to put such principles into workable practice was not so apparent. As the day went on, the conversation had broadened to reveal many practical puzzles that had to be worked through: How should decisions be made—by committee, by one person, by voting? What should be the real nature of a citywide committee—a platform for information sharing? A coordination center? A management organization? Should debate be curtailed for the sake of efficiency? And, if so, under what circumstances?

Although no one used the word "democracy" all day, the issues they were struggling with are fundamental to the formation and operation of a democratic society. With new students and universities continuing to join the group, there was a natural contest between the top-down norms of the dominant society and the democratic principles pressed by more experienced volunteers. Obviously, these are not easily resolved issues, especially in an environment where few people have experience interacting as equals to make mutually binding decisions. Yet people in this gathering saw these as problems that needed to be raised, as they would be crucial to the organization's future. Participants were actively engaged in dialogue to find the best solutions. For Together, this tug-of-war would continue for some time to come, but once this threshold of innovation had been crossed, the group's fundamentally democratic culture was well on its way to being established, and debates over principles and common practices were pretty much seen as resolved. This debate was, however, a crucial turning point in the evolution of the group's democratic culture.

Case 3: Learning the Labor Law Together

The meeting of environmentalists described in case 1 was attended mainly by successful and well-educated men. The chaotic nature of the discussion, the difficulty reaching a consensus on anything, and the failure to listen were, I argued, key features of the group's dynamics. These problems ultimately bode ill for any sort of cooperation, and indeed no new environmental groups or practices emerged until some years later. I left that meeting also wondering whether gender played a key role in structuring the interactions among the participants, questioning whether the predominance of men had skewed the day toward conflict rather than cooperation. In case 2, the Together meeting, the gender mix was almost even, and both men and women engaged in animated discussions, appearing on both sides of the top-down, bottom-up spectrum of decision-making norms.

This third and final case example comes from an evening spent at a free workshop on labor rights and computer skills, organized by a labor rights NGO in Shenzhen. At this event, both men and women were present in roughly equal numbers, but unlike the Together and environmentalist cases, the participants were not elites or young people on their way to becoming "successful" members of society through university education. Most were poorly paid factory workers who had migrated from other provinces to the coastal areas, producing goods for export through Hong Kong. Other than the gender and class dynamics it hints at, I present this case mostly as a demonstration of the challenges of democratic culture building in an NGO setting where few participants have experienced anything but the authoritarian norms and practices that dominate in China.

The setting for this event was the living room of a rented apartment that served as the office for a struggling grassroots labor NGO in Shenzhen. As a worker-initiated organization, the founder of this NGO had worked arduously to overcome language barriers, prejudice against migrants from other provinces (like himself), and the constant threat of financial collapse. Over two years, I followed the group through two office moves and several programmatic changes, visiting regularly and joining some discussions about development strategy and activities. By the time of this event, the group had successfully applied for a small grant from a foreign funder, with the help of a Chinese scholar-activist in another city. The group thus had funding to support three paid staff, all former factory workers from other provinces. It was, despite its grassroots self-identity and background, heavily influenced by the professionalized NGO model that had been promoted around the country by foreign and local "experts."[8]

On this particular Sunday evening in late May, heavy rain had kept most people from arriving on time, but by 7:00 P.M. most of the dozen or so workers who eventually showed up had all made it. We started off the evening with a short thirty-minute lesson on basic computer skills—how to start up the computer, how to log on, and how to find the internet browser. After a short break, however, we entered into the main event of the night, a lesson in Chinese labor law protections that was designed by the NGO's leader.

One of the staff members, Ms. J, had worked for a while in a Hong Kong–based labor NGO before joining this group, and many of the night's activities were clearly influenced by the kinds of interactive group activities she had learned there. After asking us to count off to three and dividing into three groups, she had us sit down at small tables, with five to six people in each group. At my table, there were three men (including myself) and three women. They were all familiar with the organization and the staff, as they all had been to more than one training session or event held there.

THE ACTIVITY AS PLANNED

We were each asked to look under our chairs for a small slip of paper. On each paper, there was a question about the Chinese labor law, with multiple choices as possible answers. Ms. J asked us to read each question aloud to our partners and discuss the answer we thought was correct, then to choose (*xuan*, the same word used in "elect") one person to write down our choices on a large sheet of white paper. When we were finished discussing and writing, we were also asked to choose a person to go up to the front of the room and explain our answers to the entire "class."

HOW THE ACTIVITY ACTUALLY WORKED

Despite what I thought were fairly clear instructions, the event did not proceed the way it had been intended. At my table, each person unfolded the slip of paper and began reading to him- or herself silently. After repeated urgings by Ms. J to choose a writer, one of the three women said, "OK, I'll write," and took up the marker we had been given. As for reading and discussing, however, that took some time. Everyone first looked only at his or her own strip of paper and read the question on it. Three people then began to read aloud simultaneously, so it was impossible to hear only one voice and focus on only one question, especially as people at other tables were doing the same thing. Eventually, Old Lee, who was sitting to my left, was the only one left reading aloud, so we all turned to him to focus on that one question. In the meantime, however, the woman with the marker and the woman next to her had already decided the answers to their two questions by themselves and had written them on the paper. By the time Old Lee had finished reading aloud and followed up by announcing his answer, everyone was listening attentively. But not everyone agreed with his answer. The next ten minutes or so were pretty chaotic, with almost everyone—the other two men and two of the women—talking over one another and disagreeing about the answers, and the woman with the marker writing down answers and others saying things like, "No, not that. This is the *real* correct answer." At different times, each of the NGO's three staff members came over to our table to remind us that time was pressing, that we needed to write our answers down, and that we needed to elect a representative to head to the front of the room to explain our answers to everyone else.

At one point, Ms. J came by and asked, "Have you chosen your representative yet? You need to pick someone, whoever you think can speak for you all. Come on, now, this is your chance to express yourself democratically, to nurture your democratic skills." Her entreaties fell on deaf ears, though. Everyone just kind of looked at her quizzically then turned back to debating the answers to our questions. When the time came to send someone from our group up, Ms. J asked, "Have you selected your representative?" No one said anything, just looked at each other. Finally, one of the two more vocal women turned to Old Lee and said, "You go! You go!" But he declined, saying, "I can't read this very quickly, I won't be a good speaker." Then the woman turned to our writer and said, "OK, you go then!" The woman with the marker hesitated, then said, "You join me, then! I don't want to go by myself!" So, the two more vocal women went up to represent our group.

When they got up there, a woman at a neighboring table laughed in a good-natured, teasing way and said, "Look, there are three big men at their table, and they have to get two women to talk for them!" Her own group's representatives were a woman and a man.

The third group's presenter was a man I had chatted with earlier in the evening. At the front of the room now, he read his questions and answers in an authoritative tone of voice. One woman in my group laughed disdainfully and said loudly to the rest of us, "How ridiculous! He sounds like a government official giving a speech!" Later, as that group's representative finished reading off his last question and answer, he admitted, "Actually, the rest of the people in my group had a different answer, but since I was the one writing it up, I wrote the answer I believe to be correct!" Although not very democratic or "representative," at least he was honest.

Later on, during the wrap up, Ms. J offered some small criticisms and observations on the night's activities. She said everyone in general had a problem picking a representative, but pointed to our group specifically, saying, "In this group there were many capable potential speakers, but everyone was so shy! That's not very useful. Some people say that humility is a traditional Chinese virtue. You have to learn to break through that tradition, to speak up for yourself when you have something to say. Humility is not a virtue that's appropriate for a modern China, and even less appropriate for an organization like us!"

In this NGO setting and others, people often questioned or debated what processes would ensure a more democratic interaction. As noted earlier, how to build and recognize a consensus, when to vote, and how to vote were all issues up for debate. While such issues were being worked out (or not), though, people often fell back on behaviors developed in other contexts or modeled on other expectations.

The man who gave only his opinion despite how it differed from his small group's consensus was engaging in a sort of "role-playing" akin to that which Anita Chan found characterized student interactions during the Cultural Revolution.[9] Although times have changed, of course, the need for roles and social scripts remains, and in uncertain situations, many people naturally rely on what they have learned or observed. For this man, playing the role of the authoritative leader and talking "like a government official giving a speech" were behaviors that were familiar—he had most likely seen them modeled before in various settings—despite how unwelcome that style was to others at this night's event.

In other organizational settings, similar attempts at spontaneous leadership were not uncommon, although—as in this labor NGO—they might be met with derision, laughter, or just cold shoulders. Democratic practices take time to develop, even in voluntary associations. In one Together meeting during a village visit, for example, one university student who was, by anyone's standards, a natural leader, tried to join in a discussion by relying on the same sorts of language and speech modes he had been accustomed to using in his capacity as a leader (*ganbu*) of several official university student clubs. As he began to enumerate the "five points" that he believed were relevant to the issue at hand, he puffed out his chest and began to speak "like a government official giving a speech." It had been a long day of hard work repairing dilapidated village housing, and we were already two hours into what would become a four-hour-long meeting. By the time he reached "point number two," some people were beginning to giggle from a combination of exhaustion and exasperation. At "point number three" a few people were laughing out loud, and somewhere around "point number five"—which, unfortunately for him, by then he had forgotten what his point was—another person laughed so hard she fell off the large raised bed boards we were all sitting on. At that, the whole group erupted in laughter, and the speaker dropped his head a bit. I felt quite sorry for him just then, especially when he turned to me, with chagrin on his face, and quietly asked, "Why are they laughing? Isn't that the way it's supposed to be done?"

CONCLUSION

Scholars following in the tradition of Tocqueville make various positive arguments for the democratizing effects of civil society organizations. The general thrust of this literature is that in associations featuring face-to-face communication, the habits and skills of democracy will be developed by an association's members and, in some fashion or another, that these habits and skills will spill over into extra-associational political life.

As Mark Warren's careful theorizing about the significance of associational type and purpose would suggest, however, not all associations are created equal, especially when it comes to their potential to nurture democratic skills and practices.[10] Evidence from Chinese GONGOs, professionalized NGOs, and even volunteer-based groups suggests that face-to-face interactions are far from "naturally" conducive to democracy building, even when people leading organizations (or the activities detailed above) consciously aim to create a more egalitarian environment and mode of cooperation. Although a clear yearning for more democratic decision-making processes is evident within Chinese civil society organizations, the culture of authoritarianism is not so easily shaken off. Without careful, considered action and organizational creativity, face-to-face interactions can also end in unresolved disagreements, inaction, and a failure to achieve shared goals.

In each of these three cases—the environmentalists' meeting, the young volunteers meeting, and the labor law education activity—there was no clearly acknowledged leader. And, in each setting, it was clear that there was little consensus on how to move forward to achieve a common goal, as most participants had little experience cooperating as equals in such a setting. When everyone was accustomed to being *laoda*, the rules of the game were unclear, and despite their common concern for the environment, many of the people present aimed only to be heard, and not to hear other viewpoints. At the day-long Together meeting, multiple voices were respected and allowed to be heard, although for those students who had previously participated only in top-down normal student clubs, it was hard to tolerate or comprehend the seeming inefficiencies inherent to such a process. At the gathering of migrant workers, discussing and building a consensus together was an elusive goal, as was choosing a representative of each small group who would honor the consensus view.

This struggle between mainstream authoritarian organizational practices and an emergent democratic counterhegemony is unlikely to be resolved easily. The challenges posed by a socially entrenched and politically hostile external environment are great. Yet as individuals gain more experience interacting as equals in the absence of a clear leader, they may indeed be able to enact the democratic ideals that draw many to join civil society organizations. Moreover, it is important to recognize that people who have grown up in an authoritarian state are able *and willing* to articulate, however vaguely, a vision for a more democratic life.

Nonetheless, the road to realizing such democratic ideals is neither clear nor straight, and over the past two decades or more, there has been an ongoing struggle over what constitutes democratic practice within civil society and what legitimate leadership and decision-making should look like. In part III, I focus on two voluntary associations—Together, introduced in this chapter, and Bridges, a youth-based rural education group—in which it appears that democratic norms and practices have the greatest chances of developing, surviving, and even thriving.

PART III

Youth-Led Voluntary Associations
as Crucibles of a Democratic
Counterhegemony

Chapter Four

REJECTING FORMALISM

Alternative Narratives of Volunteering

During the "Two Meetings" held in Beijing in March 2014, eye-level bulletin boards advertised the virtues of volunteering to visitors shopping at the Wangfujing pedestrian mall. Photographs of high school students, Beijing police officers, middle-age women, and university students depicted acts of service like cutting hair and feeding sweet tapioca balls to elderly shut-ins and administering health exams in elementary schools. Captions like "Caring for Others" served as both exhortations to ideal behavior and explanations of the photos on display. A banner strung across pedestrian bridges over main thoroughfares in the city's wealthy Sanlitun district encouraged gridlocked drivers to "Learn from Lei Feng, Contribute to Others, and Improve Yourself." A perhaps mythical Communist soldier, Lei Feng has been held up for generations of contemporary Chinese as the ultimate exemplar of selfless giving. Although the stories of Lei's volunteering are perhaps not as motivational (or as convincing) as they once were, another photo at Wangfujing spotlighted a proud, plaque-holding "Contemporary Lei Feng," an elderly gentleman who devoted himself regularly to helping people in need.

Surrounded by such images, tourists might be forgiven for assuming that China's capital is full of selfless and celebrated volunteers. Indeed, in accordance with national priorities, the Beijing branch of the Communist Youth League made "making volunteer service go into everyday life" and establishing three hundred model volunteer stations among the key goals of its 2013 work plan and "promoting volunteer service" as a key goal in its 2015 work plan.[1] Nationally, as well, inducements to volunteer abound, like the Shanghai Volunteer Regulations of 2009, which state that when hiring decisions are being made, government units should give preference to people with good volunteer records.[2] Even in far-flung and politically sensitive Tibet, regulations announced in January 2015 mandated that, when all else is equal, applicants with volunteer experience should get first priority at government jobs and places in schools.[3]

Such propaganda and preferential policies for volunteers are not simply rhetoric, however. One need only consider the incredible numbers of volunteers[4] called on to ensure the smooth running of the Beijing Olympics in 2008 to understand the power of the state to set goals and frame volunteerism for political purposes, whether that be patriotism or to show the "warmth" of the Chinese people to foreign visitors. Yet such activities— organized and approved by organs of the party-state—are often perceived as a form of semi-compulsory volunteering that generates not warm fuzzy feelings but rather a sense of detachment and even potentially resentment. As sociologist Bin Xu describes it: "The Olympics were an orchestrated event. Orchestrated events need public participation, but their major purpose is to demonstrate the state's might, the nation's image and the Party's stability in leadership transition, rather than to solve a crisis. They reproduce and reinforce state corporatism in the existing political structure. Designed and rehearsed by the state to demonstrate an image of a rising China, the Olympics needed numerous volunteers, but they were strictly selected and trained by the Youth League and other GONGOs [government-organized nongovernmental organizations] and worked in a militaristic way."[5]

University students, in particular, are a key target of state-led volunteering programs.[6] In this chapter, I argue that while the Chinese government seeks to direct the development of organized volunteerism with clearly utilitarian and political purposes in mind, volunteers in bottom-up, youth-led civil society groups have begun to articulate an aversion to the instrumentalist culture that typifies state-led programs. I focus primarily on the ideals that young volunteers in Together and Bridges bring to their organizational experiences. By comparing their participation in officially approved university student organizations (*xuesheng shetuan*) with the off-campus groups they themselves lead, I suggest that state instrumentalism overlooks and neglects youth volunteers' desire for meaningful social engagement. Although the initial motivations for volunteering vary, it is clear that these volunteers are seeking ways to connect emotionally with others, to build relationships and engage in activities that provide a sense of common purpose and belonging, and to contribute to something beyond simply their own individual benefit. Their experiences suggest that government-directed volunteering is not up to the task of building the sorts of social capital and social trust that inhere in self-directed volunteering. In turn, this ultimately limits the broader social benefits that volunteering has the potential to produce.

VOLUNTEERING AND CIVIL SOCIETY THEORY

Recent ethnographic research on contemporary volunteering challenges us to look more closely at the subjective experiences of volunteers. As one example, Nina Eliasoph's (2011) study of youth empowerment projects in the contemporary United States points out a contrast between officially pre-scribed goals and the actual experience of volunteers and the youths such projects purport to empower. Rhetorically, the volunteering programs Elia-soph studied typically aim at building bridges between people from different races, wealth, and backgrounds while empowering less fortunate youth to learn to express themselves and to master the skills necessary to participate in American democracy. Yet Eliasoph found that these programs did not produce critically thinking, active citizens of a democracy. The programs were hobbled in part by short time frames for actual program implementa-tion and the expectations of donors who prized innovation over continuity. In general, she found that the causes of the problems they sought to address went unexamined: "There was not enough time for reflective discussions, anyway. So, the youth programs all just conducted projects with which no humane person could disagree—gathering mittens and cans of tuna for the poor, but not asking why there is hunger, for example—thus severing any connections between civic volunteering and political engagement, and tend-ing to breed, paradoxically, hopelessness about finding any solutions beyond one mitten at a time."[7]

For young "at-risk" youth who were the *targets* of after-school tutoring projects, the experience of being volunteered *upon* did little to nurture either broad social trust or strong personal trust in individual volunteers: "Rather than learning to trust the stream of plug-in adult volunteers who promise to become like beloved aunties but then vanish after a few months, youth participants often learn how to distinguish the real promises that organiz-ers like Emily [a paid staff member] offer from the volunteers' usually false promises. This is a useful lesson in cultivating not too much, and not too little, but the right amount of trust in a world whose organizations often promise the sun, the moon, and the stars."[8]

Although voluntary association can in theory lead participants to better understand their own preferences and thereby contribute to molding a democratic citizenry, Eliasoph argues that superficiality of engagement in empowerment programs works to deter political reflection. Moreover, such programs tended, in practice, to suppress controversy and disagreement while producing blandly uncontroversial outputs that donors and local community leaders would appreciate: "Rather than learning how to care about 'the bigger picture,' as some organizers hope they will, youth volunteers learn to ignore politics. Instead of learning how to connect their volunteer work with larger political debates, they learn technical skills of taking notes and running meetings. Learning civic skills minus politics is likely in organizations like these, which have to accept everyone regardless of viewpoint, and have to show results of action that all audiences will consider indisputably good."[9]

Eliasoph is clear about the de-politicizing results of such projects and programs. In this context, volunteering becomes a simple activity that, at best, perhaps provides feel-good moments of doing something for charity or the less fortunate but that has little to no implications for political engagement or deepening social ties.

I suggest that some Chinese youth experience government-directed volunteering in a similar fashion to the emptiness of these American empowerment projects. Although Eliasoph's research paints a bleak image of youth-involved volunteering, the groups these Chinese youth have formed and are operating on their own are experienced as much more positive and meaningful forms of social engagements. To show how this works, I first discuss the emergence and rapid growth of government-directed volunteering in China since the student-led protests of 1989. Next I introduce the data relied on for the arguments developed here. Following this, I draw on in-depth interviews to provide accounts of the ritualized or formalistic (*xingshi hua*) volunteering common to many organizations with government background. I contrast these to young volunteers' experiences in the bottom-up, voluntary associations in which they find meaning as active participants.

GOVERNMENT-DIRECTED VOLUNTEERING IN CHINA

In China, the overarching concern with state-society relations engendered by the initial rise of GONGOs has eclipsed Tocquevillian insight into the democratic culture-building potential of voluntary associations. Even studies of the 2008 Sichuan earthquake response that note the outpouring of support from volunteers have mostly taken nongovernmental organizations (NGOs) and their professionalized staff as the key locus of investigation and have been mostly concerned with the relationship between these groups and the state.[10] Although my main interest lies in the subjective experiences of volunteers, in this section, I provide context for their contestation of government-directed volunteering by highlighting the state's aims for volunteering in the post-Mao era.

As Outi Luova explains, in the wake of the 1989 protests, the Ministry of Civil Affairs fixed upon volunteering as a way to ameliorate social tensions and address new social needs brought about by economic reform and restructuring. A portrait of the official approval granted to volunteering can be cobbled together from a variety of sources, including speeches by national-level figures, such as Vice Minister of Civil Affairs Zhang Dejiang in 1989, the reinvigoration of Learn from Lei Feng campaigns in 1990, and initiatives to establish community service (*shequ fuwu*) as a key function of the lowest levels of government. Further opinion statements from the Ministry of Civil Affairs and the State Council in 2005 and 2006 ensured that volunteers and community volunteer associations would be seen as politically legitimate and desirable.[11]

Until the 2016 Charity Law, which includes some articles concerning volunteers, government policy on volunteering had generally developed along a parallel but separate trajectory to policy on NGOs.[12] In 2006, the Communist Youth League (CYL) announced national-level regulations to manage the registration of all Chinese volunteers.[13] The ground-level practice of volunteering, however, has been governed by a patchwork of local regulations, typically based on existing legal structures and political rhetoric emanating from central government bodies. The 2010 Guangdong Province Regulations on Volunteering, for example, require that eligible volunteer groups register under the Ministry of Civil Affairs' Regulations on Social Organizations and state that government departments and other entities are permitted to organize volunteer teams within their work units.[14] The 2008 Zhejiang Province Regulations on Volunteering are similar, stressing that the regulations aim to promote "a voluntary spirit of giving, friendship, mutual aid, and progress . . . [and] the construction of a harmonious society."[15] With strong signals of top-level approval and generally supportive lower-level policy responses, over the past three decades many cities around China have seen explosive growth in government-organized volunteer associations.

In addition to the Ministry of Civil Affairs and its lower-level offices, the second major agent of government-directed volunteering is the CYL.

As Ying Xu documents, in recent years the CYL has worked tirelessly to develop volunteerism among youth as one of its key purposes, thereby promoting its own institutional legitimacy and survival. In this, they have also been incredibly successful. As one CYL official proclaimed in 2010, "youth volunteering is an extremely valuable working brand created by CYL in the last 20 years' endeavor . . . The CYL should draw on the experience of the volunteering work to promote the comprehensive work of CYL."[16] Indeed, in 2013, the CYL celebrated twenty years of organized volunteering, proclaiming that nationwide they had established volunteer associations in all provinces, including in almost three thousand cities and two thousand universities. Moreover, they boasted more than one hundred and thirty thousand volunteer service sites and had registered more than forty million volunteers. Collectively, in 2012 alone, CYL volunteers had reportedly performed nearly seven hundred million hours of volunteer service.[17]

With almost ninety million members in 2014 ranging from fourteen to twenty-eight years of age, the CYL indeed has a broad and solid base from which to encourage volunteering.[18] In dozens of interviews with university students conducted in 2012 and 2013, almost all of them were CYL members and believed that "everyone" joins the CYL in junior high school if not earlier. In keeping with its role and ambitions, at Chinese universities, the CYL takes a leading responsibility for regulating student associational life. As many of my interviewees explained and as Xu notes, for example, "students normally should seek the CYL's approval if they want to establish organizations, or reserve classrooms or other venues to organize activities."[19]

In December 2013, the CYL released its five-year Youth Volunteerism Development Plan extolling the CYL's previous achievements and looking toward a bright future through 2018. Evincing clearly utilitarian goals, the plan proclaims that youth volunteerism "has already become an important medium for mobilizing young people to participate in the construction of economic society [jingji shehui de jianshe] and an important new brand for a new era of the CYL. The coming five years are a critical period for comprehensively constructing a comfortable society [xiaokang shehui] and realizing the dream of a great renaissance for the Chinese people."[20] In their totality, these series of speeches, regulations, and guidelines from the Ministry of Civil Affairs (MOCA) and the CYL have served to legitimize, encourage, and regulate the development of government-directed volunteer associations both on and off campus. The effects of the 2016 Charity Law are yet to be seen clearly, but the law does include several articles regarding volunteers, including real-name registration, a particularly worrisome requirement for grassroots groups working on sensitive social or political issues.[21]

Extant literature has contributed significantly to documenting these processes of institutionalization and explaining policy variation among different administrative levels. As Luova notes, in general, "the party–state has utilized associations as multipurpose partners that act as mediators between the party–state and society, provide community services, and influence values, with the ultimate objective of maintaining social stability and the legitimacy of the Communist Party."[22] In a similar vein, Gladys Pak Lei Chong's (2011) study of volunteering in the 2008 Beijing Olympic Games presents a discourse analysis of the "model citizen" ideal promoted by the Chinese state. Framing her analysis using Foucault's concept of governmentality, Chong identified three emphases of volunteer participation promoted by the government: not losing face, hosting a great Olympics, and "dream and glory." Based primarily on an analysis of official volunteer training materials and, secondarily, on interviews with twenty-one volunteers, she argues that "the Chinese state succeeded in arranging things in such ways that molded, guided, and directed its citizens/volunteers to internalize [its] values and act towards its objectives."[23] By contrast, my findings here, based primarily on interviews, indicate that government-directed volunteering has left young volunteers not only affectively unfulfilled but also with an active aversion to official volunteering practices.

Indeed, as valuable and necessary as prior works' state-centered analyses are, a singular focus on state intentions for volunteering risks overlooking the subjective experience of actual volunteers and the implications for them and for Chinese society more broadly.[24] To be sure, a few scholars of China have begun such work. Friederike Fleischer's small-scale study of youth volunteering in Guangzhou focused on the subjective inspirations and motivations for volunteering, finding that television from Hong Kong was frequently cited as a source of inspiration while personal satisfaction and happiness were reasons for continued participation.[25] Similarly, Unn Målfrid H. Rolandsen's research on a party-affiliated Youth Volunteers Association in a city in Fujian looked at the motivations driving volunteer participation, concluding that "what attracts youth to the volunteer movement is the opportunity to be part of a collective where they can contribute to society, while at the same time being recognized as individuals."[26] In an exploration of rapidly changing social norms around helping behaviors, Yunxiang Yan has also detailed the risks of acting as a Good Samaritan in China, especially for young people.[27] Others have analyzed how Chinese volunteers can be "caught between the moral imperatives of altruistic sacrifice derived from China's socialist revolutionary tradition and 'neoliberal' utilitarianism derived from market rationality," ultimately left "unable to articulate their commitment in reference to either moral code."[28]

My interest lies less in volunteers' motivations and theories of individualism or altruistic sacrifice than in the sharply contrasting experiences they report when comparing their participation in government-directed volunteering projects with the bottom-up projects they organize outside of government structures. These distinctions, I argue, help us begin to understand the broader social significance of bottom-up civil society development and the limitations of top-down models. Before drawing out these arguments, however, I provide some background on the larger context of university student volunteering.

UNIVERSITY STUDENTS AND VOLUNTEERING

Every autumn, first-year university students across China find themselves away from home and in a new community with many exciting possibilities. No longer weighed down by the academic demands and pressure of the university entrance exam, many are eager to explore the extracurricular clubs (*shetuan*) the typical university offers. Some organizations offer volunteer opportunities in the community or on campus. Others, like the student union, offer the chance to make a name for oneself through formal service to one's academic department, the larger multidiscipline faculty, or the entire university. Typically, these clubs are registered officially under the school's CYL and are assigned a teacher to oversee and supervise their activities.

Most of the young Bridges and Together volunteers I interviewed joined at least one officially registered club in their first year of university. Their express motivations were varied but ran the gamut from wanting to explore a new interest or hobby to wanting to hone practical skills (*duanlian nengli*). As described in interviews, a more utilitarian motivation for some students was the opportunity to accumulate "points" that could help them qualify for scholarships. Some had calculated that serving in official leadership positions—thereby garnering even more points—would bring opportunities to build personal relations with supervising professors, the school's party leaders, and administrators as well as improving their eventual job prospects.

Although "official" on-campus student organizations form the backdrop for much of this analysis, in this chapter and throughout part III, I draw most heavily on data from observations and interviews with participants in Together and Bridges. As noted earlier, these two groups are distinctive in that their activities are almost entirely volunteer organized and led, and they operate in a mode loosely combining on- and off-campus branches. The comparison of interest in this chapter is between these groups and the typical official organizations that participants have also experienced at university or, for older volunteers, in their early work lives. Other aspects of contrast also emerged in interviews—notably hierarchy and notions of (in)equality, which I take up in subsequent chapters—but here I focus primarily on volunteers' affective search for meaningful engagement.[29]

THE FORMALISTIC VOLUNTEERING EXPERIENCE

As with the 2008 Beijing Olympics, during the Guangzhou-hosted 2010 Asian Games, the government's volunteer mobilization efforts focused prominently on university students. Several of my interviewees had "been mobilized" (*bei dongyuan*) during the lead-up to the games through official student organizations. Yet, most frequently, they described these as "formalistic" and "meaningless" exercises in following orders and meeting the demands of university authorities. One student who had taken part in several university activities described the emptiness of such gestures in almost literal terms:

> During the Asian Games, the university said each class had to send a certain number of people over to the sporting venues. A lot of times, actually, they just sent people over there just to take the photo of them at the venue. . . . Sometimes there weren't many people at the sports [events] that . . . aren't so common in China, so they'd use this kind of method [to make a good show for media]. I witnessed it myself, like a stadium with only half the seats full, the cameras focused only on the places where it looked full of people, where most people were sitting. . . . That's a kind of formalism. But, it's the government that wishes [for] . . . that kind of thing.[30]

The notion of "formalism" (*xingshi zhuyi*) is perhaps awkwardly translated into English. It has, to date, received little attention by scholars but has been common in recent Chinese discourse, even being used by government officials. In 2014, for example, after a speech by Politburo Standing Committee member Wang Qishan, the party secretary of Jilin Province Wang Rulin began offering a long-winded summary of the higher-ranked Wang's remarks. An apparently frustrated Wang Qishan told him to shorten his remarks, sarcastically saying, "You're definitely going to say how important my speech was." Pointing to the written comments in Wang Rulin's hands, he went on to castigate him further, saying, "I didn't read from a prepared speech just now. How could you have printed out so much in advance? Isn't this formalism? You don't need to read any more!"[31]

For the volunteers in this study, many understood formalism in terms of doing things for show, for politeness, and without real substance or meaning. As described by one: "For example, you come over to visit [my village], and I wait by the entrance to welcome you when you arrive. Then we set off firecrackers and shake hands and share some snacks. Just like the opening ceremony [of some event]. We'll call some people over and exchange some pleasantries, then probably ask someone to take a photograph to document [our meeting]. Then there are more pleasantries, then it's over. This is what we call formalistic."

INDUCEMENTS TO VOLUNTEERING AND FORMALISM

As anywhere in the contemporary world, the motivations behind volunteering are often structured and shaped by the larger social and political environment. Volunteering helps strengthen the applications of U.S. high school students seeking entry into top universities, for example, where admissions committees are interested in identifying young leaders who may later bring fame and fortune to their institutions. In China, similar inducements are at work in the lives of young people, but they typically begin later, during university life. Many interviewees believed formalism resulted from convention but also emphasized the tangible incentives or inducements to join government-directed volunteering programs. Even outside the university setting, such incentives were evident in activities organized by larger institutions like government agencies and even businesses. I recounted in chapter 2 the experience of a social work graduate student visiting a nursing home. Although my emphasis was on hierarchy and how it permeates the organization of much of social life in China, her account also revealed the way inducements underpin practices of formalism outside university settings. As she explained it, the elderly nursing home residents said that many groups like those she witnessed often come to give them gifts, but "they don't talk with them or anything! They just hand them something and have their picture taken." She went on to describe how on the occasion when she joined this sort of "visiting" activity: "After it was all over, someone from the company's public relations office called everyone together so we could take a group picture and they could put in a press release how many employees participated in this volunteer activity helping old people. . . . Ha ha! They tried to get me in the picture, but I felt too weird about it, so I offered to take their pictures for them. . . . The whole scene was very formalistic, like they were just there to fulfil an assignment."

As with the company employees visiting this nursing home, students who participate in government-directed volunteer activities are often drawn in by multiple incentives and pressure from the larger institutions that regulate their lives. Bridges and Together volunteers related that participation in university-organized volunteer programs—like the "Three Down to the Countryside" teaching program and the student union—is heavily motivated by the need to gain points that will help when applying for scholarships and for other purposes. Although the previously described corporate employees perhaps felt only annoyed at the demands on them to fulfill assignments, many of my student interviewees saw these sorts of inducements as adulterations of the volunteer experience, even as some acknowledged their appeal to those who think most practically (*xianshi*). One student's understanding of the incentives to participate in officially organized activities was typical of the accounts given by many others:

At university, lots of clubs bring in terms like "standing committee member," lots of things like that. I feel these are very high-ranking terms. They'll say, "I'm a standing committee member," and get extra points for that. I think that's a kind of borrowing from society, the way they bring in things like that. And they get some benefit from it, so, for example, if they want to enter the CCP they'll get priority. They can rely on those club connections. Some people just join for that stuff, because it will help them get closer to teachers or maybe get opportunities to meet people outside the university who can help them get jobs later on.

Another student who volunteered in youth-led organizations but also joined the university student union reinforced this view, drawing a sharp contrast between the organizational cultures of the two:

> The student union is more utilitarian . . . Well, of course I cannot exclude the possibility that you have pure motives, that you're working purely for the good of the organization or to improve your skills in some way, but [in the student union] it's more often about putting something on your resume. . . . You could even say it's a way to help get you a job . . . And it's good for your relations with teachers. But our starting point is to do something charitable. I personally think of these as two totally separate things. I participate at the same time in both the student union and [our group]. If I had to choose, I would definitely put [our group] as my top priority . . . In [our group] I'm much more relaxed, I don't do like in those other organizations, pursuing utilitarian goals.

For many students, participation in official organizations, even volunteer-based activities, left them feeling unsatisfied and affectively disconnected from other participants. Talk about the formalism of university-approved student clubs was used to draw a sharp contrast with Bridges and Together and underscored a desire for positive, meaningful interactions with others. When asked, "What's the difference between the two other clubs you joined at university and [your group]?" one participant replied:

> Because the Communications Club and the Loving Heart Society are both university-run groups—they're [officially-registered] student organizations, you know. . . . I feel they're more formalistic. . . . And because they're university clubs, they don't do very much. Like the Loving Heart Society—it's only active for one semester a year, or they only go like once a month to an old folks' home, and only for one day. And when we go there, it's only to take some fruit to them, and then share one piece of fruit with one old person. The club asks you to give it to them [a gesture of respect]. And then you talk with them a little. . . . It feels like the only reason you're doing this stuff is for the sake of saying you're doing something charitable.

For such people, after playing active roles as joiners and leaders in Bridges and Together, volunteering "for the sake of saying you're doing something charitable" ceased to have much appeal. These folks sometimes drew associations between charity (*cishan*) and formalism, contrasting them with the more meaningful, deeper interactions they had with others in Bridges and Together activities. When asked, "How do you think [your group] differs from the typical club?" the account given by one volunteer reflected a depth of feeling and sincerity that was evident in interviews with both groups:

> Most important is that all of [our group's] activities are organized entirely by ourselves. Although some other [university-run] clubs also organize things by themselves, more of them use connections (*guanxi*) with the government in their activities or get some money from the government for their activities, some funding. . . . But [our group] can truly let you do something useful. It offers a truly practical, real-world experience of society. For example, some schools organize "up to the mountains, down to the countryside" activities, but in my understanding sixty to eighty per cent of them are more formal-istic. . . . Like visiting a hospital and going to visit elderly people [in nursing homes]. You take a photo in the morning with the old folks, but you don't leave anything behind, and you haven't truly talked with them about anything meaningful. You can say that you haven't gone deeply into their hearts to talk about what they want to talk about. It's all very polite, with everyone say-ing "thank you"—very formalistic. But in [our group] we totally just take the elderly and students as people, allowing us to really engage with each other, and also between the elderly themselves, like a real family.

As with formalism, this kind of talk about meaningfulness (*yiyi*) was another recurring theme used to contrast typical university clubs and Bridges and Together. In this account, meaningfulness was used to describe the kinds of affective ties that often underpin social trust. Yet in other situ-ations, meaningfulness could also refer to the practical or actual production of benefits or goods that many sociologists expect to come from collective activity. Volunteers spoke with disdain or disappointment about activities that were designed only to win points or fulfill the expectations of authori-ties rather than meet a social need or provide a useful service. One woman who had joined the student union in her university described the lack of meaningfulness in such terms, even as she was resigned to doing her duty as a part of the organization:

> When [the student union] held activities, in general there wasn't much consid-eration of the activity's true meaningfulness. . . . For example, each department [within the student union] is required to do a certain number of volunteer

activities. Once you've fulfilled your quota, you can go get a prize. There's a prize, yeah. So, people go and do those really meaningless activities. Like if they went for a bicycle ride, the department head [a student leader] would say, "We can treat this as a volunteer activity and report it up." So, it would become a volunteer activity, one that promotes environmental protection. . . . Sometimes it was just a very superficial thing, you know, in terms of its meaningfulness. . . . I came to feel that the student union places a lot of importance on those sorts of prizes. I actually didn't know it was that way until after I joined. . . . But I felt like that stuff had nothing to do with me. I just tried to do my best in my role.

In the eyes of most interviewees, typical university clubs and university student union activities—like engaging in bike rides that could be labeled volunteer activities—were seen as heavily influenced by the norms of broader society, and particularly as government-style (*zhengfu leide*) volunteering. Tom Gold, writing about the cohort of people born in the 1950s, notes that for them, "Chinese communists did not define youth as a time for the individual's autonomous quest for self-identity and meaning as in the west; youth's challenge was to submit to and accept the official definition of these things in the fashion of the selfless, unquestioning soldier Lei Feng."[32] In contrast, today's youth are clearly pushing back against the government definitions of volunteering that have persisted into the twenty-first century. Indeed, what I term "government-led" or "government-directed" volunteering emerges from interviewees' narratives about their experiences with formalism and their view that it emanates from "society" or government. One young person put it in exactly such terms, emphasizing both the utilitarian nature of the activity and the authority relations embedded in its production:

For example, . . . in [our province] we have a Science Centre. [As members of an official student organization] we also recruited volunteers for them. Those were all government-style volunteers. They all gave stipends and provided meals, etc. . . . In the beginning, it was ten *renminbi*, but now it has become fifteen *renminbi* per day, plus a free lunch at noontime. That style of volunteering, that style is one in which those above give you a fixed method for doing things—you just go find people and lead them over to volunteer, then take them back at night. That's it. But there's no skill involved at all. Sometimes it even felt like all we were doing was simply killing time.

While "simply killing time" may be at worst just a boring way to spend a day, in the most blatant and potentially harmful forms of government-directed volunteering, students have been required to forgo entire classes to meet the demands of state actors. A December 2011 article in the government's paper, the English-language version of the *China Daily*, was titled "Volunteering Not Voluntary." The article details how third-year advertising and exposition students at Zhejiang University in Hangzhou balked when they were forced to "volunteer" at the World Leisure Expo that autumn rather than attend their regularly scheduled classes. One student is quoted saying, "We are not against voluntary work, but we want to have the freedom to choose when, where and for what we are doing that." Fudan University sociologist Gu Xiaoming is also cited arguing that "compulsory voluntary work of this kind is dangerous and disrespectful of students. . . . It could hurt their passion for good deeds like this, and essentially twist the original meaning of the word volunteer."[33]

EMOTIONAL TIES AND TRUST

As alluded to earlier, the meaning of the term "volunteer" is indeed contested. Even outside the most obvious forms of state-led volunteering like that experienced by the Zhejiang University students, formalistic and "meaningless" experiences were repeatedly recounted by my interviewees as generating a kind of alienation from one's fellow volunteers and from the "service targets" (*fuwu duixiang*) who were the ostensible beneficiaries of their activities.

> In other organizations, I feel it's more like simply doing work. . . . There's not a lot of deep interaction between people. The trust you have towards people in those organizations is weaker. It's not like just because you're interacting with someone closely you develop the kind of trust you have with friends. . . .
>
> It's very different. In my [other university group], we meet every week to talk about what we did last time, how it went. Then we'll assign tasks for next time to various people. And after the meeting, that's it. Seldom does anyone suggest we go out for a bite to eat or do something fun together. There's no emotional connection there.

Such formalistic and personally disconnected experiences cast strong doubt on the ability of government-directed volunteering to build social trust and social capital or, indeed, anything but the most narrowly utilitarian of social benefits. With weak, distant relations among members, such officially organized volunteering efforts moved some to question what the difference was between these groups and a remunerated work environment characterized by personal calculations and a getting-ahead mentality. In contrast, volunteering with Bridges and Together was seen to produce a much more human experience that generated strong emotional ties. Meaningful volunteering, in these groups, meant experiencing and investing heavily in nurturing a feeling of warmth, emotional ties (*ganqing*), and trust.

> Lots of people say that the atmosphere in [our group] is very warm (*hen you renqingwei*). This is one of the things that attracts people and makes them keep returning. I think the atmosphere is a lot better than university clubs. It emphasizes interpersonal interactions. . . . The things we do you can say are for the elderly, but that's not the whole story. We also interact with each other, talking late into the night, putting our hearts close to each other. . . . In the Red Cross volunteer activities [run by official university clubs], there may be these things in theory, but I think that in our activities we create a truly warm atmosphere compared to typical university student organizations.

CONCLUSION

Young Chinese volunteers' desire for more meaningful experiences is well-aligned with scholarly accounts of "modern" volunteering that emphasize subjective motivation, self-reflexivity, and autonomy.[34] Although it is true that survey-based research typically finds that in already-democratic states, associational membership and volunteering are beneficial to social cohesion and democracy,[35] to expect such benefits to emerge from government-directed volunteering in an authoritarian state may be overly optimistic. China's size and diversity, of course, almost guarantee that government-directed volunteering programs are experienced by some young volunteers as new, exciting, and personally fulfilling. Nonetheless, there is ample reason to suspect that the perceptions and experiences I report may be the dominant mode of volunteering in China. Even in the United States, where self-directed volunteering has a long history, Nina Eliasoph's work has convincingly shown that top-down "empowerment projects" do little to build trust and can leave U.S. youth learning less about the practice of democratic citizenship than about the preferences and priorities of those in power.[36] In China, a recent online survey also found that volunteering does little to build social trust but can be very effective at signaling leadership skills to party-state officials.[37]

Ethnographic evidence from Japan by Akihiro Ogawa reinforces doubts about the influence of government on volunteering.[38] Government encouragement of citizen volunteerism in approved areas of activity, Ogawa argues, is part of a neoliberal government agenda designed to cut government costs by utilizing citizens' free time and energy to provide services the state does not wish to directly fund. Moreover, through institutionalization of volunteering in the educational system, "a reality in Japan is that volunteering often sounds like it is mandatory" and—very similar to what young Chinese volunteers reported—a student's volunteering record could help with university admission as well as with "school credit, entrance examinations and employment recruitment evaluations."[39] In such a system, Ogawa argues, volunteerism becomes more a Foucauldian experience of "discipline" than a process of self-actualization holding out various possibilities of personhood and citizenship. Presaging the depoliticization argument highlighted by Eliasoph in the U.S. context, Ogawa concludes that Japanese volunteers in government-approved nonprofit organizations "would never become social activists. They are apolitical. In general, those people advocating thoughts different from the dominant political voice are labelled 'people in citizens' groups,' but not as 'volunteers.'"[40]

China's official Fourteenth Five-Year Plan, issued in 2021 with a long-term view toward 2035, pledges that "we will support and develop social work service agencies and voluntary service organizations, strengthen volunteer teams, build more volunteer service platforms, and improve the volunteer service system."[41] In 2022, after the Beijing Winter Olympics ended, Xi Jinping lauded the contributions of Chinese volunteers, proclaiming that they "offered warm services with their youthful vigor and dedication, showing the vibrant and energetic image of the Chinese youth to the world." He further pledged that China "will promote throughout society the spirit of volunteers featuring contribution, friendship, mutual support and progress and allow full play to the active role of volunteers, to facilitate social progress." Linking the party-state and volunteering, Xi also praised "all the builders, workers and volunteers, bearing in mind the trust of the Party and the people and driven by the aspirations to win glory for the country, [who] worked tirelessly and dedicatedly in their respective posts."[42] No reliable study at present indicates the extent to which volunteering in China operates mostly by either a bottom-up or top-down model. However, given the small scale of organized civil society and the powerful resources poured into capturing the "volunteer spirit" by the Chinese state in recent years, it is likely that the majority of volunteering in China today is organized by authorities and for official purposes.

One way of seeing the government's desired monopoly over volunteering can be found in the use of numbers. The government and the CYL have a deep penchant for numbers to quantify scale and progress, and the field of volunteering is no exception. News reports and official announcements are replete with ever-increasing quantitative measurements of some metric deemed important to those in charge. The public emphasis on quantifying and justifying state policy and achievements reinforces the sense of formalism inherent in government-directed volunteering rather than the meaningfulness sought by self-organized volunteers.

The bureaucratic logic behind these growing reported numbers is quite straightforward. Under pressure from above, lower-level government and government-affiliated entities need to demonstrate their adherence to the party line to ensure that their work is judged favorably. At both the organizational and individual level, "political performance" (*zhengji*) is determined in part by whether officials reach established targets. In the city of Dongguan in 2014, for example, an official Volunteers Association informed a local high school that it must register 100 percent of current students as volunteers by entering their personal information into an online database "in order to fully meet the requirement of a city and national inspection" and to meet the quota for volunteers necessary to ensure Dongguan would maintain its government-awarded Civilized City status. Online reactions were swift and negative. "Is this volunteering? In order to achieve a [government-set] target? Lots of students are unwilling," wrote one student. Another commented, "That's how they do it! In my first year of high school, it was the same." Making a broader observation about youth and their values, one teacher wrote, "Students are willing to volunteer, but they're against formalism. Formalism is poisoning our students' spirits. It's the culprit responsible for the collapse of morality in society."[43]

Young volunteers' dissatisfaction with government-directed volunteering is, of course, some distance from the demanding voices of legal rights activists like Xu Zhiyong and cultural iconoclasts like Ai Weiwei. And certainly, their private protests are not on a par with the public calls for political reform proffered by the late–Nobel Prize winner Liu Xiaobo. Yet there is power in their quiet contestation of the purposes and meaning of volunteering.

As Vaclav Havel might remind us, trenchant critiques by radical dissidents offer compelling visions for a different future, but surely no less significant in terms of an envisioned good society are the day-to-day quiet discomforts expressed by everyday young volunteers. They are, without doubt, the immediate subjects of state efforts to control and regulate voluntary helping behaviors. It is in their quiet protests against the emptiness of formalism that we can see the agency of those whose bodies and minds would be mobilized by the state. By acting in groups that they themselves lead, they are actively challenging state visions of volunteering and constructing a new narrative, one that finds meaning in reaching out to develop relationships with strangers and in working to better their society.

Chapter Five

EQUALITY AS CULTURE AND PRACTICE

The concept of equality has implications for many aspects of social life, including, among others, the philosophical underpinnings of the modern human rights regime, religious understandings of human dignity, and, as is my interest here, questions of power and authority in politics, society, and organizations. Writing about efforts to realize equality under an authoritarian regime, especially one founded on the ideals of communism, is also fraught with contradictions and ironies and, I expect, may invite no small amount of cynicism. Yet, inequality of power—expressed in relations of intraorganizational hierarchy—is a key feature of life in virtually all human societies, regardless of political regime type. China is not different in this regard, and sociological studies of modern China have spilled much ink documenting and analyzing structures of inequality and hierarchy, including before and after the Chinese Communist Party (CCP) took power in 1949.[1]

Without a doubt, throughout much of Chinese history, inequality would not only have seemed a normal but also proper part of the apparently natural order of social life.[2] As Suzanne Ogden puts it:

Although the Chinese cultural tradition supports certain aspects of equality, its dominant strain has been inegalitarian. China was, and is, a hierarchically oriented country that finds it difficult to accept egalitarianism. To this day, Chinese tend to treat people differently depending on whether they are above or below them in rank (and now, in wealth) . . . the egalitarian assumptions of

democracy, as well as those of Marxism, have not found a welcoming environment in China. . . . Nevertheless, until the reforms that began in 1979, China's
leaders tried valiantly to make equality an operating principle of "socialist
democracy" in China.[3]

To ground current understandings of equality in China and in the eyes of
many of my interviewees, we can turn briefly to the lessons left by Fei Xiaotong, perhaps twentieth-century China's most influential sociologist. In his
seminal work, *From the Soil*, Fei identified three types of power governing
life in rural China, each of which has direct implications for the pursuit of
equality in contemporary China, both rural and urban.[4] "Dictatorial power,"
in his account, was imposed from above by emperors seeking to exploit their
subjects for their own material benefit. Yet imperial governments were never
able to fully penetrate and dictate life in rural areas, and a measure of democratic power (or "consensual power," in Fei's term) also existed, as people
cooperated with others for mutual economic benefit. A third form of power
relations Fei found was what he termed "rule by elders," a process of social
reproduction in which elders use education to teach children—and anyone
younger than them—in the ways of the world, thereby ensuring continuity
in culture and the smooth functioning of society. Fei saw this as neither
dictatorial—for there was no obvious material benefit in investing so much
in children's education—nor democratic, as children had little say in how or
what they were taught.

I take Fei's analysis as a starting point to propose that even in pre-
Communist rural (or "traditional" or "imperial") China, people lived with
an awareness of multiple structures of power and inequality, albeit with an
experience of consensus being built at the village level for the purposes
of economic benefit. Presumably this limited expression of equality would
have been shared predominately by men, to the exclusion of women, and
children would have encountered a system of unequal power relations
through a top-down educational process in which they were led by elders
(teachers) rather than taught as equals (as, indeed, they largely are around
the world still today). Yet, still, the idea of people interacting as equals in
some fashion, even if for limited local economic purposes, would have been
experienced directly by some and possibly observed by those it excluded
(women and children).[5]

This limited rural tradition of equality notwithstanding, in China today
as elsewhere, the notion of equality (*pingdeng*)—in all its vagueness and

potential applications—is a distinctly modern concept. In "traditional" China—or, more precisely, in most of the dynastic periods before the twentieth century in what today is called China—people were born into and lived their lives enmeshed in a system of unequal and frequently hierarchical relationships. In the late nineteenth and early twentieth century, however, European colonization in Asia and exchanges with Japan, Europe, and the United States brought into the discourse of Chinese intellectuals Western concepts of individualism, human dignity, and equality. The early twentieth century also saw the spread of Marxism, the baseline ideological justification for the Communist Party's rule. The history of Marxism's introduction into China is complex and convoluted, and much richer than I will attempt to portray here. It is not a stretch, however, to say that the CCP introduced and spread the very modern concepts of social and political equality across contemporary China.

Marxism as interpreted by Mao Zedong, at least, insisted that the tenant farmers who worked the fields of China's wealthy landowners should not see themselves as subservient to landowners, but rather as the rightful collective masters of the land and of the country (along with urban factory workers, of course). When the CCP took power, the vast majority of Chinese rural dwellers were for the first time exposed to explicit teachings about economic (in) equality, political equality, and social equality. For example, after 1949, the newly established Communist regime banned foot-binding, abolished child marriage and arranged marriages, and gave women the right to divorce their husbands, all practical but also deeply symbolic steps toward promoting the rights of women and gender equality. To be clear, these changes did not usher into China an egalitarian utopia. The contradictions in communist ideals and the Leninist structure the CCP adopted under Mao created a strong tension between hierarchical practices and the promises of equality held out by Marx's original vision of communism. As Ogden explains, "Even under Chinese Communist Party rule, which has emphasized equality in both property and social relationships, egalitarianism has had rough going. In a sense, Leninism, with its emphasis on hierarchical structure and the subordination and obedience of individuals to those above them in the hierarchy, has trumped the Marxist concept of equality."[6] And, as many scholars have observed, Deng Xiaoping's "reform and opening" policy shift after Mao's death led to increasing inequality both in terms of income and opportunity.

Although there is thus ample reason to argue that an expansive and modern concept of equality has spread and been popularized by the CCP, today China is in many respects one of the world's most unequal societies. Income inequality in China has increased dramatically since the country embarked on market reforms in 1979. Access to education, clean drinking water, and safe food, among many others, are also areas in which unequal resources and opportunities translate into unequal life chances for people around the country. Yet despite the new forms of inequality brought on by China's embrace of a capitalist-style market economy, in more recent years the core socialist values promoted nationwide through CCP propaganda and taught in Chinese primary schools also include an express commitment to equality (*pingdeng*).[7]

In this chapter my interest lies in the ways in which young activists employ the rhetoric of equality to describe both an ideal of mutual respect and, in practical application, a justification for shared authority and decision-making practices akin to those promised by formal political equality in democratic societies. In democracies, formal political equality is guaranteed by law and made most visible during elections through the mechanism of voting under conditions of universal suffrage. In authoritarian states like China, where the vote is unavailable to most people or functionally meaningless in terms of delivering substantive political choices to voters, we can turn to other settings and processes—like those within civil society organizations—to understand how power is shared, held tightly, or contested by particular individuals or groups.

DESIRING EQUALITY

Within civil society organizations in China and elsewhere, ideals of equality are often confronted with the harsh realities of inequality. In chapter 2, I discussed the discontent with unequal power relations within Chinese government-organized nongovernmental organizations (GONGOs), normal university clubs, and many professionalized NGOs. In this chapter, I focus on the ways Bridges and Together volunteers talk about equality, hierarchy, leadership, and authority. In doing so, we can begin to see the appeal of equality as an ideal and make sense of the steps they have taken to put it into practice.

As Fei's study might suggest to readers wondering about cultural continuity in decision-making practices, the continuing force of seniority as a basis for unequal power relations was present in what Bridges and Together volunteers saw as normal organizations at university and in society. Many viewed such seniority-based inequality as a source of potential conflict and actively eschewed it in their activities and organization. In Bridges, one long-term volunteer averred: "There aren't many obstacles in communication between regular volunteers, nor between regular volunteers and older volunteers. Everyone is basically very equal. It's not like just because you have more experience, or because you have some higher leadership role in the organization, therefore you have some special authority (*tequan*). Interacting as equals helps reduce conflicts and friction and makes communication easier. One of our core principles is equality. So, it doesn't matter how much volunteering experience you have, you still approach others as equals."

Although not naming it as the sort of "rule by elders" (*zhanglao tongzhi*) that Fei saw at work in precommunist rural China, the same volunteer—and many others like her—believed that habits privileging the wisdom of "seniors" threw up building blocks to realizing equality in their groups. Articulating a view widely shared by others I interviewed, she explained how some new volunteers had internalized this traditional source of inequality and emphasized how it took time and collective effort to change their views and habits: "Probably the bigger problem is with newer volunteers, because sometimes they won't see themselves as equals to us older volunteers. They restrict themselves to a lower position. But we older volunteers work hard to help them break through those self-imposed restrictions, to help them gradually grow in their awareness and adjust their mindset to recognize the equality we share. In general, it can take six months to a year, but after returning from volunteering in the villages, they come to see themselves as our equals, and interactions between different people becomes a lot simpler."

Rather than taking instruction from elders, volunteers were often encouraged to participate (*canyu*) in decision-making and planning, both in small logistical matters and in large decisions affecting the entire organization. The concept of participation, in these organizations—although certainly not in all—was considered a practice through which the ideal of equality could be realized and unproductive hierarchical distinctions could be overcome. To make this point, one volunteer drew a contrast between a well-known NGO incubator led by intellectuals and entrepreneurs in their home city and their own youth-led group: "We're not like [the large NGO incubator] where Prof. Cheng and Ms. Li are in charge. There, if you come up with a plan for a project and share it with others, they'll bluntly point out where the problems are and say, 'You should do it this way instead.' Here, we're much more grassroots. We emphasize a more participatory approach, with everyone giving mutual support and pursuing mutual understanding."

Upon being asked why people who understand the importance of participation continue to act in a top-down fashion, the same interviewee responded by further contrasting the older liberal elites who, in the 1990s and early 2000s, were instrumental in pushing open the space for grassroots NGOs to emerge, and the younger cohort who volunteer in Bridges and Together:

> There's an assumption in your question, that they understand the importance of participation. They might understand "participation" but haven't put it into action through their behavior. It's really just a word. And maybe that word—participation—hasn't really sunk into their mind yet, doesn't take an extremely important position in their mind yet. They might say, "I'm doing this so as to save you from taking the long way around to getting to where you want to go." But one of our core cultural values is that we feel that setbacks (*cuozhe*) and failure are extremely valuable treasure. The contradiction here is that some people will say, "Well, should we give new volunteers time to make mistakes and just ignore our obligation to provide the best services? Shouldn't we be responsible to our service targets?" But, in reality, there are ways to resolve this. We use a facilitator (*xiezhuzhe*) to do this. . . . We really don't have enough resources to train people well for this role, but in the last couple of years we've come up with this idea. Some people say there's no need for such a professional sounding vocabulary, that we should develop our own terms for this. We're working on it, but we haven't come up with a better term yet.

In this approach, which has been replicated across many subgroups and branches of Bridges and Together, those with more experience were not presented as the solution-holders but rather as helpers facilitating the growth (even through failure) of newcomer volunteers. Rather than give up the notion of equality in favor of efficiency, that is, volunteers across both organizations preferred to have "elders" step back.

Yet why is this idea of equality so attractive to these young volunteers? Although there are multiple reasons that could be offered by scholars across the social sciences as well as explanations from philosophers and seminarians, many volunteers gave reasons that were both personal and practical, often interweaving their arguments with notions of equality, respect for diversity, and the practical advantages of having multiple solutions to a problem put on the table. As one Together volunteer argued, equality implied a recognition of one's personal dignity and offered a way to ensure that all volunteers would feel comfortable raising unique solutions to collective problems:

> Maybe it's just my personality, but I like to listen to different views. I can't stand it when everyone's the same, because then it's just like you're alone. And from another angle, when you make different friends you can see things about yourself that normally you're blinded to. You can understand yourself better when you look through the eyes of others. And there's no way you can accomplish anything just by yourself. The more people, the more views, and the better you can find solutions to problems. As for volunteers, volunteers shouldn't have any inequality between them. I've been to other volunteer activities, like greeting people at the train station, giving directions to people—stuff like that. I think school-organized volunteering like those things is just like the university using us as free labor. They tell you how many people they need for what specific thing, and you go do it. It makes you feel like you're a robot without a mouth. My like of diversity and multiple voices started in high school, where I think I had an idea about it, a sense about it—albeit a very fuzzy one. After joining Together, that attraction was confirmed. I really like that feeling.

Without the sense that "you and I are equal" and "our voices are all important"—recurring themes throughout many interviews—people with differing views would be cowed by the inequalities of power inherent in Fei's "rule by elders," where "you feel like you're a robot without a mouth."

OPPOSING HIERARCHY

It may be that as inequality is the status quo in many people's minds, talking of equality outside of the language of hierarchy and the inequality it implies is almost impossible. For many volunteers, hierarchy was an unavoidable aspect of mainstream culture and society. One long-term volunteer working at a foreign-owned enterprise in a major Chinese city saw hierarchy as a key feature of everyday life in China:

> It seems to me that the difference between American culture and Chinese culture, in a team, at least, is that in a foreign company like where I am now, I don't think there are very obvious hierarchical relationships. But in these so-called university organizations, their origins lie in the hierarchical

administrative system of higher education, so organizations are divided by levels as well. In multinational corporations, you can even hear people just using first names. Even directly calling the boss by his name is not inappropriate. But that would be completely inappropriate in Chinese companies. Of course, society is slowly changing, but if you go to seek someone out in a government administrative office, their title is much more important than their name.

As recounted in chapter 2, hierarchy is reflected in titles, which are generally eschewed in Bridges and Together except in rare circumstances when volunteers need to present themselves or their groups to the larger public. In their actual day-to-day work, members of both groups insisted that titles were meaningless. As one Together volunteer put it, "During the winter vacation village visit, the coordinator said to us, 'Everyone is a coordinator, not only me. You're each a coordinator.'" Such sentiments were expressed to encourage broad participation and responsibility and to remind volunteers that equality as a principle is at the core of the group's value system.

As one volunteer offered, this was far different than the norm in typical university-based clubs, where the expectation is for clearly delineated and hierarchical roles:

We don't care much about someone's role as club chair or department chair. To register our club at university, we had to give an official name list, specifying who is club chair, vice-chair, like the Communist Youth League and Student Union do. But actually, even now, I'm not sure who has these official roles in our organization. Or if I know someone is a department head, I have no idea if they are the "full" department head or a "vice" department head. Having that formal title there is just to show to outsiders, a formalistic thing. In our club we would never call someone "department head" or "club head," like they do elsewhere. We just use names, and everyone actually gets along easily. No one would get offended because we're not using their title.

The aversion to hierarchy emerges in many ways that would be unheard of in typical groups where status distinctions are pursued actively by ambitious members. In one group that was formally registered at a particular university as a club, no one wanted to be named its leader. As the leader at the time told me in an interview: "We don't have elections for formal positions in our [officially registered] club. Like, when I became the head of our club (*shezhang*), it was decided through a game of 'rock, paper, scissors.' No one wants to be the head, because the term 'club' (*shetuan*) sounds awful. It feels like if you're going to be the 'club head,' then suddenly you're going to create hierarchical relationships, and nobody wants that… Our group is special like that."

In the accounts of many volunteers, the attraction of "equality" cannot be overemphasized. Being "sensitive" to status distinctions, wanting a "special" club, and avoiding the feeling of "a gulf between people" were typical of the ways people talked about equality, even when intermingling it with a more rational assertion that equality allows for a diversity of voices to come out and thus for better solutions to problems to be discovered.

When asked why Together was able to minimize hierarchy, especially compared with other Chinese civil society groups, one volunteer attributed it to the voluntary nature of the organization:

> Other organizations are more professionalized, because they want to operate as an institution (*jigou*), and maybe the work they do requires them to have layer upon layer of a division of labor. But Together is, I think, mostly driven by volunteerism. As a group of volunteers, even if there are a couple of full-time staff in the organization, we think of ourselves as more equal and believe that formal roles would affect the way we interact as equals. When I chose to join Together, in large part it was because it was so equal, with everyone having the right to speak. And also because in our activities we emphasize diversity, with different kinds of people, but then everyone being able to talk together that way feels great. Only with more voices getting heard can we do our work even better.

Again, the belief that "formal roles would affect the way we interact as equals" points to how these volunteers are pushing back against the power inequalities produced by hierarchy. As another volunteer explained it, equality expedited mutual goodwill, which in turn allowed the freedom to be honest when they had differences of opinion:

> The way I see it is that we first become friends and then work together, and between friends there isn't anyone above or below anyone else. If one person is "above" another, then they're really not friends any longer, right? If that happens, they're no longer equal, right? But I think real friends always see each other as equals. So, when it comes to work, if you propose something that I think will work, I'll follow your proposal. But that's very different than you

proposing something that I must follow—if that were the case, then clearly you'd be a level above me, and I'd be a level below you. But here it's very different. If I've got a different view, I'll definitely speak it out so everyone can discuss it, because we don't have any hierarchy and don't need to follow anyone else's orders.

REALIZING EQUALITY THROUGH LEADERSHIP

Fei's concept of "rule by elders" speaks, in this admittedly very different contemporary context, to the question of leadership and the exercise of authority. In discussing their pursuit and embracing of equality, many interviewees talked about leadership and the authority to make decisions within their groups. Some volunteers had little contact with NGOs in society, but virtually everyone had experience in other university-based groups. Most interviewees had much to say about leaders and the wielding of decision-making authority, and to a person, they argued that the organizational cultures of Bridges and Together were strikingly different from the norms of mainstream organizations.

In speaking of the leader of a well-known environmental NGO, one long-term Bridges staff member reflected on the problem of leadership within civil society more broadly, identifying a generational divide between early leaders of grassroots NGOs and the younger people who currently were staffing and volunteering within them: "Take Ms. G., for example. Her team members complain that she's too autocratic, but she doesn't see herself that way. In a sharing session once, she said she had been fighting her earlier self for many years and that she used to be much more autocratic. She said she's old now and so much more mellow. But people in her group still feel she's extremely controlling."

In this person's analysis, the staff of the professionalized environmental NGO have been frustrated by their leader's desire to control things and her low tolerance for mistakes. Conversely, and in keeping with the broader views within Bridges and Together, she offered that mistakes are necessary for both the individual and the organization:

Those of us who do volunteering are very clear. You have to give people space to grow on their own (*zifa de qu chengzhang*), even if that means they make mistakes, and you feel disappointed and frustrated by how inefficiently things are being done. Our experience shows that you have to be patient through all this if you want to achieve a stable teamwork model. . . . This takes lots of time, to let people grow, of course. I don't know if this is what democracy is or not, but allowing each person's autonomy (*meiyige ren de zizhu*) to develop is a process, especially for people like us, having been educated as we were and growing up in this environment where, at the beginning, you don't understand any of this.

To be clear, the education and environment to which she's referring is the larger authoritarian system that characterizes most organizational and political life in China. The idea that mistakes are necessary and productive, in her view, contrasts sharply with most organizational norms and the expectations visible in many professionalized NGOs. Here the notion of personal autonomy emerges as a pathway to understanding democracy as it might be lived in the everyday sense. Her long-term affiliation (more than ten years) with her group had given her many chances not only to reflect on their practices and the implications of their work but also to compare it to other groups with which she had come into contact. In contrast to most mainstream groups, she saw leadership in her organization as a process of discussion facilitation, not imposing one's will upon others or setting the rules for the organization:

Actually, because everyone has their own opinion, nobody will really say, "Oh, I'll just do whatever the team leader says, since he's always correct." All of our decisions are arrived at after discussion. The team leader's job is to promote discussion and then, if people come up with four or five different options, to help narrow it down to a couple of better ones and then facilitate more discussion around those. That's all they're there to do, to facilitate the discussion, not to make a binding decision on the group. Because, even if they try to make a decision like that, everyone else may not fall in line, right?

In her telling—which reflected the accounts of others both in and out of leadership positions—the group's commitment to equality prevents a team leader from imposing decisions on others. Instead, decisions are made through discussion and consensus-building (a topic taken up more in chapter 6).

When prompted that in some groups, some people complain that such a process is too slow and would prefer the leader just tell them what to do, one Bridges volunteer insisted that never happens with them: "No, normally no one would ever do that, say 'Ai ya, you just decide!' Because to do so would imply that you've lost a little bit of your personal autonomy, and in our teams, the work we do doesn't belong to the team leader alone. If you did that, you'd not only be giving up your personal rights but also be abdicating your responsibility to the group to participate in planning and stuff, to raise your views on things."

Again, giving up one's "personal autonomy" and abdicating the "responsibility" to participate in planning is seen as antithetical to the group's norms and to their commitment to equality. Similarly, people in leadership positions themselves are expected to *not* impose decisions on others or insist on doing it their way because of more experience: "I can't say there's no possibility that might ever happen, but this isn't what Bridges advocates. Of course, what you say and what you do can be different, so it's possible that some more experienced volunteer might think that way. But the vast majority of people wouldn't because we always insist on not interfering in what newer volunteers have planned. It's a matter of principle, as long as the plan looks acceptable, you don't interfere. If there's an issue of safety, however, well, that's nonnegotiable, not up for discussion."

People in leadership roles are seen as equal to others in the sense that their preferences and suggestions are open to question by all other members, who, in turn have an obligation to fully participate:

> If people below the leader don't agree, it's not like in that typical autocratic (*laoda*) mode. If they don't agree, they'll speak up. The culture of our organization includes speaking up when you disagree, to raise objections if you have them. It's not a one-person show here. I think that's impossible here, because it's like we don't allow that kind of person here. Like me, in leading this next group out, I'll tell them that if they have any thoughts they should just speak them out, because they also have a responsibility to the mission, including to talk about any dissatisfactions they might have so that we can come up with an even better plan.

And, indeed, many people agree and take up such leader's entreaties to speak up. As one volunteer explained: "Before joining, I thought a leader (*lingdao*) was simply someone who led others to do things (*dailing ren qu zuoshi de ren*). Now I think a leader has to first be able to listen to and incorporate others' opinions and to be able to get others' voices out onto the table."

Taking on leadership roles does not confer automatic distinction in terms of social status or make one immune to honest feedback on poor performance. As one Together volunteer put it, there is no need to give special deference to leaders just because of their title or extra work they might do:

> In the villages, everyone's equal. It's not like because someone was part of the preparation committee so they have more power or something. It's just that someone in the preparation committee had to work a little harder, like planning transportation logistics, developing a work plan for our time there, the kinds of activities we'll do with the elderly villagers, gathering necessary tools and resources, etc. That stuff just requires more effort, but that's it. And if someone does a bad job, we can tell them straight up, tell them they need to improve in such and such a way, give our opinions, and voice out our complaints.

Another volunteer averred that leaders in these groups are relatively weak, unlike the autocratic role common in mainstream organizations or society:

> Even when we have disagreements, we talk through them. No one would take the position that "I'm the club head, you all have to do what I say." We don't have those kinds of beliefs (*guannian*) here. Everyone's very tolerant of others' views and ideas. In the village where our group goes, we have a tradition that's carried down year after year whereby the coordinator's role is kind of weak. There's no strong leader (*lingdao*) role in our group. The coordinator won't say, "Everything I say is correct." Not like back in the day (*dangnian de shihou*) when whatever Chairman Mao said was always correct.

Another participant made a similar claim, in explicit opposition to the kind of "rule by elders" Fei saw at work in an earlier era: "I haven't met many people in Together who insist on others following them. A village team coordinator usually has more experience, but at the beginning of each training, we'll remind everyone to avoid exploiting their seniority (*yilao mailao*). So, I wouldn't say that someone is particularly arrogant or overbearing because they've participated in more activities. And we also point out each other's mistakes. Like in the village visit I just organized, [another volunteer] would tell me if I was doing something badly. But really that's also assisting me to handle any problems that arise."

Lest readers think all volunteers in these groups are self-effacing saints of participation and egalitarian warmth, it is worth noting that even those who profess a commitment to equality are not always able to realize it in practice. In speaking about a leader in the group with a strong personality, one volunteer related how:

> a couple of years back we had a full-time volunteer who, maybe because of his personality, there were problems in the ways he handled things and so a lot of people had a problem with him. They felt he was too autocratic (*zhuanzhi*), that he couldn't take in others' views, that he was unwilling to listen to others and that he thought he was always right. So, some people in positions of leadership, even though they talk about openness, equality, mutual respect, they don't actually do that stuff as well as other people do. This is pretty normal, though, right? . . . I remember something a teacher told me in high school, that "In lots of places, people are governed by pigs!" Ha ha![8]

Yet these more autocratic types of personalities or approaches were, by all accounts, extremely rare in leadership roles within Bridges and Together. The groups' commitments to the pursuit of equality worked to suppress enactment of the top-down norms found elsewhere, even when many recognized that the common notion of "efficiency" was not easily achieved by such a model. As a long-term volunteer put it: "A strong leader (*lingdaozhe*)—someone with a lot of experience, authority, and charisma—might try to end discussions faster for the sake of efficiency, but that would mean that some people's views might not be respected (*debudao zunzhong*). There really is a contradiction between equality and efficiency. But we hope that, or we try to make sure that in planning activities we have a consensus, so that everyone's opinion is respected."

In these groups, making sure that "everyone's opinion is respected" is generally seen as more important than chasing efficiency, because to do otherwise would imply that some participants' views are less valued, thereby introducing an unwelcome inequality into the group's work. On the seeming trade-off between efficiency and equality, one Together volunteer argued that experience taught them that buy-in from all participants was more important than saving time:

> I think it's really a minority of people who want others to make decisions for the group as a whole on the basis of some idea of efficiency. There are such

people, but the majority of us, because of the activities we do in the villages, we have a common view that we should each participate in discussions to decide the best solutions for problems we encounter. Even if it takes longer, we'll have ownership over the decision and know that it came from us as a whole. So, no one will feel very dissatisfied because "what you decided doesn't suit me"—even if it would have saved some time.

Another volunteer made a slightly different argument against seeing the autocratic (*laoda*) model as more efficient, emphasizing the practical benefits of a flatter decision-making structure: "It might be more efficient to have a *laoda* make a decision and everyone go implement it. It would be faster, and you wouldn't have much conflict come out. But the downside of this method is that you would only use the idea of the *laoda*, even when other members might have a better idea for a solution or a more creative solution. If you don't get those other ideas out on the table and just go with the *laoda*'s idea, other people just act as implementers, not as planners or strategists."

In this view, two benefits of a nonhierarchical model emerge. Greater equality among participants means that "a more creative solution" can be found for a particular issue or project, and participants are not simply "implementers" of another's idea, a role that would limit their personal growth and development.

Reinforcing the importance of emotion (*ganqing*) for these group's volunteers, as introduced in chapter 4, one interviewee drew a straight line between recognizing the goodwill and voluntariness of volunteers' actions and the need to avoid an autocratic approach in leadership:

Most people come here with a certain kind of compassion in their hearts (*yifen aixin*) or you could say joy in their hearts. And in doing the actual work, people are giving of themselves without seeking compensation, giving things like time, energy, money, etc. And when people are working together, they're not doing it out of self-interest or a search for some benefit. So, much of what we do depends on good relationships (*ganqing*). So, if, for example, a coordinator tries to play the role of the *laoda*, it would destroy those good relationships. So, the best leader in this situation is someone with experience who can bring everyone together, who can nurture everyone and guide everyone in the work, not someone who takes on the role of *laoda*.

CONCLUSION

What motivates the drive toward equality? Overall, two factors seem to push Bridges and Together volunteers to embrace equality as a value and to find ways to put it into practice. The first is affective—an emotional affinity for or desire for equality. An antipathy for hierarchy is a recurring theme throughout this book. Many people in grassroots groups, GONGOs, and professionalized NGOs abhor the sense that they are somehow "less than" or "below" someone else. They also believe that people with differing views should be respected, as related by many of the people quoted in this chapter.

Battling the inequality imposed by mainstream norms, of course, could mean that "those below" struggle within a hierarchy with the goal of becoming "those above," trading a position of subservience for the chance to lord it over others. Yet in Bridges and Together, at least, people viewed hierarchy as an oppressive system of relationships that they preferred to avoid rather than recreate in their own groups. I relate more about the "origin story" of Bridges in chapter 6 and explain how it foreshadowed their organizational emphasis on equality. In Together, equal relations between volunteers was seen as a natural extension of the group's commitment to battling the societal discrimination faced by victims of infectious disease. Years after their founding, new volunteers in both organizations mentioned the feeling of equality experienced in the groups as one of the things that attracted them and kept them involved.

Aside from positive personal feelings, many volunteers also emphasized the practical benefits of equality. Establishing an environment in which everyone's view could be expressed and considered meant they had a greater possibility of hearing better ideas and finding more creative solutions to problems. Without that basic sense of equality, many believed, alternate views might be suppressed, and the goals of the group might not be realized to the fullest extent possible. In short, both an affective attraction to equality as a value and a recognition of its practical benefits served to maintain equality as a core value in both groups' organizational culture, even after a decade of growth and expansion.

Chapter Six

HANDLING DIFFERENCES OF OPINION
AND BUILDING CONSENSUS

Scholars have long portrayed voluntary associations like Bridges and Together as sites where people come together as equals around common goals, working to build consensus on solutions to shared problems. Given the rarity of such organizational settings in China, the question of how people confront and overcome differences of opinion in bottom-up associations is both empirically pressing and theoretically rich if our goal, as mine is here, is to consider how democratic culture can emerge in an authoritarian state. As recounted in chapter 2, social scientists inspired by Tocqueville have held that voluntary associations are critical "schools" for teaching the skills and habits that are essential to democracies. Among other things, in voluntary associations, people are said to learn how to articulate their opinions, to negotiate and compromise, and to build and recognize consensus. Yet these are not simply lessons floating out in the ether waiting to be absorbed by budding democrats. They are, rather, hard-won skills that require reflection on goals and on the practices that give tangible expression to democratic values.

Within Bridges and Together, many questions arose on a regular basis that offered choices to participants and generated significant debate over best options: How many visits should we make to particular villages in a given year? Who is a suitable volunteer for our group? What specific activities should we pursue in the villages? What is the best way to incorporate newcomers? Knowing that most "ordinary" organizations in China are run in a top-down fashion and have a clear hierarchy in place, and working on the premise that power abhors a vacuum, I was curious as to how people make decisions in the absence of a clear hierarchy of authority. Put differently, when there is no preexisting power structure, how do decisions get made? In interviews and other informal conversations, I thus asked, "When you encounter differences of opinion, what do you do?" In this chapter, I explore this question in depth.

This chapter is structured as follows: First, I introduce the origins of the Bridges work style and its early incorporation of formal training programs (something that emerged in Together only over time). I then show how both Bridges and Together teach participants certain practices and discussion skills seen as necessary for effective teamwork. Next, I focus on communication and consensus building, and then on how both groups nurture tolerance as both a personal virtue and a collective good. After considering the role of shared goals in creating workable voluntary associations, I discuss how these young Chinese volunteers talk about voting as a last resort when making decisions. I then show how these groups have redefined the role of a "leader" as a facilitator rather than as the autocratic boss common in other civil society groups. Finally, I discuss how Bridges and Together came to evolve this particular kind of participatory group culture.[1]

ORIGINS OF A WORK STYLE: THE STORY OF BRIDGES

Both Bridges and Together work in teams of roughly ten to twenty young people. In any group, differences of opinion are bound to arise. Whether it be creative differences or the stress of facing unexpected situations in new environments and with new people, both organizations have found themselves needing ways to resolve differences among team members. For Bridges, concerns about conflict resolution were present at its very founding and were consciously integrated into its "training program" for new recruits. For Together, as I show later in this chapter, conflict resolution skills have evolved more organically over time and are passed on by example within the group, with older cohorts showing newer cohorts their way. Despite their different origins, the similarity of the approach that has been embraced by both groups is striking.

Bridges can trace its beginnings to just after the turn of the new millennium, when a small group of friends who had graduated from university just a few years before were chatting together. One mentioned seeing a news report about a Hong Kong-er who had gone to a village in rural (mainland)

China and ended up staying for more than a year to volunteer as a teacher. At this time, rural China was even more remote and less developed than it is now, and the group of friends thought this was an incredibly brave and challenging thing to do, *especially* for someone from Hong Kong, where, to their minds, life was much more materially comfortable. One of the friends posed the question, "Why is it that someone from Hong Kong is doing that, coming over here and sacrificing so much of himself to benefit China, but we mainland Chinese are not?" After some soul-searching and much discussion, it was decided by this initial group of three people that they should try to get people in mainland China to do something similar. The next question was, "But who can give so much of their time?" The three of them were just starting out in their work lives and their careers, enjoying the early fruits of a hard-won university education and facing pressure from family to marry, have kids, and settle down. It seemed unrealistic that they or people in their situation would be willing to set aside their lives to spend a year in the countryside, regardless of the obvious pressing needs of disadvantaged rural schools and children. As one cofounder put it, "Chinese people are 'practical'-minded . . . Nobody would be willing to give up a year of their life doing something solely for the sake of 'serving the people.' It was that way at that time, and I don't think it's much different now [in 2014]."

Eventually, however, these friends hit upon the idea of university students. As a group that has long summer and winter holidays, that is generally qualified to tutor children, and that might have more passion for such things, university students would be ideally situated both personally and (semi-) professionally to take on the challenges of working in rural schools, even if only for relatively short periods. "So, we decided on this alternative solution," the cofounder explained: "We realized it wasn't necessary to spend six months or a year in the countryside since our goal wasn't to help increase rural students' test scores. We just wanted to expand their horizons. So, one month or so was all that was needed, and during that time we could have some outstanding individuals give those rural kids some new ways of thinking (*xin de sixiang*), new ways of seeing things (*xin de silu*). If we could do that, then we would have achieved our goal."

These friends became the founders of Bridges. But as this was also a new venture for them, they quickly realized there were many logistical considerations to address. As their discussions unfolded and plans began to emerge, someone raised the issue of the challenges of working in remote areas of China. In the early 2000s, mobile phones were becoming slightly more common, but many parts of rural China still had no or very spotty signal coverage, and transportation was far from efficient. Some rural schools they had in mind would require multiple bus rides and could take university students several hours to get to from the city. "What if they face an unexpected situation and don't know what to do? They won't be able to call us," one of the friends worried. Even though, in their late twenties, these founders were fairly close in age to the volunteers they were considering, they recognized that many university students had lived sheltered lives and perhaps still lacked a full range of life skills. And, in any case, as organizers of the teaching program, they should be responsible for ensuring that volunteers would be able to handle whatever challenges they might face.

Recognizing that disputes and disagreements would be almost inevitable, one of the group's cofounders suggested they modify the team-building training program at the multinational corporation where he worked. Some of the materials had already been translated into Chinese, and with some changes, he believed it could help build trust relationships and help team members get to know each other better before going into the field. So now, each year, just before the summer vacation begins, Bridges organizes a two-part training workshop. The first part focuses on team building, largely following the outlines of the corporate training manual, and the second part focuses on technical skills and teaching practices that new members can use during their month in the field.

Although intention does not guarantee outcome, Bridges' teamwork training program is intentionally designed to nurture better communication skills and impart lessons about managing interpersonal relations. In the words of a former leader and long-term staff member who was the daughter of working-class parents: "Sharing sessions and those kinds of emotional things are probably the most important things in the training. And we also do icebreakers and activities to go deeper into people's inner selves. These things teach you how to gradually get to know someone else, how to establish relationships with others, how to get along with others, and how to open yourself up. Even though the training also conveys some things about Bridges' values and some knowledge specific to our work, I think these are the core things that are taught."

Although Together's training program has not always featured a distinct module on "communication," it has been incorporated as a feature of both trainings and informal socialization into the organization. Participants in Together tell a very similar story to those in Bridges when it comes to the importance of being "open" and sharing one's "true" thoughts with others. As one volunteer, the son of farmers, explained: "The idea is that when you share, and I share, then we can exchange views on things and, in the process, we'll both learn something new. . . . Once, when I joined a Together training, I remember someone used the phrase, 'No Sharing, No Growth.' That is, without sharing your thoughts and experiences with others, you yourself won't experience any personal growth. That idea left a deep impression on me."

STRUCTURING SKILLS FOR TEAMWORK AND COMMUNICATION

At the practical level, both groups teach organizational and implementation skills to ensure effective and efficient activities, from predeparture planning sessions to implementation practices that emphasize a "rational" division of labor. In keeping with the corporate training program used at its origins, Bridges teaches new recruits—and reinforces it with older ones—how to hold "efficient meetings" (*youxiao huiyi*). As one person described them, "We have people in the meetings take on different roles. One person will act as 'timekeeper' [in English], to make sure the meeting doesn't drag on and that it ends in a fixed time period. The second is a recorder, to take notes, because everyone speaks about their views, right? The facilitator is the third role that has to be filled." Although formulaic, this was a system that came up repeatedly in interviews and was described as both enlightening and incredibly "useful" by volunteers.

In Together, the larger team going into a village is divided into smaller groups, dealing with things like medical care, neighboring village relations, cooking, cleaning, and other activities. A preparation team that includes around three volunteers does much of the intensive advance planning required. As one recent construction team member described it: "Before going to the village, we arrange everything in advance. We write down everything we want to do each day on a piece of cardboard and post it up. Then everyone works according to that list. But usually, the person in charge of the construction team will ask everyone's opinions about how to do things best. I feel that the preparation team really respects the regular volunteers' views." In contrast to the "formalistic" experience described in chapter 4, volunteers are asked what they want to do, instead of being assigned to specific roles or specific teams without their input.

In both groups, "discussion" (*taolun*) was seen as an essential tool for both avoiding conflict or, when it still emerged, to dissipate any tensions between group members. But unlike the meeting of environmental activists described in chapter 3, these volunteers had become habituated to weighing pros and cons in a systematic "rational" fashion as a standard practice. As one Together volunteer with more than two years' experience explained: "For each project we're proposing, we'll write everything out, line by line, all the details about what we want to do. . . . It's a very effective method because we'll come up with all kinds of different ideas. And when we talk about each one, we can talk about its feasibility, whether it's appropriate for the particular village, and whether it's meaningful."

Again, and in accordance with the broader social goals of the groups, even line-by-line rational discussion still must keep faith with the basic test of *meaningfulness*. Reflecting the persistent aversion to autocracy and awareness of the risk of only hearing one dominant voice, another participant related how "sometimes, when there's a stronger difference of opinion, we'll analyze the pros and cons of the matter, listing them out. . . . There's often a blackboard that we can write the advantages and disadvantages on. And after analyzing them, everyone can say, 'Oh, so this is the better way for us to do this.'" By the time Bridges and Together had reached their tenth anniversaries, such step-by-step rational planning had become routine in both organizations and was recounted by numerous interviewees as part of the normal process of planning activities.

COMMUNICATION AND CONSENSUS BUILDING

Talk of these normal processes of planning and implementation, however, can easily mask the much more complex, underlying process of communication that has to take place before agreement can be reached on "the better way for us to do this."

In these volunteer-based groups, communication (*goutong*) takes on a new meaning. Unlike in the examples in chapter 3, in which unidirectional instructions were given and called communication, or more subtle dynamics of power and hierarchy were on display, in these groups communication is experienced, valued, and protected as a key aspect of both individual growth and effective teamwork. Both organizations emphasize that participants should enter into dialogue on the basis of mutual respect. Diversity of opinions is not only recognized but also sought out and valued in the belief that the best ideas will come through open communication. As I will demonstrate, talking through differences and problems until a consensus is reached is crucial to these young volunteers' sense of what successful communication means.

In Together, the influence of the preparation team members is minimized, drawing a sharp contrast with the top-down leadership styles in normal organizations. A business major gave the following example: "Like when we were debating whether we should buy something to give to the old folks in the village, everyone talked it over together and decided together. It wasn't just the preparation team deciding. Everyone took part in talking about it, considering both the pros and cons before coming up with a final decision together."

Direct and open communication, although not easy for everyone, especially newcomers unaccustomed to such styles, is pursued with a passion. A pharmacology major explained:

> Typically, the method we advocate is that everyone speaks out whatever they think, that they speak clearly. Whatever anyone is dissatisfied about, or whatever objection they have, we can just state it directly. There's no need for anyone to go quietly and complain to another person, then have that person act as intermediary for the original person you disagreed with. . . . Being more direct feels better! And I think it can help you resolve problems faster, too. . . . It's more efficient. . . . Some people's personalities are different, more reticent to speak up about their objections. . . . But I think that if you don't speak up, no one will know what you're thinking. . . . If everyone speaks their mind, it can decrease misunderstandings.

In contrast to more top-down groups, a preventative medicine major noted that they are willing to spend a great amount of time on consensus building: "If there's really a conflict between two people's views that we can't resolve in a group discussion, usually we'll talk one-on-one afterwards. We'll talk about a lot of things. We'll talk and talk and talk some more, then we'll figure out a better solution than what we were able to see earlier."

The recognition of diversity inherent in their interactions can also extend to the ways decisions are made, as a law major explained: "People always have their own views about how to decide things. For example, one way is that people will sit together and take a long time to talk things over, until they don't need to talk any more, when they feel they've gotten to a resolution. But another way is that the coordinator will listen to all different views, then make a decision by herself."

In the second scenario, however—one that I found to be rare in both interviews and in observations—facilitators or coordinators of discussions were not given free rein. In sharp contrast to the labor rights training event described in chapter 3, in these groups, it was generally considered anathema to their values to have one person take charge and impose his or her own view. The law student continued by noting that "the important thing in *that* case is that the coordinator has to be open to others' opinions."

Indeed, although this volunteer thought that facilitators would sometimes make decisions by themselves, in the vast majority of interviews, both leaders and the volunteers who were not in any leadership role averred that the *leaders can set the agenda but cannot make big decisions that are binding on others*. One such volunteer, a biotechnology major, said that "the three coleaders of our group will meet before the larger meeting to discuss the agenda, the general direction of the discussion. We'll decide that together then take that agenda to the rest of the larger group for discussion. But all we do is discuss things earlier. We don't decide on what to do. The real decisions about how to do things are made only when everyone is in agreement."

Whether because of their own embracing of individualism or other factors, many volunteers described differences of opinion as natural or normal, not something that could be denied or downplayed in way that would "harmonize" weaker voices into subservience. They also displayed a strong faith in the ability to reach a consensus that could achieve buy-in from all participants. "Everyone's way of thinking is different," said one member. Another law student offered: "Since conflict is inevitable between people, when opinions are very strong sometimes you'll need to spend a great deal of time talking, and also waiting for everyone to cool down. Only then can you propose a solution that everyone will agree to."

GETTING ALL VIEWS OUT AND RESPECTING ALL VIEWS

In stark contrast to mainstream civil society group meetings in which the organization's *laoda* does most of the talking and dominates any discussion, in Bridges and Together, people go out of their way to ensure that everyone speaks—not simply that everyone *has a chance* to speak but that they actually *do* speak.

In a week-long village activity with Together, for example, I saw firsthand how participants put into practice the conviction that everyone's view should be voiced for collective consideration. After dinner was made and the kitchen team's cleanup was completed, at the end of each day's work reconstructing dilapidated homes, cementing over a rough patch in the pathways elderly villagers trod to go to nearby markets, or caring for wounds that old eyes could no longer see clearly enough to tend to, the collective group of about twenty people gathered to discuss the successes and frustrations of the day and to modify any existing plans for the rest of the work camp. Complaints were aired, suggestions made, and inspirational moments shared. But whenever a question arose as to whether any changes needed to be made—and, if so, what form those changes should take—everyone was expected to speak up and share their thoughts. Going around in a circle, one by one, each question was given to each participant, whether or not they had strong views or specific suggestions. This "letting each person speak" puzzled me at first, wondering why there wasn't a more efficient way to reach consensus sooner. But over time, and as a participant in these conversations, it became clear through my own observations and through the explanations of others that there was a commitment to ensuring that each person in the group felt their voice would be welcomed. There was an acknowledgment that some felt naturally more comfortable speaking up, whereas others were naturally more shy or hesitant and thus needed encouragement and support from the group to offer their thoughts.

This approach and commitment to getting everyone's views out was not a phenomenon restricted to Together, but rather was a common practice in Bridges as well. One Bridges volunteer (an engineering and business major) with whom I met had more than eight years of experience in the group and had been working for several years at the time of our first interview. He had points of comparison both from his current job in private business and his experience as a Chinese Communist Party (CCP) member. Like many others of his age and experience level, over time, he had developed a critical sense of what should be distinctive about nongovernmental organizations (NGOs). Although I have come to see the importance of distinguishing between NGOs and "voluntary associations," in his vocabulary—and in mine at the time of that interview—they were the same. In meetings of NGOs (like Bridges), he argued, the responsibility of any person in a leadership role was to

> ensure that everyone's thoughts have been expressed, to ask if anyone's ideas have been suppressed. If, at the end of the meeting, several people haven't expressed their thoughts and thus leave the meeting feeling depressed, then, I'm sorry, I think that meeting was a failure. Why? Because Bridges is an NGO.

It's not supposed to be top-down; it's supposed to be without hierarchy. Participants' relationships are partnerships. Even if you're the group leader, your role isn't to make policy, it's to coordinate everyone (*xietiao dajia*), to figure out how to facilitate everyone in the group to make their own contribution (*fahui ziji de zuoyong*).

Groups like this, in his estimation, by their very nature require different kinds of interactions than the normal practice of top-down management with a clear *laoda* in charge. Moreover, the values inherent to NGOs—a commitment to equality, partnership, and welcoming participation—needed to be expressed in practice. If not, such groups and the activities they engage in should be seen as "a failure."

Many others in Bridges and Together referred to these values in varying terms, but they always placed an emphasis on practices. Determining how to put their values into practice was a question people wrestled with but—in my reading, at least—were obviously succeeding at on many occasions.

Rather than viewing differences as problems or obstacles to achieving their goals, participants in both groups evinced a shared belief in the value of diverse experiences and views. At the most mundane level of meetings, for example, one Together volunteer (a Chinese medicine major) related a process that would be familiar to many Bridges participants, wherein "everyone can speak up about what they think. I really like to use the 'brainstorm' method first to get all kinds of ideas listed out. Once we do that, we can choose the better ones or choose better elements from different ideas to combine together."

Despite the emphasis on relationships and feelings (*ganqing*) noted in chapter 4, this pick-and-choose approach reflects a communicative process informed heavily by the norms of rational discourse. Such an approach was mentioned by numerous volunteers who averred that everyone had an equal right and opportunity to speak and to have their views considered. According to the preventative medicine major noted earlier: "If I have a different view, I'll be direct and raise it with the group so everyone can analyze the situation. If someone else has a different view, they can raise it, and everyone can analyze the advantages and disadvantages."

Of course, consensus requires compromise, another key skill that both groups were heavily invested in teaching. One long-time volunteer (the business major), already in his early thirties when we spoke, related how he had learned that sometimes he should go with the flow rather than insist on his own views, at least when he felt he could do so in good conscience: "I'm a pretty stubborn person. That's why my nickname is 'Hardhead.' I'll insist on my own view, but if there's a decision by the team that's opposed to my own view, I'll still follow it. I'll respect the collective decision. . . . As long as it doesn't go against the principle of doing the job well or mess the work up. If that's the case, then of course you cannot compromise, right?"

As suggested by the neo-Tocquevillian scholarship introduced in chapter 2, if the willingness to listen to others and give careful consideration to different views is a democratic virtue, both groups nurture and express this virtue in spades, training themselves to be patient and shift their perspective to understand others' points of view when conflicts arise. In Bridges, this training is explicit and purposeful, said one engineering major: "In Bridges, we have a tool called 'Feedback.' When two people have a disagreement, they'll sit back and think about it a bit, then give the other person feedback, like 'I think such and such' or 'I think you are such and such.' They'll do communication with each other like that. But in our communication, we don't have any prejudice. That is, we reason with each other's views. We've found that if you really engage in careful and well-rounded communication, in the end any problems can be resolved."

As with the willingness to carefully listen to others' views, the democratic ideal of "tolerance"—a wonderfully complicated notion—is also evoked in these groups as a virtue that members both need and can learn to put into practice through their participation. The engineering major explained:

> After coming into the Bridges environment, a lot of people become much more tolerant (baorong). I remember once, when I was in charge of one project, I had a conflict with someone else. . . . He was a stubborn person, very opinionated, I guess. . . . I was willing to talk with him directly, and gave him feedback, saying 'in my interactions with you I've found you to be such and such. . . . And although you have your views, you also need to listen carefully to the views of other people.' Later on, he came up and told me he was thankful I had said what I did, because he hadn't discovered that part of himself. . . . We all saw a big change in him, too. . . . He has become much warmer and gentler, a very different attitude than before he volunteered in the village. . . . He's now much more tolerant of people with different views.

Yet rather than only a personal virtue with implications for the individual, in these organizations, giving tangible expression to tolerance—putting it into practice—has become essential to the ways these groups function and operate. This particular coming together of equals relies on tolerance as a cultural norm within the organization as well as a lesson learned by individuals. This has not happened over night, however. As one long-term Bridges volunteer and staff member reflected on his group's evolution, it became clear that a willingness to carefully listen and tolerance were virtues that required conscious nurturing by both individuals and the group itself: "I think this 'feedback' method we have is precious. It allows us to communicate on a basis of equality, one to one with others, to understand their views, and to build a consensus. Earlier, in the beginning [of our organization], we perhaps didn't have this kind of mutual understanding. It was something that required honing over time, constantly engaging in this kind of feedback so that, eventually, everyone would try to understand each other, and to treat each other with more tolerance (*huxiang baorong*)."

Many Together branches went through a similar process in their organizational evolution. As one older volunteer, a Chinese medicine major, explained it, everyone had to work hard to learn how conflict could be handled in a way that satisfied most people and still allowed for a diversity of views to be expressed:

> When our group first started out, we thought about this problem. Everyone
> believed that differences of opinion would be inevitable at some point, so after
> discussion we decided that we would resolve any conflicts in a democratic way
> [i.e., voting], and that even if your idea wasn't taken up, the minority would
> have to unconditionally obey the decision of the majority. We thought this way
> in the beginning. Later on, after some conflicts arose in our work, we began
> to talk more one-on-one with people who had opposing views, to get them
> to voice out their dissatisfaction, to get them to talk about their ideas more.

As participants in both organizations came to understand it, reaching a consensus meant that someone would likely have to compromise; otherwise, cooperation would be impossible.

THE ROLE OF SHARED GOALS

What allows for people to overcome their differences in these groups? Aside from explicit trainings, selectivity in recruitment (which I address more in chapter 9), a belief in rational discourse, and a strong culture of mutual respect, a number of volunteers also offered a classical Tocquevillian answer: shared goals. People were willing to modify their position, when necessary, because they felt that everyone else was working toward the same end. A pharmacology major said this: "Differences of opinion? In our activities, if you disagree with something, you can go talk to the project head directly. That person will talk with the heads of the other project groups and, after discussion, will sometimes make some adjustments. We're very equal here! And, more to the point, everyone is working towards the same good goal, trying to reach it. That's why people will point out problems, because if they're identified, then we can do even better in reaching our goal. I think it's great! [Laughing]."

A preventative medicine major added: "We'll have questions, but conflict is rather uncommon. Like, I'll wonder, 'Why are we doing this in this way?' Then I'll listen to others' explanation, like 'It's for this reason' or 'It's for the elderly residents' or 'It's for better communication between volunteers,' or 'It's for increased efficiency.' . . . But as for outright conflict, no one will say, 'I disagree with you, so I'm not doing that.' I feel that in our activities everyone is thinking along similar lines, for similar goals." A physics major agreed: "Differences in approaches are there, for sure, but everyone's working towards the same goal. . . . So even with different methods, there's no inherently opposed positions, no conflict of interest, and thus no intense conflicts. When everyone's working for the same goal, it's like that."

As recounted by numerous interviewees from both groups, Bridges and Together nurture a culture of horizontal support in which participants strive to do their best in their role while keeping an eye on the broader challenges faced by related teams and the group's overall goals. When problems emerge—as they inevitably do—their default response is to offer advice and lend a hand. This idealized and idealistic mode of operating is, of course, always a work in progress and, at times, a struggle. Mistakes are made, and disputes arise. But the dedication and responsibility group members feel toward achieving their shared goals drive them to seek improvement, both in the present and with an eye toward lessons they can impart to future participants. In short, in the context of respect for differences of approach and a shared sense of common goals, compromise and mutual support are seen as necessary for successful teamwork.

VOTING: NECESSARY SOMETIMES, BUT NOT PREFERRED

In interviews, I raised the question of voting as an option to reach resolutions on thorny issues. Although almost to a person each interviewee carefully considered the question and reflected on their own experience, the consistent message was that consensus building was always to be preferred over voting. A communications major explained: "In general, we don't have any kind of voting. . . . For a problem with two possible solutions, everyone talks about it at length until a consensus view emerges. Whoever is facilitating the discussion will check with everyone to make sure they're on board. Then we have a decision."

Readers may recall the emphasis on affective ties described in chapter 4, in which Bridges and Together volunteers drew sharp contrasts with their formalistic club experiences. This emphasis on emotional ties (*ganqing*) emerged again when faced with choosing between voting and consensus building. One volunteer (the law major) offered a particularly vivid picture of the "violence" of voting as a method of conflict resolution:

> Voting is a tough thing. If we really vote [reluctant sigh] . . . Voting is like violent government over the minority. Sometimes if we don't pay attention to another person's view, to overlook his or her objections . . . then that person will take on a very passive attitude to planning or implementing our activities. Compared to talking with everyone to build a consensus, voting may be more efficient, but I feel that with such small-scale activities, involving only a dozen or so people, there's no need to place such a high value on efficiency. We want to achieve effectiveness but also ensure good emotional ties (*ganqing*) amongst our team.

Indeed, most Together and Bridges activities are organized in fairly small groups of less than twenty people. Because everyone is believed to share the same goals, small-group discussions lend themselves to consensus development, and relying on a show of hands or a secret ballot introduces a risk that trust ties between members may be challenged, that somehow the relationships so important to these volunteers might be harmed. To not be able to reach agreement and *have* to rely on voting is not considered a total failure, but it is far from the ideal interaction members want to have.

Despite the strong preference for consensus, however, members of both groups have found that voting is sometimes necessary. Across both groups, participants who described the use of voting as a last resort almost always mentioned it in the context of selecting new members. A preventative medicine major explained:

> In general, if we can come to a decision through discussion, then we'll do that. . . . Selecting new volunteers is the most likely to require voting, because it's the hardest thing to decide. It's hardest to get everyone on the same page.

There are many factors to consider, like the goals of the particular visit to the village, balancing the various personalities of participants, the local dialect, because we need local dialect speakers. . . . Some groups feel it's easiest to just vote rather than discuss for too long, so first they'll exclude the ones everyone feels are unacceptable. Next everyone will discuss the pros and cons of the remaining people and then vote. I've participated in two committees. Luckily, in the first one, we didn't need to vote. I was quite torn then, and we talked about the candidates until very, very late. But everyone finally came to a consensus. In the second one, because people had differing views on a couple of the candidates, we just voted.

As another volunteer, a management major, described it: "When choosing new volunteers, we're more likely to have stronger differences of opinion. So, the most important thing is to discuss it together. . . . If we really can't come to a consensus through discussion, then we'll have no choice but to vote. . . . In general, though, we prefer to come to a decision through discussion, not through voting."

This strong insistence on consensus building over voting was apparent in the response of another volunteer, an engineering major, who echoed the notion of "violent government" raised earlier:

If there are differences of opinion, then first everyone will express their views again and explain the reasons behind their views, to try to persuade others first. If you really insist on your view, and if we really get stuck into it, then we might choose to have a vote. But we really don't want to let it get to that point, because the ones who vote against something are the ones who will be most unable to accept the result. . . . If someone really can't accept a proposal, all they're doing is giving in to the will of the majority. . . . We might have to vote when we're recruiting new volunteers, because everyone sees different character qualities in others. When you have a fixed number of spots, it can get problematic. . . . Recently it hasn't been such a problem because we're able to get each other to see different views, but last year we had to vote, because we were interviewing over 100 people for less than 20 spots.

As discussed more in chapter 9, the fraught nature of the selection process revealed one of the moments of great uncertainty and also of great consequence for these groups. Choosing the "wrong" people not only could disrupt the democratic culture of the groups but also would risk hampering the achievement of their goals in the villages. As "everyone sees different character qualities in others," this was the moment when members were most likely to settle a disagreement by voting, even though the preference typically remained to decide by consensus. (As I describe more in chapter 8, however, voting *was* considered preferable to other selection processes when choosing new leaders for these groups.)

In both organizations, voting was recognized and recognizable as a democratic practice, whereas consensus building, thorough and inclusive discussion, and the application of other skills and methods for resolving conflict were almost never spontaneously labeled as "democratic," despite the CCP's advocacy of a party-interpreted vision of "deliberative democracy."[2] Given China's controlled media environment and politicized educational curriculum, it is possible that "democratic" practice has been reduced in many people's eyes to a system in which voting determines all. Indeed, this view would accord with the minimalist definition of democracy proffered by some political scientists. Other aspects of well-functioning democracies, including informed discussion and debate, may not be as visible to people outside such systems, or at least not to the relatively young Chinese population that is my focus. Indeed, even after many conversations and hundreds of hours of participant observation, I was frequently left with the impression that many of these young volunteers did not (yet) fully appreciate the resonances between the organizational cultures they were building and the cultural norms and practices inherent to democracy writ large.

LEADERSHIP IN AN ANTIHIERARCHICAL GROUP

Although I touched on leadership in chapter 5 when discussing the value of equality, these observations about the importance of consensus building and the recognition of diverse ways of thinking raise other complex questions about leadership. What role do older, more experienced volunteers (as one example) play in these groups? How exactly do participants avoid reproducing the top-down, hierarchical, and generally authoritarian culture that permeates so much of organizational life in China? Where should we draw the line between "experience" and "authority" to make decisions that bind others?

The role of leaders in these groups was typically seen as primarily coordinators charged with helping to facilitate decision-making and to resolve conflicts. Given their experience, their ideas and suggestions are often valued, but in most situations—or in *all* situations, according to some participants—the views of newcomers are vigorously solicited in the hopes of getting even bet-ter, innovative solutions to questions or problems that the groups are facing. Leadership roles rotate among members annually in most of the subgroups I could identify, and people occupying leadership roles are valued most highly not for their ability to direct the actions of others in an authoritative manner but for their skills and contributions as mediators, coordinators, and facilita-tors of discussions and collective decision-making.

In keeping with the groups' emphasis on communication and personal skills building, leaders are seen as facilitators, not as final authorities on matters of debate. As one long-term Bridges volunteer (a Chinese literature major) put it: "In the villages, we rely on the team members themselves to resolve any conflicts. Older volunteers will lead the team into the village, but they don't have any way to interfere in the decisions of the team. They might be able to give some guidance, some direction, but the final decisions are all made by our team members, through discussion."

The thinking in Together was quite similar, with respect for all experience levels emphasized early in formal orientations and trainings for newcom-ers, as noted by an anthropology major: "In our trainings, we don't instruct people on exactly what they should do. Everyone's personality is different, so they need to be able to compromise when there's a conflict. . . . There are all kinds of people and personalities with different ideas about how to do things. But we do encourage people to think more together. We don't say that just because someone has richer experience that everything they do is correct. . . . That person doesn't have that kind of authority. Rather, everyone will consider the pros and cons of different actions, together."

In both organizations, older volunteers are expected to step back so that newcomers and those less experienced can find their own solutions to prob-lems and propose new ideas. Yet this also requires some experimentation and reflection to find a balance that aligns with the groups' core values. In one instance, the "coordinating" function of the facilitator led to concerns that his own opinions were not being heard, that his views were being over-looked as he took on the role of *only* facilitator instead of an equal, active participant whose voice was just as important as that of others. As one of the group's members, a business studies major, explained:

In our club's meetings we take turns speaking. We like to sit on the grass, in a circle, during our meetings. Our *laoda* [a term expressing respect and affec-tion, not power-hungry dominance, in this case] will say, "OK, everyone, say what you think." He used to play a particular role of only collecting views. But we felt that wasn't good, that he should also be able to have his own opinion and not just collate and summarize the opinions of everyone else. So, over time, we made this small change, so that he also shares his thoughts, but everyone else will still go around and raise their views."

In keeping with traditional norms, of course, in most circumstances, older volunteers are still shown strong respect, and their experience can be highly valued. As one communications major described: "If someone like [an older volunteer] joins in a trip to the village, we're more likely to listen to him, because he did a great job before and can tell us about the methods they used before. He would have thought about a lot of things from more perspectives than we have, so if he suggests some good ideas, everyone will consider them together and, if we like them, we'll take them up."

As another Chinese literature major made clear, however, proposals by older volunteers will be taken up "if we like them," not automatically as simply orders from "those above." Indeed, any aspirations of assuming the role of traditional domineering *laoda* are quickly dashed by the groups' aversion to hierarchy and their dual emphasis on diversity and equality: "Nobody's voice is bigger than others. Even if an older volunteer has more experience, we won't just take up their suggestions without thinking about them carefully. . . . Even new volunteers can have valuable ideas. So, when they raise them, we will share them with everyone."

In interview after interview, members of both organizations related how leaders were expected to help participants reach a consensus while avoiding suppressing the views of any individual member. In these situations, the leader's function is to ensure that all voices are given equal respect and consideration. They expected effective leaders to step back and let others speak first. One long-term volunteer in his late twenties (a marketing major) explained that leaders of these groups are not the strong "opinion leaders" that outsiders to the group might normally expect:

Lots of people think the facilitator (*zhuchiren*) is the decision-maker. But in our meetings, they aren't. They're only a coordinator tasked with encouraging people to think over problems, to make sure the atmosphere is harmonious. Of course, they're also a participant in the meeting, but usually they'll wait until the very end to give their opinion. In most people's everyday experience, facilitators are in charge (*zhudao*), so if the facilitator speaks their mind first, everyone will think they're the opinion leader (*yijian lingxiu*) trying to lead others towards their view. That would violate our principles [of giving equal consideration to everyone's views]. . . . And, besides, as facilitator your role isn't to make decisions. That's everyone's responsibility . . . Does that mean that just because everyone's sharing their view, it becomes very messy? No, not at all. The facilitator has to make it clear that "If you want to speak, you're welcome to. Just raise your hand. When we call on you, then you can speak." Also, as facilitator, whenever someone raises a point, you have to respond to it. Others may not respond, but the facilitator definitely must. Because if you don't respond, then that person won't share their thoughts the next time around.

Note that these understandings were not discussed as idealized forms of leaders, something that people wished to have. Rather, these were presented as interviewees' understandings of how things *actually work* in their groups. Readers may contrast this with the earlier discussion in chapter 2 of GONGOs and professionalized NGOs, in which case staff typically saw the actual workings of leadership in quite negative terms but also held out a vision of an idealized leader that would remedy the ills they felt beset their organizations.

THE EVOLUTION OF GROUP CULTURE

Getting to a position in which leaders were expected to facilitate everyone's active participation was not an easy feat for either Together or Bridges. These were lessons that were hard learned over months and sometimes years of trial and error in various settings and circumstances. After all, what these groups were doing was new and groundbreaking in the context of contemporary China. And as both groups grew and new branches arose, ingrained habits were reintroduced to the collective and were put into contention with emergent cultural norms at odds with the mainstream. Despite an early and strong sense of the kinds of values the founders of both groups wanted to promote—including active participation, equality, and mutual respect—putting those values into practice required conscious effort from everyone involved.

As explained in chapter 4, the formalistic culture of most university student organizations was what most people knew best, and although they aspired to something different, making that difference a reality would require group-level and individual-level introspection and experimentation.

Even though Bridges began with a premade team-building training module, they had to find ways to modify it to fit the purposes of volunteering by young idealists, not career-oriented corporate ladder climbers. For Together, building such a group culture was perhaps even more challenging, as at the beginning, they had no such preexisting written model that could be implemented and disseminated throughout a rapidly expanding network of new branches.

For one branch of Together, the beginning stages were a learning experience and a struggle that took several months to resolve. When it first began, most members were not accustomed to speaking as equals, and some lacked the confidence to voice their opinions in the face of other, stronger personalities:

> In early meetings, some group members would simply say, "my views are about the same as hers." . . . But the meeting facilitator discovered that some people would say that, and then one-on-one would tell her that "actually, I feel that doing it his way is wrong, etc., etc." These people actually had lots of objections and opinions on how things should be done differently, but in meetings they wouldn't speak up. . . . They said they didn't speak up because "some other people were so articulate and strong-minded (*biaoxian de hen you xiangfa*), or they had so many thoughts, I just wasn't willing to say much in front of them." . . . At the very beginning, people spoke up more, but eventually it became just the same four or five people talking to each other, with others just listening. So [the objectors] said that to them it felt like "this is a listen-up, not a meet-up."

Understandably, not everyone was keen to continue in a group of supposed equals yet in which they felt their voices were excluded or marginalized. As one business major observed:

> Some of them slowly dropped out over the course of a few months, and the mood of meetings became bad, because we actually need a lot of people to do the activities but only a few people were making decisions about what would be done. So, of course, those people who didn't share their thoughts became more passive about the work. So, after going through all that, now we insist that everyone speak up, saying, "Speak up about what you think if you have some thoughts. Everyone, speak up. I'm sure there are even better ideas out there." We do it like that now.

Establishing practices whereby everyone felt empowered to speak up was not the only challenge faced. They also quickly discovered that a kind of law of big numbers applied to their group dynamics. As more people heard about the experiences of their peers, more wanted to join. As I discuss more in chapter 9, both organizations are quite competitive to enter and employ rigorous screening processes for newcomers (and interest in joining seems to have only increased over time). Incorporating newcomers was not simply a matter of choosing the right people, however. As this same volunteer (the business major) explained, they also struggled with how to reproduce and protect the group's participatory culture while also accepting more people:

> After our group brought in new people, we discovered that going another round [of everyone sharing their thoughts] was impossible. There were too many people! It took forever for everyone to get through saying their thoughts just once. . . . I think nine or ten people is OK, but once the number goes above fifteen, going around the circle for everyone to speak takes a long time. Some people would complain, because then some meetings would last until 11:30 P.M. . . . Maybe there would be a resolution then, but maybe not. If there wasn't a resolution, people would complain that it was a waste of time.

Still struggling with how to make meetings both fairly efficient and productive, they tried another tack: "After that, the style changed to one of everyone 'opening the door and seeing the mountain,' just directly getting to their point. For example, 'I disagree because of such and such reason'—very quickly. It was fast, not taking a long time and engaging in dialogue with others. Other people chose to quietly withdraw, to lessen their involvement. Actually, in some situations, some people wouldn't speak, or just wouldn't come. They'd feel that they didn't have much of an opinion but were willing to help out when help was needed."

Eventually this group (and others in the network) found models of small-group participation that allowed for people to both speak up and for an actual exchange of views and considered discussion. But getting to that place was not a direct path, nor a simple one. The horizontal decision-making practices and skills evident in both organizations were honed over time and have had to be passed on to each new incoming cohort of volunteers. Given both organizations' openness to new ideas, modifications have been made along the way—and will likely continue to be—but this has been done under the premise that their core values continue to be heralded and realized in any new practices adopted.

CONCLUSION

The ways in which differences of opinion and leadership roles are treated in Bridges and Together are, I would argue, in large part the result of the organizations' voluntary nature. As contrasted with regular university-based clubs that are often underpinned by institutional incentives, joining these groups is typically seen as a completely personal choice. Participants have the option to exit, and—as in the early days of both groups—will choose to do so when their expectations of a "participatory space" in which they can make a difference are frustrated by any number of obstacles. Yet, over time, they have evolved incredibly participatory and democratic organizational cultures that give life to each person's views and use leaders as facilitators of discussion and consensus development.

Readers might contrast these depictions of life inside Bridges and Together with a professionalized NGO working on environmental issues, one I visited several times to interview both leaders and regular workers. In this established group, boasting just under twenty staff members, a more traditional approach to leadership was still practiced, despite the top leaders' efforts to "democratize" the group by encouraging more people to speak up. In this NGO, two of the group's cofounders were relied on heavily to make decisions for the entire organization. As noted by one staff member, the daughter of factory workers, who was in her late twenties: "[Our leaders] synthesize the opinions of different people, because it would be impossible, if you're in charge, to take up everyone's suggestion. If you did that, you would never be able to make a decision and you would be very inefficient. . . . So, the final decisions get made by the two of them. . . . But I guess it's somewhat democratic in that they ask everyone's views. . . . But, anyway, in the end the final decisions they make are in the best interests of our organization."

Despite the cofounders' fervent desire to have their staff work out problems and make decisions on their own, which had been expressed to me in multiple interviews, this staff member could not move beyond the issue of perceived inefficiency to see how the NGO could function without someone "above" making the "final decisions".

Another staff member also in her late twenties (the daughter of low-level government officials) in the same NGO expressed a desire for an even stronger leader: "If I want to organize an event, for example, but in my team I have only two people and need three, I'll ask my supervisor for help finding someone. If they don't support me, and I really want to do it, I'll go ask [the elder cofounder] to help coordinate (*xietiao*) for me, to find someone to help out. This is one of the annoying things about our organization, that the [middle] management is a little weak because they're reliant on [the top leader]. So, the management level needs to improve their capabilities."

The hierarchy of a senior cofounder at the top, a management layer in the middle, and regular staff at the bottom of the organization hardened boundaries between the various staff members. In contrast to Bridges and Together, however, in this group, the meaning of "coordinate" was not to help resolve differences or build consensus, but rather to "find someone to help me out" (i.e., to *assign* another staff member the role of assistant to the speaker). Far from an association of equals, in this and other professionalized NGOs with a larger number of paid staff, the practices of bureaucracy and hierarchy were unmistakably dominant.

None of these observations should be taken to mean that even the most experienced participants in Bridges and Together were not sometimes stumped by how to bridge differences. Rather than a secret formula guaranteed to succeed, they saw intensive, reflective, and respectful communication as a challenging process. Different personalities, assumptions, and experiences can all come together to create barriers to effective discussion, and, ultimately, effective teamwork. As one Together volunteer, a business major, related, knowing when to take a break and return to the table later is also a form of wisdom in group dynamics:

One time we had a meeting about a promotional activity here, at this table, for hours and hours without any kind of resolution. The coordinator insisted that the activity had to be very formal and large-scale. Others of us didn't have any particular thoughts about it, but we weren't clear on what he meant by "large-scale" and thought it would probably be OK to just rehearse it once before we did it. But he said that we were only thinking of it from an organizer's viewpoint, that we weren't thinking of how to control the flow of the program. We still didn't get his point and had all kinds of different opinions. We couldn't even figure out what he meant, so the meeting didn't go anywhere. In the end, the coordinator said, "Oh, forget it for now. Let's go eat and talk about it again later!" Ha ha! Just like that, we ended the meeting.

Chapter Seven

NURTURING DEMOCRATIC SKILLS
AND VALUES

As recounted in part I, scholars of democratic societies have long argued that participation in voluntary associations provides opportunities to develop a broad range of skills, habits, and dispositions that support democratic culture and democratic political practice. Drawing mostly on interviews with Bridges and Together participants, in this chapter I explore how the skills and habits of democracy are indeed being nurtured in these particular voluntary associations, despite their being embedded within a larger authoritarian regime. I further discuss the values that underpin these practices and suggest that these practices and values are both interwoven and mutually reinforcing.

My initial observations of group activities impressed upon me how different Together and Bridges volunteers were from their mostly older counterparts I had encountered in other Chinese nongovernmental organizations (NGOs). The values these young volunteers' behavior seemed to reflect (e.g., trust, mutual respect, equality, humility) existed in what I earlier termed the "democratic yearnings" of other civil society organizations, but only in these youth-based voluntary groups did they seem to regularly and deeply inform actual organizational practices. The next stage of the research led me to propose doing in-depth interviews in which I hoped to elicit participants' own articulations of their values and explanations driving their behavior. As I aim to show, asking questions about how people's volunteering experience had changed them helped answer the broader question of whether these sorts of grassroots voluntary associations could generate democratic skills and habits despite the overwhelmingly authoritarian organizational culture that dominates mainstream society. What follows is an account of the lessons they believed had been imparted by their experiences and the lessons I see for broader sociological questions about the development of democratic culture.

I consider the answers they provided to two general lines of inquiry: *What have you learned from your time volunteering here?* and *How has volunteering here affected you?* In line with existing literature, most people reported learning a number of new practical skills as well as developing a heightened sense of self-efficacy, stronger communication skills and interpersonal relations, a change in their values, and an increased social awareness. In general, they were highly cognizant of the transformative effects of their volunteering experience. Indeed, the vast majority of interviewees were strikingly self-reflective, and many offered sophisticated analyses of how their participation had transformed them personally and socially.

Although my own framing of these transformations emphasizes their relevance for democratic culture, many volunteers understood the lessons learned here as opportunities for personal growth (*geren chengzhang*), without any necessary or obvious political implications (an issue to which I return later in this chapter and in chapter 9). In this chapter, I consider these lessons in democratic values and practices, referring briefly to existing literature, when relevant, but devoting the majority of the chapter to understanding the views of the speakers themselves.

This chapter proceeds as follows: I first consider these voluntary associations as a training ground for practical skills, including how to hold meetings and how to organize activities. I then show how they also serve as schools for political communication and advocacy, albeit limited by the structures of the authoritarian state. Drawing on unprompted points made by volunteers, I then show how skills are considered to be a benefit of participation, and not a set of lessons pursued out of individualistic, utilitarian motives. Next, I detail how Bridges and Together nurture communication skills in participants, not only motivating them to shed any shyness so they can articulate their views and contribute to group discussion but also showing them the importance of active listening when working toward a common goal with others.

The second half of this chapter focuses on how these groups work to expand democratic values and virtues and seek to put equality, diversity, and mutual respect at the core of their organizational cultures. I discuss questions of ingroup and outgroup trust—a feature of voluntary associations that has received much attention in the scholarly literature outside China. After that, I use interviewees' stories to describe what I call democratic virtues—that is, respect for diversity, tolerance, and compassion—and relate how they express these virtues when they aim to shift their perspective to that of others. I also propose that the broader literature should see humility as a virtue inculcated in voluntary associations. I show how these groups work to deepen participants' emotional attachments and increase empathy, and I relate how volunteering increases the quality of family ties and relationships, an impact on volunteers seldom mentioned in existing scholarship.

The chapter wraps up with a discussion of how the lessons learned in these groups combine to increase participants' sense of self-efficacy. I also consider how, for many volunteers, their working-class background has not posed a major obstacle to their full and equal participation in their groups, despite what we might otherwise expect based on studies of democratic association in the United States.

A TRAINING GROUND FOR A VARIETY OF SKILLS

Practical Meeting Skills

Since almost their very founding, both Bridges and Together have organized orientation camps and training sessions for new recruits. In Bridges' trainings, how to hold "efficient meetings" is a core module of what newcomers learn. To ensure the most effective use of time, each meeting requires a timekeeper, a notetaker, and a facilitator. As one volunteer, the son of factory workers, explained: "We emphasize working efficiently, because in the countryside we have limited time every day. But because we have a model of efficient meetings, a process, our meetings can be much faster and we can avoid discussions that go around a long way before getting to the point, and so our discussions and problem-solving are more orderly."

A division of labor and a structured meeting format allow participants to use everyone's time most wisely and to devote attention to problems that emerge in the field. One volunteer, the son of garment sellers, explained:

When we're in the villages, we have a meeting every night so that various work groups can communicate about their situation. If your meetings aren't efficient, you'll waste lots of time, time that should be used to prepare lessons and activities for the students, you know? So, the different work groups—like the education group, the public relations group, the student activities group—everyone will report and reflect on the day's activities so that everyone else can get an understanding of it. If you ran into problems that day, we'll put them on the table for discussion, drawing on the strengths of the entire team to find solutions.

Learning to prioritize tasks and set deadlines are two practical skills taught to new recruits and put into practice in both Bridges and Together. As one person, the son of carpenters, who had recently played the role of notetaker put it: "We learn how to list out the most important points and then to feed those back to others, setting a deadline for each task. This is one of the first responsibilities I had. So that's why I say these sorts of things, things we do in Bridges, are very practical and can be put directly into use."

Taking notes at meetings is only one aspect of the careful recording work these groups undertake. Both organizations recognize the challenges of maintaining group culture in a predominantly university-adjacent setting, where new recruits arrive every year and "old soldiers" graduate and move into the next stage of adulthood. In both Bridges and Together, keeping track of how issues are considered and decisions are made was thus also a tool for institutional memory and organizational improvement. One Together volunteer, the son of farmers, recounted how he had learned writing skills and struggled with the challenges of recording organizational history with future volunteers in mind: "I learned how to write activity reports that could give suggestions for later volunteers about how to run an activity, noting what did and didn't work well. I had never written anything like that before and didn't understand how to. But now I've put a lot of thought into how to do this kind of thing well."

Others articulated similar lessons, averring that their organizational skills had been greatly bolstered by their participation. One volunteer, the daughter of working-class parents, explained: "At another level, it has nurtured my own basic abilities, like organizing and planning events, teamwork and cooperation, and resolving problems through communication. All these have greatly improved. In the past I seldom organized any activities, and if I did they were pretty small scale and not very well done. But here I've tried my hand at organizing more activities, and in the process accumulated more experience and nurtured this ability." Another volunteer, the son of factory workers, offered: "Another change is in the way I do things. I'm a lot more organized and analytical in my approach now, considering the pros and cons of things—I'll analyze all that. Before, I just did things however I wanted to."

Organizing activities full of logistical and sometimes even political challenges, many volunteers found themselves learning a broad set of planning and problem-solving skills. According to one daughter of migrant workers, they learned things "like budgeting and writing different kinds of documents. Like me, I used to not know how to write a project plan, but I learned here how to do it." A daughter of working-class parents offered: "I'm more careful when I do things now, demanding of myself that I work in a more dedicated fashion. So, I think I've become more careful, more serious. Like when I'm preparing a trip to the village, I'll demand more of myself, think more carefully about the details of the projects and the entire trip. I guess I feel like I've improved my ability to do things (*zuo shi*), because I'll consider many different aspects of problems and tasks now." A son of part-time menial job workers explained: "If you had asked me before about some problem, I would not have thought about approaching it logically, thinking through it clearly, like what steps I should take to fix something. But now, if I encounter a problem, I can immediately list out the steps to resolve it in an orderly fashion, even if I [still] don't list them out in a very detailed way."

As previous literature would suggest, participants in Bridges and Together went from what many described as having "zero" practical skills to becoming thoughtful and accomplished planners, organizers, and implementers. In the case of Bridges, although these skills and practices were derived no doubt in part from the corporate teambuilding training program adapted by one of Bridges' original founders, they were put to especially effective use in the service of decidedly nonprofit goals. In reflecting on the growth they had experienced in their roles, many participants in both organizations spoke with a sense of wonder at the changes in themselves and with gratitude toward their fellow participants for helping them along this trajectory.

Developing practical skills like these, however, was not the only benefit of participating in these groups. Volunteers in both groups learned communication and advocacy skills that were directly applicable to influencing policymakers and others in positions of authority.

A Training Ground for Civic Engagement and Advocacy

In general, studies of civic engagement that focus on voluntary associations have typically aimed to explicate or understand better the relationship between individuals and associations in relation to democratic governments.[1] Drawing inspiration from Alexis de Tocqueville's analysis of U.S. democratic life in the early 1800s, much recent scholarship has been concerned with the practices through which individuals seek to affect democratic polities and, in particular, their elected representatives.[2] Although civic engagement is challenging to define, in a survey of four thousands citizens in Melbourne, Australia, for example, Damon Alexander et al. (2012) identified fifteen separate activities that they argue encapsulate the "civic virtues, civic competence, and general political involvement" central to any understanding of civic engagement.[3]

In other work, Jingyun Dai and I have shown that many of the activities Chinese environmental NGOs (ENGOs) engage in would qualify under one or more of the activities on Alexander et al.'s list. For the ENGOs we studied, these included contacting a local councilor, contacting a member of parliament, signing a petition, writing to an editor of a newspaper, attending a public meeting or consultation, discussing a pressing local issue, and participating in a web-based discussion.[4] Even under an authoritarian regime, professionalized ENGOs have found ways to lobby local government to realize the environmental protection goals that the Chinese state has publicly proclaimed for itself in recent years.

Although professionalized NGOs are predominantly not the ideal-typical voluntary associations of democratic societies, in the case of China, a country without a democratic history, the leaders and staff of the ENGOs Dai and I studied have been learning how to engage as citizens of a democracy might. To the extent that they do incorporate volunteers and work to mobilize public opinion, they are also bringing others into the realm of active citizenship. Expecting that in the future these groups could attract new members of the public into joining and supporting their advocacy activities, we anticipated that the skills and practices of civic engagement may radiate beyond just these organizations, incorporating more individuals as well as solidifying policy advocacy as a mainstay of what ENGOs regularly do.

Within Bridges and Together, volunteers are learning and mastering many of the same political communication skills Dai and I found in professionalized ENGOs and the advocacy practices identified by Alexander et al. in Australia. One daughter of migrant workers said: "Normally, before joining Together there would be lots of things we wouldn't understand how to do. Like how to approach local medical authorities or how to go do a construction project. The stuff they teach us is incredibly useful." A daughter of dock workers added: "Volunteering here gives a platform from which to grow. For example, you can learn how to talk to authorities, like the principal of a school, and how to manage public relations and publicity—skills like that, and a lot of others."

Despite the undemocratic nature of the Chinese political system, recent studies have found that the Chinese state offers some limited channels for input from its citizens, even if only to fend off social unrest by developing policies that address pressing popular concerns. For example, the Law on Legislation was updated in 2015 to mandate that most newly proposed laws should go through at least a thirty-day public comment period.[5] From the standpoint of civil society actors, there is often a desire for practical civic engagement that can help further their organizational goals and fulfill their ideals. In such a context, informal and formal channels of communication between civil society actors and state officials can help both sides meet their goals.

In Bridges and Together, volunteers' deep sense of attachment to and passion for their groups—both to their missions and to the relationships participants form—motivates them to develop new advocacy-related skills they otherwise would not easily learn. After contrasting his experience in Together to "normal" university student organizations, one volunteer (the son of a farmer and migrant worker) reflected on his initial introduction to advocacy with a sense of wonder and pride in his achievements: "I even had to reach out to local media and journalists, but I had no idea how to do that. And later, I had to do stuff like making short video clips and newsletters specially focused on our village volunteer site. I had to do all of that, and at the time I felt a lot of pressure. . . . I had to learn each piece of it, to push myself to learn those things. I thought about giving up, but in the face of so many people's expectations I just couldn't let myself do that."

Researchers trying to understand civic engagement in Britain have identified what they call "contact activism," or "actions that focus on contacting those in authority" like politicians or government officials as well as media organizations and journalists who can help draw attention to a particular cause.[6] In China's authoritarian system, learning how to "approach local medical authorities" and to "talk to authorities, like the principal of a school" is a civic skill analogous to communicating with elected officials or government actors in democratic systems, despite the obvious differences in representation and political accountability. In China, where individual officials can wield great power, conveying one's preferences to "those above" (*shangmian*) and actually having a chance of achieving one's desired result requires self-confidence, a certain linguistic facility, and also an ability to "read" cues about politics and personalities. In the absence of transparent processes ensuring equal access to all comers, the ability to initiate a conversation with authorities and to interweave one's preferred outcomes with official narratives is especially important.[7] To "reach out to local media and journalists"—all of whom are subject to strict censorship rules—and to seek favorable coverage is, like approaching government authorities, also an exercise in political communication that average people in China would have little need to attempt except in the most extreme of circumstances. In these groups, however, seeking authorities' support for their causes or media coverage for their activities are regular practices that are learned and shared with each new cohort of volunteers.

Volunteers in Together put these skills to work when, for example, trying to ensure that "Uncle Chen"[8] actually gets the monthly entitlement of oil and rice that government policy says he should receive, cajoling or shaming local officials into fulfilling their duties to these otherwise forgotten elderly. Bridges volunteers do the same when approaching teachers and principals in remote areas to request entry into the local school and when trying to obtain logistical support for the extracurricular activities they organize for rural schoolchildren. Whenever media outlets report on their work—both organizations have attracted attention over the years—and when they themselves seek to engage in semipublic or public fundraising, volunteers have to learn to craft succinct, media-ready statements about the impact of their work and to construct heart-warming appeals to motivate potential donors.

IS SKILLS BUILDING JUST UTILITARIAN?

The hard and soft skills of organizing and advocacy are, to be sure, incredibly useful to achieving the goals that Bridges and Together volunteers pursue. Yet multiple interviewees brought up, unprompted, that learning such "useful" things was not the motivation for their participation. Perhaps because of the perception of typical student clubs being highly utilitarian, they made a point of stating that their motives for participating were not rooted in strategic calculations of personal gain. They claimed their motivations were driven by sincerity in personal relationships and a morally higher set of values and ideals.[9]

Numerous people explained that while they had indeed picked up many useful skills and met many different kinds of people in Together or Bridges, they were uncomfortable talking about their participation in utilitarian terms. As one volunteer, the daughter of a farmer and a factory worker, put it: "I've definitely learned a lot of things, like how to write various kinds of reports and documents, how to organize activities. . . . I've learned lots of stuff like that. But if you ask me to talk about it like that—like 'what I've learned here'—it's kind of. . . . Well, that stuff isn't why I participate in Together. It's kind of weird to talk about it that way."

Similarly, even though building one's *guanxi* (relationship) network for personal or familial gain is both an art and a tradition in China,[10] another volunteer (the daughter of factory workers) drew a sharp contrast with the larger society's norms, emphasizing that the relationships she sought were not part of some utilitarian *guanxi*-building exercise. Rather, these relationships were valued because they helped expand her appreciation for the diversity of people she encountered and taught her how to interact with people unlike herself: "I've learned about interpersonal communication. I feel like in our organization you develop a sense of how to understand others, how to get along with a diverse group of people. There's nothing utilitarian about it, mind you. But it allows you to get to know different kinds of people, to understand people different from yourself, and through that you become more tolerant and accepting."

To her and to many others, meeting new people through volunteering was not pursued as something useful for a future job search. Rather, it was cherished because of its effect of creating more meaningful, deeper relationships and for leading her to become more tolerant and accepting, changes in herself that she viewed positively. For these volunteers, what they had learned was real in the sense of practical skills and knowledge. Yet they insisted they do not volunteer *because* of those things. Rather, it is their groups' deeper meaning system and the relationships they forge that keep them engaged and motivated.

The impressive dedication of older volunteers often inspires new recruits and nurtures an intrinsic motivation to perform well in the pursuit of the groups' mission. One volunteer (the son of farmers), for example, found his work ethic had changed after participating: "Before, I didn't know why people could work continuously on something for a month, or all night long, without stopping. They're really dedicated (*renzhen*). It's inspiring to see that, and it made me want to do the same, to take responsibility for something and see it all the way through. There's that kind of slow influence on you, so that, in time, you also want to do things really well, in a responsible way, no matter the sweat and tears you have to expend." In typical student clubs, he added, he would never have learned the variety of skills imparted in Bridges, because the motivation would have been imposed from above, not emanate from within: "In other school clubs, although there may be a few chances to learn such things, the problem is that I would have no motivation to learn those things or do those things. Because in those, it would be 'those above' forcing me to, oppressing (*yapo*) me to go learn something. But those skills I just mentioned, the prerequisite for my learning those was that I myself wanted to learn them."

COMMUNICATION SKILLS

Since at least the 1990s, debate over associational life in developed democracies has highlighted concerns about a loss of face-to-face contact between organizational members. In part, this loss is attributed to the rise of national organizations that seem to have displaced local, community-based groups and to the increased prevalence of nominal membership that allows people to donate money instead of engaging in more active forms of participation like attending a meeting.[11]

Regardless of how accurate this portrayal of the dissolution of civil society in democratic countries may or may not be—and with the emergence of newer forms of community action, it may not be—the situation in China is quite different. Given the Chinese Communist Party's (CCP's) fears of large groups organizing outside its control, most grassroots NGOs in China operate primarily at a local level, eschewing large-scale and nationwide activities. Indeed, many groups consciously keep themselves small to avoid drawing the ire of authorities.[12] By extension, such groups often involve a great deal of personal interaction among participants. Together and Bridges are typical in this regard. Operating with less than five full-time paid staff, the vast majority of both organizations' work is handled by volunteers interacting directly with other volunteers in subgroups of around fifteen to twenty-five regular members. Periodic trainings and citywide or regional meetings bring together larger numbers from time to time, but most regular discussions and decisions take place in these smaller subgroups.

Such intensive face-to-face interaction nurtures a broad range of communication skills in participants. Responding to the question, "Has participating in this group changed anything about you?" numerous participants spontaneously offered that volunteering had improved their ability to articulate their views and also their ability and willingness to actively listen to people with different opinions. These skills are difficult to disentangle from the broader values of equality and mutual respect that the organizations advocate and nurture in their members, but for the sake of analytical clarity, I treat skills and values separately here.

ARTICULATING ONE'S VIEWS

Readers may recall the reticence of some factory workers to speak up in the labor rights NGO training session recounted in chapter 3 and, in chapter 2, the ways in which hierarchy inhibited government-organized NGO (GONGO) staff and others from daring to express their opinions or offering suggestions to "those above." By contrast, participating in Bridges and Together inspired many people with the self-confidence to speak up and to express themselves much more freely. One daughter of migrant workers said: "Before joining, I wasn't very good at going up to others and initiating an interaction. I was pretty passive. But here everyone is so pro-active (*zhudong*), and I've gradually learned to be so, too." A son of small restaurant owners further explained:

> I think my personality has changed quite a bit, probably. From childhood I was always very quiet and introverted, you might even say a little autistic. I had lots of thoughts but just kept them to myself, so I wasn't very good at expressing myself (*biaoda ziji*). But then, after joining Together, our group leader said 'Everyone speak up. Whatever thoughts you have, you can raise them. At that time, I really wanted to work with everyone. It felt like we were a group working together for the same goal. So, I forced myself to get out a few sentences. And then, gradually, I could speak a little more and then finally I got the courage to speak out my own thoughts. So, what Together has given me is this, the courage to speak in front of others.

Another volunteer, the son of warehouse workers, recounted a similar change, especially in front of large groups and in formal settings: "The change in me has been huge. . . . Before, when I ran for a board member spot on the Youth Volunteers Committee [an official university club], I got up on the stage and my whole body was shaking. My mind went blank, and I just talked nonsense. Now, I still feel nervous when I first get up on the stage, but then I relax and do a great job. I've got the guts now to speak in front of others."

China is a country of incredible economic inequality, a problem especially apparent when contrasting the rural, relatively poorer and isolated parts of the country from the bigger cities where most universities are located. For volunteers from working-class families in rural areas, an initial intimidation and fear of the unknown could be overcome through participation, building their self-confidence as well as trust in others. The daughter of a driver and a farmer put it this way: "Together has helped me grow a lot. I used to be a very reserved person. When I arrived in the city for university [from a small rural community], I was super cautious in my dealings with people, quite afraid of others, actually. Now I'm much more open and much better able to open myself up and express myself to others. . . . I'm very outgoing now."

Overcoming natural shyness and a reserved personality was mentioned over and over again by Bridges and Together volunteers, despite how, in my experience, the vast majority of Bridges and Together volunteers I encountered in interviews and in group settings were articulate and thoughtful speakers.

For those who saw themselves as having found their voice through participation, however, they seldom differentiated between being able to express themselves clearly and finding the confidence to speak up. Indeed, in large gatherings, like one annual meeting of Together that I attended, it was not uncommon for people to preface their (semi-)public remarks with a caveat like one person offered: "Please forgive my poor Mandarin. If you don't understand [my heavy accent], please let me know and I'll try again." Because many volunteers come from areas of the country where standard Mandarin is not the native dialect, distinctive accents abounded in many larger meetings. Yet, despite the humility inherent in their apologies in advance—which I and others took as deeply sincere—their efforts to speak publicly demonstrated a (learned) self-confidence and an eagerness to contribute to group discussions.

ACTIVELY LISTENING TO THE VIEWS OF OTHERS

Although writing letters to elected officials and expressing one's views in a public forum are the prototypical *political* communication skills mentioned in studies of democratic societies, volunteers in Bridges and Together frequently cited active listening (*lingting*) as a key communication skill they had learned. This type of listening should be distinguished from the relatively neutral (and common) "hearing of sound" (*ting*), because it implies an active intentionality, and a willingness and openness to consider another person's views.[13] The "proactive" culture noted by the daughter of migrant workers could, of course, refer only to self-expression. But a gathering of active self-expressers, as seen in the meeting of environmentally minded leaders recounted in chapter 3, will take a group only so far. Without anyone actually listening carefully to and considering the views of others, very little can be accomplished in a group of any size.[14]

Indeed, aside from developing volunteers' skills of verbal self-expression, participating in Bridges and Together also nurtured an appreciation for the value of actively listening to others. One long-term volunteer (the son of working-class parents) with eight years' experience was particularly frank about the transformative impact on his willingness to listen to others:

> I learned to really listen (*lingting*) here. I used to be a pretty impatient and stubborn person. When people had a different view to mine, I would get angry quickly. I realized that this isn't a very good model for communication (*gout-ong*), and now I wait for others to finish talking. I really listen to understand how they're thinking. The first time I went down to the village, one of my team members was stammering, saying "I mean . . . I mean . . . What I'm saying is. . . ." When he finished, I just blew up at him. Later on, I realized that in doing so I made it impossible to continue the conversation. And then he told me, "Actually, you don't have a lot of confidence in your own view, otherwise you wouldn't be so impatient to push it on others." So, I learned how to first listen to others' views, then consider them, then express my own views to them. Later, when I had returned from the village, I realized I had become more patient.

Another long-term volunteer in his late twenties, the son of middle-class parents, had been a leader in his university's student union for three years. After joining Bridges, he recalled a similar change in himself and connected the practice of active listening to respect for the dignity of others and a recognition of the importance of mutual respect in discussion and debate:

> Actually, Bridges changed me a lot. One major thing it changed was that it taught me to respect others' views (*zunzhong bieren de yijian*). Previously, when I was in year two, in the student union I exercised a pyramid-like management style. "I'm the head of this, and whatever I say goes!" I have a pretty dominating personality. . . . So, at the beginning, I really didn't respect

other people's opinions. Actually, it wasn't that I didn't respect them. It was that I wasn't willing to listen (*lingting*), you know? If you said something that touched on one of my thoughts, I thought I knew what you wanted to say and wouldn't let you finish. If I didn't want to listen, I just didn't listen. It was only after joining Bridges that I realized that if you want to work with others in a team, to do something together, even if they respect you greatly, and even if you already have thought of what you're going to do, you still have to respect their views, and you must learn to really listen (*lingting*). Because if you want others to grow together with you,[15] and if you want everyone to feel comfortable working with you and to feel a sense of accomplishment in doing so, you have to listen to them.

At the company where he works now, he is on the receiving end of his earlier top-down communication style, and the lessons he learned in Bridges are getting reinforced: "Now, I find that when I try to talk with my boss, he just won't listen to me. It makes me feel miserable. It's really tough. I just want to say, 'Even if you think you know what I'm going to say, just let me say it!' But he doesn't. And it feels just awful."

It may be that active listening is a skill in short supply in mature democracies as well. Yet in places like China, the authoritarian model of decision-making encourages a *laoda* to dominate, and active listening is considered far less important than obedience to the dictates of the leader. Since that's what these young people have grown up with, learning to listen actively to others is a challenging skill to master and apply in their associational lives. As readers may recall from chapter 3, participants in the meeting of environmentalists and in the labor rights training activity struggled—and ultimately failed—to listen and consider the views of their peers. Both of those events were organized and run by the norms of professionalized NGOs, not as products of bottom-up voluntary associations. Those experiences provide another example of how the lack of democratic associational models in an authoritarian state creates special challenges for developing the skills and habits of democracy. Yet despite the broader top-down norms of the society in which they were raised, the youth in Bridges and Together have, over time, cobbled together a habit of interaction that nurtures both the confidence to speak up and the confidence to listen actively to others.

The various kinds of communication skills and practices detailed here account for but one aspect of the transformative impact of volunteering in these grassroots voluntary associations. To be clear, such skills could be put to use in for-profit corporate settings as well as in the service of an authoritarian state's bureaucracy. We can presume that China's party-state, as a whole, would be more than happy to employ people with such skills, assuming it could put them to work towards its own political purposes. Yet, as I aim to show next, what distinguishes the lessons learned in these groups is—as volunteers themselves confirmed—both the skills and the combination of values that underpins the honing of those skills.

EXPANDING DEMOCRATIC VALUES

Equality, Diversity, and Mutual Respect

In both voluntary associations, an obvious feature of their organizational culture is a belief in the equality and dignity of all participants. As explained in chapter 5, the notion of equal worth was upheld as a common ideal in their rhetoric, yet it was also one that volunteers worked to put into practice. In tandem with this belief in equality was the valuing of diverse life experiences, voices, and perspectives, and a conviction that mutual respect should inform how people treat each other in discussions, debates, and activities of small groups and in larger gatherings. In interviews, many people spoke of equality, diversity, and mutual respect as interconnected values or elided their distinctions.

In contrast to the hierarchical organizations described as normal university clubs in chapter 4, Together and Bridges served as spaces of equality in ways that many participants had never experienced. A volunteer from rural China, the son of farmers and one of five children, spoke with amazement at the way equality could be expressed in his group: "In Together, you'll meet lots of senior brothers and sisters [upper-year students], but they treat you just like a regular friend. And you'll see them as a regular friend, too. So, there's an equality there, an equality in our relationships. As equals, senior volunteers will tell you how they've done some things, but just through normal chatting with you. They talk with you in a way that makes you realize, 'Wow, so it's possible that people can communicate with each other in a non-hierarchical fashion, without being constrained by age or seniority.'"

The rejection of hierarchy common to these groups emerges, as here, in contrast to the age-based distinctions that are prevalent in mainstream society, even between university students in different years of study. Many Bridges and Together volunteers shared his excitement at not needing to follow the social convention of addressing those further along in their studies as "elder sister" (*shijie*) or "elder brother" (*shixiong*), a custom viewed as distancing them from their only slightly older peers, especially when accompanied by an expectation of automatic deference.

Both groups draw new recruits from a mix of top universities and lesser-known schools, bringing volunteers into contact with others who occupy a different stratum in China's educational hierarchy and presumably are following a different career trajectory. The contrast in associated prestige offers yet another opportunity to reconsider assumptions about hierarchy and to develop an increased awareness and appreciation of diversity. The son of state-owned enterprise manager offered:

> Lots of different kinds of people enter Bridges. [Unlike me,] they're not all artistic and literary types (*wenyi qingnian*). But I discovered that they also have things that make them special, things that you've never come in contact with before but which are still really important and even beautiful. For example, like [another volunteer]—she studied at a technical institute that doesn't require such high scores to enter, unlike our university. Before entering Bridges, I thought people there weren't very smart, I suppose. That's just how I saw things. But after getting to know her, I realized she's really interesting. She's really able to observe others carefully and see clearly tiny things that others might miss. Meeting so many different kinds of people can help you break through your prejudices, to slowly tear down some of the mistaken ideas you have, and to see that other people can have qualities that deserve your respect.

The complex interrelations between diversity and equality—or, more specifically, the path between exposure to a diverse social world and a deeper appreciation of equality—led a number of volunteers to recount their learning journeys in similar terms. As one Together volunteer (the daughter of government cadre father and working-class mother) put it: "I guess I'm not so judgmental now. I tend to look at things as independent, and with respect. . . . I guess it's the diverse culture in the group that has given everyone a kind of real-life experience that shows us how different we are from each other. We're open to recognizing the existence of that diversity, and I understand that you and I are the same. So, my starting point now is that you and I are equal. We're just doing different things in different ways."

A number of people experienced this impulse to strive for equality after reflecting on how the mainstream discourse on volunteering—one featuring the enactment of "charity" on those less fortunate—contrasted with the lessons they had learned from the ostensible targets of their "good works." Rather than seeing herself as somehow superior to poor villagers and thus deserving of praise for her selfless sacrifice, one person, a daughter of middle-class parents, came to see how much she had learned and benefited from their interactions:

> There is one really large change that was pretty obvious. The first time I went to the village, after coming back I had a very different understanding of the term "volunteering." Before I went, I thought what I was doing as a volunteer was a grand and admirable thing, very meaningful. But afterwards, I felt that I shouldn't think of it that way. In my original thinking, it was like I put myself on a higher level than our "service targets" (*fuwu duixiang*), like I was contributing something to them, helping them. But, afterwards, I realized I shouldn't think that way because we're all equal. And also, after going to the village several times, I feel that the old folks there actually give me a tremendous amount.

As one son of breakfast shop owners related it, his own prejudices about social rank and value had to be reexamined when he began to question who benefits more from "volunteering":

> I've changed a lot. Before coming into contact with Together, I thought that volunteers and the group they were serving were very different. I guess I felt like volunteers, like me, were superior, one level up from the people we were supposed to be helping. At the beginning, I had that kind of idea, like "You're the ones being helped. I'm the one helping you." But later on, I had a very different outlook on this. I was surprised at how good the old folks were towards us. And later on, I realized that what I was giving them was far outweighed by what they were giving me.

Another volunteer (a daughter of working-class parents) explained that her participation had transformed her understanding of charity (*gongyi*),[16] prompting her to reevaluate the moral hierarchy implied in the mainstream discourse on volunteering:

> My understanding of charity has changed. Before, I probably thought, like most people do, that doing "charity" meant doing good things for other people,

helping others. And those "others" would be pitiful, weak, marginalized groups (*ruoshi qunti*). But then after joining Together, I started thinking a lot more about what 'charity' means. I don't think it's just going to help other people in need. Because I feel that my relationships with the villagers is really friendship, that we're truly friends. And sometimes it strikes me that I'm actually learning a lot from them. That is, I don't put myself up on some pedestal anymore, like "I'm so fantastic because I'm doing charity," like I'm some highly virtuous person. I see "charity" more objectively now, just a normal thing that I do.

These various lessons in equality were not simply abstract values with implications for how the speaker should treat others. They also served as motivations to explore new practices and to reflect on society more broadly. A daughter of vegetable vendors shared her dream of escaping the standardized life plan of "school-to-job-to-house-buying-to-marriage" that she saw as not just common but as oppressively so: "If everyone followed the same path in life, just think how many 'model' people China would be producing, how uniform everyone would be, like pieces of mass-produced candy that are all exactly the same size. . . . People ought to be able to choose their own life paths, to pursue their own ideals."

Rejecting a decades-long government practice of producing and praising model villages, model factories, model workers, model students, and model volunteers,[17] she worried such strict uniformity would not only work to suppress individuality and personal freedoms but also would stifle new possibilities for individual and social fulfillment by refusing to allow people to "pursue their own ideals."

Trust and Openness

One of Tocqueville's main concerns with democracy was a fear that it could lead to a collapse of community and the sacrifices needed to construct and maintain the common good. Individualism, he believed, "disposes each citizen to isolate himself from the mass of his fellows and withdraw into the circle of family and friends; with this little society formed to his taste, he gladly leaves the greater society to look after itself."[18] Participation in associations, by contrast, could stave off the worst implications of individualism and equality taken to extremes, because "feelings and ideas are renewed, the heart enlarged, and understanding developed only by the reciprocal action of men one upon another."[19]

The ideas of "feelings and ideas" being renewed and "the heart enlarged" are commonly translated into contemporary language and academic studies as the concept of trust. Following the early insights of Tocqueville, a number of recent studies have found that participation in voluntary associations does indeed help facilitate generalized social trust. One large-scale survey of civic involvement in Europe and the United States, for example, found that people active in voluntary organizations are not only more politically engaged but also exhibit higher levels of trust toward others, even people outside their own groups.[20]

In China, although government-driven reforms since 1978 have been limited mostly to the economic realm, the rise of individualism[21] has clearly generated fears of the selfishness that concerned Tocqueville so. In Xi Jinping's recent anticorruption campaign, unbridled greed and self-interest are the vices in which guilty officials are typically said to have indulged. Celebrities are often judged negatively for their selfish behavior and lack of contribution to the social good.[22] These criticisms have become commonplace in Chinese society, especially by netizens in China who respond with outrage to tales of moral failure by their fellow Chinese.

Against the backdrop of extreme self-interest and disregard for the rights and welfare of others, both Bridges and Together work in ways that build trust and mutual respect among their members, making it a priority in training programs for newcomers as well as a norm and habit developed through regular participation. Many volunteers spoke of the need to trust others to fulfill the groups' goals and discussed how their participation increased their capacity to trust others. As the son of migrant workers put it:

> When you speak to others from the heart, and you get a similar response, you'll begin to identify with this person, right? Following from that, the internal relationships in the small group will be good, because people trust each other. Like, "When I told you something, you found something that resonated with you, and I was moved." Or others agree that you should do something in a certain way, and they support you. When that happens, I'll feel like you're the sort of person who deserves my trust. . . . I think this is incredibly important in Bridges, because before meeting here people don't know each other. Yet we need to cooperate with each other in the villages for a month. If there's no trust, it would be just like co-workers in a company—you do your work, I'll do mine. The effectiveness would be much lower, I believe.

A daughter of working-class parents offered:

[After participating for some time] I also realized that I was slowly opening up, becoming less uptight, and able to express my true self better. I discovered that from early on I tended to cover up my real self, to hide myself, and I felt that I had been living in a very false way. But from the time I joined, I felt like I was being more sincere, like I was beginning to open up. It feels like here I can express myself however I want, and others will be very accepting of that. And they'll also help you improve yourself so that you can create a better you.

As has been found in democratic countries, the trust built in these organizations is not limited to within-group trust. Participants also related being open to strangers and others in ways that they would not have were it not for their experience in these groups. A son of farmers explained: "I've become a lot more open to others, willing to share my thoughts. When I knew there wasn't any danger in doing so, it was easier for me to open up and speak up. Since learning to do so, I've gone to other organizations and shared my experiences, too, and now I find it much easier to do." Another son of migrant workers added: "The way I used to be, if you and I were meeting as strangers, sitting down to talk here, I wouldn't have been able to say much at all. In the past, I just couldn't. Now I see it as problem of perspective. It's like if I'm the host or something, I'll pro-actively approach strangers to talk with them. But most people, if they meet up in a group where everyone are strangers, they won't go to talk with each other in that way." Similarly, a son of warehouse workers explained that "[joining Together] has made me more outgoing, more able to talk with anyone. At the beginning, I wasn't like that at all. Now I'm very willing to talk with others, more easy-going with strangers."

It is worth remembering that these volunteers are in their youth. Previously, it was theorized that older generations might be more trusting of strangers, but a recent study of general social trust in Germany and Sweden has argued against this, finding that it is actually younger generations that report higher trust levels.[23] In China, there is also reason to suspect that younger people might be inclined to be more trusting, regardless of how active or inactive they are in voluntary associations, as people born in the 1980s and 1990s have not experienced the kinds of traumatic political turmoil of their parents' and grandparents' generations. For those older generations, massive state- and party-led events like the Anti-Rightist Campaign and the Cultural Revolution led to deep cultural traumas and frayed social ties. Unlike South Africa and some other contemporary societies torn by divisive conflict, however, China has never undertaken a Truth and Reconciliation process to collectively recognize and try to move past the turmoil of the first few decades of CCP rule. Despite the continuing impacts of those events on Chinese politics and society more broadly, at the individual level many families are reluctant to expose old wounds by talking about them openly—especially in families where some elders were both victims and victimizers. As a result, even the most basic facts about those periods are unknown to many of the younger generation. This gap in intergenerational knowledge transmission has negative repercussions, to be sure, but it also has inoculated many in the younger generation against the harshest realities of life under authoritarianism, allowing at least some of them to experience their youth as a time of idealism and optimism about the future. This beautiful naivete has allowed them to take for granted the promises of socialism and to push forward, in their own ways, with pursuing the dream of a morally better world.

SHIFT IN PERSPECTIVE, RESPECT FOR DIVERSITY, INCLUSIVITY, TOLERANCE, AND COMPASSION: DEMOCRATIC VIRTUES AND WHAT NURTURES THEM

Tocqueville's observation that voluntary associations help "enlarge" the heart—bridging gaps and building empathy toward others—can also be seen in Bridges and Together as an increased generosity of spirit toward others. One person, the son of farmers, saw this as a major change in himself: "One transformation in me is that I've become more willing to think about others. . . . Like, if you say you're doing something, I'll want to help you and wonder if there's anything I can do for you. . . . I used to think only of myself."

Some articulated this approach to collaborating with others in terms of being able to "shift one's perspective" (huanwei sikao), a marked transformation in themselves that they attributed to the culture of their groups. A child of self-employed restaurant owners explained what "shifting one's perspective" means in these groups, relating how he applies this approach to many different settings, in the village, with his peers at university, and when dealing with administrators at school:

> I've learned to shift my perspective, to think about things from others' point of view. For example, I'll try to think about what we're doing from the old folks' perspective, whether they'll think it's suitable or not. . . . I think being able to shift my perspective will be extremely important in my future, when I'm planning more things or responsible for more projects. . . . For example, now when I go seek a professor to apply to use a university common space for an activity or some other resources, I'll think about it from the professor's perspective. They might be concerned with our safety during the event, so I'll think in advance about how to respond to that concern. . . . And, another example is that each year we do a publicity event, showing some short video clips, to attract new members. We use a PowerPoint to explain some things that we do, what the villages are all about. When I did that last time, I was in charge of preparing for the event, and so I tried to shift my perspective to that of the audience, knowing that many of them may not have studied medicine. So, I'll try to think, from their point of view, what's the best way for me to explain things so that they can understand more easily. . . . This is something that's emphasized in Together's trainings, something we learn to do.

Indeed, "shifting one's perspective" was a skill a number of people spontaneously mentioned they had developed through their participation. For some, such as the daughter of working-class parents, this practice was a tool for making sense of views and opinions that contradicted their own: "I used to be more narrow-minded, believing I was always right. But at Bridges I discovered that a lot of things should be considered from different angles, seen from the viewpoints of different people. In the process, I realized that no matter what direction something is developing, there's a rationale behind that direction that should be respected." A son of farmers offered: I've learned how to understand other people better. In the past, I wouldn't give much thought to other people's perspective. But now, sometimes, when considering a problem, I'll shift my perspective to see things from someone else's point of view, to try to understand why they would do something a certain way. And, I guess, I'll consider different angles of a problem now. I never thought this much before. Ha ha!"[24]

For others, shifting one's perspective was a practice that enhanced their compassion for others' problems and improved their tolerance for what they had originally perceived as others' shortcomings. The son of breakfast-shop owners explained: "Being together in the villages, you learn to put yourself in others' shoes. Like with my parents—I used to just take for granted everything they did for me, like paying my tuition, giving me spending money, and other stuff. But after returning from the village, I gradually realized that at my age, I should be able to take a little bit of that burden off their shoulders." Another son of working-class parents offered: "Now I seek to understand others better. I think a big characteristic of Together is that the people who have participated, afterwards they—regardless if it's an immediate or gradual change—everyone seeks to understand, to proactively try to understand other people. For example, sometimes, some people may be late. I used to get angry at that because they're late. But since participating in Together, I've changed. That is, maybe they really have . . . lots of reasons, lots of unforeseeable circumstances. And, so, I've slowly changed. I'm a lot calmer now."

One Together volunteer, the son of a factory worker and a domestic helper, connected respect for others and diversity: "I've learned to respect others (*zunzhong bieren*), because the participants in Together are all different in their own ways. In my first village trip, there were participants from Japan and people from different universities. Since people's values are different (*jiazhiguan butong*), it was easy to run into conflict and arguments. But all those people with different views can still be together, and actually become great friends. Maybe it's because they respect each other's differences. And by working towards mutual understanding and communication, we created a great atmosphere. Actually, that shouldn't be hard to understand, right?"

In talking about diversity—"I've learned to respect others (*zunzhong bieren*), because the participants in Together are all different in their own ways."—many people spoke in the same breath about respect for the individuals who embody those differences. Others, like the daughter of working-class parents, used the word "tolerance" (*kuanrong*).

I've become a lot more tolerant (*kuanrong*) now, too. [How so?] Well, because I've seen a lot of things now. I encountered lots of friction in trying to communicate with others. . . . But now I understand better how to consider others' views, to try to solve problems together. . . . In the past, if I saw someone doing something badly, I would immediately accuse them, yell at them, tell them what they were doing was wrong. But now I'll think a lot more about why they're doing things that way, why they're doing things badly, and how I ought to communicate my views to them. I'm not like before. I'm more tolerant now.

HUMILITY AS A DEMOCRATIC VIRTUE

In Benjamin Franklin's autobiography, he reflected on how when he was twenty-two years old, he conceived a goal for himself of living a virtuous life. At that still young age, he first listed out twelve key virtues he aspired to inculcate in himself but soon realized he needed to add another—humility: "My List of Virtues contain'd at first but twelve: But a Quaker Friend having kindly inform'd me that I was generally thought proud; that my Pride show'd itself frequently in Conversation; that I was not content with being in the right when discussing any Point, but was overbearing & rather insolent; of which he convinc'd me by mentioning several Instances;—I determined endeavouring to cure myself . . ., and I added Humility to my List, giving an extensive Meaning to the Word.[25]

Although humility is not typically listed as a democratic virtue nurtured through participation in voluntary associations, the experience of Bridges and Together volunteers suggests that perhaps it should be. A number of people mentioned how one of the key ways in which their volunteering had changed them was that it made them more humble. While volunteering boosted their self-confidence and increased their self-efficacy, as I illustrate, working in these groups also brought them into contact with peers who had obviously stronger abilities, better ideas, or more innovative solutions to problems.

As the daughter of a farmer and a factory worker put it: "There are lots of super-capable people in Together, and so, in comparison, I've found that I can make lots of mistakes on this or that. I think a bigger change in me is that I'm in a state of constant learning now. . . . From my first contact with the group to now, to probably in the future, too, I guess you could say that I'm more humbly learning from others, that I'm a lot more willing to learn from others."

A son of middle-class parents observed that his former "arrogance" had been tempered by his work in the group:

> The first change in me is that I've learned to respect others' opinions. The second is about arrogance. . . . My sharp edges have been smoothed out. I used to be a real show-off. You might still find me this way, right? But, before, if you gave me a small flame, I could build it into the sun. I used to be very provocative, argumentative (*shandongxing hen qiang*). Now, though, I'm a little better. Because now I understand that that a person cannot move forward alone. Sometimes you need to step back a little, to let others have their chance to shine. That's the only way that others are willing to work with you,

to grow with you. Otherwise, if you're constantly suppressing other people, it's the same as if you're disregarding the rights of others.

The virtue of humility, as practiced within these voluntary associations, could also be identified in the ways the older volunteers stepped back to let the newcomers make their own mistakes or find new methods of resolving problems, as recounted in chapter 5. Why it has not yet been identified in the scholarly literature as a virtue inculcated through associational participation, I do not know. It was, however, one of the most obvious and recurring themes in discussions with Bridges and Together volunteers.

DEEPENING ATTACHMENTS AND INCREASING EMPATHY

As another interpretation of Tocqueville's enlarged heart might suggest, among the benefits of voluntary association participants in Together and Bridges also counted the close ties they developed with other volunteers and their ostensible "service targets" (*fuwu duixiang*), a term that came to some of them through the spread of social work as a discipline in Chinese universities. Although the broader sociological literature typically uses the term "social capital" to denote the increased networks that result from associational participation, I have deliberately chosen this more affective terminology of "attachments" and "empathy" because this phrasing more closely aligns with the understandings put forth by my interviewees. To be clear, while "meeting new people" was also mentioned by many volunteers as a fun part of their experience, the message they sought to convey in discussing this aspect of volunteering related much more strongly, in their views, to the development of emotional ties (*ganqing*) and to affectively meaningful connections with others. Recalling the differences recounted in chapter 4 between typical university clubs and these bottom-up associations, the daughter of a farmer and a truck driver from rural China highlighted the emotional fulfillment and sense of community she experienced in her group: "It's been my good fortune to be a part of this organization. . . . I've really enjoyed the mutual understanding, mutual support, and team spirit everyone shares."

A Together participant who was the daughter of middle-class parents and never knew her grandfather explained: "When I go into the village, I don't feel like I'm a 'volunteer.' I feel quite relaxed and happy to go there. . . . There are some villagers there that are very warm (*qinqie*). It kind of feels like they're my grandparents. It's not exactly the same kind of thing as family, but there's a kind of warmth and caring there. There are even some older women there that I can joke around with, like I would with friends."

A son of farmers offered that he had begun to value the personal relationships he used to take for granted: "I think it's made me cherish more the friends and family I have around me, who support me. Before, I guess I didn't see those things. I didn't really see them."

FAMILY TIES AND VOLUNTEERING

Although I have found little in preexisting literature about the impact of volunteering on family life, a number of people cited closer family relationships as a benefit of their volunteering. I draw attention to it here to highlight the ways in which volunteering in these groups has deepened and expanded participants' compassion for others—one impact of civil society engagement that some theorists have seen as key element for building an inclusive democratic society in which the rights and concerns of others deserve careful consideration alongside one's own. One volunteer from Together (the daughter of working-class parents) found that spending time with the elderly in rural villages allowed her more patience with her grandparents than she had before: "I began to see why my mother often said we should go to my grandparents' house to visit. I used to think just sitting around beside the old folks couldn't make them happy. But after returning from the village, I got how old folks sometimes actually aren't looking for anything other than having their grandchildren spend a bit of time chatting with them. So nowadays I do visit them more frequently."

Another Together volunteer (the son of working-class parents) related how he had found the confidence to express affection to the older members of his family, something not often seen in his home community: "Before, I used to seldom speak to my grandfather. It would just be polite, you know? But now it's the same as if I'm talking with the old folks in the villages. I'll go up to him and hug him, which is pretty uncommon since generations are normally divided so heavily. Other adults will say, 'What are you doing? How can you so casually touch your grandfather like that?' But I don't care. I think it's great! My grandfather doesn't normally have anyone around him who will show him any affection, any physical contact."

Yet another volunteer (a son of breakfast-shop owners) found it easier to talk with his parents: "After joining Together, I slowly came to realize that I was getting along better with my parents, that communication between us had become a lot easier."

Many of my interviewees from Together and Bridges were from inland or rural areas of China, often the children of farmers or migrant workers who struggled mightily to generate enough income to support their families. In China's poorest regions, when young parents leave their villages to go to urban centers for factory work, they are often unable to ensure childcare, education, or medical care for themselves or for their children in their adopted cities. Facing tough choices about what is best for their children, some parents decide to leave them in the care of their grandparents, seeing them only once a year during Chinese New Year holidays and communicating from a distance by mobile phone video chats.[26] Children like these—growing up separated from their parents, raised by grandparents or sometimes looking after themselves from a very young age—are increasingly recognized as collective victims of China's economic development model.[27]

One of these "left-behind children," a daughter of migrant workers, believed that her volunteering experience helped her understand her parents' predicament better and brought them closer:

My way of thinking about things has changed. I didn't used to feel that close to my parents. They were always away from home, so there was a gap between us. I never got why they had to go away for work instead of staying in our hometown to raise their child. I used to feel like I was all alone, like no one cared for me. Ha ha. But after participating in Together, after getting to know the old folks in the villages, I saw that they really were all alone and realized that at least I still have my parents. And so I came to see that what my parents were doing wasn't easy. I slowly came to understand them better. Now I will try to communicate with them more, whereas in the past I had so much resentment towards them that I was hard-pressed to even phone them once a month. Ha ha. Now I call home frequently, to show them I care, not like when I used to just ignore them. I think this was a huge change in me. Ha ha.[28]

This rather unexpected impact on family relations may be understandable, given the obvious and intense impacts of volunteering on participants' ability to communicate, to shift their perspective, and to empathize with others. However, in extant literature I have found no natural leap to include family members in volunteers' wider orbit of more meaningful relations. The effect observed here may have been due to their exposure to children's needs (and their parents and grandparents) in the case of Bridges or to the plight of socially isolated and marginalized elderly infectious disease sufferers in the case of Together. Alternatively, because volunteers in both organizations saw these changes as affecting their interactions with strangers, teachers, and employers—a broad swath of out-group people with whom they interacted regularly—applying the lessons learned through volunteering to their own blood ties may simply have been an extension of the same dynamics.

Whether in their families or with other out-group people, in the accounts offered by many Together and Bridges volunteers, an expanded orbit of empathy and compassion was a clear result of their participation—a change that many recounted as making a positive difference in their lives.

SELF-EFFICACY

Increases in self-confidence, organizational and interpersonal skills, and visibly positive outcomes—both for oneself and in one's relationships with others—combine to bolster the self-efficacy of participants in such voluntary associations. "Self-efficacy" is a term that encompasses individuals' objective skillsets and their attitude and outlook. There is a voluminous literature on self-efficacy in psychology, with Albert Bandura arguing that "a strong sense of efficacy enhances personal accomplishment in many ways. People with high efficacy approach difficult tasks as challenges to be mastered rather than as threats to be avoided. . . . They set themselves challenging goals and maintain strong commitment to them. They maintain a task-diagnostic focus that guides effective performance. They heighten and sustain their efforts in the face of failure. . . . They approach threatening situations with assurance that they can exercise control over them."[29]

Without utilizing the term itself, the volunteers with whom I spoke gave almost textbook articulations of how their experiences had strengthened their sense of self-efficacy. One young man, a former engineering student and the son of working-class parents, started volunteering in Bridges about fourteen months before I spoke with him. He depicted his journey toward increased self-efficacy not only as challenging but also one of the most significant lessons he had learned through volunteering:

> If there was a problem I couldn't figure out, I would ask the older volunteers
> for help. But they wouldn't directly give you an answer. They would constantly
> ask you, over and over again, "What do you think about this? How do you
> think it should be done?" I used to get very angry every time I had to ask them

for help, because they wouldn't give you a direct answer, but just say "How do you think it ought to be done?" and "So try it that way and see." But I eventually realized that in this process I would gradually figure things out for myself. So, actually it was really helping me in the end. . . . At first, I didn't like it, but slowly, at the end, I just stopped asking them and thought about the problem myself. And I realized that this is actually the best way to go about it. After all, the older volunteers can't always be right beside me.

Having participated in Together for seven months, an accounting student and the son of farmers said: "It was Together's values that led me to become more proactive in tackling problems. I feel now that there's nothing that can't be overcome, that difficulties aren't insurmountable problems. I'm more proactive now in the way I see problems, more optimistic. I used to be very introverted, but in Together I've become more 'open' [in English]."

A son of construction workers offered that he had found the confidence to take on new challenges without a crippling fear of failure: "After they join, a lot of people change in pretty obvious ways, including myself. I used to be very reticent to speak. The biggest change in me is that now, when I am confronted with a problem, I no longer get so anxious that I want to run away. Now, the harder something is, the more I want to tackle it head on. At the very least, I won't run away from it."

Reported increases in self-efficacy took a range of forms, from a finance major who was no longer afraid to clean and cook live fish—"I had always asked my mother to do it"—to a son of restaurant workers who credited his volunteering with giving him the bravery to speak to strangers—"Before, I wouldn't dare look at people in the eyes when talking to them, and, when I did speak, I would get all red in the face." Some changes were of a very personal nature—one volunteer proudly proclaimed that participation in his group had helped him get through daily life: "Now, my obsessive-compulsive cleanliness disorder is much better!"

Others around them noticed these changes, too. A finance major from a working-class family explained:

One time when a granny from the village called me at my house, I got a fright! I can't really speak much Hakkanese [the dialect in that village]. In the village we can speak face to face, but really it's more like "chickens talking to ducks" and also using body language to express ourselves. But on the phone it's completely language dependent. . . . My parents heard me speaking in broken

Hakkanese that day, and they felt that I had changed. In the past, when at home I was always very dependent on others, like a kid who wouldn't grow up. But they started to see that after joining Together, I could do those things and make others remember me, that there were people in the world [outside the family] with whom I was establishing relationships. So, my parents started seeing me not as a child who understands nothing, but rather as someone who can pursue things that they [also] find meaningful.

Other scholars have articulated how participation in such organizations can lead to increases in self-efficacy and eventually to increased political participation. Verba et al. (1995), for example, argue that "someone who routinely writes letters, gives speeches, or organizes meetings will be more likely to feel confident about undertaking these activities in politics. The individual who, for example, commands verbal skills—a wide vocabulary, an ability to formulate and articulate an argument—will be more effective and persuasive when he or she decides to speak up. . . . Those who possess civic skills, the set of specific competencies germane to citizen political activity, are more likely to feel confident about exercising those skills in politics and to be effective . . . when they do."[30]

While the explicit linkage to "citizen political activity" that these scholars assert is not such an easy leap to make in an authoritarian country, the increase in self-efficacy recounted by volunteers in Bridges and Together is visible and meaningful in their immediate nonpolitical lives and in the pursuit of their organizational missions. As demonstrated earlier in this chapter, volunteers are already nurturing the ability to talk with authorities and the media. Time will tell how or whether these skills translate into broader political participation, and, if so, what form that participation will take.

CLASS AND PARTICIPATION IN VOLUNTARY ASSOCIATIONS

As some readers may see it, this chapter has largely confirmed Tocqueville's early insights into the importance of voluntary association for teaching skills and habits that are productive of democratic culture. My own view in this is to concur, that, yes, these groups are distinctive in the ways they lay the groundwork for democratic society and thus could support democratic institutions in a more democratic future China. Yet one aspect of these volunteers' experience is worth highlighting, both for what it tells us about theories of democratic political participation and for the possibilities it implies for democratic development in China. Throughout this chapter, I have noted the gender and class background of most interviewees whom I have quoted directly. I have done this intentionally, to highlight the sophisticated self-reflections and critical insight offered by these volunteers *despite* many interviewees' relatively underprivileged backgrounds and family status.

Shifting the focus to yet another historical period and social context may help us see better why this class dimension is important. Here I would draw attention to and a sharp contrast with Jane Mansbridge's study of two U.S. "micro-democracies" in the 1970s.[31] Her groundbreaking work—albeit still in the tradition of Tocqueville—illuminated the salience of class background for understanding the limits to participation and the educative impacts of associational democracy in the United States. In Mansbridge's "Selby," a small town in the U.S. state of Vermont, and "Helpline," a social-service-providing NGO in an unnamed U.S. city, participants' class background was a crucial variable affecting attendance and willingness to speak at meetings as well as observed and self-reported levels of political self-efficacy. In Selby's annual town hall meetings, where tax matters and other public policies were decided, working-class residents were less likely than wealthier citizens to attend, in part because of a structural impediment—many of them worked hourly wage jobs, and joining the hours-long meeting would have meant the loss of almost a full-day's income.

Even when they were able to attend, in both Selby and at Helpline people from working-class backgrounds spoke less at meetings, although in one-on-one interviews with Mansbridge, Selby residents spoke just as long as white-collar residents. Insecurity and discomfort with publicly debating the pros and cons of potential decisions were also evident in both settings. As one Helpline staff member put it, "I never liked talking ideas. I really have a hard time. I can talk to you; you're only one person and I only have to deal with one head, but where there's a lot of people, like, I find myself repeating myself."[32] In the town-hall meetings, Selby residents reported that "they feel more subject to ridicule (. . . 'They'll say, "She's a fool!" '; 'I haven't got the education to decide on that stuff'; 'If you go there and speak up, they make fun of you') and are less likely to convince anyone."[33]

In Helpline, a "radical collective" that attracted NGO staff with a professed commitment to equality, power relations were seen as heavily biased toward the better-educated, middle- and upper-middle class staff who accounted for the vast majority of members. When asked who holds most influence in the organization, one of only three working-class staff (in a forty-one-person organization) explained to Mansbridge that "I'll put the most talkative people [at the center of power]," because "they know how to talk."[34] Another believed that the concentration of power in the hands of the higher class–background majority "ties into with money. Most of the people you see up here had enough money to go to college for four years, or wherever they went, and learn how to use a lot of big words. (laugh) That has a lot to do with it! You really have to play word games!'" Comments such as these, coupled with their responses to related survey questions, led Mansbridge to conclude that "this comparative lack of confidence in their verbal skills goes a long way toward explaining the tendency of the working-class members to attend fewer meetings, speak less frequently at meetings, and in other ways exercise less power in the organization as a whole."[35]

The working-class reticence to engage and discomfort with public speaking that Mansbridge identified in the United States more than forty years ago is also evident in the *initial* experiences recounted by many Bridges and Together volunteers in China. Aside from the examples recounted in this chapter, numerous individuals described themselves as quiet, shy, uncomfortable talking to strangers, and not adept at public speaking before joining.

Although class in China is as difficult to define as in other societies, the vast majority of my interviewees had parents who were engaged in a variety of lower-wage and frequently insecure jobs, including dock workers, farmers, and construction workers. Almost all my interviewees were either current university students or recent university graduates, yet the majority did not hail from top-ranked national universities but rather from lower-ranked institutions, including some that only recently had been "upgraded" to university status. Many of them were among the beneficiaries of China's massive expansion of higher education in the early 2000s, the period when both Together and Bridges were founded.[36] That growth brought into universities millions of teenagers from second- and third-tier cities—as well as rural areas—who might otherwise have missed out on the chance to study beyond high school. As is the case with many Together and Bridges volunteers, this new wave of students also included many who were the first in their families to attend university.

Despite the similarities in family background and in prevolunteering experiences and personalities, the contrast between the working-class people

Mansbridge encountered—a few of whom had "some college"—and the dynamics related by Together and Bridges volunteers could not be starker. Over and over again, my interviewees narrated a process of self-reflection and self-discovery, with encouragement from their peers, that gave them the confidence and courage to find their voice and become an active and equal participant in the groups' activities. Across dozens of interviewees, this did not seem to be a "trained" narrative resulting from a standard story each member was expected to memorize. Conversations flowed, rather, from a discussion of their backgrounds and initial motivations to a methodical reflection on their experience as volunteers. In asking them wide-ranging and sometimes abstract questions about organizational culture and dynamics, I frequently observed that many interviewees had not thought in such terms before but—in accordance with the norms and practices of their groups—were quite open to exploring the questions I posed and keen to give sincere, considered responses.

What was clear was that while working-class backgrounds did likely contribute to a strong initial reticence toward public speaking, participation in these voluntary associations nurtured the self-confidence and skills necessary to participate fully as members of the group, helping working-class young people shed their inhibitions and persuading them that their views were both valuable and deserving of others' consideration.

In considering class divisions as obstacles to full participation, I would also draw a contrast with the kinds of "empowerment talk" that Nina Eliasoph documented in her study of empowerment projects that were designed, at least rhetorically, to help those less fortunate in the contemporary United States.[37] Whereas her research found those groups to be rich in rhetoric but starved of actual empowerment outcomes for both (adult) organizers and the youth they sought to empower, volunteers in Bridges and Together recounted a great deal of skills development and enjoyed a space in which they could nurture and give practical expression to their greatest ideals. In the cases of Mansbridge's Helpline and Eliasoph's organizations, however, I would emphasize that both sorts of groups should be properly characterized as professionalized NGOs dependent on donors' largesse and approval, and not the ideal-typical voluntary associations approximated most closely by Bridges and Together. Not only do Bridges and Together talk the talk of empowerment—if not using exactly that term in translation—they also walk the walk, providing platforms for personal growth that have truly transformative effects on participants.

CONCLUSION

Clearly, Bridges and Together produce volunteers with high levels of self-efficacy. Both men and women, as well as people from different regions and family backgrounds, described their experiences in Bridges and Together as transformative, nurturing skills and abilities that they otherwise would not have developed. Commonly mentioned new skills were how to hold efficient and effective meetings, set deadlines, write and manage a budget, draft a project proposal, plan through the details of an event, approach and interact with local authorities, and design and implement a promotional activity (e.g., to attract new members). Some of these skills were learned as a matter of course because of participants' desire to accomplish larger goals. Others were taught intentionally as a part of the organizations' regular training programs.

In addition to developing skills, participating in these organizations also provided opportunities for the expansion and expression of democratic values and virtues like tolerance and—as I suggested earlier—humility as well as teaching participants about the value of diversity, mutual respect, and trust. Many participants recounted dramatic changes in themselves and even improved relationships with nonvolunteer family members.

Readers may reasonably ask if many of these lessons are not things that could be learned elsewhere, in other organizational settings. Perhaps normal university clubs could engender the same sorts of changes that Bridges and Together do. The perspectives offered in chapter 4 comparing normal university clubs and these bottom-up associations, however, suggest that Bridges and Together offer sharp contrasts to the official university clubs that most people join. As opposed to the formalistic and utilitarian experiences many reported in normal university clubs, these bottom-up groups serve as sites for practical skills development and for the expression of a set of ideals that are seen only in rhetoric—if at all—in typical student groups.

One might also suggest that these are simply common growing-up processes that every university student goes through during the transition period between high school and work life. In the views of my interviewees, however, their experiences are profoundly different from what their nonparticipant peers go through at university. As one education major from rural China (the daughter of a driver and a farmer) put it:

> Some [nonparticipants] do change, but most don't change a bit. They stay the same, personality-wise, from the beginning of university till the end. Some

might fall in love and then break up, so that can make them grow a little. But for most people. . . . Like in my dormitory, very few people have had much personal growth. Looking back carefully, from when we entered university to now, I think only a few people have experienced any real personal growth. I think it's because they haven't come into contact with very much new stuff. They just stay isolated on campus. For students from other areas, especially, they have even less outside contact. They only know their classmates in the same year.

Another volunteer (the son of middle-class parents) painted a similar picture of normal university life, one devoid of much outside stimulation or awareness of social problems: "Participating here brings about personal growth. . . . From a regular high school student to a regular university student who only knows about studying, a person who only cares about having a materially better life, to someone who can also care about other things, someone who thinks not only of one's own small family but also the larger society. It nurtures a shift in perspective on what's important and what's possible."

The (now) mainstream rhetoric of "personal growth,"' with its focus on the individual, is perhaps misleading and maybe even masks what these groups do for young volunteers. A key aspect of the transformations they induce, intimated by the two participants just quoted, derives from the fact that both organizations expose previously sheltered high school students to the sometimes-harsh realities of the adult outside world. Despite coming from mostly working-class backgrounds, many felt their eyes had been opened to the great levels of inequality and social injustice experienced by many in China only after volunteering with these groups. Or perhaps it was not that they were unaware, but that they lacked the vocabulary to articulate their awareness and the confidence to speak out about their observations. In this book's conclusion, I show how these experiences of personal growth expanded their insight into complex social and political phenomena, inspiring a more critical analysis of the world around them and, in some, a desire to address other social problems through deeper involvement in civil society. In the next two chapters, however, I first discuss how these groups work to maintain and reproduce their distinctive organizational cultures through the careful selection of leaders and newcomers.

(S)ELECTING NEW LEADERS

Democracy may have many different definitions, but a key feature of most is that leadership positions are determined by some sort of election process, ideally with a high degree of openness as to who is qualified to stand for election. As Larry Diamond and Marc Plattner have argued, in national political systems, the design of electoral systems holds key implications for many core aspects of political life, including "the breadth and legitimacy of representation, the capacity of the system to manage conflict, the extent of public participation, and the overall responsiveness of the system."[1] Taking the large-scale system down to the microlevel, we can also see that the ways in which leaders are selected or elected within voluntary associations and civil society more generally can have immense implications for the fortunes of a group and its work.

As in other parts of the world, professionalized Chinese nongovernmental organizations (NGOs) populated and run mostly by paid staff are structured to a great degree like for-profit businesses. The larger the group, the more likely it is to have fixed staff roles, like an executive director, project officers, administrative assistants, and accountants. In the North American nonprofit world, the head of a professionalized NGO of a certain scale is typically chosen by a board of directors and paid a salary to oversee the group's operations. As most Chinese NGOs are quite young—with grassroots groups blossoming mostly only after the turn of the twenty-first century—their original founders frequently are also their current leaders.[2] As years pass by, we would expect the head to step down, retire, or leave the organization in some other fashion, raising particularly thorny leadership succession questions.[3]

For voluntary associations, even though typically they may have no or few paid staff positions, leadership is still needed to set priorities, organize events, keep everyone in communication, recruit and train new volunteers, and tackle many other jobs that professionalized NGOs rely on paid staff to do. Volunteers, however, can choose to enter or exit the organization at will, unlike in professionalized NGOs that expect long-term, contractual commitments from their paid staff.[4]

Since NGOs, whether professionalized or volunteer driven, represent a new organizational form in China, a great deal of ground-level learning and experimentation is taking place. Many NGO participants spend a significant amount of time and energy trying to find the organizational structure and practices that best fit the needs and mission of the group. Reflecting a rapidly changing society, the pace and intensity of experimentation can seem almost meteoric when viewed from the outside.

Over several years of intermittent observation, I often was puzzled by the challenge of answering questions that seemed ostensibly quite straightforward: Who is in charge? Who is responsible for what? How did they get into that position? In a number of groups, people were frequently changing roles, and every few months, a group might restructure itself so that new jobs were created and old ones were abandoned or merged. After some time, I began to realize that these frequent changes were in part due to necessity (because of financial or other considerations), in part due to outside influences (training programs, salons, and scholar-activists that brought new ideas), and in part due to initiative from within a group's own participants.

In this chapter, I thus deal with questions of leadership and authority, focusing primarily on Together and Bridges. Showing the diversity of ways in which people come to be in leadership positions reveals much about the dynamism and spirit of experimentation within Chinese civil society. More fundamentally, however, I shed light on how civil society participants view the role of leaders as well as their attitudes toward authority.

The chapter begins with an introduction to the kind of "formalistic" elections that university students in China are most likely to encounter in on-campus organizations, like student unions and other university-supported clubs. These elections set the backdrop to the experimentation pursued in Bridges and Together and are key to understanding these groups' novelty in the Chinese context as well as the ways they have struggled to institutionalize their alternative value systems.

The main sections of the chapter draw attention to a number of tensions and choices faced by both groups as they consider how to best distribute authority and responsibilities within their organizations. First, for both Bridges and Together, a tension exists between relying on accumulated experience to inform the group's work and the commitment to welcoming and nurturing new ideas. Another three tensions are presented through examples of three Together efforts to engage in what I call "experimenting toward elections": (1) the choice between allowing any interested volunteers to take up particular areas of work and the urge to select the most suitable people through elections; (2) the tension between keeping voting open to all newcomers and the idea of weighting votes to give more experienced participants a larger say; and (3) the choice between a closed nomination process that privileges experienced or favored candidates and an open system that allows everyone to have a chance to self-nominate or nominate others.

A final tension for both Bridges and Together emerges in the struggle to stay committed to open elections while also wanting to ensure that voters are as informed as possible before casting their ballot.

The chapter concludes with an account of one professionalized NGO's innovative attempt to hold elections for its leadership, something that would be considered radical in almost any country today, much less in China, given the remunerative nature of professionalized NGO employment and the power inequalities built into supervisor–subordinate relations. As readers shall see, however, this approach ultimately did not satisfy many staff members' expectations of what a democratic election should be.

THE NORM IN LEADERSHIP SELECTION: FORMALISM INSTITUTIONALIZED

To appreciate the novelty of how these voluntary associations have experimented toward democracy in deciding their leadership, it is important to keep in mind the top-down and formalistic elections they are most familiar with from other organizations. To be clear, elections and attempts at democratic participation in China have a long, if tumultuous history. Reflecting on his experience of factory-level forums in the 1960s, one of Joel Andreas's (2019) interviewees depicted a scene that would have been strikingly familiar to my interviewees some four decades later: "Everything was already decided in advance; they just let everyone go there and raise their hands. . . . They would let you support them, but they wouldn't let you undermine them. The basic things, the principal things were decided internally, so democracy was just a form; it didn't have any practical content."[5]

As I will show, although Bridges and Together have gradually adopted elections to choose leaders, many participants were reluctant to characterize their selection of leaders as relying on any formal process. When discussing the actual process of elections, a number of people studiously avoided anything that resembled the institutionalized or formalistic norms of typical student unions and other groups they may have joined on campus. When asked, for example, whether people campaigned when running for an upperlevel position in a recent election, one Together participant said:

> Actually, that wasn't necessary. Most of the candidates had all nominated themselves through writing a self-nomination letter and sending it to everyone else, so that everyone could understand them better. It wasn't really done through any kind of formal process (*zhengshi de yizhong xingshi*). Because, normally, we interact a lot and are already pretty familiar with each other from doing things like publicity events on campus or other activities. So, we knew each other pretty well. For us, saying "campaigning" is . . . that kind of formality is a bit overboard. We'll talk about our thoughts, but using the word "campaigning" is too formal. We prefer to just express our thoughts, that's all.

By contrast, the election processes of normal university student organizations reflected the mainstream authoritarian practices of hierarchy and formalism. One extensive recounting of a student union election by a former Bridges leader, "V", was typical of the experiences shared by others. While at university, V sought and was (s)elected to serve as chair of the student union. But, as he explains, the nomination process for such positions is strictly controlled, so that at any point, one level or another of the university authorities could have nixed his rise to the chair:

v: Leaders of the student union are approved first by the outgoing chair of the student union, then the supervising professor, then the party secretary of the university—like this. Level by level, they have to be given approval by university authorities.

ajs: Was there an election?

v: Yes, there was an election, a process, you know. But in China, it's very formalistic. There's a student representative general meeting where you go up to make a speech, dressed very formally. (Laughing) Just like the style of the National People's Congress. Most importantly, the people going up have already been preselected (*yijing neiding de le*). You have to post your résumé publicly, on bulletin boards or walls within the school so all your classmates can see it, then they vote. At the formal election, the dean will come out, at the general meeting. And you go up and give your speech. It's that kind of event.

AJS: How many student representatives attend the general meeting?

v: At that time, we had two or three hundred people, all from different faculties within the university, the student class leaders from other departments, the party secretaries, people like that. (Laughing) It's China, you know. All that stuff is very formalized. It's like that all through the university.

AJS: Were votes recorded on ballots or by counting of hands?

v: Some items require a counting of hands. Like, at the student union general meeting, some things are written on the agenda and need to be voted on. For example, "The student canteens are restructuring and need to raise prices. Does everyone vote to approve a price change?" And people raise their hands. Stuff like that. Just like at the National People's Congress. The second type of agenda item is the election of student cadres (*xuesheng ganbu*). Our names are written on a ballot, and then you check off the one you want to choose. And, basically, it's those people on the list—all of them get chosen. Then you walk out onto the stage, like it's very open and fair (*gongkai gongzheng*) [said dismissively]. And you fold up your ballot and place it into the ballot box. After that, they count the votes and announce who got how many votes, and those are the ones that are elected.

AJS: Does anyone not get elected?

v: Yeah, there will be one or two that don't get elected. But then later they'll get appointed as alternates, and then from alternates they'll be put on the committee anyway. So, in reality it doesn't matter if you don't get elected initially, because you'll still get on there.

The formalism inherent in "that kind of event" was noted numerous times by other participants, and many used a similarly dismissive tone when observing that such things are run "like it's very open and fair." Nonetheless, and although Bridges and Together volunteers frequently insisted that they eschewed the formalistic style of typical student organizations, they did indeed mirror some of the practices of student union general meetings and other electoral forums. What distinguishes the processes they employ is not the trappings of elections, but rather the belief that the process of choosing leaders should be *truly* "open and fair." The earnestness of their belief, moreover, has led them to engage in active and regular reflection both as individuals and as organizations. This reflection, in turn, has led to changing practices in branches of both organizations. But the goal over more than a decade remained the same—to craft organizational practices that embody and express their democratic visions and values.

TENSION BETWEEN ACCUMULATED EXPERIENCE AND NEW IDEAS

Embracing bottom-up initiatives is tough for any group that has been up and running for a while. Stretching back to Max Weber, sociologists who study processes of institutionalization have long recognized that as an organization grows and becomes more complex, it tends toward greater bureaucracy, a phenomenon that can stifle individual creativity and make the entire organization rule bound and slow to adapt to changing circumstances.

The core philosophies behind Bridges and Together are welcoming of any innovations that help further the missions and goals of the group. Yet, even with explicit commitments to inclusiveness, both groups have struggled with the tension between utilizing the experience of older volunteers and the desire for more active bottom-up participation that offers personal growth opportunities for newcomers. In both organizations, experimentation in how they select leaders has been key to striking that balance. Some positions are elected, some are appointed, and yet others are simply open to anyone who volunteers.

The ways organizations choose their leaders serve as windows into their participants' values. Although the specific structures vary a bit, both Bridges and Together have numerous branches or subgroups that are formally or informally based at universities. Neither organization's administrative centers have sought to fix a particular method for their various branches to select branch leaders. One interviewee explained: "Together's [upper-level leaders] don't govern the clubs at all, how we operate internally, they don't manage (*guan*) us like that. They won't control you like that. Students have the autonomy (*zizhu*) to do things however they want. . . . It's all under the control of the club members. Whatever you consider is best, they'll only give you suggestions. Some clubs elect their club leaders as they feel like, whomever they feel would be best. In others, some older volunteers will go to talk with the new people they feel would be best. There are these different models."

In branches where older members go "to talk with the new people," the older members effectively invite and approve particular new members to take leadership roles, a process that is seen as perfectly acceptable and reasonable. Others have developed election processes to manage leadership transitions, but the key for these participants is that the central offices do not seek to determine how local branches operate, leaving those decisions to the judgment of local groups.

A conversation with one of Together's founders reinforced this view, one I saw and heard from many average volunteers: "We don't get involved with how individual clubs select their leaders. I don't think we'd ever tell them what kind of structure or process they should have. We just let them decide for themselves what kind of structure they want. But surely it's also common that different clubs learn from each other, see each other's structures when they meet up at district meetings or read other districts' reports. I haven't asked everyone to follow the same structure for their districts or the clubs within the districts. They can do that however they want."

Indeed, some branches have developed a system of regular elections, whereas others rely on a more traditional top-down appointment system for new leaders. In many cases, however, a mixture of both is at play. This mixture reflects an ongoing tension between the outside organizational practices that most participants are familiar with and a desire to make these voluntary groups more participatory and democratic. Of course, such a tension is not simply between "democratic" and "authoritarian." A practical concern faced by people in any volunteer-based organization is also present here— that is, learning how to find a balance between older and newer members in the workings of a group that has annual, predictable turnover because of changes in life circumstances like university graduation, entry into the job market, and family obligations.

What is particularly noteworthy, though, are the simple yet powerful statements about dignity and equality that inform the ways participants understand these groups. In talking about choosing new leaders, many participants discussed the need to balance the experience of older volunteers with a commitment to ensuring space for more active bottom-up participation and offering a growth experience to newer members. Although many people articulated a need to preserve existing knowledge and the accumulated wisdom of older participants, the same people typically expressed a genuine concern for ensuring that new members had opportunities to learn and innovate, even if that meant making mistakes along the way.

Within Bridges, the selection of leaders within village site teams takes place after everyone has first been divided into different teams. This preparatory period is also when new members and old members begin to get a sense of each other's strengths, personalities, and interests. One long-term leader of Bridges sees this as a crucial time for pursuing a democratic ideal, albeit one that is hard to realize: "In principle, each site's leadership is chosen by democratic election. But the older volunteers might use different ways to exert some influence. However, I personally wish we could guarantee it be democratic, not to be influenced by the outside."

Another older volunteer sees a role for people like himself to guide newcomers:

> We have an election before going down to the countryside. Of course, we older volunteers will make some evaluations about who will be more suitable, based on our previous experience. And so we'll have our priority list. But more importantly we let them choose by themselves, choose who will be their main team leader, who is responsible for public relations and other matters. . . . Groups going to other sites don't interfere in the election. And a first precondition is that the person has to be willing to do it. We do make some evaluations, but the key thing is that the new volunteers vote. . . . We [older volunteers] will try to get to understand each person a little. Then we'll give some suggestions to individuals, like "I think you're better suited for this. . . . When the time comes, you should run for this position."

One volunteer with just over a year's experience felt that Bridges had found a good balance between guidance given by older volunteers and the enthusiasm and judgments newcomers might make. In her view, all site teams should have some support from older volunteers, but ultimately the choice of leadership roles was settled by election, so newcomers—the majority in most site teams—would have the opportunity to make their choices freely:

> We give each site team a lot of freedom to decide what roles people will play. Basically, we just let them decide on their own, internally. In general, we abide by two principles: First is that older volunteers will take the lead, with two assistants, to observe and get to know their team well, get to know the new

volunteers in the team. Then they'll know which ones are more suited for which positions, because they're very experienced in how teams operate, so they'll recommend some people take on certain roles. But, in the end, there's also a voting process. So it's not like the older volunteers just tell people what role they should do and don't consider popular opinion. . . . In the end, we'll respect a person's wishes and the votes of the team. Another way is that older volunteers don't interfere at all. In those teams the team members vote and make the decisions on their own, and the older volunteers' active participation is much lower.

Both models have their advantages. For example, older volunteers might be great at sizing people up, based on their own experience, and might be better at assigning different tasks to different people. On the other hand, for groups that decide completely freely, it's a very tangible reflection of the group's opinion, because of someone's proactive approach and high level of participation. But there's a risk there, that they may not really understand themselves very well and may not understand the actual responsibilities of a particular role, so they may not be very suitable for it. This is all a process of figuring it out. . . . Both models have their advantages and disadvantages.

Another volunteer's experience in Bridges led him to see older volunteers as much more deferential. Even if they offered their opinions early on, during the actual election process, they would—and in his case did—step back, not participating in the actual voting:

We were chosen by election. During training, the older volunteers . . . kind of stood on the sides observing us to see what every person was good at and what kind of role they could take on. Then on the day of the election, we did it in rounds, choosing the overall team leader first, then the curriculum leader and these other more important roles.

Others on my team nominated me. The older volunteers don't have the right to participate in the election, the right to vote or to speak. They just listen in, because otherwise new volunteers would be too easily influenced by them.

He saw this act of stepping back as purposeful, and based on the older volunteers' presumed bad experience with top-down models, he felt that "it's intentional. Because maybe they've suffered in the past by being overly influenced by the volunteers that came before them. . . . In general, Bridges has evolved this kind of thing. . . . What emerged in the previous two or three years is continued on down, but what everyone feels isn't suitable is changed."

Similar to Bridges, the first level of leadership selection within Together happens in the preparatory stages, when volunteers are still in the cities. In these groups, as in Bridges, familiarity with the local site and previous experience are considered to be important knowledge that should be respected as plans are being laid: "The preparation team is mostly more experienced people, and those who want to join it. And they need to be more familiar with the villages, especially with the old people there, the ones who have closer relationships with them."

Another volunteer's understanding is similar, but in her view, experienced people are best qualified to be on the initial preparatory team: "In general, you need to be more experienced. In our club, in the first semester, new people coming in don't have much experience. In the second semester, because they haven't even visited a village yet, we wouldn't let them be in the preparation team. But once they've visited a village, if they're interested, they can then join the preparation team. But, in many cases, the responsibilities of the preparation team are pretty intense, so you have to consider whether you're able to guarantee the quality of the work before you sign up."

Within individual Together branches, or clubs, the organization's regular leadership is sometimes selected by appointment: "Currently, in our group, they're chosen by the outgoing representatives, through discussion. . . . But it depends on whether people are willing, their personal preference, because there are many things we have to coordinate. So, do you have the ability to do it well? But basically it's decided by those outgoing district representatives and the district leaders."

Yet even under such an appointment system, the groups still retain an emphasis on the individual choices of volunteers, personal freedom, and organizational openness, which they embrace and rely on to attract and maintain their memberships. In one Together group, although its internal leadership roles were traditionally appointed, at the time of one interview in 2012, the group had recently shifted to become more open to enthusiastic newcomers:

Mostly it's the outgoing group of key leaders that identify and recruit the new ones. By key leaders I mean the club leader (*shezhang*), the extramural liaison, and some of the others who are interested in guiding (*zhudao*) the club. But nowadays, sometimes if you aren't one of the ones who were selected by the outgoing group, if there's a group of people who want to stand up and help out, they can quickly become part of it, one of the key leaders. So, there aren't a lot of formal restrictions or formalistic rules (*xingshi de jushu*). It's really free (*ziyou*). That's one of the things I like about our club.

As contrasted with the utilitarian motives of other, typical youth-based organizations and their top-down culture, the core principle of voluntariness was emphasized in numerous interviews concerning the selection of new leaders. As one Together volunteer highlighted: "The first condition is that you're willing to do it. In general, the older volunteers will discuss who they think is more suitable and then go ask that person if they're willing to do it. Then they basically decide it. But first it's whether you're willing to do it, and second it's whether the older ones think you're suitable or not."

The organizational cultures of both Bridges and Together hold it to be self-evident that no one should be forced against their will to take a particular role or shoulder a particular responsibility. This principle of voluntariness—"whether you're willing to do it"—came up time and time again in interviews about choosing leaders. Its importance, I believe, stems from the conviction of these young people that each individual should have autonomy (*zizhu*) over his or her decisions and actions. The contrast implied is deeper than simply the absence of self-direction suffered by many in normal organizational life. Rather, for many of these young people, participation in these organizations provided one of their first chances in life to ask—and to be asked—what they themselves wanted to do. Having studied hard for years in high school with one goal imposed largely by society and their families—to obtain a spot at university—many found it to be novel and extremely attractive to be given the choice of how to devote their time.

EXPERIMENTING TOWARD ELECTIONS

This experimentation and evolution is best exemplified by the ways in which these voluntary associations have sought to incorporate elections into their leadership selection process. Although not always consistent between groups or across levels within the organizations, the general tendency is toward more openness and democratic processes throughout the organizations. At a practical level, this openness to experimentation has resulted from the need to find the right balance between experience and innovation. Just as importantly, and not unrelated to practical concerns, is a more idealistic vision of the groups' values and ongoing efforts to realize those in practice. In both Bridges and Together, although virtually all upper-level leadership positions were elected by the time the groups reached their tenth anniversaries, the selection of leaders in lower-level positions was subject to experimentation. Although some leadership questions could be resolved by simply volunteering—one group's members ask each other, "Who wants to do this?"—other positions might be appointed by those already in leadership roles. In general, however, the process of experimentation has trended toward open nominations followed by open elections.

Together's more complicated structure has allowed for more opportunities to arise for elections to be held, or for appointments to made, than within Bridges. Bridges does not have any official branches (but it does have numerous local-level clubs), whereas Together has multiple branches, including some registered university clubs, at or near universities across several areas in southern China. Although many of these branches utilized a mixture of leadership selection practices, none of the groups I spoke with had switched from elections back to top-down appointments or simply volunteering once elections had been implemented for particular roles.

In this section, I present three cases in which Together branches struggled to find the most suitable (s)election process for their groups, a phenomenon that I term "experimenting toward elections."

Case One: Selection Through Election but Also Still Just Volunteering

The case of one Together branch is illustrative in that it followed a clear trajectory from appointing or volunteering to be the main group leader to one in which elections were held. As one older but still active local leader related: "When I became club leader it was just because everyone felt I could do it, so I just did. Everyone supported me (*dajia renke le ni*). Now the club leader is elected. Everyone votes. That was changed just this year, because everyone felt like this might encourage everyone to be more proactive, so they wanted to do it this way."

Whether because of personal charisma or proven capabilities, in this particular group's earlier period, people relied on their "feeling" to select someone into the main leadership role. And—in keeping with the principle of voluntariness—because this interviewee was also willing to take up the role, he was appointed by this "felt" consensus to the position of club head. With time, however, in this as in other branches, more people began to show interest in joining Together activities. The group's culture of openness also eventually seemed to require that a method be found to encourage others to be "proactive" in taking on leadership positions. Still, when I spoke with this particular group, the election of the club head continued in parallel with volunteering for other lower-level department positions (e.g., project manager, extramural liaison): "When I was chosen as leader, everyone just sort of agreed that 'you'd be good at it, so you go be club leader, and others can go be department heads'—like that. But this year's group feels that it would be better to elect the club leader, so they did it this way this time. However, the department heads are still done the old way—if you want to do it, if everybody feels it's a good idea, then you're it."

For these groups, there is no template for figuring out what positions should be elected and what should be done simply through volunteering. As noted earlier, Together's central office issues no rules about this, and as many others confirmed, the various Together groups take different approaches. What was common across all of the ones I encountered, however, was an emphasis on improvement and experimentation. Trying to find the best results while still staying true to the groups' core values, especially openness, helped ensure a constant flow of innovation.

Case Two: Weighted Voting but Also Open Voting

Another Together group went through a similar evolution, coming up with a voting formula that privileged experience while still giving average members a chance to have their voices heard. As one former leader explained:

> Now we're electing people, but when I was chosen, I was directly appointed by the outgoing board of directors. Now it has changed so that we hold elections. About fifty people participated in the election—all the club's directors and all the average members came together. Before that, we fixed a time so that anyone who was interested in running could sign up to become a candidate. Then all the candidates gave a speech, and all the directors then got one and a half votes. The regular members got one vote. There were a bunch of others there, too, guests from other universities' Together clubs, all Together members, and some of the people who graduated but used to be in our club. They all got one vote, too.

For this group, giving directors (twelve in all) an extra half-vote was part of the solution to balancing experience and openness to new ideas and new perspectives. At the same time, others who were not actual members of the current group were also invited to take part, as their input was valued: "There were about four or five people from other schools that night. Actually, we didn't publicize it to other schools, but since they were there they could vote, because they had also been there from the very beginning for all the speeches, too."

Giving more votes to tried and true insiders—the directors—but also giving votes to other clubs' members who just happened to be curious and eager to join in presented no contradiction in this particular Together branch. Rather, it fit with the organization's larger value system—recognizing contributions and the "wisdom" of older volunteers (the directors) while also staying open to those who were motivated by their sincerity of purpose, even if they were perhaps formally outsiders to the group. (Indeed, avoiding drawing too-tight boundaries was generally recognized across both Together and Bridges as central to their self-identity as open and inclusive organizations.)

This particular election was held in the same spirit of openness and voluntariness that runs throughout the justifying principles of the groups. As another volunteer described it:

> It was interesting because there was a question-and-answer session. Everyone who was there could ask a question of any of the candidates who had spoken, and the candidates responded on the spot. . . . Seven people signed up to run. It was all voluntary; they wanted to sign up. And, from the start, we didn't go in any order. Whoever wanted to stand up to give their speech could go up. We didn't set any maximum time limit on them, but we did set a minimum of three minutes per person. Most people took around five minutes.

Again, this emphasis on voluntariness—"they wanted to sign up"—recurs as a way to distinguish these groups from the formalistic rituals of other organizations and to distinguish the values embedded in Together. No one was pressured into doing anything they did not want to do. They signed up because of the sincerity with which they approached the group's work and their identification with its goals and values.

Yet while the commitment to openness meant that anyone could ask questions, older volunteers played a special advisory role. As another volunteer, "Z", recounted:

z: The question-and-answer session took more time. Everyone talked for about ten minutes, I think, so the whole thing lasted for more than two hours. . . .

That's because, too, after their speeches, each of the department heads came up on stage to talk briefly about the candidate, to evaluate their strengths and weaknesses as they understood them from working with them over the past year.

AJS: Wouldn't that be kind of awkward, standing up and saying "So-and-so is good in these ways, but also bad in other things"?

z: It was OK. . . . They were trying to comment more objectively, you know, setting aside personal feelings or whatever. . . . And, beforehand, we had held a meeting and asked the department heads to be more objective in their comments. Because as department heads, they should know about how the candidates work. So, then we wrote down our votes on ballots and tallied them up on the spot.

This particular club structured itself with multiple "heads," in the end electing three people to help lead and represent it in any meetings of the larger regional organization. The very idea of elections came about in part because of the growth in the club's membership. Crucially, however, it also arose out of an increasing awareness by the directors—the highest level of leadership at the local level—that they may be missing out on identifying talent and might have a limited perspective. As one leader explained it, rather than risk developing blind spots caused by seeing only from the top, the board of directors sought to move to an election model that recognized value in diverse viewpoints:

> Several people thought we should be more creative and proposed this reform. . . . We on the board of directors thought . . . since there are so many activities all the time, people hanging out together, doing work together, it seemed that we could see more than others. But then sometimes it's actually the regular members that are doing a lot of the work together, even more than what we can do. So maybe the regular members look at things from another perspective . . . What they can see would be different. So, by using this kind of electoral method, we could come up with a more authoritative (*quanwei*) way of figuring out who would be more suitable.

Despite relying on the language of hierarchy and traditional authority (*quanwei*), this interviewee took care to emphasize that their method for selecting leaders should be distinguished from the model used in typical university-based student organizations: "Other clubs at our university don't work this way at all. . . . Their leaders are all internal appointments (*neiding de*). Even if there's a formalistic election, most of them operate so that the outgoing leaders just directly appoint the incoming ones."

Some readers may argue that the allocation of one-and-a-half votes to a minority of members and only one vote to others is fundamentally undemocratic in that it goes against the principle of equality. Such a process, though, has its historical roots—although one unlikely known to these young people— in the debates held during the 1989 protest movements in Beijing and other Chinese cities. As Daniel Kelliher has documented, at that time, most student protestors and established intellectual elites were demanding full liberalization of individual rights but only a limited form of democracy, one in which educated urban Chinese would be at the fore, while poorly educated workers and most people living in rural areas were deemed to be still "unready" for the full responsibilities of democratic citizenship.[6] The rationale was, in part, that urban residents were more educated and sophisticated than their country brethren. They would, therefore, be able to understand China's interests and political dynamics more fully, exercising informed judgments for the benefit of the entire country. Rural residents, in contrast, were viewed as more susceptible to manipulation by others. Urbanites were also vastly outnumbered by rural residents in 1989, and restricting their political power would help ensure that people perceived as "country bumpkins" could not ride roughshod over urbanites' interests. Such a division had even earlier, if foreign, precedents, of course, in the U.S. system, which initially limited the right to vote to only white, landowning males, extending full suffrage to male and female citizens without regard to race only in the mid-twentieth century. Even Sun Yat-sen, the "Father of Modern China" who led the overthrow of the Qing dynasty in 1911, had promoted the idea that his newly founded Republic of China needed a period of "political tutelage" during which China's massive peasantry would first be instructed in democratic politics by educated elites.

Despite precedence for this sort of weighted voting in recent Chinese history, when I asked other interviewees about the partial- versus full-vote system mentioned in the previous group, most responded with incredulity, claiming never to have heard of such a system. In their own groups, they insisted, each person was given one vote, regardless of their status or length of service.

Case Three: From Closed to Open Nomination Processes

As any student of politics knows, voting is only one measure of democracy. China implemented nationwide voting in villages years ago. But, as observers have noted, the method of selecting candidates can predetermine election results, often in favor of those already in power. One local Together branch confronted this problem early on. Given Together's larger scale and geographic spread, it relies on a district representative system when convening certain planning meetings. The selection of district representatives is one of the ways in which voting has been utilized to choose the best person from each district to join these higher-level meetings.

One representative explained how, in her district, volunteers had made changes over time to help promote fairness and equality within the group:

> Every district is a little different. Here in our city, it's gradually improving (*gaijin*). In my case, the first time I was the district representative, there were a total of six board members in our district. At the end of each year, the board members would nominate six people to be the next district representative. Everyone who had gone through training to become a coordinator, and also the extramural liaison, could all vote. But average volunteers couldn't vote. They could be there to watch the election, but they didn't have the right to vote. So, the board put all the names up on a big screen, and everyone who was qualified could vote.
>
> When I became the district representative, I didn't stand up to give a speech. It just depended on everyone's regular interactions with me, how familiar they were with me. After all, there weren't that many of us, and in the previous year, we had had a lot of contact and gotten to know each other well.

Such a method eventually came to be seen as too exclusionary and out of step with the group's larger emphasis on equality and inclusiveness. After reflection, her group decided to make a change:

> When I finished my first year and it came time to choose the next year's representative, the six district board members didn't nominate anyone. Everyone whose term was up—those six board members and myself—we all came together for a meeting. At that time, I said we should ask everyone below (*xiamian de quanbu ren*) if they had any interest in standing for office, for taking up one of these roles. . . . Anyone who wanted to join could speak up

and say so. That was one option we had. Another way was that any of the coordinators could nominate someone they thought was suitable.

After some discussion, they decided to utilize both methods: "It's better now, because now that we've changed the process, you can not only vote for others but also nominate yourself if you want. So, we can get better, more suitable people, maybe. . . . It seems everyone feels this is better. . . . Because, you know, no one wants to be told what to do by those six people. That's the way I understand it, at least."

The aversion to hierarchy—even when the language of hierarchy is ubiquitous ("everyone below")—and the desire for openness are again key themes and provide motivation for innovating within the organization. The idea that "no one wants to be told what to do by those six people"—despite "those six people" being liked and trusted—was a common refrain heard not only here but also in other interviews. Moving past a controlled nomination system to one in which everyone, especially "those below," could affect the outcome was seen as helping to get "better, more suitable people, maybe." Although uncertainty persists ("maybe"), the sense is that "everyone feels this is better" with a more open nomination process. As with other interviewees, this volunteer relied on the language of emotion ("feels," *ganjue*) to describe a process that also involved reason and aimed at producing the generally desirable outcome of getting "better, more suitable people" to represent the district.

GETTING READY FOR DEMOCRATIC ELECTIONS

Although the overall trend in both Bridges and Together was toward elections, in interviews I found it was generally only the most experienced participants that introduced the term "democracy" into our conversations. Perhaps this was because the transformation toward elections was noticeable only to older participants who had some points of comparison. Crucially, however, some of the older participants had also developed a very sophisticated understanding of the importance of an informed "electorate."

One experienced Bridges participant in his early thirties believed that all Bridges groups should aspire to democratic elections for leadership positions: "Every team is different. In general, those teams with higher quality (*suzhi*) will ensure the process is democratic. They all want to make sure this is guaranteed in their organization. Most of them can ensure it, but I can't say all of them can have this kind of process. But what we aspire to is that they can all use democratic methods, that they will elect the team leaders themselves."

In his analysis, though, the quality (*suzhi*) of some groups was still too low to make for a very democratic process.[7] Aside from low *suzhi*, or cultural norms that inhibited democracy, he also pointed to the question of *when* democratic elections should be held: "But there's a problem here. In reality, democracy, it . . . there's a key aspect, the so-called deliberative democracy (*shenyi minzhu*).[8] It's not about just voting, I think. Actually, we need to learn more to fully understand this issue. . . . But, in fact, we haven't always created this kind of a platform for understanding each other. In the past, they held elections before they had gone into the countryside. They had had only limited contact with one another, which was a problem."

Voting *too early* for team leaders, when team members had only "limited contact with one another," meant that volunteer teams had insufficient information on which to make their judgments. Rather than going simply with first impressions, he hoped that volunteers could take more time to get to know one another further through discussion about the strengths and weaknesses of each candidate. The solution they hit on to address this problem involved facilitating intensive and creative interactions among team members, before they voted and before they left for the countryside:

> At the beginning of our team building training program, two small groups are assigned to each site, and in each of the small groups the members are pretty familiar with each other. It's a three-day intensive training program. And then there's a swap. From within the two small groups, we older volunteers will pick the people we think are most central, the ones with the biggest leadership ability, and switch them out to the other group. And we'll tell them "You're leaving that group forever." This is to train their ability to accept change, to get accustomed to a new environment. Then we bring both groups back together. This is a huge trick! But, actually, the point is to let the core members get to know each other as much as possible and for the members to get to know them, too. But this isn't the end of it. We'll still have more training afterwards. And in those trainings we break up the groups, so everyone gets a chance to know others. Older volunteers will also try to organize some get-togethers on the weekend to talk about the projects. Then, just before we go down to the countryside, we'll have a strategy meeting where the older volunteers will talk about the conditions in the village they're going to. . . . So, we hope to create an environment in which they can get to know each other well. A lot of times we might fail, but that's the ideal.

Even though this had been attempted and incorporated recently, he still worried about how to ensure openness to newcomers and new ideas when site teams finally elected their leaders: "In the training session we older volunteers might say what we expect the camp leadership team to do. But in fact, a site's older volunteers can influence newer volunteers more."

As within Together, volunteers in Bridges have debated over this dilemma for some time. Although voting occurs on the basis of "one person, one vote," older volunteers still needed to check their influence at times:

> There's something funny (*haowan*) about this aspect of our group culture. There's a point of view that holds that older volunteers should not vote. That is, Bridges has a very strong cultural preference, that every teaching site team will go through their own growth experience. From one angle, we don't want older volunteers to interfere or to play a leading role (*bushi zhudao xingde*), but rather to only assist each team. But we always have a hard time doing this. Sometimes, older volunteers strongly recommend their own views to the team. And this frequently leads to some conflict or tension. . . . I feel Bridges' culture is special in this way. In all of China's NGOs, it has a lot of research value! Ha ha! It's not very common.

Indeed, my observations of other NGOs in China accorded with his own. What participants in Bridges (and Together) were doing was far from "common" in Chinese civil society.

ELECTING YOUR BOSS? EXPERIMENTING WITH DEMOCRACY IN A PROFESSIONALIZED, BUT STILL IDEALISTIC, NGO

Bridges' and Together's experiments toward democracy occurred in special circumstances, and notably in volunteer- and youth-based organizations. In China, these two organizations are exceptional in many ways. In the typical professionalized NGO, as recounted in chapter 2, top-down norms and hierarchical authority structures are the rule. Yet even in some of these "normal" Chinese NGOs, many participants aspire to democratic governance and democratic ideals. In one unusual case, an environmental NGO based in the country's southwest, an otherwise typical Chinese NGO has undertaken its own experiment toward democracy.

Just after the turn of the century, when many grassroots NGOs were being launched, the founding leadership of a group I call Greenthumb envisioned their fledgling NGO as a place that would one day be led and driven by a young generation of committed environmentalists. Started by a few friends, most of whom were already in their forties or older, members of this group decided early on that they wanted to hand over the reins to younger people as soon as possible.

Greenthumb's early emphasis on youth is worth understanding in its own right, as it emanated not from the stereotypically self-confident post-1980s or post-1990s generation, but rather from an older cohort of well-educated Chinese Communist Party members who were thinking down the road about who would tackle China's long-term environmental issues. These patriotic progressives took environmental protection as their main concern but saw youth as key to realizing their vision of a cleaner and safer environment. They had a strong shared sense that addressing China's environmental concerns would require the energies and dedication of the younger generation. As one cofounder related:

> When we were learning how to run projects, we didn't use young people, we used a few dozen professors, experts in environmental issues. After a while, asking them to help out this way, we discovered that, first, they didn't have a very strong sense of responsibility towards society. Their outlook on life, their values were crystal clear: "I just want to get paid for what I do for you." Of course, that's understandable. But if that's all there is to it, it seemed to us like our organization wouldn't last very long. Secondly, . . . if we brought young people on board, we would have to start from scratch, training them about the issues we work on. But the same was true of the experts—they all had their positions in universities or research centers, but the only extra thing they had over young people was what their specific specialty was, and most of that wasn't of any use to us. Also, they were always doing it part time and couldn't guarantee when the work would be finished. So eventually we came to the conclusion that we should nurture our own team. But who? I thought at first we should match up one young person with one expert, but then I wondered why we actually needed the experts when we could let the young people learn how to do things themselves. . . . So, then, we started saying to incoming new people, if you young people don't grow into these positions, it will be a hopeless situation for both China's environmental problems and for our organization itself. It can't be enough just for us older people to be concerned about these issues. So, since then we've constantly focused on developing young people.

Although this emphasis on youth was seemingly shared among all the founders, Greenthumb's approach to leadership, succession, and its vision for the group's future was largely shaped by Dr. Chen, one of the older founders.[9] Dr. Chen is an academic with experience in a number of government-appointed and government-affiliated positions. As with many others who are drawn to NGOs in China, he also envisions NGOs as a space for democratic participation and innovation. After getting the group off the ground and running it fairly smoothly for several years, Dr. Chen and another founder, Lu Jie, decided it was time to extricate themselves from daily operations and let the next generation of leaders take their place. Six years or so after Greenthumb's founding, and after some deliberation, they decided to implement an election, asking the current staff of about twenty people—mostly in their twenties—to vote for two out of three people that Dr. Chen and Lu Jie would nominate to run.

Again, the absence of a preexisting indigenous model for NGOs in China led to surprising innovations. As a professionalized NGO, with paid staff and the normal organizational structure that NGOs around the world have adopted, Greenthumb is much like environmental NGOs one could find elsewhere in China. Indeed, they also first considered promoting from within, as might be the norm in other places. Dr. Chen explained:

> In our board of directors, we had been discussing this a lot, since we founders and senior people want to move to the backstage. The future development of our NGO will require leadership from young people. We were often talking about, wondering what we should do. Of course, objectively speaking, Lu Jie and I, the directors, we might all feel, we might all trust that one particular person would do a great job, right? But we also worried, "If we nominate someone to be the new head of the organization, will other people follow that person (*fu bu fu ni*)?" Doing it that way could introduce all sorts of conflicts.

Even with such a visionary and truly open-minded leader as Dr. Chen at the helm, as demonstrated by this quote, he also relies on the language of hierarchy to describe future potential leaders. "Will other people follow that person?" is rendered more literally as "Will they obey you or not?" (*fu bu fu ni?*). Although obedience can imply respect for someone's authority, experience, or wisdom, it can also imply subservience. In asking whether current staff would turn to one of their own and then "obey" them as a new leader, the Greenthumb directors had hit on a key problem of staffing their NGO with only young people. More accurately, they had discovered that the young people on their staff—most were in their twenties at the time and virtually all held postgraduate degrees—were unlikely to transfer the deference and respect they had given to Dr. Chen to someone on their level, regardless of the change in job title. Authority amongst one's peers, in this setting, would not be so easily won.[10] They had all come in as rough equals, and none of them could easily see who amongst them should stand above the others.

Recognizing that promoting from within would be problematic, the directors considered going into the market, to hire someone from outside. But this came with its own risks, as Dr. Chen explained: "I spent about a year thinking about how to do this best. We could go out and try to find someone from outside the organization. But what if we hired someone new, and their way of thinking and our existing team's thinking didn't match up? What if people didn't agree with their ways of doing things? So, in the end, *ai ya*. . . . Anyway, we really struggled over which way to go."

Confronting this leadership succession challenge eventually gave birth to the idea of holding an election from within the current staff. Of course, most NGOs would typically choose one of the two methods they had rejected— either promoting from within or bringing someone else in altogether. From its very beginnings, though, the management and leadership within Greenthumb had taken an unusual character.

Actually, the origins of this idea of electing someone goes back a long way. When we first got off the ground, we originally had three full-time staff. Back then, because there were so few of us, we had what we called a rotation system. Each staff person in the center would be in the office for half a year while the other took care of fieldwork for half a year. . . . But after each of the three had gone through one cycle, we felt there was a problem with our method. It seemed that there was about a six-month "familiarity" process, whether that meant getting familiar with all aspects of the group's operations or it meant getting used to sitting in the leader's chair. In six months, some people might need only two months before they pretty much got a handle on things, but someone else might need six months before they felt they could do the job. But, just as they felt comfortable in a role, their time was up, six months had passed, and they needed to change to another role. We did this for a year and a half or two years until we realized it wasn't working. So we started asking ourselves what we should do, what kind of method should we adopt? We thought about this continuously after that, all the way through to last year when we held the election.

The rotation system originally implemented was hoped to create a new model of organization. It was adopted to ensure that everyone took equal responsibility for the new group's success, because it required everyone to be familiar with various work issues but also because it avoided creating one single head who held authority over others. When the six-month rotation period proved too short, however, their democratic yearnings led them to the idea of holding an election.

Greenthumb is unusual in Chinese civil society in that not only would it eventually hold an election but also from its very founding the idea of "handover" to others was in the minds of its leaders. The kind of "founders syndrome" faced by nonprofits in the United States and elsewhere exists in China, as well, but the fragile political position of most grassroots NGOs and the lack of supportive legal frameworks for creating financial stability mean in part that the lifecycle of many NGOs is quite short, and their survival is often contingent upon one or two people's personal fortunes. The motivation of Greenthumb's founders for having an election to choose leaders—and for making sure they were young leaders—was tied to fears that their organization and the mission of tackling China's environmental problems could fall victim to this same dynamic. As one director explained:

> I don't know if you've seen it or not, but the founders of NGOs in China are incredibly influential in their organizations and in society, extremely influential individuals. So, if the founder leaves the NGO or for some reason isn't there any more, the organization quickly collapses. It totally relies on that one person's . . . what is it called? That one person's charisma. They depend on that one person to run the whole organization, to lead it. And because below him there aren't any capable young people being nurtured, as soon as the founder leaves, it just collapses. We've seen it reported on in magazines, that Chinese NGOs maybe exist for a year or two, maybe three years, but then just collapse (*zisheng zimie le*).

The idea of holding an election itself was intriguing to regular staff members. But, as Together volunteers had discovered, one key to a satisfactory election is an open nomination process. As one Greenthumb staff person explained:

> Prior to the election, Lu Jie and Dr. Chen both talked to everyone individually, to tell us we were going to have an election like this. And they privately asked

us our views. They asked if we could nominate three people, who would we nominate. And then they asked what these people's strengths and weaknesses were, and why we would nominate them. . . .

I think it was pretty fair, you know? Three people were nominated in the end, three pretty suitable people. And each of them went up to say what they would do if they were chosen. You could say they didn't know in advance which of them would be chosen. . . . Basically, it was an open. . . . I felt it was a fair process, anyway. After they had spoken, everyone started asking questions of each of the three people, asking, "If we elect you, what will you do?" Lots of questions like that. . . . Then we voted for two of the three.

In general, the process seemed acceptable to this person. Having been at least consulted, and having the chance to ask questions was viewed positively. The election, however, did not go off as smoothly as the directors and others had hoped: "But one of the three didn't know he would be nominated and hadn't prepared. . . . And he didn't want to do it. . . . When he stood up to speak, he said he didn't want to be a co-head. . . . So, we had no choice, really, because we were electing two people out of three, and one of them said he didn't want to do it."

Although Bridges' experience had taught their volunteers that they should avoid calling for a vote too early, Greenthumb's directors had perhaps rushed the nomination process. And unlike Together's lessons learned, they did not open it up to all staff but rather "consulted" them on their views and then presented them with three names to choose from. In another contrast to Bridges and Together, they also failed to consider the principle of voluntariness, and overlooking the fact that one of their nominees was uninterested in the job meant that the election results were inevitably seen as predetermined. Asked whether the two new co-heads were democratically elected, one staff member hesitated but then gave an incisive evaluation of the process:

Yes, we voted for them. But it's like sitting down to a meal. If there are five different dishes, I can choose the two I like. But if there's only one dish, I can only eat that one dish. As you can see for yourself, a lot of the people in our organization are new. They haven't been here very long. They were asked to elect others before they even had time to figure out what's going on, what we do here. So, you can say it was "democracy with no choice" (bei minzhu),[11] because democracy should be like when you have five dishes you can actually choose what you want. When you don't have multiple dishes, you can't choose, but you still have to vote. But, yes, we had a vote.

The sense that the vote outcome was predetermined was strengthened by the fact that one of the nominees had been considered for leadership for some time. As one of the directors explained, "One of the two elected leaders became our deputy head four years ago. So, this last election was a way of reaffirming her in that position."

In seeking to "reaffirm" their previously favored staff member through an election, the directors left regular staff members with a sense that they should know who to vote for: "Actually, subconsciously, everyone knew that these were the ones being groomed for that position, you know? And because people had already talked about it, they knew that the founders favored them. Everyone knew how it was. So, you could say it was very democratic, but you could also say it was democracy with no choice (*bei minzhu*)."

The concept of "democracy with no choice" (*bei minzhu*) might better be understood as something done *to* someone, not the proactive, taking control of one's destiny that idealized visions of democratic processes sometimes evoke. This likely emerged after inspiration from the Hu Jintao era rhetoric of a "harmonious society," in which dissidents and civil society actors punished for speaking out were said, with a kind of dark sarcasm, to have "been harmonized" (*bei hexie*) by the state.[12] Rather than voting for their preferred candidates, the regular staff I spoke with described voting as going along with the suggestions of the directors, their bosses. Although these same people also showed sincere respect for the directors, their resentment at having been pushed into conferring democratic legitimacy onto the new co-heads was also palpable in interviews.

Lest readers imagine that these were the grumblings of petty jealousies or disappointed dreams of leadership, most staff seemed to view the choices as reasonable. As one said: "Actually, when we had the election most of us had not been here very long; we lacked experience. But [the two we elected] had been here the longest and were better suited for those positions, both in managing things in the organization and in dealing with people and issues outside of the organization."

In any case, several noted, despite the election and the attempted handover of authority, most staff believed the original directors were still the *real* bosses: "Everyone was very clear that in the end, even after the vote, Dr. Chen would still be boss (*shuo le suan*). So, you can say that everyone took the election very seriously, but everyone also knew that in the end Dr. Chen would still be in charge."

Another staff member concurred, explaining that the new co-heads still had to find their own feet and that problems in the transition were inevitable: "Actually, two of the founders are still the decision-makers, but they're always hoping that a younger group will slowly replace them as leaders and managers. So now we have two co-heads. So, there are two wristwatches. But how do you know which one is correct? This kind of problem has emerged. If the two of them don't coordinate their positions well, if they're not working on the same time, then those of us below might not know what to do. There's this kind of effect."

Looking for "correct" guidance from those above is an ingrained response nurtured through the norms of the larger organizational world in which Greenthumb is embedded. Even in this NGO, a presumed carrier of democratic values, and even after investing time and effort to have an election, the staff continued to rely on the language of authoritarian organizational culture when conceptualizing relationships in their workplace. Ultimately, achieving the main goal of the election—to identify and put into place a new younger leadership and thus ensure the NGO's long-term success—proved elusive. The new co-heads' formerly same-level colleagues were not ready to accept them as equals, and Dr. Chen and other directors still found themselves in demand to adjudicate disputes and offer authoritative guidance.

As with Bridges and Together, we can see in Greenthumb the same propensity for experimentation and the struggle to find a balance between the experience of older people and the desire to attract and keep newer people engaged. Despite problems with the process, it would be unfair and unwise to see Greenthumb's election as simply an experiment gone wrong. Greenthumb's efforts were, by any standard, incredibly innovative and unusual. With no extant democratic models available in China's mainstream organizational culture, and in a context in which youth are frequently considered deserving of less authority than their elders, Greenthumb's leaders were bold in their vision and attempts to put youth at the forefront of their group.

CONCLUSION

How to select new leaders for groups that have operated for a decade or more is a question many civil society groups have faced. In voluntary associations, especially, easy exit complicates this question further. As Bridges and Together draw most heavily on university students, the natural cycle of student organizations means that new people can be recruited each year, but it also means that some must leave and move on to other things after graduation. Throughout the lives of both Together and Bridges, early founders and volunteers have played crucial roles in keeping the groups running, helping them survive through crises of various sorts, and eventually even helping win them legal registration at their local Ministry of Civil Affairs office in the 2010s. Tied into southern China's network of NGO activists through connections with a top-tier university, the original leaders of both groups—and many of those selected through the processes described in this chapter—have been exposed to the latest thinking from within China and from abroad about how (professionalized) NGOs should be managed.[13] As with many other civil society groups in China, their organizational lives have been characterized by uncertainty—continuously under financial pressure, sometimes under political suspicion, frequently moving offices in search of cheaper rent and a more convenient location for volunteers, and trying to recruit volunteers and staff members who will devote themselves to their mission with low or sometimes no compensation. Until very recently, these groups were not even legal in the strictest sense of the word.

In tackling the issue of leadership and leadership selection in the ways they have, Bridges and Together are true pioneers in China. Although they have been connected to a national, regional, and even international network of professionalized NGOs, they have had no more-experienced role models or examples to follow in how to run bottom-up voluntary associations. Their various directors and boards have sought advice from others (myself included) on all the problems they face. But because they are doing what no one else has done before in contemporary China—at least no widely known others—most of their advisers have not been able to offer any ready-made solutions. They are, by virtually any measure, self-made organizations.

As distinct from professionalized NGOs and government-organized NGOs (GONGOs), since their inception these voluntary associations have continuously sought the best ways to put their democratic values into practice while still pursuing their service missions. As I have shown in this chapter, this has not been easy. Without templates to follow, whether in organizational survival or democratic self-management, they have innovated with a number of methods, and, in the process, they have confronted questions that are fundamental to any democratic society. The one I tackled in this chapter has mainly focused on the issue of leadership selection. But in searching for an answer to this, these organizations have also tackled many related problems: How does anyone build consensus in a group with differing opinions? How can a voluntary association committed to the principle of equality benefit from the rich experiences of older volunteers while balancing that with the enthusiasm and innovations brought by newcomers? How can a group recognize when consensus has been reached? When should people turn to voting, and, indeed, on what matters is a vote necessary? These are all questions Bridges and Together have struggled with over time, finding their own solutions and developing a set of practices that more fully reflect their fundamental democratic ethos.

Although participants in non-volunteer-based associations may have similar "democratic yearnings," as I showed in chapter 2, and as exemplified in the example of Greenthumb, for professionalized NGOs and GONGOs, the pathways to democratic management are unclear. While even the leaders of such groups might aspire to a new model of organizational culture, their political positioning, financialized management structures, and the broader environment offer little incentive and space for escaping the top-down norms and practices that characterize mainstream organizational life. By contrast, the voluntary nature and distinctive generational profile of Bridges and Together have allowed them more freedom to experiment and have driven them toward an alternative model of self-governance.

Lest readers think it is somehow inevitable that all youth-based, voluntary associations in China (or elsewhere) nurture such bottom-up, participatory, and ultimately democratic organizational cultures, in the next chapter I consider the question of who joins these groups. More precisely, I consider the question of who is *allowed* to join, as with each new year both Bridges and Together turn away many more applicants than they can accept. In answering this question, we see another way in which these groups lay claim to democratic values.

Chapter Nine

SELECTING NEWCOMERS AND
SCREENING FOR COMMON VALUES

In many sociological studies of voluntary associational life, "Who joins?" is a key and perennial question. Scholars typically try to develop profiles and discern characteristics that describe "typical" volunteers as, for example, young or retired, religious or secular.[1] My purposes, by contrast, are to understand a different set of issues. Having spent time with and having interviewed many Bridges and Together members, it became clear that a key question for these particular voluntary organizations is not "Who joins?" but rather "Who is *allowed* to join?"

Each year, both Bridges and Together attract far more new applicants than they are able to absorb. Unlike the ambitions of many Chinese nongovernmental organizations (NGOs) whose leaders aspire to make their group the biggest, the most influential, the most well-known, or some other superlative, both Bridges and Together have made conscious decisions to emphasize quality over quantity in the work they do. Rather than exponentially grow their volunteer numbers each year and risk losing their sense of common purpose and shared values, they are highly selective when choosing newcomers. Selectivity is necessary not only for ensuring that the groups' activities meet their self-imposed high standards but especially for protecting the culture of the organizations from the potentially destructive influence of newcomers who are steeped in the norms of official organizations rather than democratically run voluntary groups.

For youth-based volunteer groups with inevitable turnover, the selection of newcomers presents both a recurring challenge and a regular opportunity to reflect on (and reaffirm) group values. To be sure, both Bridges and Together, like most grassroots civil society groups in China, work with limited human and financial resources.[2] Each year, however, after periodic assessments of their activity needs and the numbers of new recruits they will be able to absorb, they are faced with tough choices. All organizations, and perhaps especially voluntary associations, may start out with one set of common values and norms only to have those supplanted by newcomers with other priorities and practices.[3] Taking in "unsuitable" newcomers risks moving the group in directions that existing volunteers would find unacceptable.

In Bridges and Together, the ways participants talk about who is a right fit for their group—and who is not—reveal how their values inform the choices they make when facing a new pool of applicants. Their choices are largely driven by their commitment to a culture of openness and mutual respect, and when choosing newcomers they aim to find people who share their values and who can carry those values forward into the future.

ABILITIES CAN BE HONED, BUT VALUES ARE KEY

Both Bridges and Together aim to accomplish something tangible in their activities, whether that be repairing an elderly villager's roof or opening the eyes of a youngster to the joys of learning a foreign language. For both groups, volunteers' individual abilities play a clear second fiddle to their attitudes. Useful skills and abilities are desirable but not sufficient. As one young man put it, "there are those who might have great ability and strong opinions, but you feel like they wouldn't be able to get along with others. Those are the types likely to be rejected." One volunteer who interviewed new applicants at Bridges explained why she believed ability should be a secondary consideration: "As long as you don't have bad motives and don't have problems communicating with others, that's good enough for me. Because I myself used to be a person with mostly weak abilities and skills. My improvements have come because Bridges has trained me and taught me. Bridges gives you a growth opportunity (*chengzhang de jihui*) to let you go discover your own potential. So, my own standards for newcomers are kind of low, because they should have the same chance that I had."

In multiple interviews with volunteers in differing sites and roles, people described volunteering in Bridges and Together as unique environments offering a rare "growth opportunity" and the chance to "discover your own potential." Indeed, these were considered to be valuable enough to be protected against an alternative standard that prioritized whatever skills or abilities potential participants might bring to the group. The belief that newcomers "should have the same chance that I had" was also pervasive. If growth opportunities were valuable to current volunteers, a sense of basic equality and fairness meant that the organizations should not privilege narrow or utilitarian goals if doing so meant denying newcomers the chance to grow. These deeply committed volunteers saw the value of the groups not simply in what they could claim as tangible accomplishments—numbers of classes taught or dilapidated houses fixed—but also, and perhaps even more so, in the kinds of unique personal growth opportunities they offered to participants. Other normal groups would welcome the strongest and most impressive candidates, but the value systems underlying Bridges and Together meant that another set of criteria was even more important.

EXPERIMENTING WITH THE SELECTION PROCESS

Just as experimentation in the selection of leaders has tended toward more open, democratic election methods, both Bridges and Together have engaged in reflective experimentation to screen new volunteers for conscientiousness, dedication, and the democratic values and habits that distinguish them from other groups.[4] Over time, Bridges' selection process evolved, extending beyond the standard practices borrowed from the original corporate training manual and questions that hiring managers the world over would find familiar. While retaining concerns about qualifications and personal strengths, in recent years Bridges has also begun to incorporate new questions and creative activities that reveal whether a candidate will be a good fit. A senior leader explained:

> We initially referenced the standards used by the multinational corporation in their job interviews, in their management trainings. They looked for different kinds of abilities, like how you understand and solve problems, your teamwork spirit, your ability to learn new things, your communication skills. In our interviews we'll ask questions like, "What do you think our motto means?"— to see to what extent you identify with us. Then we'll ask, "What do you think your biggest advantage to date has been? Your biggest accomplishment? Your biggest tragedy or difficulty?"

But now we've added another round, called "leaderless small groups." We seat six to eight people together in a small circle. Then we give them a question to discuss, and they need to come up with a small group proposal for us. This is mainly to see how well they express themselves, how well they listen to others (*lingting*), whether they're able to accept others' opinions, their work attitude, and their ability to hold a meeting.[5]

Although practical skills and abilities are important, multiple interviewees confirmed that even more important are things like listening skills and respect for others. In both Bridges and Together, newcomers are expected to engage with others and proactively contribute to the common efforts of the groups. When asked what sorts of folks are not suitable, a longtime leader of Bridges explained that the group was not interested in "passive people (*bu jiji de ren*). That is, people who don't actively express themselves or solve problems. For people who don't speak a word—we'll ask them a question at the end, 'Why didn't you express your views just now?' To give them a final chance. If they don't say anything, they won't pass." While seeking newcomers who are not afraid to speak up, he was equally adamant that Bridges volunteers were not keen on "people who can't hear other's views (*buneng tingqu bieren yijian*), people who lack a spirit of cooperation." In other words, both the ability to articulate one's own views and to carefully and respectfully consider the views of others were key criteria for acceptance.

Both Bridges and Together struggle with how to select for the best possible outcomes while staying true to their goals of openness and diversity. Striking a balance between valuing experience and openness to newcomers—with the latter's attendant emphasis on opportunities for personal development and skills building—is a running concern and ongoing challenge. As one leader put it:

We also look at their personal qualities because we've discovered that these things will influence the future development of their abilities. Of course, it's all relative to what we've seen and known about in the past, so selection outcomes depend a lot on the personal experience of the interviewers.

Our bottom line for evaluating new applicants is, "You're a Bridges volunteer. Would you be willing to work alongside this person?" If they're exceptional individuals in all ways, but you're not really willing to work with them, you can write that down on their application evaluation form. Ha ha! . . . This easily leads to only selecting people like yourself, but in the end we feel like there are all types of people, so all types of people will still join in.

The question of who should interview applicants was raised spontaneously by numerous Bridges and Together volunteers as we discussed these challenges. As individuals and as organizations, they had begun to recognize the dilemmas wrought by interviewer bias and the desire for efficiency in the selection process. While searching for ways to overcome these problems, they also were eager to ensure participation by more junior volunteers: "In the past we've asked fairly new volunteers to serve as interviewers, but in reality their experience is just too limited. So, next year, we might allow only experienced people to be the so-called head interviewer, the one to give a score, and we'll let other newer people sit on the side and take notes and help out, and they wouldn't need to go through a special training. That way, we could just put our training energies and time into the head interviewer instead. This is what we're thinking about, anyway."

One of the newer volunteers appreciated such problems, but saw the very opportunity to conduct interviews as beneficial to more junior volunteers and in line with the group's broader emphasis on personal development:

> We've discovered that when people leave, it's easy for us to lose that experience, and we end up relying on volunteers with only one year's experience to do the actual interviews, to explore (*tansuo*) by themselves. For example, this year, when I was interviewing people, I wasn't really clear on how to do it. I did it only by exploring what needed doing as I was doing it, and I found there were lots of things left out. It's a little inevitable, because of insufficient experience, but this lack of experience is also a great growth opportunity for the volunteers that serve as interviewers. On the other hand, I feel like because this interview is so consequential for the applicants, I think that we should be more standardized (*guifanhua*). It would be fairer that way, and we'd be more professional because we would be more principled in the way we choose new people.

SINCERITY AND MUTUAL RESPECT

While "standardization" was raised by a few interviewees as a possible direction for the next evolution of selection processes—but not without some reservations—much more common was an emphasis on finding the right cultural fit with the organization. Sincerity of purpose and mutual respect were highly sought-after character traits, even when applicants had little to no direct skills they could offer in the groups' actual work.

Sincerity of purpose—rather than doing things formalistically "for show" or to get ahead—is key to admission in Bridges and Together. Again rejecting the utilitarianism seen as underpinning participation in normal student organizations, one long-term leader lamented the state of volunteering as commonly understood: "It seems like nowadays everyone seems to think that volunteering is just some kind of fashionable thing. People who just want an experience, or extra credit at school, or some certificate."

Although "sincerity" was a shared core value, how does one identify who is and who is not sincere? It was often understood as visible in the ways that applicants treated others: "For example, are you punctual? And how do you—when you're interacting with others, how do you treat other people? Through other interactions with them, we can see how sincere they are. These attitudes will be reflected in those interactions. You can even tell a lot about their attitude by how seriously they take the signup process, like if they leave a lot blank."

Another volunteer interpreted sincerity of purpose as having the proper motivations: "Those who don't get it, who want to just go have fun—they'll probably be rejected. The same with those guys who just want to go meet girls, that type, the kind with impure motives (*mudi bu chun*)." Many interviewees insisted that "we don't have any [fixed] standards," but then would go on to describe the following scenario in some fashion or another: "We'll ask them a few basic questions, then we'll discuss it later on. How do we feel about this person? Do they really have the heart to put into doing public welfare work (*gongyi*)? Or are they just looking to try out something new, looking for a new experience? Will they just join one camp and then not come again?"

Others were more direct: "There are a few simple standards. First, they need to be able to express themselves clearly because they're going to teach. Second, they need to be . . . umm . . . more "open" [in English]. Third, they shouldn't be too selfish . . . People who are selfish, they'll show it."

A long-time Together volunteer admitted that setting clear standards was hard, but reflected a concern that showed how they valued interactions with other people over more utilitarian calculations:

> We've been struggling over this. Some people are just not suitable, so you can eliminate them quickly. Others are generally suitable but have some problems. . . . Deciding to eliminate them can be a really tough decision. As for our standards, [they include] sincerity, diligence (*yongxin*) in looking after the old villagers, and how they would treat the old folks. And also how

sincere they are in interacting with other campers. And another one is "purity of purpose" (*mudi danchun*). We don't want those who are coming just to experience an activity. Their motivations should be purer than that.

This emphasis on sincerity could be interpreted in multiple ways, but a key aspect in most interviews was a focus on mutual respect and honesty, rather than participating simply as a means to an end as they might in normal, formalistic, university-run organizations. As another volunteer put it, "We haven't really set fixed standards. The most important thing is to see if everyone gets along well. That is, if they're really coming with sincerity. It's about their attitude."

Even in the absence of formal standards, consensus about respect for others was widespread: "We've discussed standards before, but we haven't made any formal ones yet. I think it just depends on how we feel about the person. Ha ha! Yeah, that's pretty much what it is. We have a face-to-face meeting for us to see how we feel about them. The preparation team meets with all the applicants together. . . . And, for example, if you're playing with your mobile phone the whole time and not listening, we definitely won't pick you, because clearly your attitude isn't very serious."

THE ENDURING IMPORTANCE OF EQUALITY

Discussing the selection of newcomers reinforced that most Bridges and Together participants felt a strong aversion to hierarchy and would actively work to reaffirm the importance of equality between individuals where they could. Given the formality of most interview settings—and a structured interview's attendant associations with preexisting power relations—a number of Together branches even sought to avoid the formality and hierarchy implied by terms like "interview":

Choosing newcomers is really a pain! It's not difficult to do the interview, but we feel it's just awful in general, because it feels like we're way up high (*gaogao zaishang*), and the people we're interviewing are down below us. But, in general, although maybe all interviews are the same, we try our best not to make the atmosphere too stiff (*jiang*), and so we don't call it an "interview." We just say we're going to have a "face-to-face meet-up" (*jianmianhui*) with potential volunteers. I think there's a little bit of an awkward feeling there . . . But we haven't thought of any better method to use yet! Ha ha!

Trying to create a more casual atmosphere is designed to put applicants on the same level as older volunteers, introducing them to the culture and goals of the group. At these "face-to-face meet-ups": "We don't do one-on-one interviews with applicants. Everyone sits down together for a chat, just like we're chatting now. That way the new applicants and old volunteers get to know one another better. . . . We don't care so much about having a formalistic interview, because most interviews are too stressful for applicants."

Relaxed "chats," rather than "interviews," also reveal the personalities of potential applicants and show them another way of conducting interviews that they are unlikely to have experienced before.

> Our interview process includes self-introductions and playing some games together. Then we show a video about Together and another one about one of the villages. Then we break into small groups for discussion. A lot of times we don't use the term "interview" (*mianshi*) but rather "face-to-face chats" (*miantan*), which are just like chatting normally, like you and I are doing now in our interview, chatting about life, about all kinds of things. This helps us get to know an applicant's personality and how they conduct themselves, . . . The feedback we get from them is that it's not that bad, that it's very different from other interviews.

In deciding who is invited to join, the applicant-interviewee dynamic is not the only process in which hierarchical norms are actively avoided. The presence of older and newer volunteers as interviewers can also drive a search for equality of opinion, with the "elders" of the groups expected to respect the decisions made by those holding the most responsibility for the activity, even when the decision-makers are younger or less experienced. Just as Bridges has struggled to find the right mixture of old and new interviewers, Together branches have evolved different methods to ensure a good balance is struck:

> In our interviews, decisions are made by the original four leaders of the club, plus some "old soldiers" who have previously volunteered. Maybe they're in their third or fourth year, or even people who have graduated already. We'll do the interviews together, and they'll join us in the discussions of who to choose. Although all of us will discuss any questions of suitability, the old soldiers don't have power to make the final decision. That falls to the four of us in the preparation team. They can only give their opinions for us to consider. Everyone agrees that the final decision-making power should be in the hands of the preparation team.

PARTY MEMBERS WELCOME, BUT CHECK YOUR
OFFICIOUSNESS AT THE DOOR

Unlike many government jobs or certain university-backed club positions, Chinese Communist Party (CCP) membership and prior leadership roles in the party did not bolster one's chances of admission into Bridges and Together.[6] Indeed, for some, an applicant's prior experience as an official "student leader" (*xuesheng ganbu*) risked disadvantaging them, especially if it taught them to be obnoxiously assertive or to "talk like a government official" (*da guanqiang*). Humility, in many interviewees' eyes, was in short supply with these sorts of applicants.

One interviewee applied three times before he was accepted into Bridges, discovering to his surprise that his formal qualifications did not advantage him in the application process: "They didn't explain anything about why I failed on the first two attempts. At that time, I was even class leader (*banzhang*), a student official. And because I was a student official, I thought I was really good, you know? So, getting rejected was really puzzling to me. Ha ha!"

Although CCP membership was not an explicit negative criterion for entry, behaving "like a government official" was frequently cited as a red flag in interviews and interactions with applicants. The connection between party membership and officiousness was evident in the ways volunteers talked, frequently implying the existence of an acculturation process or affinity for officiousness that came with party membership. For one fairly junior leader, a lack of sincerity, officiousness, and party membership easily went hand in hand with the kinds of people who were unsuitable for Together:

> I personally look at how I feel about a person, because there are many types of people. I prefer those people who are warmer in person, the way they talk to you, those who seem more sincere in talking with you. I prefer those over people who like to talk like a government official (*xihuan da guanqiang*) or, you could say, people who don't seem like they're very sincere, those who are stricter in their speech.
>
> I'll give you a real-life example. Once, I went to a group interview for new applicants. This one person said, "I'm a party member, so I have a responsibility and obligation to do this or do that, and I feel like I could go help others, blah blah blah. . . . The second part of what he said sounded OK, but the first part sounded frightening! I felt like when he imagined participating in the work camp he wasn't acting on his own, his motivation wasn't coming from his

heart (*bushi fazi neixin de xiangfa qu zuo*). So, it seemed like we should think about what kind of influence this person would have on the elderly villagers and on other campers. Taking that under consideration, we easily saw that we wouldn't want this person to join.

Recently we've had a lot of new applicants say, "I'm a party member." I just think that's really awful! I don't think party members are unsuitable. Not at all. We have a lot of volunteers who are party members. But when people empha-size that stuff intentionally, it's clear their motivation isn't coming from their own hearts. It's like they're doing this not from some sincere motivation of their own, and it makes you feel like they're really not suitable for this. Because there are other people who really want to go visit the old villagers, and people who really want to do good work in the village. Even if they don't really know what they're doing, their motivations are their own. When you compare those two types, the difference is truly stark.

The culture of "officialness" is one into which many university students are strongly socialized. This culture came up repeatedly in interviews with Bridges and Together volunteers. Another volunteer related how selection committees struggle to break through the "formalities" most applicants bring to the interview process. Since a "formal" version of self-presentation is pervasive in the most influential university clubs and is on display across the major institutions students have encountered, applicants to Bridges and Together often turn to such models almost by default.

One long-term volunteer described her group's struggles to get appli-cants to drop their "formal" selves and show their real personalities and motivations:

In our most recent interview meeting, [another leader] wanted to make it more relaxed, like a chat just talking about how the applicants heard of our organization, stuff like that. Anyway, it turned out to be a lot more relaxed than the last one. In that one, the chair asked questions, and all the applicants felt like they had to answer the same question, one by one, or risk losing the chance to join. So, they started giving very official responses and got really anxious.

They took it as a formal interview and started trying to show their best face rather than just showing us their sincerity. . . . Everyone from first-year to fourth-year students sign up, right? So, I guess some of them have partici-pated in a lot of other club activities, in a lot of interviews or they have some off-campus work experience. They'll start telling you about how they've participated in this club or that club and done X, Y, and Z. Those people are more ambitious and utilitarian when they're talking with you.

For example, this guy we came across this year said he had been in a lot of activities before and that he had heard of our organization very early on. . . . I don't remember all of what he said, but when we had our group interview meeting, he was full of himself, thinking that he had done a lot of club activities before and so he knew better than others. . . . He actually even told [a senior leader] to hush so that he could speak, which was kind of rude. During the whole event, he kept trying to make himself look super capable at everything. We didn't accept him in the end, because we worried that he would act like he knew everything, that he would be too full of himself.

The Volunteer Who Didn't Work Out: A Cautionary Tale

A number of more experienced volunteers were able to relate stories of people who did not turn out to be good fits for their groups. In this next account, a new volunteer demonstrated great leadership potential but ultimately could not continue in the organization. In this case, a young university volunteer had entered a Together branch early in its development, when the group was still finding its feet and figuring out how to work together. As recounted by a long-time member of the group, after trying to work with others in the group for some time, the volunteer gradually withdrew out of frustration:

He said he always had different views than the rest of us, and when he brought his view up, it would always start a debate, but eventually his view would always be rejected. In reality, it's true that he usually had a very different idea than the rest of us. It made him depressed [*yumen*] and depressed us, too, so he just chose to lessen his involvement, showing up only occasionally to help a little. . . . At that time, we were all really torn about this (*jiujie de*). Eventually, those of us left just kept on with the work, and it got better slowly. Actually, I think even I am very different from the others in my views. Everyone is different. But . . . he wasn't able to accept the views of others. He felt things should be done a certain way, and why won't we all do it that way? He was unwilling to change, or, at least, that's what I saw in him. . . .

He wanted everyone to trust his opinion (*xinren ta*), but at the same time, he frequently challenged and doubted others (*zhiyi bieren*). . . . He really had lots of ideas (*you hen duo xiangfa*). If you say that the model our group worked under lacks a spiritual leader [*jingshen*], I think he would be a good choice to play that role, if he were willing to. But it was hard for him to find anyone willing to work with him, to follow him. So, he had power [in English], lots of ideas, and if he wanted to do something, he could plan it very carefully; he was capable. All that was true, but the problem was that he couldn't find anyone who was willing to work with him. So, I wasn't surprised that he eventually withdrew from the group. It wasn't that everything he proposed was unacceptable to others. It was more that he seldom would sit down and calmly explain his reasons to others (*xinping qihe qu gen bieren manman chanshu tade yijian*). He always spoke very emotionally and let his temper flare when talking to other volunteers. No one liked that, and after a while, no one felt like bothering with him any longer. He was a complicated guy, this one. Eventually, he just decided to withdraw from our group.

For this group and others, stories such as this served as a cautionary tale emphasizing the importance of the selection process and also reinforcing, reminding, and clarifying what their shared values are. Someone unable to "sit down and calmly explain his reasons to others" would be an ill fit for these sorts of groups. Someone who "wanted everyone to trust his opinion" but "frequently challenged and doubted others" would not be the kind of equal partner these groups could welcome, despite his skills and leadership potential. Yet such a story should not be interpreted to mean that these groups do not have a place for charismatic leadership. A number of my interviewees as well as volunteers I observed in activities were clearly charismatic leaders; all kinds of personalities were visible in these groups. The key difference, it seemed, was in the ability of those varied personalities to find value in others' ideas and approaches in such a way that no one person would rise to a position of dominance at all times and in all matters.

CONCLUSION

For volunteers in both Bridges and Together, respect for others and tolerance for different opinions were essential for success in the groups. Bundled together with talk of "sincerity" and humility, these values were screened for whenever newcomers applied to join. But while openness, sincerity, and mutual respect characterize these groups, this does not mean that all participants are able to articulate those values equally succinctly or fluently. More experienced participants, on the whole, were able to identify these traits to me and possessed the specific vocabulary that I have used in this chapter to re-present their stories to the reader. For many younger, less experienced volunteers, although the words did not always flow naturally from their lips, these values were clearly deeply *felt*. In initial interviews, I generally began asking something like, "What kinds of people are you looking for in applicants?" This line of questioning elicited fairly general responses, especially from newcomers who—I presume—had previously not had the chance or the need to articulate such opinions to anyone outside their group. After some attempts asking about this topic, I learned that switching the question around to ask, "What kinds of people are *not* suitable?" elicited much more spirited responses from most interviewees, like the following: "Who is unsuitable? The kind of person that everyone feels isn't right. . . . Some people, the way they speak, you can tell. For example, in the self-introduction period, they'll ask you something, then they'll say, 'I think I can do this kind of work.' And then they'll continue on to say, 'I think you're not doing this well,' or 'you're not doing that well,' or 'you need to improve in such and such way.'"

Relating broader sentiments I heard frequently in interviews with other volunteers, this speaker was not implying that his group had no need to improve. Rather, the concern was that this kind of applicant would be too arrogant and felt a need to show off their expertise or qualifications as a way of winning admission into the group. Although that sort of self-promotion was expected in "official" settings and in normal on-campus student organizations, Bridges and Together volunteers were not interested in having that sort of attitude in their groups.

That this speaker also asserted that "everyone" feels a certain way about such know-it-all's reveals two things. First, there is a strong sense that the values of the group are indeed shared by other members. In conversation after conversation, the values articulated as important to individual interviewees and presented as those of the group were noticeably consistent. The second thing such statements reflect is discomfort with assumed authority, a recurring theme in Bridges and Together and one in accord with the rejection of formalism discussed in chapter 4. In short, assuming a superior perspective before even having direct experience with their actual volunteer activities was almost sure to lead to rejection in both groups.

Screening for newcomers' values in the ways described here is a key strategy that allows Bridges and Together to maintain and reproduce their distinctive organizational cultures. Although the process for newcomer selection has evolved over time—as with the selection of new leaders—the emphasis on particular values and virtues has persisted and has come to form a core part of participants' self-identity as members of the groups. While there is a risk of selecting people too much like oneself—as one interviewee noted—the criteria used are designed not to avoid ideas current members might disagree with, but rather to ensure open attitudes, humility, and tolerance of different ideas.

PART IV
Conclusion and Implications

CONCLUSION

Implications for Democratic
Development in China and Beyond

Consolidating the "lessons learned" from the arguments and observations made in the preceding chapters has long seemed like an impossible task. In this concluding chapter, I consider three things: First, I consider the question of where groups like Together and Bridges go from here. More specifically, I look at how volunteers in these organizations imagine their futures and how their experiences might affect the larger society that surrounds them. Second, I consider the implications of this study for what we know about civil society in China more broadly and briefly revisit questions of democratization and democratic culture. Third, I conclude with some thoughts on what future research avenues this book highlights for both China and authoritarian regimes more generally.

GOING AGAINST THE GRAIN: VOLUNTEERS LOOKING FORWARD

Studies of democratic societies often suggest that the structure of civil society associations will normally mimic the larger political institutions of the nation, reproducing practices like rotating leadership, accountability mechanisms, and equitable representation in decision-making. In these places, democratic culture is seen to be ensured by and reproduced within civil society. In an authoritarian state like China, however, the democratic culture being nurtured in Bridges and Together goes against the grain of mainstream political norms and practices. If these participants try to take their emphasis on equality, voice, and mutual respect, for example, into society more broadly—into their job, other organizations, or even some government office—would they not face an uphill battle?

Volunteering in Bridges and Together served to hone practical skills, build community, and nurture other changes in individual participants. As we know from studies of other societies, volunteering, particularly for university students, can also raise awareness about issues other than the one that initially attracted volunteers, expanding their commitment to civic engagement and desire to tackle social injustices and inequalities.[1] In Bridges and Together, encountering inequality and injustice in one area of life—in these cases, around infectious disease and educational inequality—also engendered a heightened sensitivity toward broader inequalities and injustices. Many interviewees reported experiencing an awakening to problems and possibilities that had previously been hidden or obscured to them. As one Bridges volunteer put it: "Bridges opened a window for me, to see myself and to see those around me, but also to see lots of different problems in society. All I had ever done before was study, study, study. None of what I read in my books had anything to do with what was happening in society, but volunteering here has been like a way to really go deep into society, a way that's different from just working at a job. It's helped me become aware of things like the public interest sector (*gongyi hangye*)."

Drawing inspiration from the work at hand in Bridges, this volunteer began to look more critically at other aspects of life in contemporary society and to learn about less commonly known work, like that of the public interest sector. This awareness of alternatives to for-profit work or state-sector work was also mentioned by other long-term volunteers, often alongside an expanded sense of citizenship and empowerment. One Together volunteer found that volunteering had not only increased his self-confidence but also given his life a clear direction, inspiring him to better the world around him: "I've changed tremendously here. When I first arrived at university, I had no goals. I just went about daily life passing time. But after joining Together, I've had a purpose in my heart. For now, it's only a short-term goal, to graduate, to grow up, and to contribute something of value. I didn't use to feel like anything I did had any social value, made any contribution. But now I feel like I've found my worth, and I know I can make my contribution to society."

A law student from a working-class family also felt that Together inspired broader awareness of social problems, not just the particular issue of elderly infectious disease sufferers: "Together expands the concern people have for society. . . . It teaches you that there are lots of things we can do about the things that concern us. I know a number of people who were Together volunteers at university and then went on to work in public interest groups, doing this kind of stuff. So, it has this effect, helping you see things, expanding your desire to push for greater social progress."

Different people envisioned different ways to "push for greater social progress." Although a number of those on the cusp of graduation mentioned possible work in civil society organizations, this young man saw possibilities in more mainstream jobs. He envisioned pursuing a career that would provide financial security for his family as well as a chance to work toward something more socially beneficial: "If possible, I think I might work as a lawyer. That's a more flexible occupation, but the prerequisite for that is that you have some financial security so that you don't get influenced by the evils of society, so you don't work just to chase money or personal interest, helping other people do bad things. . . . I think I might try to become a judge, because that's more stable, and I could do something to try to support fairness and justice (*gongping zhengyi*), some public interest things."

This explicit emphasis on finding work that benefits society is not out of line with decades-long Communist Party entreaties that young (and old) people should "serve the people" (*wei renmin fuwu*). Yet the goals articulated by these young people went far beyond parroting the language of the state. They had their own ideas and visions about what trying to "support fairness and justice" might mean.

Of course, it may be that people drawn to volunteering may have a "prosocial personality" or inclination to see and help others in general.[2] One volunteer (the daughter of farmers) felt that her experience had reinforced her original desire to address some of China's social ills: "I used to think I ought to do something to help society, but I'm even more determined now, I'd say. I want to be able to contribute in some way, to try to change some of the bad things in society."

Whether people with prosocial personalities were more inclined to join these groups or not, many interviewees believed that volunteering had emboldened them to forge a distinctive new career path, one in which they could pursue their social justice ideals. In China, as in many countries, students typically enter university with a preset major, normally determined by their university entrance examination score. For high-scoring students, especially, choices are shaped by family pressures, advice from teachers and peers, and personal inclinations. Making a momentous career decision while still in high school means many young people, lacking broader life experience, are often not fully aware of their personal preferences and the opportunities they might have later. Volunteering in these groups opened many people's eyes to other possible futures. One volunteer (the son of working-class parents) in his final year of university claimed that his entire career plans had changed because of his time volunteering:

> I feel extremely fortunate to have found Together since I started university. During my time in Together, I've continuously participated in lots of activities and experienced lots of different things (*ganshoudao hen duo dongxi*). . . . In the past, I always thought I wanted to be a doctor and worked really hard towards that goal, choosing medicine as my major when I took the university entrance exam. But after coming into contact with Together, I realized that I like this stuff even more. Like sociology—what you're doing—or service type stuff. I think my personality is more suited for this kind of stuff.

Although his parents and peers would consider it unwise to forego the financial rewards and social status of a medical doctor, he averred, "when I graduate, I most likely will pursue a career in some kind of service work, not medicine." Others discovered the existence of the broader public interest sector through their volunteering and were determined to participate even after graduation. As one volunteer put it:

> Joining Bridges led me to pay more attention to public interest (*gongyi*) activities. Like [the activist scholar] and [the NGO] you mentioned earlier. In the past, I would never have heard of them. But because of Bridges, I've started attending some exchanges between Bridges and other organizations. When I went listen to [various talks and salons], I discovered that there was a group of people doing those sorts of things and started coming in contact with the world of NGOs. It hasn't dramatically changed my life, but in the future I will make some time to do more public interest things. Not full time working at an NGO, but I'll do something for civil society.

VOICES OF OLDER VOLUNTEERS

Volunteers who had already graduated were particularly well placed to discuss how they saw their volunteer experience affecting their work lives. A number of them reported they were already striving to take the skills they had developed into their workplaces.

One early volunteer in Bridges reflected on the question of whether the organization's values and practices could be applied in other settings:

> Actually, in the early days of Bridges, we used to tell volunteers that this kind of atmosphere could only work inside our own circle. We would tell them that by no means should they try to be "open" [in English] with their parents or to give them critical feedback [on things they felt their parents could do differently]. Because in reality, we're a pretty alternative (*linglei*) group of people. But in recent years, I've begun to think that grassroots groups like us are growing quite rapidly, and so this kind of organizational culture will be welcomed and understood by more people. Even in the school where I teach now, I've tried some of our team-building approaches, and they work!

Indeed, at the time of this interview, Guangdong province was experiencing a discernible expansion of grassroots nongovernmental organizations (NGOs), and new ideas about organizational management and alternative values were circulating rapidly through this growing community. Despite feeling some degree of success at team building in his workplace, another volunteer believed the type of culture Bridges promoted would face difficulty spreading beyond the NGO community: "It would be difficult to influence the broader society, I think. Once volunteers graduate, they have to be in that society. Otherwise, they won't survive. Unless they go into a workplace that's alternative like us, or if they create another kind of culture in their workplace. But that would be very rare."

Another volunteer offered a similarly negative assessment, highlighting the financial drives she assumed underpinned most jobs "in society": "I don't think most people in society can accept the way we do things. Spending time together in villages, separated from the outside world, everyone is working towards a common goal in a very pure way. But society is different. Even if everyone is working together on a job, they're expending that effort just for money, so it would be difficult to develop the same kind of emotional connection."

Still, others had also found ways to apply the skills and ways of thinking they developed through volunteering to their new workplaces. One former Together volunteer who entered a rapidly growing company made a position for himself in training and team building within the staff. Although his original passion was for the artistic work the company did, he found himself frustrated at the lack of coordination and the lack of teamwork among his colleagues: "So, I decided I should bring in the skills I developed as a

CONCLUSION AND IMPLICATIONS

coordinator" through volunteering, he explained, and the company's owner, whom he described as "not a good manager," was happy to have him do so. In exchange, his boss also let him off work from time to time to help out in trainings and to return for short volunteering stints in the village.

One Bridges volunteer who had found full-time work at a government-organized NGO (GONGO) recounted how the culture of the organization was typical of those described in chapter 2. "During meetings, the leadership would say 'this is bad' and 'you can't do things this way.' And everyone would just say, 'Yes. Ok.' No one would raise any opposing views," she explained. She expressed surprise that her fellow staff members— many of them in the younger generation like herself—seemed to have no thoughts on the work they were tasked with, at least in meetings. Then, she discovered that in private many of them *did* have other ideas about how things should be done. They just didn't feel comfortable speaking up: "The midlevel people wouldn't dare say anything to the president and vice president of the organization. They only knew how to say, 'Yes, yes. No problem.' They would never say, 'No, I can't do that.' So, it was just like they could only obey, obey, obey. It's really interesting, right? So, slowly, I've been slowly trying to get a few of them to say, 'No,' to know what it feels like to say, 'No.'"

While teaching lower-level staff to "say no" was perhaps not what the GONGO's leadership had hoped she would bring to the job when they hired her, it was her volunteering experience that had appealed to them. "They were hoping I could help inject some life into the organization. The top leader was quite open-minded in his attitude, and he hoped I could bring some of my experience into play," she said. Although not everyone in the organization seemed ready to accept her efforts to change the organizational culture, she found that training volunteers offered an opportunity to introduce some of Bridges' emphasis on equality and volunteering. The initial volunteers she encountered liked her methods, and so the leadership asked her to design and lead training for a large group of volunteers from a local university. When we spoke, she was optimistic and eager to see what changes her approach would bring to the larger group, but she saw many obstacles to changing the staff culture. As at other GONGOs and professionalized NGOs, "the staff turnover here is really high. The atmosphere isn't very harmonious or open, so everyone has lots of complaints," she confided.

For another recent graduate, the world that had opened up through volunteering had also given her a new outlook on what her future might hold and the confidence to chart her own course forward: "I've started living life consciously. In our group, you really begin to think about what kind of life you want to lead, what direction you want to go in, what you want to pursue. I joined the student union after starting university because I wanted something a bit more exciting in my life. But I never thought much about what I could do in the future. Here, though, I've been able to learn about civil society, public interest, the whole sector."

For these young people, "living life consciously" is a product of their participation, one that offers a path to a previously unimagined kind of social and civic engagement. Rather than "study, study, study" with no experience of life beyond books, participating in these sorts of organizations brings them into contact with real-world inequalities and injustices, many for the first time. Struggling but ultimately accomplishing their goals increases their self-efficacy, teaching them that "there are lots of things we can do about the things that concern us." For many who had already graduated, their focus was no longer only on the seemingly straightforward issues that motivated their groups' original founders but had expanded to encompass other social issues. Learning about the possibilities in civil society offered them a new vision for their future, one that would allow them to leave their mark on the world by continuing to volunteer or by bringing their carefully nurtured democratic practices and values into their work and social lives. Given the strength of the party-state's pervasive hegemonic authoritarianism, they will surely face substantial challenges if they seek work in professionalized NGOs and GONGOs. At the same time, however, their values and practices are likely to resonate deeply with the democratic yearnings of others employed in those types of organizations.

One long-term volunteer reflected on the impact of Bridges' approach and, unprompted by me, tied it to democracy:

I think the bigger impact Bridges has is that it shows people there's an alternative to mainstream life, an alternative way of living with others, of working with others. Maybe one day there will be an opportunity for something different to arise. I do believe education can influence society. I also believe that democracy requires education, and we're doing our part class by class, small group by small group, to realize that kind of alternative life. Maybe that's not the official view or predominant view within Bridges, but that's how I see it. I hope this view will be gradually understood and adopted by others.

Although neither group tracked the careers of volunteers after they left university in any systematic way, an early Bridges volunteer who later worked as a paid staff member recounted how a number of volunteers had gone on to find employment within the civil society sector. One young man joined a local incubator organization providing training for new activists and financial and administrative support for newly launched grassroots NGOs. The leader of that incubator had previously attended Bridges trainings to learn what they were doing, and the volunteer-turned-staff-member brought some Bridges ideas and practices into the trainings they gave to new groups. Others had gone on to work for labor rights NGOs, environmental groups, and arts-focused groups. One founded an LGBT rights group after graduating from university, joining with other like-minded young people in another city.

Such pathways to continued activism were common in both Bridges and Together. Other former volunteers went to work for NGO incubators, labor rights groups, and schools teaching migrant workers' children in cities where they were unable to attend local, publicly funded schools. One Together volunteer was hired by a wealthy businessman to manage and oversee a team of about one hundred social workers in a newly established social work organization the businessman had founded to help those less fortunate in his hometown. A few volunteers went to work for newly established philanthropic foundations, with entrepreneurs who quickly recognized their team management and project design skills as well as their experience working to address pressing social problems. People from both groups went on to study for higher degrees in medicine, education, social work, and finance, among other fields. While some went to work in private companies or multinational corporations, others went into civil service positions at some level of government. Whatever they were doing after leaving university, many older volunteers continued to support the groups in some fashion, including donating money or helping to train new volunteers.

EVERYDAY DEMOCRACY AND ITS IMPLICATIONS FOR CHINA

Many scholars and politicians around the world, including in China, proclaim democracy as a universal aspiration and right of all people. Yet how this goal is achieved is a matter of great debate. The most influential democratic revolutions of the modern era—the French and American ones—were accomplished through massive bloodshed and violence. Persuasion played a role, but only in that discussion and consensus building were necessary to gather sufficient numbers of revolutionaries and rebels to make an effective challenge to the existing monarchical power. And, of course, in France and the United States, the promise of democracy that began in the eighteenth century has followed a long and winding road to deliver the more expansive but still imperfect democracies French and American citizens enjoy today.

In the case of China, there is currently no apparent widespread and organized political opposition to the Chinese Communist Party's (CCP's) rule, not within civil society nor inside the party itself, discussions of "internal party democracy" notwithstanding. Yet this does not mean change is not afoot, especially if we take the long view of deeper cultural change that I have suggested. In this, I agree with the late political scientist Roger Boesche, who explained that in Alexis de Tocqueville's analysis, "Violent and sudden revolution—again, what we ordinarily think of when we use the word *revolution*—can never be successful, that is, can never quickly bring a far-reaching transformation of societies' generating principles. This can only be done slowly over a time span that includes many generations and perhaps even centuries. A political revolution that changes the rulers at the top can occur rapidly, and might even redress important grievances, but the developments that are authentically revolutionary need at least decades to ripen."[3]

The analysis and arguments put forth in this book do not help us identify a forthcoming moment of tremendous and radical change or upheaval, nor do they lead to an obvious prediction of when or if China will experience a sudden political transformation on the grand scale of other modern revolutions. Rather, the lessons I have tried to draw out in this book hint at the kind of slow but "far-reaching transformation of societies' generating principles" that Boesche saw as truly revolutionary in the Tocquevillian sense. Rather than seeing civil society as a trap laid by Western countries plotting to overthrow the government of the People's Republic of China, as one former high-ranking official warned in an official party-approved journal in 2011,[4] the processes at work are much more internal to China. Championing values like democracy, equality, and freedom as core to Chinese socialism and pursuing rapid integration with the global economy (although perhaps in fits and starts) over the past four decades, the party has overseen China's opening to the values, experiences, and logics of modernity. With millions of Chinese young people studying abroad, traveling for leisure, and accessing a global repository of knowledge and lifestyle alternatives on the internet—all developments that are nigh impossible to reverse or stamp out completely—the democratic yearnings that have drawn many people into civil society will continue to develop and seek pathways to be realized.

Overall, this book has been a study of the cultural underpinnings of democracy. A number of scholars have argued that transitions to democracy depend little on democratic cultural leanings.[5] In line with Liang Qichao's judgment of a century ago and the CCP today that China is not yet ready for full-scale democracy, scholars like Lucian Pye might argue that some obstinate cultural affinity for autocracy would prevent any successful democratic transition from taking hold in China (views greatly undermined, of course, by the experience of Taiwan).[6] My interest and contention are more in line with Juan Linz and Alfred Stepan, who argued that democratic consolidation, once a transition to democracy had been completed, required democratic cultural supports to succeed over the longer term.[7] Indeed, I would argue that democratic culture—a value system emphasizing equality, tolerance, and dignity, among others—and its attendant practices are just as important as democratic political institutions writ large for creating and sustaining democracy. As we have seen in recent years across a range of long-standing and newer modern democracies—including the United States, Thailand, and others—without these cultural underpinnings (and without their continual renewal) the political institutions and structures that are most recognizable as "democratic" are at risk of collapsing. I leave to others the work of discovering or exploring the formal institutional pillars of democracy as they may emerge in China.

The values, virtues, and practices of what I have called "everyday democracy" that we can find in voluntary organizations like Together and Bridges are at the heart of democratic culture. To be clear, the democratic organizational culture that emerged in Together and Bridges is surely the result of multiple influences. As discussed earlier—and in addition to the long-term trends in broader Chinese society—these influences include (1) their location in the relatively open province of Guangdong, where proximity to Hong Kong through family, media, academic exchanges, and interactions with INGOs introduced new ways of thinking about social issues as well as new approaches to taking actual action; (2) the relative youthfulness of their volunteers and their openness to postmodern values; and (3) the original moral visions of the founders as well as the moral aspirations of the young volunteers, who were constantly experimenting, questioning, and deepening the culture of democracy that they imagined was possible and that they had brought forth through their own actions.

It is difficult to say where Together and Bridges will go in the future. Basic tenets of organizational sociology—from Max Weber to Robert Michels to neo-institutionalists like William Dimaggio and Walter Powell[8]—would suggest that they might easily become increasingly bureaucratized and similar to the professionalized NGO model that dominates much of the contemporary world. At least in my period of study, however, both groups were aware of such pressures and fiercely protective of the very different organizational cultures they had inculcated through careful trial and reflection. From the standpoint of organizational sociology, my data offer an intriguing and perhaps counterintuitive least-likely case of democratic development in that these small, volunteer-based organizations managed to nurture democratic ideals and develop innovative practices to realize them despite the pressures of the surrounding authoritarian context. My decision in this book to engage most directly with Tocqueville and Antonio Gramsci rather than Weber and Michels was an intentional choice (not an omission), however, as I see important lessons for broader scholarship in political sociology and processes of democratic culture building.

Along with academic research by others—and exemplified in the lived experiences of people in Taiwan, who have enjoyed democratic self-rule for the better part of three decades now—I hope this book helps put to rest the idea that "Chinese culture" or "Asian culture" is somehow incompatible with democracy. In keeping with observations by Andrew Nathan and Tian-jian Shi[9] and others interested in how modernization—particularly through urbanization and education—spurs democratic political yearnings, I hope to have shown that there is a desire in China for living out the basic principles of freedom and equality that are fundamental to democratic practice and democratic society.[10] Despite the recurring railing of some Chinese critics against "little emperors" (the only children born due to China's decades-long one-child policy) and the perceived selfishness of the younger generation, the experiences of young volunteers in Bridges and Together, in particular, show that the desire for freedom and equality is not solely restricted to the level of the individual. It also reflects a desire to find a more democratic way of interacting with others, in community, and to give life to the ideals of mutual respect and dignity.

In much of this book, I have drawn almost entirely on interviews and observations with participants in Chinese civil society groups, as they are well positioned to observe and comment on the organizational norms in broader Chinese society. Their perspectives reveal the democratic aspirations and frustrations of many people active within Chinese civil society and reflect the prevalent top-down norms that carry over from mainstream organizational life. Crucially, their experiences suggest that if anything approximating a democratic culture is ever to be developed within an authoritarian society, it is unlikely to come from the typical professionalized NGO, and even less likely from the typical GONGO.

In developing the idea of the authoritarian society, I have aimed to show that the most common practices in Chinese civil society mimic those of the associational and organizational life most Chinese have experienced. At its worst, it is a top-down, hierarchical system with little room for any action other than obedience and any voice other than compelled consent. While these are common experiences of participants in GONGOs and in many professionalized NGOs, the chapters on Bridges and Together present an alternative vision of what civil society in China can create. The young people in these groups are laying the foundational cornerstones of democratic culture in China. Their achievements in doing so are—by their own accounts and in my observations—life-changing and impressive, especially given the norms of the larger society in which they are embedded. To secure a foundation for real democracy in China, however, their efforts are surely not enough. Their numbers are tiny compared with the larger population, and although some are already emerging as exemplars and thought leaders in their early work lives, it will take the collective efforts of many others to break through the authoritarian norms and practices that are so deeply entrenched in mainstream organizational life. Even if Bridges and Together volunteers seek to continue their social change-making in GONGOs and government agencies, they might ultimately find that such mainstream organizations prove too entrenched in authoritarian organizational culture to be transformed by their more democratic ideals and practices. Whether that quite likely scenario ultimately leads to frustration and disillusionment or a renewed effort to find another pathway to effecting social change is an open question for future inquiries to address.

LESSONS AND QUESTIONS FOR CHINA AND BEYOND

Extant contemporary literature linking civil society to processes of democratization has typically employed a state-society relations approach, investigating civil society organizations as (potential) agitators against an authoritarian state. Although this framing has been instructive, it has nonetheless generally sidestepped the question of whether civil society in authoritarian regimes can help produce the habits of the heart that Tocqueville saw as essential for a well-functioning democracy. Keeping one eye on Tocqueville while bringing in Gramsci's concept of hegemony, however, helps us better see the nature of the organizational culture at work within civil society groups in an authoritarian regime.

In a long-standing authoritarian state like China's, strong autocratic leadership, hierarchical structures, and the stifling of dissent within civil society organizations mirror the exercise of power in the larger political sphere, reflecting a distinctly sociological kind of hegemonic authoritarianism. Yet, as Gramsci would lead us to expect, the exercise of power in this way also rubs up roughly against a nascent counterhegemony, one that seeks a more democratic way of collaborating that acknowledges each individual's dignity and allows participants to work together as equals.

That participants in Chinese GONGOs, professionalized NGOs, and even university student clubs working across diverse fields of activity share common complaints about authoritarian practices indicates the breadth and depth of the dominant hegemony and the nascent counterhegemony. As other scholars have pointed out, we should not expect groups that are internally undemocratic to nurture democratic culture or practices. Yet—and crucially—in democratic societies, democratic norms and practices are culturally (and politically) available resources that actors can activate and mobilize to push back against authoritarian encroachment. In contrast, the model of civil society that the Chinese state allows and promotes works to reinforce authoritarian structures and practices rather than to challenge them. The state's antipathy to self-directed voluntary associations and the attendant democratic skills and practices that might develop in them further constrains the possibility for challenge. Ultimately, given the strength of China's party-state, the contestation between these two cultural poles is unlikely to be resolved easily. Indeed, in any authoritarian society, the entrenched privileging of hierarchy, autocracy, and the suppression of dissent may be the paramount obstacles preventing civil society from achieving its potential as a site for democratic culture building.

My analysis of the spectrum of Chinese civil society forms suggests that in authoritarian states—as in democracies—it is likely that democratic norms and practices have the greatest chance of developing, surviving, and thriving in voluntary associations where people seek to come together as equals for collective goals. Future research aimed at understanding the resistance to top-down models of organizational culture may thus be better served by focusing on truly voluntary associations rather than the GONGOs supported by authoritarian states and globalized models of professionalized NGOs that even China has accepted.

Direct references by interviewees to "democracy" are not especially numerous in this book. Some readers may find this lack of explicit or frequent discussion of democracy to be, on the surface, a paradox of the experiences of youth volunteers in Bridges and Together. In the larger context of contemporary Chinese political life, however, avoidance of the term makes sense, especially given the suppression of free speech, assembly, and the experiences of "fake" voting that volunteers have seen in top-down staged elections. As I have sought to illustrate across several chapters, regardless of how muted their understanding of political democracy is, small "d" democracy underpins much of their idealism and motivation for participating in such groups. As noted earlier, democratic culture requires more than just a handful of idealistic young people to develop and spread throughout a society. Ultimately, however, it must start somewhere, and the participants in these groups show how it is indeed in formation in contemporary China.

Bridges and Together are, to my knowledge, the largest such youth-based, youth-led groups of their kind in China today, dwarfed in scale only by government-directed groups like the Communist Youth League. Still, given the immensity of China's population, their membership represents but a tiny fraction of a percent of China's citizenry. To be sure, the transformative experiences recounted by Bridges and Together volunteers in the preceding chapters may be impressive at the level of personal growth, but—beyond what they mean personally for the relatively few individuals involved—do they amount to even a hill of beans in the face of an immensely powerful authoritarian state and the norms and practices it promotes? Perhaps so. Although they are a minority in terms of scale and numbers, they are the cultural vanguard of bottom-up youth-based social change movements. As one of my interviewees alluded to, while their efforts are seemingly tiny, the value of this "spark" of cultural change is that it might actually start a prairie fire.

The population of youth-based, youth-led groups in China is small—arguably fewer than one hundred, although firm numbers are virtually impossible to identify due to restrictions on survey research. What distinguishes Bridges and Together from the 2018–2019 neo-Marxist student groups that dared to criticize China's economic and political system and many other groups is (1) their ostensibly apolitical nature—they are voluntary groups that emerged around issues of specific social problems rather than a critique of the larger political-economic or social system; and (2) at fifteen years and running when the bulk of my research concluded, they had experienced longevity that few other groups have been able to achieve. Rather than short-lived gatherings that end in state repression, like the neo-Marxist groups and several others, Bridges and Together have managed to survive despite changes in China's political leadership and in NGO policy.

Other actors in Chinese civil society—including the leaders of profession-alized NGOs, as noted earlier—sometimes also embrace democratic values in rhetoric, but empirical realities show that researchers need to distinguish between "espousing" or "aspiring to" democratic values and doing the actual work needed to bring those values to reality. Other small and scattered youth-based groups I encountered in my fieldwork—including ones focused on LGBT issues and gender equality—often identified with human rights discourses and a democratic vision (broadly understood) for the future. Over the course of almost two decades of field-based research in Chinese civil society, however, I found none that were able to create the kind of dem-ocratic organizational culture that Bridges and Together have built.[11] A com-parative study might be better able to place those sorts of failures alongside the success of these two groups, but differing time frames, organizational strategies, and volunteer bases would make for an unstable comparison.

Despite the successes of Together and Bridges in nurturing democratic culture, the uphill challenges faced by groups like these cannot be under-estimated. The CCP's influence in ideological, cultural, and political terms looms like a mammoth over any alternative visions civil society actors might have for their future. Further research into hegemonic authoritarianism as a phenomenon would benefit from pursuing any number of questions: How do age and generational differences affect the willingness to experiment with more democratic organizational cultures? Are online groups more likely to operate under a more dispersed leadership style? Is government funding for GONGOs a key factor driving the continuation of authoritarian organiza-tional practices? Can foreign aid and philanthropic initiatives prioritize vol-untary associations in authoritarian states and still see the kinds of "results" they hope to achieve? Most broadly, at what point does the development of democratic culture lead to demands for systemic change?

In the case of China, hegemonic authoritarianism builds on a longer tradi-tion of Confucian paternalism. Many other societies around the world—even the world's oldest democracies—also have cultural legacies of paternalism, monarchy, or other forms of imagined or historical traditions on which hegemonic authoritarianism (and counterhegemonies) could be established and justified. I will have failed terribly in the writing of this book if readers take away the idea that the culture of democracy is alive and well in today's democratic societies. Recent failings in the United States to maintain long-standing norms of civility in Congress, for example, are one of many indicators of the fragility of democratic culture. The authoritarian norms inherent to mainstream organizations in China are not unique to China, and many instances can be found in the United States, Australia, and other mature democracies where people in positions of leadership have overstepped their authority, benefited personally at the expense of the public good, and engaged in outright illegal (not to mention unethical) corruption. As I wrote in the introduction, however, those kinds of actions are still (for the time being, at least) considered outside the norm, and democratic societies have developed legal as well as other means to handle such abuses of power and infractions of democratic practice.

Although democratic societies have the cultural resources to push back against authoritarian encroachment, the experiences and views of Chinese civil society actors may also lend fresh eyes through which to view the importance and value of democratic norms, values, and virtues. Aside from the civic engagement skills Together and Bridges volunteers have developed, their discovery of the importance of listening and humility, for example, offers lessons in democratic virtues that citizens of developed democracies would greatly benefit from learning or relearning where they have been lost. Likewise, the ways in which authoritarian regimes teach and prepare youth for life under authoritarianism offer lessons in caution for democratic societies that might otherwise underestimate or disregard the need for democratic values, practices, and virtues to be disseminated and renewed through the education system. Most broadly, this study of China should make clear that civil society organizations can be as effective at producing (and reproducing) a culture of authoritarianism as they can be at producing the democratic norms and practices needed to support a flourishing democratic political system.

The lessons we can take away from this study obviously extend to other authoritarian societies as well as China. Given variations in historical experiences with autocracy, paternalism, and democracy, further research could help determine how the practices of hegemonic authoritarianism might vary across different societal contexts. The varieties of authoritarianism that exist today suggest that some ruling groups would be more or less successful at nurturing authoritarian norms and practices broadly throughout society. It may be the case that one-party states like China's are particularly effective at imbuing civil society with the state's preferred configuration of power and suppressing counterhegemonic discourses. It may be that such effectiveness is more apparent in wealthier, more technologically advanced states or those better able to exert tight controls over education and media. Research that explores these possibilities would reveal both commonalities and differences in the form hegemonic authoritarianism can take and would deepen understandings of civil society, democratization, and authoritarianism globally.

SOME REFLECTIONS ON FIELDWORK, RE-PRESENTATION, AND ETHICS

I never set out to write a book about democratic culture. When I began China-based fieldwork for my doctoral dissertation in the Sociology Department at Yale in 2005, I intended to do a somewhat-straightforward study of relations between newly emerging grassroots nongovernmental organizations (NGOs) and the Chinese state. I was curious as to how and why they were allowed to operate or even exist at all. At that time, grassroots NGOs in China were a barely known phenomenon in or outside of academia, and in China they were considered to be an oddity at best, both few in number and possibly deserving of suspicion. I had expected to focus on environmental NGOs and labor rights groups, with questions prepared about legal registration status, financial support, corporate social responsibility (CSR) practices, and media relations. Although registration and financial support became key aspects of what I explored when I first arrived on the ground in China, the other issues quickly fell to the wayside as it became clear to me that CSR was of little relevance for many of the grassroots labor groups I encountered and that media ties were tenuous if not avoided altogether by an assortment of different groups (for various reasons).

In short, I wasn't planning to do the research that culminated in this book but rather stumbled upon it. Although I had been intrigued by Antonio Gramsci in a political sociology class taught by Chris Rhomberg at Yale, I was a skeptic of Alexis de Tocqueville's relevance for contemporary American society and politics. Having been born and raised mostly in the United

States, I had seen for myself corruption within the nonprofit sector, petty personalities and jealousies in volunteer-based groups, and a disappointing effort by American civil society groups to stop the U.S. invasion of Iraq after September 11, 2001. Perhaps, I thought, Tocqueville's insights had made sense for an earlier era of American associational life, but based on my personal experience, I saw little reason to think nineteenth-century ideas about democratic culture could still hold sway in the twenty-first century.

Joining civil society activities in China forced me to rethink what Tocqueville had seen on his travels around the United States. As recounted in chapter 3, my confusion and frustration in a meeting of would-be environmentalists led me to wonder what was happening to prevent such gatherings from producing the changes many participants obviously wanted to see. After witnessing the same dynamics unfolding in other settings, questions about organizational culture began to percolate in my mind. When I first encountered Together and Bridges and their much more democratic and participatory cultures, the contrast between these two different modes of association were striking, leading to the many questions that drove this research forward for another decade and more. I was further confounded when I spoke of my initial observations to a few trusted U.S. colleagues and advisers, most of whom reacted with skepticism and confusion, saying they had not noticed such dynamics in their own work in China (although they were typically working in very different formal academic settings and on topics unrelated to civil society). At the same time, however, a varied assortment of Chinese civil society participants—who I came to understand often saw themselves as "those below"—immediately recognized the tensions and dynamics that I reflected back to them after my initial observations. They not only believed these were problems—especially because they contrasted so greatly with what they imagined civil society *should* be—but also had a great deal to say about them and were keen to find a willing listener. As is hopefully clear to readers by now, it is the observations and experiences of these "lower-level" civil society participants that ultimately generated the research presented in this book and informed many of the questions I pursued in its development.

TRUST AND TRUST BUILDING

As I wrote previously in the *American Journal of Sociology*, despite the dearth of generalized social trust that I found in the research undertaken for my dissertation, building relationships with Chinese civil society participants, although not immediate, took surprisingly little effort.[1] People were eager to tell their stories, to express their frustrations and anxieties, and to encourage others to take up similar efforts. This was true both on topics related to state-society relations (the focus of that *AJS* article) and on questions about organizational culture. Being non-Chinese, moreover, I was not suspected as an internal Chinese spy or security official come to check up on them. Yet as a U.S. citizen, I walked a political tightrope between Chinese government authorities afraid of grassroots groups and on the lookout for American spies and U.S. government officials seeking to encourage and support NGO expansion. Ultimately, several key Chinese government officials came to see my research as nonthreatening, a judgment that allowed me to continue my inquiries and activities and provided me access to higher-level government offices—and, I supposed, allowed me to continue over the years to travel to China and talk with a variety of people. Nonetheless, trust building sometimes requires a multilayered unfolding of relationships. On the topic of government–NGO relations, I frequently treated initial conversations and meetings with new people as only hints into their experience and views, data that were then confirmed or modified through subsequent interactions. With the relatively young volunteers in Bridges and Together—and even with staff in government-organized NGOs (GONGOs) and professionalized NGOs—however, the topic of organizational culture was one that almost everyone was keen to talk about with few reservations. I can only presume this enthusiasm was due in no small measure to their experiences of hierarchy and repression inside mainstream organizations and their eagerness to repudiate the same.

COMMUNICATING ACROSS UNCERTAINTIES

I am not a trained translator, but I think the process of communicating across languages—and uncertainties of views—deserves more attention than it typically receives in studies such as this. Although it was only in the latter stages of fieldwork that I began recording interviews, pages and pages of verbatim transcripts show that "average people" seldom speak in the properly constructed sentences that academics value and wish ourselves to use without effort. Stammering, stuttering, midsentence pauses, and injections of "I'm thinking" and "I'm listening" phrases are as common in Chinese conversations (*Dui, dui, dui . . .* ; *Zheige, zheige . . .* ; *Neige shenma . . .*) as they are in English (Really?; Um . . . ; I see . . .) or in Spanish (*Este, este* . . .). The challenge for students here (myself included) is to look past these interjections and also to look into them. Sometimes they may convey a lack of self-confidence, or they are used to bide time while the speaker organizes and then clarifies their thoughts. At other times, they may reflect the speaker's search for more precise vocabulary to describe a particular concept or phenomenon.

At the same time, cultural differences (even between regions of China) generated particular linguistic peculiarities. The plural we is sometimes used when the speaker only means himself or herself, or conversely uses I to mean we. Not unlike how U.S. speakers of English often use "they" to refer to an unspecific generalized social person, many of my interlocutors use he, she, or it (all rendered in one speech sound as *ta*) to refer to a generalized other or to a general phenomenon. Both of these practices occasionally required some clarification during interviews. In translating, when referencing a hypothetical person, I generally translated *ta* as they, because it was clear the speaker meant a type of person. When it was clear the speaker meant a particular individual, and when I did not ask to clarify the person's sex, I randomly chose between he and she in my translations.[2]

Pinning people down on specifics was also challenging at times. As a general observation, many of my interviewees used tentative language to talk about things they were quite certain about. Words like "perhaps," "maybe," "sometimes," "probably," "possibly," and other qualifying adjectives were sprinkled throughout many conversations. In rendering these in English, I have tried to stay true to what I believe the speakers intended to convey, translating these words only when they were obviously (to me) relevant rather than risk confusing my readers as to the speaker's actual intention.

Because Mandarin was not the first dialect (or perhaps language, as some debate exists over which term is most appropriate) of most of my interviewees, interviews were often truly interactive and interpretive. Few people I interviewed spoke the standard northern Chinese Mandarin (*putonghua*) they were supposed to have been taught in school. Accents and variations in grammar and vocabulary abounded. Whether because of dialect influences or the relative formality of the interview setting, instead of colloquial words like *suoyi* (so, therefore), which is common in standard spoken Mandarin, a few interviewees used *yushi* (thereupon, consequently)—a formal word common in writing—while *he* or *gen* (and) was occasionally rendered in the typically more formal *yiji*. The word *shei* (who) was voiced by some as *sai*. In time references, *qunian* (last year, or the year just passed) became *shang-nian* (the year above) for many native Cantonese speakers. Generally, the "sh" sound in the officially approved version of Mandarin is pronounced as "s" in many southern Chinese dialects. Some interviewees, perhaps nervous at being formally interviewed and also hyperaware that their native dialect does not have a curled-tongue "sh" sound, sometimes overcompensated when speaking Mandarin by using the "sh" sound when only a simpler "s" sound was required (e.g., *shi* instead of *si*). Or it may have been that their Mandarin was so seldom used that they were unsure which use was correct. Vowel sounds changed as well, so that *man man* (slowly), for example, sounded like *mon mon* or *an* became *ong*. Short "i" sounds became long "e" sounds. The consonant sound "r" became "l." Word order also differed between dialects and influenced the way people spoke. As contrasted with "standard" Mandarin, for example, the words "actually" (*qishi*) or "first" (*xian*) sometimes appeared at the very end of a sentence. And the five tones of Mandarin officially recognized by Chinese educational authorities were often rendered quite differently by native speakers of other dialects, especially southern Chinese dialects that can have many more tone variations than standard Mandarin.

Having spent many years talking with people from southern China, a number of these linguistic differences were fairly familiar to me. More challenging, and perhaps universal to researchers in any context, were the spaces between speakers' thoughts. Such gaps convey nuance and subtleties that require the interviewer to actively listen for what is *not* said as much as for what *is* said. Knowing the background and context of speech is crucial to having a productive conversation and also for the analysis that, for some questions, would come much later in the research process. I took it as my task to understand the underlying assumptions of the interviewee's worldview as well as to make these explicit at times and to ask interviewees for their reflections on the same.

In translating from Chinese into English, I realized that during in-depth conversations in Chinese it is common for the subject or object to be implied rather than repeated. In writing, it seems to me that using brackets to insert these missing elements into a sentence would serve as much to distract readers as to clarify meaning. In re-presenting their voices in this book, I have tried to use brackets sparingly, only inserting these elements into the English rendering when it seemed necessary for smoother reading.

Happily, many of the interviews I conducted were quite relaxed, with occasional good-natured laughter helping to moderate the otherwise formal interview format. Especially with Together and Bridges participants, because in their activities they frequently interacted with people from very different backgrounds and language or dialect traditions, a few initially awkward introductions were quickly ameliorated by their willingness to deepen mutual understanding and bridge differences.

RESEARCH DESIGN AND QUALITATIVE FIELDWORK: ON THE VALUE OF EXPLORING

As noted earlier, this research was conducted over a period of more than a decade, most intensively from 2005 through 2017 (and continuing, less formally, with occasional conversations and check-ins stretching into 2023). During this time, I engaged in participant observation in numerous NGO gatherings that brought together leaders of groups in different fields. I also took part in training programs focused on the professionalization of the NGO sector. I volunteered both as a conference organizer and a regular participant in two grassroots NGOs. I occasionally acted as a translator and interpreter for other NGOs. The fields I covered ran the gamut from women's rights groups to environmental NGOs, migrant worker associations, and HIV/AIDS groups to education groups, children's welfare groups, autism groups, and NGOs working on other social issues. Although the majority of my long-term exposure was to groups based in southern China, I also met with groups in or from most other areas of the country.

Discerning readers will see that for some people this is not an ideal sociological study in several key respects. There is no randomly drawn sample of organizations or individuals. There is no paired-set comparison involving young volunteers in government-directed volunteering programs on the one hand versus volunteers in bottom-up voluntary associations on the other. Had I been able to approach the book's various topics in such a clean methodological fashion, I would perhaps be able to convince more readers of my arguments. For example, had I asked volunteers in GONGOs and professionalized NGOs exactly the same set of questions as volunteers in youth-led, bottom-up voluntary associations, I might persuade more people that the former generally failed to inculcate democratic culture, whereas the latter were exceptionally well-suited to doing so. For these failings, I blame both my inclinations to wander through the wilderness in search of the clearing as well as the practical and political challenges of researching a topic of such sensitivity in an authoritarian state. That said, the actual circumstances of GONGOs and bottom-up voluntary associations sometimes were so drastically different that asking the same set of questions simply would not have made sense to many of my interviewees.

Navigating the uncertainties of an emerging and rapidly changing field and discovering what questions I could ask—while giving consideration to both the political and personal sensitivities of the individuals involved—required long periods of immersion, observation, reflection, and trial and error. In a more open society, and on a more developed topic of inquiry in the particular setting, I might have been better able to design this study more intentionally.

Despite these limitations, I believe my ability (and privilege) to take a longer length of time, to remain open to new research questions and puzzles, and to develop deeper relationships with my research subjects generated understandings that otherwise would have been difficult, if not impossible, to achieve.

STRUGGLES WITH CONFIDENTIALITY AND ETHICS

It has taken me many years to be able to write this book. The normal obstacles were part of that, of course, like starting a new job in a new country (twice), being overwhelmed with teaching six new courses in my first two years as an assistant professor, not having a junior faculty sabbatical, trying to publish articles in a department that didn't know how to count books, and applying for grants to obtain tenure and continue on with my academic career. Aside from these issues—and my own insecurity about whether what I thought I understood was actually right—a persistent challenge across the years has been how to write this book without imposing an undue burden on my informants, without breaching their confidentiality, without bringing unwanted political attention to their activities, and without depicting them as they are *not*. Many of my earlier academic articles were translated (not by me) in whole or in part and circulated online in China, and I presume that my future work will be as well.

Knowing we are no longer in an era when what scholars outside China write about China never makes it back to China, since 2007 I have sought counsel from many senior academics in sociology, at informal gatherings, at round-tables during annual meetings of the American Sociological Association, and whenever it seemed I could find people who had written about sensitive topics in sensitive ways. Ultimately, my search for an answer to my queries never bore satisfactory fruit, perhaps because the activist-scholars I typically met often saw their work as liberating (for others), or because their life experience was working in a free society where they believed no one would be hauled away due to their research findings. Teaching research ethics and methods for years in Hong Kong also did not help me uncover an answer to my most basic questions: Should I write about this stuff, or is doing so too risky for those involved? What is my ethical obligation?

After many years struggling with these questions, I came to the conclusion that I should publish what I can and that I can only do my best to ensure the confidentiality of the people who helped me along the way. Indeed, my main interlocutors have often confirmed they are keen for me to write what I have seen and thought, to tell and frame their stories in ways that will make people think about their practices and actions. My concern remains, however, that we cannot predict how others, especially authorities, will interpret this work, what lessons they will draw from it, and what actions they may or may not take. Nonetheless, in this book (and in other writings), I have taken steps to anonymize speakers where possible, without wholly sacrificing some of the texture that lends richness to the views they have expressed. I have also removed as many details about gatherings, specific incidents, and experiences as I could—hopefully without completely sanitizing the scenes and situations that struck me as deeply revealing and meaningful. Ultimately, I have not made some things explicit in my writing because of my unresolved reservations about publishing, hoping that perhaps in the future I can revisit these more publicly. I leave it to readers to judge whether and where I have succeeded or failed on all these counts.

THE VALUE OF THE SCHOLAR

For future researchers, I end by noting that one part of the scholar's privilege is that we have the time—for it is our job—and money (when we have research funding, at least) to travel between different sites, to talk to a variety of different actors, and to reflect more broadly on how what we see, hear, and experience help draw a bigger picture of what is happening in society. At times, however, both in the interview and writing process, I wondered what more any scholarly analysis I constructed could add to what my interviewees voiced to me. Some of the most powerful analyses in this project came directly from my research subjects. Their depth of self-reflection was at times astounding. In a way, this is not surprising. Many of the people depicted in this book are leaders in a brave new world, forging pathways that their peers may one day follow. Their vision is often powerful, and their stories are compelling. After facing somewhat of an existential dilemma over the value of the sociological researcher, I have reached the conclusion that my role in this project must be less grand than I (or my employer) might wish. I have now to content myself with collecting multiple voices into one space, to putting these stories into a larger sociopolitical context as best I can, and to suggesting a few (hopefully) critical questions and thoughts about their implications for larger social and political change.

NOTES

INTRODUCTION

1. On GONGOs, see Elizabeth Economy, *The River Runs Black: The Environmental Challenge to China's Future* (Ithaca, NY: Cornell University Press, 2004); Kenneth W. Foster, "Associations in the Embrace of an Authoritarian State: State Domination of Society?," *Studies in Comparative International Development* 35, no. 4 (December 1, 2001): 84–109, https://doi.org/10.1007/BF02732709; Tony Saich, "Negotiating the State: The Development of Social Organizations in China," *China Quarterly* 161 (2000): 124–41, https://doi.org/10.1017/S0305741000003969; Jonathan Unger, "Bridges: Private Business, the Chinese Government and the Rise of New Associations," *China Quarterly* 147 (1996): 795–819, https://doi.org/10.1017/S0305741000051808; and Gordon White, Jude Howell, and Xiaoyuan Shang, *In Search of Civil Society: Market Reform and Social Change in Contemporary China* (Oxford: Clarendon Press, 1996). On more independent grassroots groups, see Timothy Hildebrandt, *Social Organizations and the Authoritarian State in China* (Cambridge: Cambridge University Press, 2013); Anthony J. Spires, "Contingent Symbiosis and Civil Society in an Authoritarian State: Understanding the Survival of China's Grassroots NGOs," *American Journal of Sociology* 117, no. 1 (July 1, 2011): 1–45, https://doi.org/10.1086/660741; and Xin Zhang and Richard Baum, "Civil Society and the Anatomy of a Rural NGO," *China Journal* 52 (July 2004): 97–107, https://doi.org/10.2307/4127886.
2. Larry Jay Diamond, *Developing Democracy: Toward Consolidation* (Baltimore: Johns Hopkins University Press, 1999); Pamela Paxton, "Social Capital and Democracy: An Interdependent Relationship," *American Sociological Review* 67, no. 2 (April 1, 2002): 254–77, https://doi.org/10.2307/3088895; and Robert D. Putnam, *Bowling Alone: The Collapse and Revival of American Community* (New York: Simon & Schuster, 2000).
3. Richard Madsen, "The Public Sphere, Civil Society and Moral Community: A Research Agenda for Contemporary China Studies," *Modern China* 19, no. 2 (April 1, 1993): 190, https://doi.org/10.2307/189379.

4. As I argue in chapter 2, however, this is not universally accepted as an inevitable function of civil society.

5. Of course, failure in a classroom is always a possible outcome, as simply showing up for class does not guarantee students learn much of anything.

6. Jun Zi, "Cheng Long jingshi yanlun: Zhongguoren bixu bei guan" (Jackie Chan's Shocking Statement: Chinese People Must Be Controlled), *Kan Zhongguo* (*Vision Times*), April 20, 2009, https://www.secretchina.com/news/b5/2009/04/20/289041.html.

7. Lucian W. Pye, *The Spirit of Chinese Politics: A Psychocultural Study of the Authority Crisis in Political Development* (Cambridge, MA: MIT Press, 1968); and Lucian W. Pye, *Asian Power and Politics: The Cultural Dimensions of Authority* (Cambridge, MA: Belknap Press, 1985).

8. Kathleen M. Blee, *Democracy in the Making: How Activist Groups Form* (Oxford: Oxford University Press, 2012), 139.

9. Stephanie Bräuer, "Becoming Public: Tactical Innovation in the Beijing Anti-Domestic Violence Movement," *Voluntas: International Journal of Voluntary and Nonprofit Organizations* 27, no. 5 (October 1, 2016): 2106–30, https://doi.org/10.1007/s11266-015 -9610-2; Jingyun Dai and Anthony J. Spires, "Advocacy in an Authoritarian State: How Grassroots Environmental NGOs Influence Local Governments in China," *China Journal* 79 (January 2018): 62–83, https://doi.org/10.1086/693440; and Samantha Keech-Marx, "Airing Dirty Laundry in Public: Anti-Domestic Violence Activism in Beijing," in *Associations and the Chinese State: Contested Spaces*, ed. Jonathan Unger (Armonk, NY: M.E. Sharpe, 2008), 175–99.

1. DEMOCRACY IN CHINA: A CENTURY OF DEBATE

1. Hong Kong, for example, was won by the British as a prize after defeating Qing troops in the Opium War that ended in 1843. Later, foreign concessions in coastal cities effectively negated Chinese control of even more territory.

2. Andrew J. Nathan, *Chinese Democracy* (New York: Knopf, 1985), 49.

3. Quoted in Nathan, *Chinese Democracy*, 60.

4. Quoted in Jerome B. Grieder, *Intellectuals and the State in Modern China: A Narrative History* (New York: New York Free Press, 1981), 167.

5. Quoted in Nathan, *Chinese Democracy*, 61.

6. Jue Fang, "A Program for Democratic Reform," *Journal of Democracy* 9, no. 4 (1998): 9–19, https://doi.org/10.1353/jod.1998.0064; and Yu-shih Mao, "Liberalism, Equal Status, and Human Rights," trans. Shi Heping, *Journal of Democracy* 9, no. 4 (1998): 20–23, https://doi.org/10.1353/jod.1998.0071.

7. Qinghua Wang and Gang Guo, "Yu Keping and Chinese Intellectual Discourse on Good Governance," *China Quarterly* 224 (December 2015): 985–1005, https://doi.org /10.1017/S0305741015000855; Keping Yu, "Zhongguo gongmin shehui yanjiu de ruogan wenti" [Several Issues in the Study of Chinese Civil Society], *Journal of the Party School of the Central Committee of the Communist Party of China* 11, no. 6 (2007): 14–22; and Keping Yu, *Democracy Is a Good Thing: Essays on Politics, Society and Culture in Contemporary China* (Washington, DC: Brookings Institution, 2009).

8. Jun Zi, "Cheng Long jingshi yanlun: Zhongguoren bixu bei guan" [Jackie Chan's Shocking Statement: Chinese People Must Be Controlled], *Kan Zhongguo* (*Vision Times*), April 20, 2009, https://www.secretchina.com/news/b5/2009/04/20/289041.html.

9. Suzanne Ogden, *Inklings of Democracy in China in China* (Cambridge, MA: Harvard University Asia Center, 2002), 68.

10. Andrew J. Nathan, "Chinese Democracy: The Lessons of Failure," *Journal of Contemporary China* 2, no. 4 (September 1993): 4, https://doi.org/10.1080/10670569308724182.

11. Thomas P. Bernstein, "Village Democracy and Its Limits," *Asien* 99 (2006): 30.

12. John James Kennedy and Dan Chen, "Election Reform from the Middle and at the Margins," in *Local Governance Innovation in China: Experimentation, Diffusion, and Defiance*, ed. Jessica C. Teets and William Hurst (London: Routledge, 2014), 154–73.

13. Joshua Hill, *Voting as a Rite: A History of Elections in Modern China*, Harvard East Asian Monographs 417 (Cambridge, MA: Harvard University Asia Center, 2019).

14. Bruce J. Dickson, *The Dictator's Dilemma: The Chinese Communist Party's Strategy for Survival* (New York: Oxford University Press, 2016).

15. Although it is possible that exercises in voting could lead to greater questioning of the purpose of elections, only a focused study of voters' experiences could establish whether that is the case, and such a claim is beyond the scope of my current data.

16. Bernstein, "Village Democracy and Its Limits," 29.

17. Linda Chao and Ramon H. Myers, "The First Chinese Democracy: Political Development of the Republic of China on Taiwan, 1986–1994," *Asian Survey* 34, no. 3 (March 1994): 213–30, https://doi.org/10.2307/2644981; and Andrew J. Nathan, *China's Crisis: Dilemmas of Reform and Prospects for Democracy*, Studies of the East Asian Institute (New York: Columbia University Press, 1990).

18. Chao and Myers, "The First Chinese Democracy," 221.

19. Yun-han Chu, "China and East Asian Democracy: The Taiwan Factor," *Journal of Democracy* 23, no. 1 (2012): 55, https://doi.org/10.1353/jod.2012.0011.

20. Nathan, *Chinese Democracy*, 65.

21. Jintao Hu, "Speech by Chinese President Hu Jintao at Yale University," New Haven, CT, April 21, 2006, http://ph.china-embassy.org/eng/xwdt/t259486.htm.

22. For a comprehensive account of the Charter 08 movement, see Jean-Philippe Béja, Hualing Fu, and Eva Pils, *Liu Xiaobo, Charter 08, and the Challenges of Political Reform in China* (Hong Kong: Hong Kong University Press, 2012), http://site.ebrary.com/id/10597160.

23. Samson Yuen, "Friend or Foe? The Diminishing Space of China's Civil Society," *China Perspectives* 3 (2015): 51–56.

24. Thomas Gold, "Tiananmen and Beyond: The Resurgence of Civil Society in China," *Journal of Democracy* 1, no. 1 (1990), 31.

25. Ogden, *Inklings of Democracy in China*, 36.

26. Heath B. Chamberlain, "On the Search for Civil Society in China," *Modern China* 19, no. 2 (April 1, 1993): 199–215, https://doi.org/10.2307/189380; Philip C. C. Huang, "'Public Sphere'/'Civil Society' in China? The Third Realm Between State and Society," *Modern China* 19, no. 2 (April 1, 1993): 216–40, https://doi.org/10.2307/189381; Richard Madsen, "The Public Sphere, Civil Society and Moral Community: A Research Agenda for Contemporary China Studies," *Modern China* 19, no. 2 (April 1, 1993): 183–98; Mary Backus Rankin, "Some Observations on a Chinese Public Sphere," *Modern China* 19, no. 2 (April 1, 1993): 158–82, https://doi.org/10.2307/189378; William T. Rowe, "The Problem of 'Civil Society' in Late Imperial China," *Modern China* 19, no. 2 (April 1, 1993): 139–57, https://doi.org/10.2307/189377; and Frederic Wakeman Jr., "The Civil Society and Public Sphere Debate: Western Reflections on Chinese Political Culture," *Modern China* 19, no. 2 (April 1, 1993): 108–38, https://doi.org/10.2307/189376.

27. Timothy Brook and B. Michael Frolic, *Civil Society in China* (Armonk, NY: M.E. Sharpe, 1997); Elizabeth Economy, *The River Runs Black: The Environmental Challenge to China's Future* (Ithaca, NY: Cornell University Press, 2004); Mary Gallagher, "China: The Limits of Civil Society in a Late Leninist State," in *Civil Society and Political Change in Asia: Expanding and Contracting Democratic Space*, ed. Muthiah Alagappa (Stanford, CA Stanford University Press, 2004), 419–52; Qiusha Ma, "The Governance of NGOs in China Since 1978: How Much Autonomy?," *Nonprofit and Voluntary Sector Quarterly* 31, no. 3 (September 1, 2002): 305–28, https://doi.org/10.1177/0899764002313001; Tony Saich, "Negotiating the State: The Development of Social Organizations in China," *China Quarterly* 161 (2000): 124–41. https://doi.org/10.1017/S0305741000003969; Phillip Stalley and Dongning Yang, "An Emerging Environmental Movement in China?," *China Quarterly* 186 (2006): 333–56, https://doi.org/10.1017/S030574100600018X; Jessica C. Teets, *Civil Society Under Authoritarianism: The China Model* (New York: Cambridge University Press, 2014); Jonathan Unger, "Bridges: Private Business, the Chinese Government and the Rise of New Associations," *China Quarterly* 147 (1996): 795–819. https://doi.org/10.1017/S0305741000051808; Jonathan Unger, ed., *Associations and the Chinese State: Contested Spaces*, Contemporary China Books/Australian National University (Armonk, NY: M.E. Sharpe, 2008); Jonathan Unger and Anita Chan, "China, Corporatism, and the East Asian Model," *Australian Journal of Chinese Affairs*, no. 33 (January 1, 1995): 29–53, https://doi.org/10.2307/2950087; Gordon White, Jude Howell, and Xiaoyuan Shang, *In Search of Civil Society: Market Reform and Social Change in Contemporary China* (Oxford: Clarendon Press, 1996); Fengshi Wu, "New Partners or Old Brothers? GONGOs in Transnational Environmental Advocacy in China," *China Environmental Series*, no. 5 (2002): 45–58; and Naihua Zhang, "Searching for 'Authentic' NGOs: The NGO Discourse and Women's Organizations in China," in *Chinese Women Organizing: Cadres, Feminists, Muslims, Queers*, ed. Ping-Chun Hsiung, Maria Jaschok, and Cecilia Milwert (Oxford: Berg, 2001), 159–79.
28. Alexis de Tocqueville, *Democracy in America* (New York: Harper Perennial, 1988), 287.
29. Jingyun Dai and Anthony J. Spires, "Advocacy in an Authoritarian State: How Grassroots Environmental NGOs Influence Local Governments in China," *China Journal* 79 (January 2018): 62–83. https://doi.org/10.1086/693440; May Farid, "Advocacy in Action: China's Grassroots NGOs as Catalysts for Policy Innovation," *Studies in Comparative International Development* 54, no. 4 (December 2019): 528–49, https://doi.org/10.1007/s12116-019-09292-3; Chloe Froissart, "Using the Law as a 'Harmonious Weapon': The Ambiguities of Legal Activism in Favour of Migrant Workers in China," *Journal of Civil Society* 10, no. 3 (July 3, 2014): 255–72, https://doi.org/10.1080/17448689.2014.941086; Diana Fu, "Fragmented Control: Governing Contentious Labor Organizations in China," *Governance* 30, no. 3 (July 2017): 445–62, https://doi.org/10.1111/gove.12248; Diana Fu, *Mobilizing Without the Masses: Control and Contention in China* (Cambridge: Cambridge University Press, 2017); Diana Fu and Greg Distelhorst, "Grassroots Participation and Repression Under Hu Jintao and Xi Jinping," *China Journal* 70, no. 1 (October 30, 2017): 100–122, https://doi.org/10.1086/694299; Thomas E. Kellogg, "Western Funding for Rule of Law Initiatives in China," *China Perspectives* 2012, no. 3 (September 2012): 53–59; and Weijun Lai et al., "Bounded by the State: Government Priorities and the Development of Private Philanthropic Foundations in China," *China Quarterly* 224 (December 2015): 1083–92, https://doi.org/10.1017/S0305741015000123X.

30. Tianjian Shi, *Political Participation in Beijing* (Cambridge, MA: Harvard University Press, 1997).

31. Shi, *Political Participation in Beijing*, 274.

32. For a comprehensive overview of the concept's use in American political science, see Lucian W. Pye, "Political Culture Revisited," *Political Psychology* 12, no. 3 (September 1991): 487, https://doi.org/10.2307/3791758.

33. Lucian W. Pye, *The Spirit of Chinese Politics*, new ed. (Cambridge, MA: Harvard University Press, 1992).

34. Lucian W. Pye, *Asian Power and Politics: The Cultural Dimensions of Authority* (Cambridge, MA: Belknap Press, 1985).

35. Tianjian Shi, "Cultural Values and Democracy in the People's Republic of China," *China Quarterly* 162 (2000): 540–59, https://doi.org/10.1017/S0305741000008249.

36. Shi, "Cultural Values and Democracy in the People's Republic of China," 557.

37. Shi, *Political Participation in Beijing*, 251.

38. Gabriel A. Almond and Sidney Verba, *The Civic Culture: Political Attitudes and Democracy in Five Nations* (Princeton, NJ: Princeton University Press, 1963).

39. Andrew J. Nathan and Tianjian Shi, "Cultural Requisites for Democracy in China: Findings from a Survey," *Daedalus* 122, no. 2 (1993): 98.

40. Nathan and Shi, "Cultural Requisites for Democracy in China," 116.

41. Nathan and Shi, "Cultural Requisites for Democracy in China," 98.

42. Baogang He, "Democratisation: Antidemocratic and Democratic Elements in the Political Culture of China," *Australian Journal of Political Science* 27, no. 1 (March 1992): 122, https://doi.org/10.1080/00323269208402185.

43. Bin Xu, *The Culture of Democracy: A Sociological Approach to Civil Society*, Cultural Sociology (Medford, MA: Polity, 2022).

44. Madsen, "The Public Sphere, Civil Society and Moral Community"; Craig J. Calhoun, *Neither Gods nor Emperors: Students and the Struggle for Democracy in China*, Asian Studies Sociology (Berkeley: University of California Press, 1997); and Guobin Yang, "Achieving Emotions in Collective Action: Emotional Processes and Movement Mobilization in the 1989 Chinese Student Movement," *Sociological Quarterly* 41, no. 4 (2000): 593–614.

45. Xu, *The Culture of Democracy*, 8.

2. CIVIL SOCIETY UNDER HEGEMONIC AUTHORITARIANISM

1. See, for example, C. R. Henderson, "The Place and Functions of Voluntary Associations," *American Journal of Sociology* 1, no. 3 (1895): 327–34; and Seymour Martin Lipset, "The Social Requisites of Democracy Revisited: 1993 Presidential Address," *American Sociological Review* 59, no. 1 (1994): 1–22, https://doi.org/10.2307/2096130.

2. Roger Boesche, *Tocqueville's Road Map: Methodology, Liberalism, Revolution, and Despotism* (Lanham, MD: Lexington Books, 2008).

3. Alexis de Tocqueville, *Democracy in America*, trans. George Lawrence (New York: Harper Perennial Modern Classics, 1988), 513.

4. Tocqueville, *Democracy in America*, 189.

5. Archon Fung, "Associations and Democracy: Between Theories, Hopes, and Realities," *Annual Review of Sociology* 29 (December 31, 2003): 516, https://doi.org/10.2307/30036978.

6. Michael W. Foley and Bob Edwards, "The Paradox of Civil Society," *Journal of Democracy* 7, no. 3 (1996): 46, https://doi.org/10.1353/jod.1996.0048.

7. Muthiah Alagappa, "Civil Society and Political Change: An Analytical Framework," in *Civil Society and Political Change in Asia: Expanding and Contracting Democratic Space*, ed. Muthiah Alagappa (Stanford, CA: Stanford University Press, 2004), 41.

8. Kareem Elbayar, "NGO Laws in Selected Arab States," *International Journal of Non-Profit Law* 7, no. 4 (2005): 3–27.

9. Melissa Hooper, "Russia's Bad Example" (Washington, DC: Free Russia Foundation /Human Rights First, February 2016), http://www.4freerussia.org/wp-content/uploads /2016/03/Russias-Bad-Example.pdf.

10. Negar Katirai, "NGO Regulations in Iran," *International Journal of Not-for-Profit Law* 7, no. 4 (2005): 28.

11. Janjira Sombatpoonsiri, "'Authoritarian Civil Society': How Anti-Democracy Activism Shapes Thailand's Autocracy," *Journal of Civil Society* 16, no. 4 (2020): 333–50, https://doi.org/10.1080/17448689.2020.1854940.

12. Szu-chien Hsu and Muyi Chou, "Cellularized Civil Society: Public Participation in Community Governance," in *Evolutionary Governance in China: State-Society Relations under Authoritarianism*, ed. Szu-chien Hsu, Kellee S. Tsai, and Chun-chih Chang, Harvard Contemporary China Series (Cambridge, MA: Harvard University Press, 2021), 98–128.

13. Jo Crotty and Sergej Ljubownikow, "Creating Organisational Strength from Operationalising Restrictions: Welfare Non-Profit Organisations in the Russian Federation," *Voluntas: International Journal of Voluntary and Nonprofit Organizations* 31 (September 15, 2020): 1148–58, https://doi.org/10.1007/s11266-020-00271-0.

14. Yun Fan, "Taiwan: No Civil Society, No Democracy," in *Civil Society and Political Change in Asia: Expanding and Contracting Democratic Space*, ed. Muthiah Alagappa (Stanford, CA: Stanford University Press, 2004), 164–90; Yun Fan, "Activists in Political Environment: A Microfoundational Study of Social Movements in Taiwan's Democratic Transition" (PhD diss., Yale University, 2000); and Sunhyuk Kim, "South Korea: Confrontational Legacy and Democratic Contributions," in *Civil Society and Political Change in Asia: Expanding and Contracting Democratic Space*, ed. Muthiah Alagappa (Stanford, CA: Stanford University Press, 2004), 138–63.

15. Edward Aspinall, "Indonesia: Transformation of Civil Society and Democratic Breakthrough," in *Civil Society and Political Change in Asia: Expanding and Contracting Democratic Space*, ed. Muthiah Alagappa (Stanford, CA: Stanford University Press, 2004), 61–96; and Sheri Berman, "Civil Society and the Collapse of the Weimar Republic," *World Politics* 49, no. 3 (April 1, 1997): 401–29.

16. Of course, scholars studying established democracies have also understood civil society and associational life as a rich and complex phenomenon with profound implications for state-society relations. Kenneth T. Andrews et al., "Leadership, Membership, and Voice: Civic Associations That Work," *American Journal of Sociology* 115, no. 4 (January 2010): 1191–242, https://doi.org/10.1086/649060; Robert D. Putnam, *Bowling Alone: The Collapse and Revival of American Community* (New York: Simon & Schuster, 2000); Robert D. Putnam, Robert Leonardi, and Raffaella Y. Nanetti, *Making Democracy Work: Civic Traditions in Modern Italy* (Princeton, NJ: Princeton University Press, 1994); Chris Rhomberg, *No There There: Race, Class, and Political Community in Oakland* (Berkeley: University of California Press, 2007); Sidney Verba, Kay Lehman Schlozman, and Henry E. Brady, *Voice and Equality: Civic Voluntarism*

in American Politics (Cambridge, MA: Harvard University Press, 1995); and Mark E. Warren, *Democracy and Association* (Princeton, NJ: Princeton University Press, 2001).

17. See, for example, Kathleen M. Blee, *Democracy in the Making: How Activist Groups Form* (New York: Oxford University Press, 2012); Nina Eliasoph, *Making Volunteers: Civic Life After Welfare's End* (Princeton, NJ: Princeton University Press, 2011).

18. Pamela Paxton, "Social Capital and Democracy: An Interdependent Relationship," *American Sociological Review* 67, no. 2 (April 1, 2002): 254, https://doi.org/10.2307 /3088895.

19. Larry Jay Diamond, *Developing Democracy: Toward Consolidation* (Baltimore: Johns Hopkins University Press, 1999), 228.

20. Theda Skocpol, "Advocates Without Members: The Recent Transformation of American Civic Life," in *Civic Engagement in American Democracy*, ed. Morris P. Fiorina and Theda Skocpol (Washington, DC: Brookings Institution Press, 1999), 461–509; Joshua Cohen and Joel Rogers, *Associations and Democracy* (London: Verso, 1995); and Putnam, Leonardi, and Nanetti, *Making Democracy Work*.

21. Fung, "Associations and Democracy," 521.

22. Fung, "Associations and Democracy," 519–20.

23. Putnam, *Bowling Alone*.

24. Skocpol, "Advocates Without Members," 500.

25. Alagappa, "Civil Society and Political Change," 46.

26. Nina Eliasoph, *Avoiding Politics: How Americans Produce Apathy in Everyday Life* (Cambridge: Cambridge University Press, 1998), https://doi.org/10.1017/CBO9780511583391; Jason Andrew Kaufman, *For the Common Good? American Civic Life and the Golden Age of Fraternity* (New York: Oxford University Press, 2002); and Nancy L Rosenblum, *Membership and Morals: The Personal Uses of Pluralism in America* (Princeton, NJ: Princeton University Press, 2018); and Skocpol, "Advocates Without Members."

27. Tocqueville, *Democracy in America*, 287.

28. Tocqueville, *Democracy in America*, 308.

29. Tocqueville, *Democracy in America*, 308.

30. Antonio Gramsci, *Selections from the Prison Notebooks of Antonio Gramsci* (repr., London: Lawrence & Wishart, 2005), 261.

31. Gramsci, *Selections from the Prison Notebooks* 244.

32. Stuart Hall, "Introductory Essay: Reading Gramsci," in *Gramsci's Political Thought: An Introduction*, ed. Roger Simon (Electric Book Company, 2005), 9.

33. This is not to discount, of course, the impact of increasing inequality on the state's efforts to manage economic development and the population's perception of the regime's legitimacy.

34. Ernesto Laclau and Chantal Mouffe, "Socialist Strategy: Where Next?," *Marxism Today* 25 (1981): 21.

35. Roger Simon, *Gramsci's Political Thought: An Introduction*, completely rev. (London: Lawrence & Wishart, 1991), 45.

36. Laclau and Mouffe, "Socialist Strategy," 20.

37. Tim Carrigan, Bob Connell, and John Lee, "Toward a New Sociology of Masculinity," *Theory and Society* 14, no. 5 (September 1985): 551–604, https://doi.org/10.1007 /BF00160017; R. W Connell, *Gender and Power: Society, the Person and Sexual Politics* (Sydney: Allen and Unwin, 1987); and R. W. Connell and James W. Messerschmidt, "Hegemonic Masculinity: Rethinking the Concept," *Gender and Society* 19, no. 6 (December 2005): 829–59, https://doi.org/10.1177/0891243205278639.

38. Connell and Messerschmidt, "Hegemonic Masculinity," 832.
39. Connell, *Gender and Power*, 184.
40. Stuart Hall, "Postscript: Gramsci and Us.," in *Gramsci's Political Thought: An Introduction*, ed. Roger Simon (London: Lawrence & Wishart, 2005), 118.
41. Hall, "Introductory Essay," 10.
42. Eli Friedman, *Insurgency Trap: Labor Politics in Postsocialist China* (Ithaca, NY: Cornell University Press, 2014); Jude Howell, "Shall We Dance? Welfarist Incorporation and the Politics of State–Labour NGO Relations," *China Quarterly* 223 (September 2015): 702–23, https://doi.org/10.1017/S0305741015001174; Ke-hsien Huang, "Governing an 'Undesirable' Religion: Shifting Christian Church-State Interactions in Post-Mao China," in *Evolutionary Governance in China: State-Society Relations Under Authoritarianism*, ed. Szu-chien Hsu, Kellee S. Tsai, and Chun-chih Chang, Harvard Contemporary China Series (Cambridge, MA: Harvard University Press, 2021), 362–86; Stein Ringen, *The Perfect Dictatorship: China in the 21st Century* (Hong Kong: Hong Kong University Press, 2016); Wen-Hsuan Tsai and Xingmiu Liao, "Institutional Changes, Influences and Historical Junctures in the Communist Youth League of China," *China Quarterly* 248 (2021): 161–80, https://doi.org/10.1017/S0305741021000813; and Ge Xin and Jie Huang, "Party Building in an Unlikely Place? The Adaptive Presence of the Chinese Communist Party in the Non-Governmental Organizations (NGO)," *Journal of Contemporary China* 31, no. 135 (2022): 428–44, https://doi.org/10.1080/10670564.2021.1966901.
43. Jason Brownlee, "Portents of Pluralism: How Hybrid Regimes Affect Democratic Transitions," *American Journal of Political Science* 53, no. 3 (2009): 515–32; and Seraphine F. Maerz, "Simulating Pluralism: The Language of Democracy in Hegemonic Authoritarianism," *Political Research Exchange* 1, no. 1 (January 1, 2019): 1–23, https://doi.org/10.1080/2474736X.2019.1605834.
44. Theodor W. Adorno et al., *The Authoritarian Personality* (New York: Norton, 1982).
45. For a strong argument for why we should see China as a dictatorship, however, see Ringen, *The Perfect Dictatorship*.
46. Mary Gallagher and Blake Miller, "Who Not What: The Logic of China's Information Control Strategy," *China Quarterly* 248 (2021): 1011–36, https://doi.org/10.1017/S0305741021000345.
47. Timothy Hildebrandt, *Social Organizations and the Authoritarian State in China* (Cambridge: Cambridge University Press, 2013); Anthony J. Spires, "Contingent Symbiosis and Civil Society in an Authoritarian State: Understanding the Survival of China's Grassroots NGOs," *American Journal of Sociology* 117, no. 1 (July 2011): 1–45. https://doi.org/10.1086/660741; and Jessica C. Teets, *Civil Society Under Authoritarianism: The China Model* (New York: Cambridge University Press, 2014).
48. Juan J. Linz, "An Authoritarian Regime: The Case of Spain," in *Mass Politics: Studies in Political Sociology*, ed. Erik Allard and Stein Rokkan (New York: Free Press, 1964), 251–83, 374–81.
49. Robert Alan Dahl, *On Democracy*, Yale Nota Bene Book (New Haven, CT: Yale University Press, 2000); Larry Jay Diamond, *The Spirit of Democracy: The Struggle to Build Free Societies Throughout the World* (New York: Holt Paperback, 2009).
50. Marlies Glasius, "What Authoritarianism Is . . . and Is Not: A Practice Perspective," *International Affairs* 94, no. 3 (May 1, 2018): 517, https://doi.org/10.1093/ia/iiy060.
51. Andrew J. Nathan, "Authoritarian Resilience," *Journal of Democracy* 14, no. 1 (2003): 6–17, https://doi.org/10.1353/jod.2003.0019; and Daniela Stockmann and

Mary E. Gallagher, "Remote Control: How the Media Sustain Authoritarian Rule in China," *Comparative Political Studies* 44, no. 4 (April 1, 2011): 436–67, https://doi.org /10.1177/0010414010394773.

52. Sada Aksartova, "Promoting Civil Society or Diffusing NGOs? U.S. Donors in the Former Soviet Union," in *Globalization, Philanthropy, and Civil Society: Projecting Institutional Logics Abroad*, ed. David C. Hammack and Steven Heydemann (Bloomington: Indiana University Press, 2009), 160–91; and Paxton, "Social Capital and Democracy."

53. Heath B. Chamberlain, "On the Search for Civil Society in China," *Modern China* 19, no. 2 (April 1, 1993): 199–215. https://doi.org/10.2307/189380.

54. Data for 1988 from Ministry of Civil Affairs, *Minjian zuzhi linian tongji shuju (2005)* [Historical Statistical Data on Civil Organizations], accessed October 2, 2005, http:// www.chinanpo.gov.cn/web/showBulltetin.do?id=20151&dictionid=2201; and data for 2021 from Ministry of Civil Affairs, accessed September 11, 2021, http://www.gov.cn /xinwen/2021-02/09/content_5586274.htm.

55. Timothy Hildebrandt, "The Political Economy of Social Organization Registration in China," *China Quarterly* 208 (2011): 970–89, https://doi.org/10.1017/S0305741011001093; Anthony J. Spires, Tao Lin, and Kin-man Chan, "Societal Support for China's Grass-Roots NGOs: Evidence from Yunnan, Guangdong and Beijing," *China Journal* 71 (January 1, 2014): 65–90, https://doi.org/10.1086/674554; and Jessica C. Teets, "Post-Earthquake Relief and Reconstruction Efforts: The Emergence of Civil Society in China?," *China Quarterly* 198 (2009): 330–47, https://doi.org/10.1017/S0305741009000332. A new wave of repression under the current Xi Jinping government, however, has forced more outspoken NGOs to scale back their activities or risk imprisonment; see Samson Yuen, "Friend or Foe? The Diminishing Space of China's Civil Society," *China Perspectives* 3 (2015): 51–56.

56. Timothy Brook and B. Michael Frolic, *Civil Society in China* (Armonk, NY: M.E. Sharpe, 1997); Gladys Pak Lei Chong, "Volunteers as the 'New' Model Citizens: Governing Citizens through Soft Power," *China Information* 25, no. 1 (March 1, 2011): 33–59, https://doi.org/10.1177/0920203X10393212; Jingyun Dai and Anthony J. Spires, "Advocacy in an Authoritarian State: How Grassroots Environmental NGOs Influence Local Governments in China," *China Journal* 79 (January 2018): 62–83. https://doi.org /10.1086/693440; Elizabeth Economy, *The River Runs Black: The Environmental Challenge to China's Future* (Ithaca, NY: Cornell University Press, 2004); Mary Gallagher, "China: The Limits of Civil Society in a Late Leninist State," in *Civil Society and Political Change in Asia: Expanding and Contracting Democratic Space*, ed. Muthiah Alagappa (Stanford, CA: Stanford University Press, 2004), 419–52; Chao Guo and Weijun Lai, "Community Foundations in China: In Search of Identity?," *Voluntas: International Journal of Voluntary and Nonprofit Organizations* 30, no. 4 (August 1, 2019): 647–63, https://doi.org/10.1007/s11266-017-9932-3; Hildebrandt, *Social Organizations and the Authoritarian State*; Weijun Lai and Anthony J. Spires, "Marketization and Its Discontents: Unveiling the Impacts of Foundation-Led Venture Philanthropy on Grassroots NGOs in China," *China Quarterly* 245 (2021): 72–93, https://doi.org /10.1017/S0305741020000193; Spires, "Contingent Symbiosis and Civil Society"; Jonathan Unger, *Associations and the Chinese State: Contested Spaces*. Contemporary China Books/Australian National University (Armonk, NY: M.E. Sharpe, 2008); and Fengshi Wu, "Environmental Activism in Provincial China," *Journal of Environmental Policy and Planning* 15, no. 1 (March 2013): 89–108, https://doi.org/10.1080/15239 08X.2013.763634.

57. See, for example, Kerstin Martens, "Mission Impossible? Defining Nongovernmental Organizations," *Voluntas: International Journal of Voluntary and Nonprofit Organizations* 13, no. 3 (September 1, 2002): 271–85, https://doi.org/10.1023/A:1020341526691.

58. Erica Frantz, *Authoritarianism: What Everyone Needs to Know* (New York: Oxford University Press, 2018), 118.

59. Carolyn Hsu, "Beyond Civil Society: An Organizational Perspective on State–NGO Relations in the People's Republic of China," *Journal of Civil Society* 6, no. 3 (2010): 259–77, https://doi.org/10.1080/17448689.2010.528949; and Fengshi Wu, "New Partners or Old Brothers? GONGOs in Transnational Environmental Advocacy in China," *China Environmental Series*, no. 5 (2002): 45–58.

60. Armine Ishkanian, "Self-Determined Citizens? New Forms of Civic Activism and Citizenship in Armenia," *Europe-Asia Studies* 67, no. 8 (September 14, 2015): 1203–27, https://doi.org/10.1080/09668136.2015.1074981; Natascha Mueller-Hirth, "South African NGOs and the Public Sphere: Between Popular Movements and Partnerships for Development," *Social Dynamics* 35, no. 2 (September 1, 2009): 423–35, https://doi.org/10.1080/02533950903076568; Shelley Feldman, "Paradoxes of Institutionalisation: The Depoliticisation of Bangladeshi NGOs," *Development in Practice* 13, no. 1 (February 1, 2003): 5–26, https://doi.org/10.1080/0961452022000037955; and Islah Jad, "NGOs: Between Buzzwords and Social Movements," *Development in Practice* 17, no. 4–5 (August 1, 2007): 622–29, https://doi.org/10.1080/09614520701469781.

61. Mette Halskov Hansen, "Learning to Organize and to Be Organized: Student Cadres in a Chinese Rural Boarding School," in *Organizing Rural China—Rural China Organizing: Rural China Organizing*, ed. Ane Bislev and Stig Thogersen (Lanham, MD: Lexington Books, 2012), 110.

62. Yan Zhu, "Being Student Leaders or 'Ordinary' Students: Children's Emotional Experiences of Relationships with Others in a Chinese School," *Emotion, Space and Society* 40 (August 1, 2021): 100810, https://doi.org/10.1016/j.emospa.2021.100810.

63. A similar class leader system exists in Taiwan and is akin to the prefect system common in schools in Australia and the United Kingdom. Although these various practices deserve their own careful treatments and comparative analyses, my point is that hierarchical authority systems are experienced from a very young age on an almost daily basis.

64. Mette Halskov Hansen, *Educating the Chinese Individual: Life in a Rural Boarding School* (Seattle: University of Washington Press, 2015), 96.

65. Anthony J. Spires, "Chinese Youth and Alternative Narratives of Volunteering," *China Information* 32, no. 2 (2018): 203–23, https://doi.org/10.1177/0920203X17752597.

66. Kjeld Erik Brødsgaard and Gang Chen, "China's Attempt to Professionalize Its Civil Service," EAI Background Brief (Singapore: East Asian Institute, National University of Singapore, December 16, 2009), https://research.nus.edu.sg/eai/wp-content/uploads/sites/2/2017/11/BB494.pdf.

67. Outi Luova, "Community Volunteers' Associations in Contemporary Tianjin: Multipurpose Partners of the Party-State," *Journal of Contemporary China* 20, no. 72 (November 2011): 773–94, https://doi.org/10.1080/10670564.2011.604500.

68. Deborah Davis, ed., *The Consumer Revolution in Urban China* (Berkeley: University of California Press, 2000); Andrew B. Kipnis, "Introduction: Chinese Modernity and the Individual Psyche," in *Chinese Modernity and the Individual Psyche*, ed. Andrew B. Kipnis (New York: Palgrave Macmillan, 2012), 1–16, https://doi.org/10.1057/9781137268969_1; Kevin J. O'Brien, "Rightful Resistance," *World Politics* 49, no. 1 (October 1, 1996): 31–55,

https://doi.org/10.2307/25053988; Yunxiang Yan, "Introduction: Understanding the Rise of the Individual in China," *European Journal of East Asian Studies* 7, no. 1 (April 1, 2008): 1–9, https://doi.org/10.1163/156805808X333893; Yunxiang Yan, "The Chinese Path to Individualization," *British Journal of Sociology* 61, no. 3 (September 14, 2010): 489–512, https://doi.org/10.1111/j.1468-4446.2010.01323.x; and Li Zhang and Aihwa Ong, eds., *Privatizing China: Socialism from Afar* (Ithaca, NY: Cornell University Press, 2008).

69. Spires, Tao, and Chan, "Societal Support for China's Grass-Roots NGOs"; and Guobin Yang, *The Power of the Internet in China: Citizen Activism Online*, Contemporary Asia in the World (New York: Columbia University Press, 2009).

70. Eva Pils, "The Party's Turn to Public Repression: An Analysis of the '709' Crackdown on Human Rights Lawyers in China," *China Law and Society Review* 3, no. 1 (August 17, 2018): 1–48, https://doi.org/10.1163/25427466-00301001; and Yuen, "Friend or Foe?"

71. Anthony J. Spires, "Regulation as Political Control: China's First Charity Law and Its Implications for Civil Society," *Nonprofit and Voluntary Sector Quarterly* 49, no. 3 (2020): 571–88, https://doi.org/10.1177/0899764019883939; Anthony J. Spires, "Built on Shifting Sands: INGOs and Their Survival in China," in *Authoritarianism and Civil Society in Asia*, ed. Anthony J. Spires and Akihiro Ogawa (New York, NY: Routledge, 2022), 218–34.

72. Mark Sidel, "Managing the Foreign: The Drive to Securitize Foreign Nonprofit and Foundation Management in China," *Voluntas: International Journal of Voluntary and Nonprofit Organizations* 30, no. 4 (August 2019): 664–77, https://doi.org/10.1007/s11266-018-9988-8.

73. Huihui Gong, Haiyan Jiang, and Joe C. B. Leung, "The Changing Relationship Between the Chinese Government and Non-Governmental Organisations in Social Service Delivery: Approaching Partnership?," *Asia Pacific Journal of Social Work and Development* 29, no. 2 (April 3, 2019): 120–32, https://doi.org/10.1080/02185385.2018.1525762; Howell, "Shall We Dance?"; and Fengrui Tian and Julia Chuang, "Depoliticizing China's Grassroots NGOs: State and Civil Society as an Institutional Field of Power," *China Quarterly* 250 (2022): 509–30, https://doi.org/10.1017/S0305741022000157.

74. Samson Yuen, "Negotiating Service Activism in China: The Impact of NGOs' Institutional Embeddedness in the Local State," *Journal of Contemporary China* 27, no. 111 (May 4, 2018): 406–22, https://doi.org/10.1080/10670564.2018.1410976.

75. Michael Gow, "The Core Socialist Values of the Chinese Dream: Towards a Chinese Integral State," *Critical Asian Studies* 49, no. 1 (January 2, 2017): 92–116, https://doi.org/10.1080/14672715.2016.1263803.

76. In the following quotes, I purposely keep my translation as close to the original language as possible rather than opting for more conventional English-language renderings.

77. Katja Levy and Knut Benjamin Pissler, *Charity with Chinese Characteristics: Chinese Charitable Foundations Between the Party-State and Society*, Elgar Studies in Law and Society (Cheltenham: Edward Elgar, 2020); Spires, "Regulation as Political Control"; and Yuen, "Friend or Foe?"

78. Glasius, "What Authoritarianism Is."

79. Joseph Fewsmith, "Balances, Norms and Institutions: Why Elite Politics in the CCP Have Not Institutionalized," *China Quarterly* 248 (2021): 265–82, https://doi.org/10.1017/S0305741021000783.

80. As a regular volunteer in the NGO, my role on this particular occasion was as the interpreter. I had known some members of the group quite well by this time and had

established a degree of trust that I believe encouraged them to be more forthcoming than they may otherwise have been with the typical "outside" visitor. In this instance, however, the small group's *laoda* was clearly interested in presenting a picture of merry cooperation, knowing that the larger organization's top leader would eventually be reading the expert's report.

81. Richard Madsen, *Morality and Power in a Chinese Village* (Berkeley: University of California Press, 1986), 29.

82. Joel Andreas, *Disenfranchised: The Rise and Fall of Industrial Citizenship in China* (New York: Oxford University Press, 2019), 77.

3. STRUGGLING TO COME TOGETHER AS EQUALS

1. Jingrong Wu, ed., *Ying-Han Cidian* [A Chinese-English Dictionary] (Beijing: Shangwu Yishuguan, 1989), 239.

2. *Merriam-Webster's Collegiate Dictionary*, 10th ed. (Springfield, MA: Merriam-Webster, 1997), 233.

3. In this instance, to describe relationships as complicated (*fuza*) is to imply that the people in the relationships disagree with one another to some unspecified extent.

4. I recognize, of course, that communication norms are frequently gendered and that this varies across context and culture. This question, however, deserves focused treatment of its own.

5. Their quandary is akin to what Kathleen M. Blee, *Democracy in the Making: How Activist Groups Form* (New York: Oxford University Press, 2012) found in her study of small activist groups in Philadelphia, where participants' freedom to enter and exit could determine the lifespan of the organizations as well as transform their missions in unexpected ways. See chapter 4 for more on the points system in Chinese universities.

6. Although I would not be able to see or articulate it myself until much later in my fieldwork, the term *lingdao* (leader), typically seen as associated with the hierarchy and inequality of typical student groups, was often studiously avoided by participants in Together and Bridges.

7. Blee, *Democracy in the Making*, 2012.

8. Anthony J. Spires, "Lessons from Abroad: Foreign Influences on China's Emerging Civil Society," *China Journal* 68 (July 2012): 125–46.

9. Anita Chan, *Children of Mao: Personality Development and Political Activism in the Red Guard Generation* (London: Macmillan, 1985).

10. Mark E. Warren, *Democracy and Association* (Princeton, NJ: Princeton University Press, 2001).

4. REJECTING FORMALISM:
ALTERNATIVE NARRATIVES OF VOLUNTEERING

1. China Communist Youth League Beijing Committee, "Beijing gongqingtuan 2013nian gongzuo yaodian," [Beijing Communist Youth League Important Work Points for 2013] March 6, 2013, http://www.bjyouth.gov.cn/zdgz/102285.shtml; and China Communist Youth League Beijing Committee, "Beijing gongqingtuan 2015nian gongzuo yaodian,"

[Beijing Communist Youth League Important Work Points for 2015] September 17, 2015, http://www.bjyouth.gov.cn/zdgz/716787.shtml.

2. Shanghai Municipal Government, "Shanghai shi zhiyuan fuwu tiaoli," [Shanghai City Volunteer Service Regulations] 2009, http://shnu.volunteer.sh.cn/LinkClick .aspx?fileticket=NLen58qwyJY%3D&tabid=12590&language=zh-CN.

3. Weihua Liao, "Xizang chutai zhiyuan fuwu tiaoli zhaolu gongwuyuan youxian luyong zhiyuanzhe" [Tibet Releases Volunteer Service Regulations: Volunteers Get Priority for Civil Servant Jobs], *Fazhi Ribao* [*Legal Daily*], January 24, 2015, http://epaper .legaldaily.com.cn/fzrb/content/20150124/Article03006GN.htm.

4. Although the government reported that more than one million people had initially signed up, in the end, Beijing's Olympics Committee took only about seventy-four thousand volunteers from China along with a smattering of others from other countries. See Zhen Lai, "2008 nian Beijing aoyunhui zhiyuanzhe renshu bi jihua zengjia jin 5000" [The Number of Volunteers for the 2008 Beijing Olympics Exceeded Plans by Almost 5000 People], July 16, 2008, http://www.gov.cn/jrzg/2008-07/16 /content_1047053.htm.

5. Bin Xu, "Consensus Crisis and Civil Society: The Sichuan Earthquake Response and State–Society Relations," *China Journal* 71 (January 2014): 91–108, https://doi.org /10.1086/674555.

6. Yongling Zhang and Jing Lin, "Volunteerism in China (I): National Policies, Student Responses, and Two Case Studies of Self-Organized Volunteer Programs: Guest Editors' Introduction to Part I," *Chinese Education and Society* 41, no. 3 (May 1, 2008): 3–13, https://doi.org/10.2753/CED1061-1932410300.

7. Nina Eliasoph, *Making Volunteers: Civic Life After Welfare's End* (Princeton, NJ: Princeton University Press, 2011), 12.

8. Eliasoph, *Making Volunteers*, 233.

9. Eliasoph, *Making Volunteers*, 233.

10. See, for example, Jessica C. Teets, "Post-Earthquake Relief and Reconstruction Efforts: The Emergence of Civil Society in China?," *China Quarterly* 198 (2009): 330–47. https://doi.org/10.1017/S0305741009000332.

11. Outi Luova, "Community Volunteers' Associations in Contemporary Tianjin: Multipurpose Partners of the Party-State," *Journal of Contemporary China* 20, no. 72 (November 2011): 773–94, https://doi.org/10.1080/10670564.2011.604500.

12. For an overview of regulations on domestic NGOs before passage of the 2016 Charity Law, see Anthony J. Spires, "Contingent Symbiosis and Civil Society in an Authoritarian State: Understanding the Survival of China's Grassroots NGOs," *American Journal of Sociology* 117, no. 1 (July 2011): 1–45.

13. Central Committee of the China Communist Youth League, "Zhongguo zhuce zhiyuanzhe guanli banfa," [Management Methods for the Registration of Chinese Volunteers] 2006, http://www.ccyl.org.cn/notice/200612/t20061224_12206.htm.

14. Guangdong People's Congress, "Guangdongsheng zhiyuan fuwu tiaoli" [Guangdong Province Volunteer Service Regulations]," 2010, http://www.gdzyz.cn/zcfg/zcfglist!zcfgShow .do?districtId=b0dc9771d14211e18718000aebf5352e&headType=shouye&pageNo=17.

15. Zhejiang Province People's Congress, "Zhejiang sheng zhiyuan fuwu tiaoli," [Zhejiang Province Volunteer Service Regulations] 2008, http://hszh.tx.gov.cn/web /zcfg/20150108/093550.html.

16. Quoted in Ying Xu, "Chinese Communist Youth League, Political Capital and the Legitimising of Volunteering in China," *International Journal of Adolescence and Youth* 17, no. 2–3 (June 2012): 98, https://doi.org/10.1080/02673843.2012.656195.

17. Anonymous, "Qingnian zhiyuanzhe xingdong 20 nian zhuce zhiyuanzhe chao 4000 wan" [20 Years of the Youth Volunteer Movement: Registered Volunteers Exceed 40 Million], *Renmin Ribao [People's Daily]*, December 3, 2013.

18. Weitao Liu, "Zaizhi 2014 niandi quanguo gong you gonqingtuan 8821.9 wan ming," [At the End of 2014 the Nation Had a Total of 88,219,000 Communist Youth League Members] *People's Daily [Renmin Ribao]*, May 4, 2015, http://paper.people.com.cn /rmrb/html/2015-05/04/nw.D110000renmrb_20150504_5-04.htm.

19. Xu, "Chinese Communist Youth League," 97.

20. Central Committee of the China Communist Youth League, "Zhongguo qingnian zhiyuanzhe xingdong fazhan guihua (2014–2018)," [China Youth Volunteer Action Development Plan 2014-2018] December 2, 2013, http://news.youth.cn/gn/201312 /t20131202_4315922.htm.

21. Anthony J. Spires, "Regulation as Political Control: China's First Charity Law and Its Implications for Civil Society," *Nonprofit and Voluntary Sector Quarterly* 49, no. 3 (2020): 571–88, https://doi.org/10.1177/0899764019883939.

22. Outi Luova, "Divergent Trajectories Among Chinese Community Volunteer Associations and Urban Governance: Comparing Four Districts in Tianjin," *Journal of Comparative Asian Development* 12, no. 3 (December 2013): 775, https://doi.org/10.1080 /15339114.2013.863563.

23. Gladys Pak Lei Chong, "Volunteers as the 'New' Model Citizens: Governing Citizens Through Soft Power," *China Information* 25, no. 1 (March 1, 2011): 34–35, https://doi.org /10.1177/0920203X10393212.

24. One exception to this is Xu, "Chinese Communist Youth League," 107, whose discussion of the CYL does note some critical voices and that "the CYL had been bureaucratic and lacked communication channels between the CYL and the volunteers."

25. Friederike Fleischer, "Technology of Self, Technology of Power: Volunteering as Encounter in Guangzhou, China," *Ethnos* 76, no. 3 (September 2011): 300–325, https:// doi.org/10.1080/00141844.2011.565126.

26. Unn Målfrid H. Rolandsen, "A Collective of Their Own: Young Volunteers at the Fringes of the Party Realm," *European Journal of East Asian Studies* 7, no. 1 (March 2008): 103, https://doi.org/10.1163/156805808X333938.

27. Yunxiang Yan, "The Good Samaritan's New Trouble: A Study of the Changing Moral Landscape in Contemporary China," *Social Anthropology* 17, no. 1 (February 18, 2009): 9–24, https://doi.org/10.1111/j.1469-8676.2008.00055.x.

28. Rundong Ning and David A. Palmer, "Ethics of the Heart: Moral Breakdown and the Aporia of Chinese Volunteers," *Current Anthropology* 61, no. 4 (August 1, 2020): 396, https://doi.org/10.1086/710217.

29. The desire for "meaningful" social engagement as a motivation for volunteering is a phenomenon also noted by Fleischer, "Technology of Self, Technology of Power." My interest, however, is in highlighting the ways in which volunteers use the concept of "meaningfulness" to draw contrasts with government-directed volunteering.

30. Indeed, this volunteer perceived what scholars saw in the 2008 Beijing Olympics, a media spectacle orchestrated by the government to create a positive image of China. See Chong, "Volunteers as the 'New' Model Citizens."

31. Qiang Xiao, "Wang Qishan jiaoting jilin shuji: zhe bushi xingshi ma?," [Wang Qishan Tells the Jilin Provincial Party Secretary to Stop: Isn't this Formalism?] *China Digital Times*, March 11, 2014, http://chinadigitaltimes.net/chinese/2014/03.

32. Thomas B. Gold, "Youth and the State," *China Quarterly* 127 (September 1, 1991): 601, https://doi.org/10.2307/654678.

33. Junqian Xu, "Volunteering Not Voluntary," *China Daily*, December 1, 2011, http://www
.chinadaily.com.cn/2011-12/01/content_14192894.htm.

34. E. Gil Clary et al., "Understanding and Assessing the Motivations of Volunteers: A
Functional Approach," *Journal of Personality and Social Psychology* 74, no. 6 (1998):
1516–30; and Lesley Hustinx and Frans Lammertyn, "Collective and Reflexive Styles
of Volunteering: A Sociological Modernization Perspective," *Voluntas: International
Journal of Voluntary and Nonprofit Organizations* 14, no. 2 (June 2003): 167–87.

35. Paul Dekker and Andries Van den Broek, "Civil Society in Comparative Perspective: Involvement in Voluntary Associations in North America and Western Europe,"
Voluntas: International Journal of Voluntary and Nonprofit Organizations 9, no. 1
(1998): 11–38.

36. Eliasoph, *Making Volunteers.*

37. Jessica C. Teets et al., "Volunteerism and Democratic Learning in an Authoritarian
State: The Case of China," *Democratization* 29, no. 5 (July 4, 2022): 879–98, https://
doi.org/10.1080/13510347.2021.2015334.

38. Akihiro Ogawa, "Invited by the State: Institutionalizing Volunteer Subjectivity in
Contemporary Japan," *Asian Anthropology* 3 (2004): 71–96.

39. Ogawa, "Invited by the State," 86–87.

40. Ogawa, "Invited by the State," 90.

41. "Outline of the People's Republic of China 14th Five-Year Plan for National Economic
and Social Development and Long-Range Objectives for 2035" (Center for Security and Emerging Technology, 2021), 124, https://cset.georgetown.edu/wp-content
/uploads/t0284_14th_Five_Year_Plan_EN.pdf.

42. Jinping Xi, "Speech at the Beijing 2022 Winter Olympics and Paralympics Review and
Awards Ceremony," April 8, 2022, http://jm.china-embassy.gov.cn/eng/zgxw/202204
/t20220411_10666791.htm.

43. Anonymous, "Xuexiao fa tongzhi yaoqiu gaozhongsheng 100% zhuce wei zhiyuanzhe
zao tucao" [School Issues Notice Requiring 100 percent of High School Students to
Register as Volunteers, Meets with Anger], *Zhongguo Jingjiwang* [*China Economic Net*],
April 9, 2014, http://big5.ce.cn/gate/big5/edu.ce.cn/xw/201404/09/t20140409_1533986.
shtml. Ogawa, "Invited by the State," also recorded similarly critical responses in Japanese media to government efforts to incentivize student volunteering.

5. EQUALITY AS CULTURE AND PRACTICE

1. For the now-classic pre-Communist exploration of the nature of power and (in)equal-
ity in China, see Fei Xiaotong, "From the Soil: The Foundations of Chinese Society"
(1947), in Xiaotong Fei, *From the Soil, the Foundations of Chinese Society: A Translation of Fei Xiaotong's Xiangtu Zhongguo, with an Introduction and Epilogue,* trans. Gary
G. Hamilton and Zheng Wang (Berkeley: University of California Press, 1992). There
is also a voluminous literature from more recent years on how the move to a more
market-based economy has rewritten the rules for social mobility and power in China,
with debates often focusing on the economic returns to Communist Party membership, personal connections, and prereform employment status. See, for example, Joel
Andreas, *Rise of the Red Engineers: The Cultural Revolution and the Origins of China's
New Class,* Contemporary Issues in Asia and the Pacific (Stanford, CA: Stanford University Press, 2009); Yanjie Bian, "Guanxi and the Allocation of Urban Jobs in China,"
China Quarterly 140 (1994): 971–99, https://doi.org/10.1017/S0305741000052863;

Xiaowei Zang and Nabo Chen, "How Do Rural Elites Reproduce Privileges in Post-1978 China? Local Corporatism, Informal Bargaining and Opportunistic Parasitism," *Journal of Contemporary China* 24, no. 94 (July 4, 2015): 628–43, https://doi.org/10.1080/10670564.2014.975956; and Victor Nee, "The Emergence of a Market Society: Changing Mechanisms of Stratification in China," *American Journal of Sociology* 101, no. 4 (January 1996): 908–49, https://doi.org/10.1086/230784.

2. Fei, *From the Soil*.
3. Suzanne Ogden, *Inklings of Democracy in China* (Cambridge, MA: Harvard University Asia Center, 2002), 32.
4. See Fei, *From the Soil*, 108–19.
5. Under communist rule, in both rural and urban China, scholars have in recent years identified a number of processes and institutionalized mechanisms in which notions of equality, voice, and rights to participate in collective decision-making processes are apparent. Although my focus in this chapter is on ideas and ideals of equality, these related phenomena of participatory governance and institutionalized political participation are explored more fully in works such as Diana Fu and Greg Distelhorst, "Grassroots Participation and Repression Under Hu Jintao and Xi Jinping," *China Journal* 70, no. 1 (October 30, 2017), 100–122, https://doi.org/10.1086/694299; and Jonathan Unger, Anita Chan, and Him Chung, "Deliberative Democracy at China's Grassroots: Case Studies of a Hidden Phenomenon," *Politics and Society* 42, no. 4 (2014): 513–35, https://doi.org/10.1177/0032329214547344.
6. Ogden, *Inklings of Democracy in China*, 31–32.
7. Michael Gow, "The Core Socialist Values of the Chinese Dream: Towards a Chinese Integral State," *Critical Asian Studies* 49, no. 1 (2017): 92–116. https://doi.org/10.1080/14672715.2016.1263803.
8. I have no reason to suspect this volunteer had ever read George Orwell's *Animal Farm*, but I wondered if that teacher had.

6. HANDLING DIFFERENCES OF OPINION
AND BUILDING CONSENSUS

1. When offering longer quotes in this and subsequent chapters, I frequently note the speaker's gender presentation, undergraduate major, or their parents' occupations to show the diversity of volunteers' backgrounds. I observed no clear patterns in the class backgrounds or majors from which volunteers in Bridges or Together were drawn. No clear gender distinctions were apparent, either. However, a survey of participants—beyond the scope of what I could do in this study—may show otherwise. Notably, a large number of the volunteers I was invited to interview were from working-class backgrounds and from second- or third-tier cities, but without more representative data, I cannot attest to whether this means that *most* of the volunteers in Bridges and Together shared these characteristics.
2. Baogang He and Mark E. Warren, "Authoritarian Deliberation: The Deliberative Turn in Chinese Political Development," *Perspectives on Politics* 9, no. 2 (June 2011): 269–89, https://doi.org/10.1017/S1537592711000892; Ethan J. Leib and Baogang He, eds., *The Search for Deliberative Democracy in China* (Basingstoke: Palgrave Macmillan, 2006); and Elizabeth J. Perry, "The Populist Dream of Chinese Democracy," *Journal of Asian Studies* 74, no. 4 (November 2015): 903–15, https://doi.org/10.1017/S002191181500114X.

7. NURTURING DEMOCRATIC SKILLS AND VALUES

1. Damon Timothy Alexander et al., "Civic Engagement and Associationalism: The Impact of Group Membership Scope Versus Intensity of Participation," *European Sociological Review* 28, no. 1 (February 1, 2012): 43–58, https://doi.org/10.1093/esr/jcq047; Robert D. Putnam, *Bowling Alone: The Collapse and Revival of American Community* (New York: Simon & Schuster, 2000); Robert D. Putnam, Robert Leonardi, and Raffaella Y. Nanetti, *Making Democracy Work: Civic Traditions in Modern Italy* (Princeton, NJ: Princeton University Press, 1994); Alexis de Tocqueville, *Democracy in America*, trans. George Lawrence (New York: Harper Perennial Modern Classics, 1988); and Lars Torpe, "Democracy and Associations in Denmark: Changing Relationships between Individuals and Associations?," *Nonprofit and Voluntary Sector Quarterly* 32, no. 3 (September 2003): 329–43, https://doi.org/10.1177/0899764003254594.
2. Archon Fung, "Associations and Democracy: Between Theories, Hopes, and Realities," *Annual Review of Sociology* 29 (December 31, 2003): 515–39. https://doi.org/10.2307/30036978.
3. Alexander et al., "Civic Engagement and Associationalism," 48. Sidney Verba, Kay Lehman Schlozman, and Henry E. Brady, *Voice and Equality: Civic Voluntarism in American Politics* (Cambridge, MA: Harvard University Press, 1995) also include some similar forms of "contact" in their study of political participation in the United States.
4. Jingyun Dai and Anthony J. Spires, "Advocacy in an Authoritarian State: How Grassroots Environmental NGOs Influence Local Governments in China," *China Journal* 79 (January 2018): 62–83, https://doi.org/10.1086/693440.
5. As an example, the government solicited comments in 2016 on the pending Charity Law and INGO Law, a process that did seem to affect the language adopted in their final versions.
6. Charles Pattie, Patrick Seyd, and Paul Whiteley, "Citizenship and Civic Engagement: Attitudes and Behaviour in Britain," *Political Studies* 51, no. 3 (October 2003): 443–68, https://doi.org/10.1111/1467-9248.00435; see also Verba, Schlozman, and Brady, *Voice and Equality*, for "contact" as a form of political participation in the United States.
7. Examples of using state rhetoric in the service of Chinese NGOs' goals can be found in the realm of the environment, see Dai and Spires, "Advocacy in an Authoritarian State"; women's rights, see Keech-Marx, "Airing Dirty Laundry in Public: Anti-Domestic Violence Activism in Beijing," in *Associations and the Chinese State: Contested Spaces*, ed. Jonathan Unger (Armonk, NY: M.E. Sharpe, 2008), 175–99; and other areas where quiet activism has proven effective.
8. In keeping with the emphasis on close personal relationships, volunteers often call elderly villagers using kinship terms.
9. In their survey of U.S. political participation, Verba, Schlozman, and Brady, *Voice and Equality*, also found high levels of "social gratification" and "civic gratification" among those who were politically active.
10. Mayfair Mei-hui Yang, *Gifts, Favors, and Banquets: The Art of Social Relationships in China*, The Wilder House Series in Politics, History and Culture (Ithaca, NY: Cornell University Press, 1994); and Mayfair Mei-hui Yang, "The Resilience of Guanxi and Its New Deployments: A Critique of Some New Guanxi Scholarship," *China Quarterly* 170 (2002): 459–76, https://doi.org/10.1017/S000944390200027X.
11. Marc Morjé Howard and Leah Gilbert, "A Cross-National Comparison of the Internal Effects of Participation in Voluntary Organizations," *Political Studies* 56, no. 1

(March 2008): 12–32, https://doi.org/10.1111/j.1467-9248.2007.00715.x; Matthew A. Painter and Pamela Paxton, "Checkbooks in the Heartland: Change Over Time in Voluntary Association Membership," *Sociological Forum* 29, no. 2 (June 2014): 408–28, https://doi.org/10.1111/socf.12090; Putnam, Leonardi, and Nanetti, *Making Democracy Work*; and Theda Skocpol, "Advocates Without Members: The Recent Transformation of American Civic Life," in *Civic Engagement in American Democracy*, ed. Morris P. Fiorina and Skocpol (Washington, DC: Brookings Institution Press, 1999), 461–509.

12. Timothy Hildebrandt, *Social Organizations and the Authoritarian State in China* (Cambridge: Cambridge University Press, 2013); and Anthony J. Spires, "Contingent Symbiosis and Civil Society in an Authoritarian State: Understanding the Survival of China's Grassroots NGOs," *American Journal of Sociology* 117, no. 1 (July 2011): 1–45.

13. Active listening (*lingting*) should also be distinguished from the "do-as-you're-told" listening (*ting hua*) that parents often seek to impose when admonishing naughty children and the "following orders" listening (*tingcong*) of hierarchical, superior-subordinate relationships in the military or workplace. One common definition of *lingting* on Wikipedia-like Baidu argues that it implies a hierarchical relationship; see "Lingting shi shenme yisi" [What Does Lingting Mean?]," Baidu, accessed May 28, 2024, https://zhidao.baidu.com/question/332087490110675485.html. Given the antihierarchy value commitments of Together and Bridges volunteers, however, this definition would seem to be out of touch with their experience. Or it may simply be the tyranny of language that constrains them to using the words available to them, even if those words do not faithfully represent their intended implications.

14. Developing and deepening our understanding of deliberative democracy, the political theorist Mary Scudder (2023) has explicated the importance of listening for democratic decision-making more broadly. As she notes, "in order for the substantive rejection (or acceptance) of a deliberative input to be democratically valid, it must come after that input was fairly considered. And for that . . . listening is essential." See Mary F. Scudder, *Beyond Empathy and Inclusion: The Challenge of Listening in Democratic Deliberation* (New York: Oxford University Press, 2023), 6. In language that closely approximates the implications of "active listening" (*lingting*) as described here, Scudder further argues that "simple listening becomes *listening toward democracy* when we listen for the purpose of considering what others have to say" (Scudder, *Beyond Empathy and Inclusion*, 16). She, however, links it to democracy in ways that participants in Together and Bridges, for example, were not necessarily always considering.

15. His earlier assumption—"if you want others to grow together with you"—is a reflection of how both Bridges and Together encourage participants to invest in others' personal growth, while also acknowledging that as organizations, the personal growth of volunteers has become a core part of their "contribution" to Chinese society.

16. I have intentionally translated *gongyi* here not as "public welfare" or "public benefit" but as "charity," mainly because the practices she was criticizing better fit the hierarchical norms implied by recent critical discourses on Euro-American understandings of "charity." For a more nuanced discussion of various meanings of *gongyi* in China, see Fengshi Wu, "An Emerging Group Name 'Gongyi': Ideational Collectivity in China's Civil Society," *China Review* 17, no. 2 (June 2017): 123–50.

17. See, for example, Gladys Pak Lei Chong, "Volunteers as the 'New' Model Citizens: Governing Citizens Through Soft Power," *China Information* 25, no. 1 (March 1, 2011): 33–59, https://doi.org/10.1177/0920203X10393212; and Rya Butterfield, "Rhetorical

Forms of Symbolic Labor: The Evolution of Iconic Representations in China's Model Worker Awards," *Rhetoric and Public Affairs* 15, no. 1 (2012): 95–125.

18. Tocqueville, *Democracy in America*, 506.

19. Tocqueville, *Democracy in America*, 515.

20. Howard and Gilbert, "A Cross-National Comparison."

21. Yunxiang Yan, "Introduction: Understanding the Rise of the Individual in China," *European Journal of East Asian Studies* 7, no. 1 (April 1, 2008): 1–9. https://doi.org /10.1163/156805808X333893; and Yunxiang Yan, "The Good Samaritan's New Trouble: A Study of the Changing Moral Landscape in Contemporary China," *Social Anthropology* 17, no. 1 (February 18, 2009): 9–24. https://doi.org/10.1111/j.1469-8676.2008.00055.x.

22. Bill Birtles, "Fan Bingbing: Missing Chinese Actress Not 'Socially Responsible,' Report Says," *ABC News*, September 12, 2018, http://www.abc.net.au/news/2018-09-12 /report-says-chinese-star-fan-bingbing-not-socially-responsible/10234304.

23. Dietlind Stolle, "Bowling Together, Bowling Alone: The Development of Generalized Trust in Voluntary Associations," *Political Psychology* 19, no. 3 (1998): 215.

24. As in some other situations, the laughter with which this volunteer concluded his own self-assessment indicated a bit of embarrassment at what he saw as his earlier moral failing, but it also served to emphasize the change he saw in himself since joining the group.

25. *Autobiography of Benjamin Franklin*, ed. Charles W. Eliot (New York: Collier and Son, 1909), available at https://www.gutenberg.org/cache/epub/148/pg148.html Accessed May 28, 2024.

26. Yumei Gan, Christian Greiffenhagen, and Christian Licoppe, "Orchestrated Openings in Video Calls: Getting Young Left-Behind Children to Greet Their Migrant Parents," *Journal of Pragmatics* 170 (December 2020): 364–80, https://doi.org/10.1016/j.pragma .2020.09.022.

27. Lamei Wang and Judi Mesman, "Child Development in the Face of Rural-to-Urban Migration in China: A Meta-Analytic Review," *Perspectives on Psychological Science* 10, no. 6 (November 2015): 813–31, https://doi.org/10.1177/1745691615600145; and Jing-zhong Ye and Lu Pan, "Differentiated Childhoods: Impacts of Rural Labor Migration on Left-Behind Children in China," *Journal of Peasant Studies* 38, no. 2 (March 2011): 355–77, https://doi.org/10.1080/03066150.2011.559012.

28. As was sometimes the case in other one-on-one interviews, the laughter documented here—"Ha ha"—reflected not humor but rather the speaker's sense of vulnerability or awkwardness at discussing something embarrassing, sensitive, or uncomfortable.

29. Albert Bandura, "Perceived Self-Efficacy in Cognitive Development and Functioning," *Educational Psychologist* 28, no. 2 (1993): 144–45.

30. Verba, Schlozman, and Brady, *Voice and Equality*, 305.

31. Jane J. Mansbridge, *Beyond Adversary Democracy* (Chicago: University of Chicago Press, 1980).

32. Mansbridge, *Beyond Adversary Democracy*, 200.

33. Mansbridge, *Beyond Adversary Democracy*, 109.

34. Mansbridge, *Beyond Adversary Democracy*, 201.

35. Mansbridge, *Beyond Adversary Democracy*, 200–201.

36. The total enrolment of undergraduate students in China rose almost 27 percent annually from 1998 to 2004 alone; see Yinmei Wan, "Expansion of Chinese Higher Education Since 1998: Its Causes and Outcomes," *Asia Pacific Education Review* 7, no. 1 (2006): 19.

37. Nina Eliasoph, *Making Volunteers: Civic Life After Welfare's End* (Princeton, NJ: Princeton University Press, 2011).

8. (S)ELECTING NEW LEADERS

1. Larry Jay Diamond and Marc F. Plattner, "Introduction," in *Electoral Systems and Democracy*, ed. Larry Jay Diamond and Marc F. Plattner, A Journal of Democracy Book (Baltimore: Johns Hopkins University Press, 2006), ix–xxvi.

2. Anthony J. Spires, Tao Lin, and Kin-man Chan, "Societal Support for China's Grass-Roots NGOs: Evidence from Yunnan, Guangdong and Beijing," *China Journal* 71 (January 1, 2014): 65–90, https://doi.org/10.1086/674554.

3. In some Chinese NGOs, however, this question of leadership succession has already become a concern.

4. In the United States and other countries, of course, formal leaders of voluntary organizations are often elected positions with fixed terms. Although fulfilling one's elected term may generally be seen as a moral obligation, sudden departures do occur and generally leavers are only socially sanctioned, with no legal action expected.

5. Joel Andreas, *Disenfranchised: The Rise and Fall of Industrial Citizenship in China* (New York: Oxford University Press, 2019), 77.

6. Daniel Kelliher, "Keeping Democracy Safe from the Masses: Intellectuals and Elitism in the Chinese Protest Movement," *Comparative Politics* 25, no. 4 (July 1993): 379–96, https://doi.org/10.2307/422032.

7. See for more on *suzhi*—and its contestation in contemporary China—see Andrew Kipnis, "Suzhi: A Keyword Approach," *China Quarterly* 186 (June 2006): 295–313, https://doi.org/10.1017/S0305741006000166; and Delia Lin, *Civilising Citizens in Post-Mao China: Understanding the Rhetoric of Suzhi*, Routledge Contemporary China Series 169 (New York: Routledge, 2017). Note that for this speaker, the inability to hold democratic elections was an indication of low quality in other volunteer groups.

8. Although "so-called" (*suo wei de*) is sometimes used in Chinese and in English to imply skepticism about a certain term or appellation, here I believe the speaker's intention is to use it to introduce what to him (and many others) was a relatively new concept and to signal that he was going to use an important term that may require some explication.

9. Although I heard almost no one in the group refer to Dr. Chen as their *laoda*, this was, I came to see, because of the respectful way that he treated the NGO's staff. In turn, many respected or even revered him, seeing him as both a patient teacher and kind fatherly figure.

10. I was told the same, in virtually these exact terms, in interviews with Greenthumb staff conducted immediately after the election.

11. An alternative translation here might be "forced democracy."

12. Linus Hagström and Astrid H. M. Nordin, "China's 'Politics of Harmony' and the Quest for Soft Power in International Politics," *International Studies Review* 22, no. 3 (September 1, 2020): 507–25, https://doi.org/10.1093/isr/viz023; and James Leibold, "Blogging Alone: China, the Internet, and the Democratic Illusion?," *Journal of Asian Studies* 70, no. 4 (2011): 1023–41, https://doi.org/10.1017/S0021911811001550.

13. On the foreign influences inspiring training programs for Chinese NGOs, see Anthony J. Spires, "Lessons from Abroad: Foreign Influences on China's Emerging Civil Society," *China Journal* 68 (July 2012): 125–46; and Cecilia Milwertz and Fengxian Wang, "Masculine Modernity Trumps Feminine Tradition: A Gendered Capacity-Building Operation in China," *Gender, Technology and Development* 17, no. 3 (November 1, 2013): 259–80, https://doi.org/10.1177/0971852413498731.

9. SELECTING NEWCOMERS AND SCREENING FOR COMMON VALUES

1. For China, however, in the absence of a large-scale and rigorous survey, even such basic data can be elusive.
2. Anthony J. Spires, Tao Lin, and Kin-man Chan, "Societal Support for China's Grass-Roots NGOs: Evidence from Yunnan, Guangdong and Beijing," *China Journal* 71 (January 1, 2014): 65–90, https://doi.org/10.1086/674554.
3. Kathleen M. Blee, *Democracy in the Making: How Activist Groups Form* (New York: Oxford University Press, 2012), 2012.
4. The striking eagerness and ability of so many of these young people to engage in critical self-reflection was revealed in many of these conversations. More than a few people anticipated my questions as they thought and talked through these problems with me.
5. These sorts of small-group decision-making exercises are decidedly imports to China. I participated in similar exercises as a jobseeker in the United States in 1998. Much later, in 2010, I found myself on the other side of the desk, observing students in Guangdong as part of a panel of judges helping to select study-abroad candidates funded by a foreign foundation. Perhaps unsurprisingly, given the unusual qualities of Bridges and Together volunteers, not a few of the students in the running for these study opportunities were also Bridges or Together volunteers. Although I found no one who could say for sure where Bridges' "leaderless small-group" process had originated, I know at least two people who reported back to their fellow Bridges and Together volunteers on their experience of interviewing for this fellowship.
6. Virtually all of my Bridges and Together interviewees were Communist Youth League members, having been "automatically" signed up by their teachers during junior high if not even earlier in elementary school.

CONCLUSION

1. Aaron Einfeld and Denise Collins, "The Relationships Between Service-Learning, Social Justice, Multicultural Competence, and Civic Engagement," *Journal of College Student Development* 49, no. 2 (2008): 95–109, https://doi.org/10.1353/csd.2008.0017.
2. David H. Smith et al., "Conducive Motivations and Psychological Influences on Volunteering," in *The Palgrave Handbook of Volunteering, Civic Participation, and Nonprofit Associations*, ed. David Horton Smith et al. (London: Palgrave Macmillan, 2016), 702–51, https://doi.org/10.1007/978-1-137-26317-9_31.
3. Roger Boesche, *Tocqueville's Road Map: Methodology, Liberalism, Revolution, and Despotism* (Lanham, MD: Lexington, 2008), 89.
4. Benshun Zhou, "Zou zhongguo tese shehui guanli chuangxin zhi lu," [Taking the Road of Social Management Innovation with Chinese Characteristics] *Qiushi* 10 (2011), http://www.qstheory.cn/zxdk/2011/2011010/201105/t20110513_80501.htm.
5. See, for example, Giuseppe Di Palma, *To Craft Democracies: An Essay on Democratic Transitions* (Berkeley: University of California Press, 1990).
6. Lucian W. Pye, *The Spirit of Chinese Politics: A Psychocultural Study of the Authority Crisis in Political Development*, New ed. (Cambridge, MA: Harvard University Press, 1992).

7. Juan J. Linz and Alfred C. Stepan, *Problems of Democratic Transition and Consolidation: Southern Europe, South America, and Post-Communist Europe* (Baltimore: Johns Hopkins University Press, 1996).
8. Paul J. DiMaggio and Walter W. Powell, "The Iron Cage Revisited: Institutional Isomorphism and Collective Rationality in Organizational Fields," *American Sociological Review* 48, no. 2 (April 1983): 147, https://doi.org/10.2307/2095101; and Robert Michels, *Political Parties: A Sociological Study of the Oligarchical Tendencies of Modern Democracy*, 2nd ed. (1968; repr., New York: Free Press, 1962).
9. Andrew J. Nathan and Tianjian Shi, "Cultural Requisites for Democracy in China: Findings from a Survey," *Daedalus* 122, no. 2 (1993): 95–123.
10. Modernization theory and its implications for contemporary China is a topic that deserves a considered, separate theoretical treatment of its own with additional data that is beyond the scope of this current project.
11. That does not mean they do not exist, of course. In other work, I have expounded on the challenges of conducting this kind of "sensitive" research. See Anthony J. Spires, "Contingent Symbiosis and Civil Society in an Authoritarian State: Understanding the Survival of China's Grassroots NGOs," *American Journal of Sociology* 117, no. 1 (July 2011): 1–45, https://doi.org/10.1086/660741.

APPENDIX: SOME REFLECTIONS ON FIELDWORK, RE-PRESENTATION, AND ETHICS

1. Anthony J. Spires, "Contingent Symbiosis and Civil Society in an Authoritarian State: Understanding the Survival of China's Grassroots NGOs," *American Journal of Sociology* 117, no. 1 (July 2011): 1–45.
2. The role of gender and gendered dynamics is, at this point, woefully understudied in research on Chinese civil society. I hope that others can take up this task in the future, however, because surely many things are going on here that would enhance our understanding of a number of phenomena.

REFERENCES

Adorno, Theodor W., Else Frenkel-Brunswik, Daniel J. Levinson, and R. Nevitt Sanford. *The Authoritarian Personality*. New York: Norton, 1982.

Aksartova, Sada. "Promoting Civil Society or Diffusing NGOs? U.S. Donors in the Former Soviet Union." In *Globalization, Philanthropy, and Civil Society: Projecting Institutional Logics Abroad*, ed. David C. Hammack and Steven Heydemann, 160–91. Bloomington: Indiana University Press, 2009.

Alagappa, Muthiah. "Civil Society and Political Change: An Analytical Framework." In *Civil Society and Political Change in Asia: Expanding and Contracting Democratic Space*, ed. Muthiah Alagappa, 25–60. Stanford, CA: Stanford University Press, 2004.

Alexander, Damon Timothy, Jo Barraket, Jenny M. Lewis, and Mark Considine. "Civic Engagement and Associationalism: The Impact of Group Membership Scope Versus Intensity of Participation." *European Sociological Review* 28, no. 1 (February 1, 2012): 43–58. https://doi.org/10.1093/esr/jcq047.

Andreas, Joel. *Disenfranchised: The Rise and Fall of Industrial Citizenship in China*. New York: Oxford University Press, 2019.

——. *Rise of the Red Engineers: The Cultural Revolution and the Origins of China's New Class*. Contemporary Issues in Asia and the Pacific. Stanford, CA: Stanford University Press, 2009.

Andrews, Kenneth T., Marshall Ganz, Matthew Baggetta, Hahrie Han, and Chaeyoon Lim. "Leadership, Membership, and Voice: Civic Associations That Work." *American Journal of Sociology* 115, no. 4 (January 2010): 1191–242. https://doi.org/10.1086/649060.

Anonymous. "Xuexiao fa tongzhi yaoqiu gaozhongsheng 100% zhuce wei zhiyuanzhe zao tucao [School Issues Notice Requiring 100 percent of High School Students to Register as Volunteers, Meets with Anger]." *Zhongguo Jingjiwang [China Economic Net]*, April 9, 2014. http://big5.ce.cn/gate/big5/edu.ce.cn/xw/201404/09/t20140409_1533986.shtml.

——. "Qingnian zhiyuanzhe xingdong 20 nian zhuce zhiyuanzhe chao 4000 wan" [20 Years of the Youth Volunteer Movement: Registered Volunteers Exceed 40 Million]. *Renmin Ribao [People's Daily]*, December 3, 2013.

Aspinall, Edward. "Indonesia: Transformation of Civil Society and Democratic Break-through." In *Civil Society and Political Change in Asia: Expanding and Contracting Democratic Space*, ed. Muthiah Alagappa, 61–96. Stanford, CA: Stanford University Press, 2004.

Bandura, Albert. "Perceived Self-Efficacy in Cognitive Development and Functioning." *Educational Psychologist* 28, no. 2 (1993): 117–48.

Béja, Jean-Philippe, Hualing Fu, and Eva Pils. *Liu Xiaobo, Charter 08, and the Challenges of Political Reform in China*. Hong Kong: Hong Kong University Press, 2012. http://site.ebrary.com/id/10597160.

Berman, Sheri. "Civil Society and the Collapse of the Weimar Republic." *World Politics* 49, no. 3 (April 1, 1997): 401–29.

Bernstein, Thomas P. "Village Democracy and Its Limits." *Asien* 99 (2006): 29–41.

Bian, Yanjie. "Guanxi and the Allocation of Urban Jobs in China." *China Quarterly* 140 (1994): 971–99. https://doi.org/10.1017/S0305741000052863.

Birtles, Bill. "Fan Bingbing: Missing Chinese Actress Not 'Socially Responsible,' Report Says." *ABC News*, September 12, 2018. http://www.abc.net.au/news/2018-09-12/report-says-chinese-star-fan-bingbing-not-socially-responsible/10234304.

Blee, Kathleen M. *Democracy in the Making: How Activist Groups Form*. New York: Oxford University Press, 2012.

Boesche, Roger. *Tocqueville's Road Map: Methodology, Liberalism, Revolution, and Despotism*. Lanham, MD: Lexington, 2008.

Bräuer, Stephanie. "Becoming Public: Tactical Innovation in the Beijing Anti-Domestic Violence Movement." *Voluntas: International Journal of Voluntary and Nonprofit Organizations* 27, no. 5 (October 1, 2016): 2106–30. https://doi.org/10.1007/s11266-015-9610-2.

Brødsgaard, Kjeld Erik, and Gang Chen. "China's Attempt to Professionalize Its Civil Service." EAI Background Brief. Singapore: East Asian Institute, National University of Singapore, December 16, 2009. https://research.nus.edu.sg/eai/wp-content/uploads/sites/2/2017/11/BB494.pdf.

Brook, Timothy, and B. Michael Frolic. *Civil Society in China*. Armonk, NY: M.E. Sharpe, 1997.

Brownlee, Jason. "Portents of Pluralism: How Hybrid Regimes Affect Democratic Transitions." *American Journal of Political Science* 53, no. 3 (2009): 515–32.

Butterfield, Rya. "Rhetorical Forms of Symbolic Labor: The Evolution of Iconic Representations in China's Model Worker Awards." *Rhetoric and Public Affairs* 15, no. 1 (2012): 95–125.

Calhoun, Craig J. *Neither Gods nor Emperors: Students and the Struggle for Democracy in China*. 1st pbk. print. Asian Studies Sociology. Berkeley: University of California Press, 1997.

Carrigan, Tim, Bob Connell, and John Lee. "Toward a New Sociology of Masculinity." *Theory and Society* 14, no. 5 (September 1985): 551–604. https://doi.org/10.1007/BF00160017.

Central Committee of the China Communist Youth League. "Zhongguo qingnian zhiyuanzhe xingdong fazhan guihua (2014–2018)." [China Youth Volunteer Action Development Plan 2014-2018] December 2, 2013. http://news.youth.cn/gn/201312/t20131202_4315922.htm.

——. Zhongguo zhuce zhiyuanzhe guanli banfa. [Management Methods for the Registration of Chinese Volunteers] 2006. http://www.ccyl.org.cn/notice/200612/t20061224_12206.htm.

Chamberlain, Heath B. "On the Search for Civil Society in China." *Modern China* 19, no. 2 (April 1, 1993): 199–215. https://doi.org/10.2307/189380.

Chan, Anita. *Children of Mao: Personality Development and Political Activism in the Red Guard Generation*. London: Macmillan, 1985.

Chao, Linda, and Ramon H. Myers. "The First Chinese Democracy: Political Development of the Republic of China on Taiwan, 1986–1994." *Asian Survey* 34, no. 3 (March 1994): 213–30. https://doi.org/10.2307/2644981.

China Communist Youth League Beijing Committee. "Beijing gongqingtuan 2013 nian gongzuo yaodian." [Beijing Communist Youth League Important Work Points for 2013] March 6, 2013. http://www.bjyouth.gov.cn/zdgz/102285.shtml.

——. "Beijing gongqingtuan 2015 nian gongzuo yaodian." [Beijing Communist Youth League Important Work Points for 2015] September 17, 2015. http://www.bjyouth.gov.cn/zdgz/716787.shtml.

Chong, Gladys Pak Lei. "Volunteers as the 'New' Model Citizens: Governing Citizens Through Soft Power." *China Information* 25, no. 1 (March 1, 2011): 33–59. https://doi.org/10.1177/0920203X10393212.

Chu, Yun-han. "China and East Asian Democracy: The Taiwan Factor." *Journal of Democracy* 23, no. 1 (2012): 42–56. https://doi.org/10.1353/jod.2012.0011.

Clary, E. Gil, Mark Snyder, Robert D. Ridge, John Copeland, Arthur A. Stukas, Julie Haugen, and Peter Miene. "Understanding and Assessing the Motivations of Volunteers: A Functional Approach." *Journal of Personality and Social Psychology* 74, no. 6 (1998): 1516–30.

Cohen, Joshua, and Joel Rogers. *Associations and Democracy*. London: Verso, 1995.

Connell, R. W. *Gender and Power: Society, the Person and Sexual Politics*. Sydney: Allen and Unwin, 1987.

Connell, R. W., and James W. Messerschmidt. "Hegemonic Masculinity: Rethinking the Concept." *Gender and Society* 19, no. 6 (December 2005): 829–59. https://doi.org/10.1177/0891243205278639.

Crotty, Jo, and Sergej Ljubownikow. "Creating Organisational Strength from Operationalising Restrictions: Welfare Non-Profit Organisations in the Russian Federation." *Voluntas: International Journal of Voluntary and Nonprofit Organizations* 31 (September 15, 2020): 1148–58. https://doi.org/10.1007/s11266-020-00271-0.

Dahl, Robert Alan. *On Democracy*. Yale Nota Bene Book. New Haven, CT: Yale University Press, 2000.

Dai, Jingyun, and Anthony J. Spires. "Advocacy in an Authoritarian State: How Grassroots Environmental NGOs Influence Local Governments in China." *China Journal* 79 (January 2018): 62–83. https://doi.org/10.1086/693440.

Davis, Deborah, ed. *The Consumer Revolution in Urban China*. Berkeley: University of California Press, 2000.

Dekker, Paul, and Andries Van den Broek. "Civil Society in Comparative Perspective: Involvement in Voluntary Associations in North America and Western Europe." *Voluntas: International Journal of Voluntary and Nonprofit Organizations* 9, no. 1 (1998): 11–38.

Di Palma, Giuseppe. *To Craft Democracies: An Essay on Democratic Transitions*. Berkeley: University of California Press, 1990.

Diamond, Larry Jay. *Developing Democracy: Toward Consolidation*. Baltimore: Johns Hopkins University Press, 1999.

——. *The Spirit of Democracy: The Struggle to Build Free Societies Throughout the World*. 1st Holt pbk. ed. New York: Holt, 2009.

Diamond, Larry Jay, and Marc F. Plattner. "Introduction." In *Electoral Systems and Democracy*, ed. Larry Jay Diamond and Marc F. Plattner, ix–xxvi. A Journal of Democracy Book. Baltimore: Johns Hopkins University Press, 2006.

Dickson, Bruce J. *The Dictator's Dilemma: The Chinese Communist Party's Strategy for Survival*. New York: Oxford University Press, 2016.

DiMaggio, Paul J., and Walter W. Powell. "The Iron Cage Revisited: Institutional Isomorphism and Collective Rationality in Organizational Fields." *American Sociological Review* 48, no. 2 (April 1983): 147. https://doi.org/10.2307/2095101.

Economy, Elizabeth. *The River Runs Black: The Environmental Challenge to China's Future*. Ithaca, NY: Cornell University Press, 2004.

Einfeld, Aaron, and Denise Collins. "The Relationships Between Service-Learning, Social Justice, Multicultural Competence, and Civic Engagement." *Journal of College Student Development* 49, no. 2 (2008): 95–109. https://doi.org/10.1353/csd.2008.0017.

Elbayar, Kareem. "NGO Laws in Selected Arab States." *International Journal of Non-Profit Law* 7, no. 4 (2005): 3–27.

Eliasoph, Nina. *Avoiding Politics: How Americans Produce Apathy in Everyday Life*. Cambridge: Cambridge University Press, 1998. https://doi.org/10.1017/CBO9780511583391.

——. *Making Volunteers: Civic Life After Welfare's End*. Princeton, NJ: Princeton University Press, 2011.

Fan, Yun. "Activists in Political Environment: A Microfoundational Study of Social Movements in Taiwan's Democratic Transition." PhD diss., Yale University, 2000.

——. "Taiwan: No Civil Society, No Democracy." In *Civil Society and Political Change in Asia: Expanding and Contracting Democratic Space*, ed. Muthiah Alagappa, 164–90. Stanford, CA: Stanford University Press, 2004.

Fang, Jue. "A Program for Democratic Reform." *Journal of Democracy* 9, no. 4 (1998): 9–19. https://doi.org/10.1353/jod.1998.0064.

Farid, May. "Advocacy in Action: China's Grassroots NGOs as Catalysts for Policy Innovation." *Studies in Comparative International Development* 54, no. 4 (December 2019): 528–49. https://doi.org/10.1007/s12116-019-09292-3.

Fei, Xiaotong. *From the Soil, the Foundations of Chinese Society: A Translation of Fei Xiaotong's Xiangtu Zhongguo, with an Introduction and Epilogue*. Trans. Gary G. Hamilton and Zheng Wang. Berkeley: University of California Press, 1992.

Feldman, Shelley. "Paradoxes of Institutionalisation: The Depoliticisation of Bangladeshi NGOs." *Development in Practice* 13, no. 1 (February 1, 2003): 5–26. https://doi.org/10.1080/0961452022000037955.

Fewsmith, Joseph. "Balances, Norms and Institutions: Why Elite Politics in the CCP Have Not Institutionalized." *China Quarterly* 248 (2021): 265–82. https://doi.org/10.1017/S0305741021000783.

Fleischer, Friederike. "Technology of Self, Technology of Power: Volunteering as Encounter in Guangzhou, China." *Ethnos* 76, no. 3 (September 2011): 300–325. https://doi.org/10.1080/00141844.2011.565126.

Foley, Michael W., and Bob Edwards. "The Paradox of Civil Society." *Journal of Democracy* 7, no. 3 (1996): 38–52. https://doi.org/10.1353/jod.1996.0048.

Foster, Kenneth W. "Associations in the Embrace of an Authoritarian State: State Domination of Society?" *Studies in Comparative International Development* 35, no. 4 (December 1, 2001): 84–109. https://doi.org/10.1007/BF02732709.

Frantz, Erica. *Authoritarianism: What Everyone Needs to Know*. New York: Oxford University Press, 2018.

Friedman, Eli. *Insurgency Trap: Labor Politics in Postsocialist China*. Ithaca, NY: Cornell University Press, 2014.

Froissart, Chloe. "Using the Law as a 'Harmonious Weapon': The Ambiguities of Legal Activism in Favour of Migrant Workers in China." *Journal of Civil Society* 10, no. 3 (July 3, 2014): 255–72. https://doi.org/10.1080/17448689.2014.941086.

Fu, Diana. "Fragmented Control: Governing Contentious Labor Organizations in China." *Governance* 30, no. 3 (July 2017): 445–62. https://doi.org/10.1111/gove.12248.

——. *Mobilizing Without the Masses: Control and Contention in China*. Cambridge: Cambridge University Press, 2017.

Fu, Diana, and Greg Distelhorst. "Grassroots Participation and Repression Under Hu Jintao and Xi Jinping." *China Journal* 70, no. 1 (October 30, 2017): 100–122. https://doi.org/10.1086/694299.

Fung, Archon. "Associations and Democracy: Between Theories, Hopes, and Realities." *Annual Review of Sociology* 29 (December 31, 2003): 515–39. https://doi.org/10.2307/30036978.

Gallagher, Mary. "China: The Limits of Civil Society in a Late Leninist State." In *Civil Society and Political Change in Asia: Expanding and Contracting Democratic Space*, ed. Muthiah Alagappa, 419–52. Stanford, CA: Stanford University Press, 2004.

Gallagher, Mary, and Blake Miller. "Who Not What: The Logic of China's Information Control Strategy." *China Quarterly* 248 (2021): 1011–36. https://doi.org/10.1017/S0305741021000345.

Gan, Yumei, Christian Greiffenhagen, and Christian Licoppe. "Orchestrated Openings in Video Calls: Getting Young Left-Behind Children to Greet Their Migrant Parents." *Journal of Pragmatics* 170 (December 2020): 364–80. https://doi.org/10.1016/j.pragma.2020.09.022.

Glasius, Marlies. "What Authoritarianism Is . . . and Is Not: A Practice Perspective." *International Affairs* 94, no. 3 (May 1, 2018): 515–33. https://doi.org/10.1093/ia/iiy060.

Gold, Thomas B. "Tiananmen and Beyond: The Resurgence of Civil Society in China." *Journal of Democracy* 1, no. 1 (1990): 18–31.

——. "Youth and the State." *China Quarterly* 127 (September 1, 1991): 594–612. https://doi.org/10.2307/654678.

Gong, Huihui, Haiyan Jiang, and Joe C. B. Leung. "The Changing Relationship Between the Chinese Government and Non-Governmental Organisations in Social Service Delivery: Approaching Partnership?" *Asia Pacific Journal of Social Work and Development* 29, no. 2 (April 3, 2019): 120–32. https://doi.org/10.1080/02185385.2018.1525762.

Gow, Michael. "The Core Socialist Values of the Chinese Dream: Towards a Chinese Integral State." *Critical Asian Studies* 49, no. 1 (January 2, 2017): 92–116. https://doi.org/10.1080/14672715.2016.1263803.

Gramsci, Antonio. *Selections from the Prison Notebooks of Antonio Gramsci*. Reprint, London: Lawrence & Wishart, 2005.

Grieder, Jerome B. *Intellectuals and the State in Modern China: A Narrative History*. New York: New York Free Press, 1981.

Guangdong People's Congress. Guangdongsheng zhiyuan fuwu tiaoli.[Guangdong Province Volunteer Service Regulations] 2010. http://www.gdzyz.cn/zcfg/zcfglist!zcfgShow.do?districtId=b0dc9771d14211e18718000aebf5352e&headType=shouye&pageNo=17.

Guo, Chao, and Weijun Lai. "Community Foundations in China: In Search of Identity?" *Voluntas: International Journal of Voluntary and Nonprofit Organizations* 30, no. 4 (August 1, 2019): 647–63. https://doi.org/10.1007/s11266-017-9932-3.

Hagström, Linus, and Astrid H. M. Nordin. "China's 'Politics of Harmony' and the Quest for Soft Power in International Politics." *International Studies Review* 22, no. 3 (September 1, 2020): 507–25. https://doi.org/10.1093/isr/viz023.

Hall, Stuart. "Introductory Essay: Reading Gramsci." In *Gramsci's Political Thought: An Introduction*, by Roger Simon, 7–10. London: Lawrence & Wishart, 2005.

——. "Postscript: Gramsci and Us." In *Gramsci's Political Thought: An Introduction*, by Roger Simon, 114–30. London: Lawrence & Wishart, 2005.

Hansen, Mette Halskov. *Educating the Chinese Individual: Life in a Rural Boarding School.* Seattle: University of Washington Press, 2015.

——. "Learning to Organize and to Be Organized: Student Cadres in a Chinese Rural Boarding School." In *Organizing Rural China—Rural China Organizing: Rural China Organizing*, ed. Ane Bislev and Stig Thogersen, 107–19. Lanham, MD: Lexington, 2012.

Havel, Václav. "The Power of the Powerless." Trans. Paul Wilson, 1978. https://hac.bard.edu/amor-mundi/the-power-of-the-powerless-vaclav-havel-2011-12-23. Accessed May 20, 2024.

He, Baogang. "Democratisation: Antidemocratic and Democratic Elements in the Political Culture of China." *Australian Journal of Political Science* 27, no. 1 (March 1992): 120–36. https://doi.org/10.1080/00323269208402185.

He, Baogang, and Mark E. Warren. "Authoritarian Deliberation: The Deliberative Turn in Chinese Political Development." *Perspectives on Politics* 9, no. 2 (June 2011): 269–89. https://doi.org/10.1017/S1537592711000892.

Henderson, C. R. "The Place and Functions of Voluntary Associations." *American Journal of Sociology* 1, no. 3 (1895): 327–34.

Hildebrandt, Timothy. "The Political Economy of Social Organization Registration in China." *China Quarterly* 208 (2011): 970–89. https://doi.org/10.1017/S0305741011001093.

——. *Social Organizations and the Authoritarian State in China.* Cambridge: Cambridge University Press, 2013.

Hill, Joshua. *Voting as a Rite: A History of Elections in Modern China.* Harvard East Asian Monographs 417. Cambridge, MA: Harvard University Asia Center, 2019.

Hooper, Melissa. "Russia's Bad Example." Washington, DC: Free Russia Foundation/Human Rights First, February 2016. http://www.4freerussia.org/wp-content/uploads/2016/03/Russias-Bad-Example.pdf.

Howard, Marc Morjé, and Leah Gilbert. "A Cross-National Comparison of the Internal Effects of Participation in Voluntary Organizations." *Political Studies* 56, no. 1 (March 2008): 12–32. https://doi.org/10.1111/j.1467-9248.2007.00715.x.

Howell, Jude. "Shall We Dance? Welfarist Incorporation and the Politics of State–Labour NGO Relations." *China Quarterly* 223 (September 2015): 702–23. https://doi.org/10.1017/S0305741015001174.

Hsu, Carolyn. "Beyond Civil Society: An Organizational Perspective on State–NGO Relations in the People's Republic of China." *Journal of Civil Society* 6, no. 3 (2010): 259–77. https://doi.org/10.1080/17448689.2010.528949.

Hsu, Szu-chien, and Muyi Chou. "Cellularized Civil Society: Public Participation in Community Governance." In *Evolutionary Governance in China: State-Society Relations Under Authoritarianism*, ed. Szu-chien Hsu, Kellee S. Tsai, and Chun-chih Chang, 98–128. Harvard Contemporary China Series. Cambridge, MA: Harvard University Press, 2021.

Hu, Jintao. "Speech by Chinese President Hu Jintao at Yale University." April 21, 2006, New Haven, CT, 2006. http://ph.china-embassy.org/eng/xwdt/t259486.htm.

Huang, Ke-hsien. "Governing an 'Undesirable' Religion: Shifting Christian Church-State Interactions in Post-Mao China." In *Evolutionary Governance in China: State-Society Relations Under Authoritarianism*, ed. Szu-chien Hsu, Kellee S. Tsai, and Chun-chih Chang, 362–86. Harvard Contemporary China Series. Cambridge, MA: Harvard University Press, 2021.

Huang, Philip C. C. "'Public Sphere'/'Civil Society' in China?: The Third Realm Between State and Society." *Modern China* 19, no. 2 (April 1, 1993): 216–40. https://doi.org/10.2307/189381.

Hustinx, Lesley, and Frans Lammertyn. "Collective and Reflexive Styles of Volunteering: A Sociological Modernization Perspective." *Voluntas: International Journal of Voluntary and Nonprofit Organizations* 14, no. 2 (June 2003): 167–87.

Ishkanian, Armine. "Self-Determined Citizens? New Forms of Civic Activism and Citizenship in Armenia." *Europe-Asia Studies* 67, no. 8 (September 14, 2015): 1203–27. https://doi.org/10.1080/09668136.2015.1074981.

Jad, Islah. "NGOs: Between Buzzwords and Social Movements." *Development in Practice* 17, no. 4–5 (August 1, 2007): 622–29. https://doi.org/10.1080/09614520701469781.

Katirai, Negar. "NGO Regulations in Iran." *International Journal of Not-for-Profit Law* 7, no. 4 (2005): 28.

Kaufman, Jason Andrew. *For the Common Good? American Civic Life and the Golden Age of Fraternity*. New York: Oxford University Press, 2002.

Keech-Marx, Samantha. "Airing Dirty Laundry in Public: Anti-Domestic Violence Activism in Beijing." In *Associations and the Chinese State: Contested Spaces*, ed. Jonathan Unger, 175–99. Armonk, NY: M.E. Sharpe, 2008.

Kelliher, Daniel. "Keeping Democracy Safe from the Masses: Intellectuals and Elitism in the Chinese Protest Movement." *Comparative Politics* 25, no. 4 (July 1993): 379–96. https://doi.org/10.2307/422032.

Kellogg, Thomas E. "Western Funding for Rule of Law Initiatives in China." *China Perspectives* 2012, no. 3 (September 2012): 53–59.

Kennedy, John James, and Dan Chen. "Election Reform from the Middle and at the Margins." In *Local Governance Innovation in China: Experimentation, Diffusion, and Defiance*, ed. Jessica C. Teets and William Hurst, 154–73. London: Routledge, 2014.

Kim, Sunhyuk. "South Korea: Confrontational Legacy and Democratic Contributions." In *Civil Society and Political Change in Asia: Expanding and Contracting Democratic Space*, ed. Muthiah Alagappa, 138–63. Stanford, CA: Stanford University Press, 2004.

Kipnis, Andrew B. "Introduction: Chinese Modernity and the Individual Psyche." In *Chinese Modernity and the Individual Psyche*, ed. Andrew B. Kipnis, 1–16. New York: Palgrave Macmillan, 2012. https://doi.org/10.1057/9781137268969_1.

——. "Suzhi: A Keyword Approach." *China Quarterly* 186 (June 2006): 295–313. https://doi.org/10.1017/S0305741006000166.

Laclau, Ernesto, and Chantal Mouffe. "Socialist Strategy: Where Next?" *Marxism Today* 25 (1981): 17–22.

Lai, Weijun, and Anthony J. Spires. "Marketization and Its Discontents: Unveiling the Impacts of Foundation-Led Venture Philanthropy on Grassroots NGOs in China." *China Quarterly* 245 (2021): 72–93. https://doi.org/10.1017/S0305741020000193.

Lai, Weijun, Jiangang Zhu, Lin Tao, and Anthony J. Spires. "Bounded by the State: Government Priorities and the Development of Private Philanthropic Foundations in China." *China Quarterly* 224 (December 2015): 1083–92. https://doi.org/10.1017/S030574101500123X.

Lai, Zhen. "2008 nian beijing aoyunhui zhiyuanzhe renshu bi jihua zengjia jin 5000" [The Number of Volunteers for the 2008 Beijing Olympics Exceeded Plans by Almost 5000 People]. July 16, 2008. http://www.gov.cn/jrzg/2008-07/16/content_1047053.htm.

Latham, Kevin. "Media, the Olympics and the Search for the 'Real China.'" *China Quarterly* 197 (March 2009): 25–43. https://doi.org/10.1017/S0305741009000022.

Leib, Ethan J., and Baogang He, eds. *The Search for Deliberative Democracy in China*. Basingstoke: Palgrave Macmillan, 2006.

Leibold, James. "Blogging Alone: China, the Internet, and the Democratic Illusion?" *Journal of Asian Studies* 70, no. 4 (2011): 1023–41. https://doi.org/10.1017/S0021911811001550.

Levy, Katja, and Knut Benjamin Pissler. *Charity with Chinese Characteristics: Chinese Charitable Foundations Between the Party-State and Society*. Elgar Studies in Law and Society. Cheltenham: Edward Elgar, 2020.

Liao, Weihua. "Xizang chutai zhiyuan fuwu tiaoli zhaolu gongwuyuan youxian luyong zhiyuanzhe" [Tibet Releases Volunteer Service Regulations: Volunteers Get Priority for Civil Servant Jobs]. *Fazhi Ribao* [*Legal Daily*], January 24, 2015. http://epaper.legaldaily.com.cn/fzrb/content/20150124/Article03006GN.htm.

Lin, Delia. *Civilising Citizens in Post-Mao China: Understanding the Rhetoric of Suzhi*. Routledge Contemporary China Series 169. New York: Routledge, 2017.

Linz, Juan J. "An Authoritarian Regime: The Case of Spain." In *Mass Politics: Studies in Political Sociology*, ed. Erik Allard and Stein Rokkan, 251–83, 374–81. New York: Free Press, 1964.

Linz, Juan J., and Alfred C. Stepan. *Problems of Democratic Transition and Consolidation: Southern Europe, South America, and Post-Communist Europe*. Baltimore: Johns Hopkins University Press, 1996.

Lipset, Seymour Martin. "The Social Requisites of Democracy Revisited: 1993 Presidential Address." *American Sociological Review* 59, no. 1 (1994): 1–22. https://doi.org/10.2307/2096130.

Liu, Weitao. "Zaizhi 2014 niandi quanguo gong you gonqingtuan 8821.9 wan ming." [At the End of 2014 the Nation Had a Total of 88,219,000 Communist Youth League Members] *People's Daily* [*Renmin Ribao*], May 4, 2015. http://paper.people.com.cn/rmrb/html/2015-05/04/nw.D110000renmrb_20150504_5-04.htm.

Luova, Outi. "Community Volunteers' Associations in Contemporary Tianjin: Multipurpose Partners of the Party-State." *Journal of Contemporary China* 20, no. 72 (November 2011): 773–94. https://doi.org/10.1080/10670564.2011.604500.

——. "Divergent Trajectories Among Chinese Community Volunteer Associations and Urban Governance: Comparing Four Districts in Tianjin." *Journal of Comparative Asian Development* 12, no. 3 (December 2013): 443–64. https://doi.org/10.1080/15339114.2013.863563.

Ma, Qiusha. "The Governance of NGOs in China Since 1978: How Much Autonomy?" *Nonprofit and Voluntary Sector Quarterly* 31, no. 3 (September 1, 2002): 305–28. https://doi.org/10.1177/0899764002313001.

Madsen, Richard. *Morality and Power in a Chinese Village*. Berkeley: University of California Press, 1986.

——. "The Public Sphere, Civil Society and Moral Community: A Research Agenda for Contemporary China Studies." *Modern China* 19, no. 2 (April 1, 1993): 183–98. https://doi.org/10.2307/189379.

Maerz, Seraphine F. "Simulating Pluralism: The Language of Democracy in Hegemonic Authoritarianism." *Political Research Exchange* 1, no. 1 (January 1, 2019): 1–23. https://doi.org/10.1080/2474736X.2019.1605834.

Mansbridge, Jane J. *Beyond Adversary Democracy.* Chicago, IL: University of Chicago Press, 1980.

Mao, Yu-shih. "Liberalism, Equal Status, and Human Rights." Trans. Shi Heping. *Journal of Democracy* 9, no. 4 (1998): 20–23. https://doi.org/10.1353/jod.1998.0071.

Martens, Kerstin. "Mission Impossible? Defining Nongovernmental Organizations." *Voluntas: International Journal of Voluntary and Nonprofit Organizations* 13, no. 3 (September 1, 2002): 271–85. https://doi.org/10.1023/A:1020341526691.

Merriam-Webster's Collegiate Dictionary. 10th ed. Springfield, MA: Merriam-Webster, 1997.

Michels, Robert. *Political Parties: A Sociological Study of the Oligarchical Tendencies of Modern Democracy.* 2nd ed. 1968. Reprint, New York: Free Press, 1962.

Milwertz, Cecilia, and Fengxian Wang. "Masculine Modernity Trumps Feminine Tradition: A Gendered Capacity-Building Operation in China." *Gender, Technology and Development* 17, no. 3 (November 1, 2013): 259–80. https://doi.org/10.1177/0971852413498731.

Mueller-Hirth, Natascha. "South African NGOs and the Public Sphere: Between Popular Movements and Partnerships for Development." *Social Dynamics* 35, no. 2 (September 1, 2009): 423–35. https://doi.org/10.1080/02533950903076568.

Nathan, Andrew J. "Authoritarian Resilience." *Journal of Democracy* 14, no. 1 (2003): 6–17. https://doi.org/10.1353/jod.2003.0019.

——. *China's Crisis: Dilemmas of Reform and Prospects for Democracy.* Studies of the East Asian Institute. New York: Columbia University Press, 1990.

——. *Chinese Democracy.* New York: Knopf, 1985.

——. "Chinese Democracy: The Lessons of Failure." *Journal of Contemporary China* 2, no. 4 (September 1993): 3–13. https://doi.org/10.1080/10670569308724182.

Nathan, Andrew J., and Tianjian Shi. "Cultural Requisites for Democracy in China: Findings from a Survey." *Daedalus* 122, no. 2 (1993): 95–123.

Nee, Victor. "The Emergence of a Market Society: Changing Mechanisms of Stratification in China." *American Journal of Sociology* 101, no. 4 (January 1996): 908–49. https://doi.org/10.1086/230784.

Ning, Rundong, and David A. Palmer. "Ethics of the Heart: Moral Breakdown and the Aporia of Chinese Volunteers." *Current Anthropology* 61, no. 4 (August 1, 2020): 395–417. https://doi.org/10.1086/710217.

O'Brien, Kevin J. "Rightful Resistance." *World Politics* 49, no. 1 (October 1, 1996): 31–55. https://doi.org/10.2307/25053988.

Ogawa, Akihiro. "Invited by the State: Institutionalizing Volunteer Subjectivity in Contemporary Japan." *Asian Anthropology* 3 (2004): 71–96.

Ogden, Suzanne. *Inklings of Democracy in China.* Cambridge, MA: Harvard University Asia Center, 2002.

"Outline of the People's Republic of China 14th Five-Year Plan for National Economic and Social Development and Long-Range Objectives for 2035." Center for Security and Emerging Technology, 2021. https://cset.georgetown.edu/wp-content/uploads/t0284_14th_Five_Year_Plan_EN.pdf.

Painter, Matthew A., and Pamela Paxton. "Checkbooks in the Heartland: Change Over Time in Voluntary Association Membership." *Sociological Forum* 29, no. 2 (June 2014): 408–28. https://doi.org/10.1111/socf.12090.

Pattie, Charles, Patrick Seyd, and Paul Whiteley. "Citizenship and Civic Engagement: Attitudes and Behaviour in Britain." *Political Studies* 51, no. 3 (October 2003): 443–68. https://doi.org/10.1111/1467-9248.00435.

Paxton, Pamela. "Social Capital and Democracy: An Interdependent Relationship." *American Sociological Review* 67, no. 2 (April 1, 2002): 254–77. https://doi.org/10.2307/3088895.

Perry, Elizabeth J. "The Populist Dream of Chinese Democracy." *Journal of Asian Studies* 74, no. 4 (November 2015): 903–15. https://doi.org/10.1017/S002191181500114X.

Pils, Eva. "The Party's Turn to Public Repression: An Analysis of the '709' Crackdown on Human Rights Lawyers in China." *China Law and Society Review* 3, no. 1 (August 17, 2018): 1–48. https://doi.org/10.1163/25427466-00301001.

Putnam, Robert D. *Bowling Alone: The Collapse and Revival of American Community.* New York: Simon & Schuster, 2000.

Putnam, Robert D., Robert Leonardi, and Raffaella Y. Nanetti. *Making Democracy Work: Civic Traditions in Modern Italy.* Princeton, NJ: Princeton University Press, 1994.

Pye, Lucian W. *Asian Power and Politics: The Cultural Dimensions of Authority.* Cambridge, MA: Belknap Press, 1985.

——. "Political Culture Revisited." *Political Psychology* 12, no. 3 (September 1991): 487. https://doi.org/10.2307/3791758.

——. *The Spirit of Chinese Politics.* New ed. Cambridge, MA: Harvard University Press, 1992.

——. *The Spirit of Chinese Politics: A Psychocultural Study of the Authority Crisis in Political Development.* Cambridge, MA: MIT Press, 1968.

Rankin, Mary Backus. "Some Observations on a Chinese Public Sphere." *Modern China* 19, no. 2 (April 1, 1993): 158–82. https://doi.org/10.2307/189378.

Rhomberg, Chris. *No There There: Race, Class, and Political Community in Oakland.* Berkeley: University of California Press, 2007.

Ringen, Stein. *The Perfect Dictatorship: China in the 21st Century.* Hong Kong: Hong Kong University Press, 2016.

Rolandsen, Unn Målfrid H. "A Collective of Their Own: Young Volunteers at the Fringes of the Party Realm." *European Journal of East Asian Studies* 7, no. 1 (March 2008): 101–29. https://doi.org/10.1163/156805808X333938.

Rosenblum, Nancy L. *Membership and Morals: The Personal Uses of Pluralism in America.* Princeton, NJ: Princeton University Press, 2018.

Rowe, William T. "The Problem of 'Civil Society' in Late Imperial China." *Modern China* 19, no. 2 (April 1, 1993): 139–57. https://doi.org/10.2307/189377.

Saich, Tony. "Negotiating the State: The Development of Social Organizations in China." *China Quarterly* 161 (2000): 124–41. https://doi.org/10.1017/S0305741000003969.

Scudder, Mary F. *Beyond Empathy and Inclusion: The Challenge of Listening in Democratic Deliberation.* New York: Oxford University Press, 2023.

Shanghai Municipal Government. "Shanghai shi zhiyuan fuwu tiaoli." [Shanghai City Volunteer Service Regulations] 2009. http://shnu.volunteer.sh.cn/LinkClick.aspx?fileticket=NLen58qwyJY%3D&tabid=12590&language=zh-CN.

Shi, Tianjian. "Cultural Values and Democracy in the People's Republic of China." *China Quarterly* 162 (2000): 540–59. https://doi.org/10.1017/S0305741000008249.

——. *Political Participation in Beijing.* Cambridge, MA: Harvard University Press, 1997.

Sidel, Mark. "Managing the Foreign: The Drive to Securitize Foreign Nonprofit and Foundation Management in China." *Voluntas: International Journal of Voluntary and Nonprofit Organizations* 30, no. 4 (August 2019): 664–77. https://doi.org/10.1007/s11266-018-9988-8.

Simon, Roger. *Gramsci's Political Thought: An Introduction.* Completely rev. London: Lawrence & Wishart, 1991.

Skocpol, Theda. "Advocates Without Members: The Recent Transformation of American Civic Life." In *Civic Engagement in American Democracy,* ed. Morris P. Fiorina and Theda Skocpol, 461–509. Washington, DC: Brookings Institution Press, 1999.

Smith, David H., Boguslawa Sardinha, Alisa Moldavanova, Hsiang-Kai Dennis DONG, Meenaz Kassam, Young-joo Lee, and Aminata Sillah. "Conducive Motivations and Psychological Influences on Volunteering." In *The Palgrave Handbook of Volunteering, Civic Participation, and Nonprofit Associations,* ed. David Horton Smith, Robert A. Stebbins, Jurgen Grotz, and Jurgen Grotz, 702–51. London: Palgrave Macmillan, 2016. https://doi.org/10.1007/978-1-137-26317-9_31.

Sombatpoonsiri, Janjira. "'Authoritarian Civil Society': How Anti-Democracy Activism Shapes Thailand's Autocracy." *Journal of Civil Society* 16, no. 4 (2020): 333–50. https://doi.org/10.1080/17448689.2020.1854940.

Spires, Anthony J. "Built on Shifting Sands: INGOs and Their Survival in China." In *Authoritarianism and Civil Society in Asia,* ed. Anthony J. Spires and Akihiro Ogawa, 218–34. New York: Routledge, 2022.

——. "Chinese Youth and Alternative Narratives of Volunteering." *China Information* 32, no. 2 (2018): 203–23. https://doi.org/10.1177/0920203X17752597.

——. "Contingent Symbiosis and Civil Society in an Authoritarian State: Understanding the Survival of China's Grassroots NGOs." *American Journal of Sociology* 117, no. 1 (July 2011): 1–45. https://doi.org/10.1086/660741.

——. "Lessons from Abroad: Foreign Influences on China's Emerging Civil Society." *China Journal* 68 (July 2012): 125–46.

——. "Regulation as Political Control: China's First Charity Law and Its Implications for Civil Society." *Nonprofit and Voluntary Sector Quarterly* 49, no. 3 (2020): 571–88. https://doi.org/10.1177/0899764019883939.

Spires, Anthony J., Tao Lin, and Kin-man Chan. "Societal Support for China's Grass-Roots NGOs: Evidence from Yunnan, Guangdong and Beijing." *China Journal* 71 (January 1, 2014): 65–90. https://doi.org/10.1086/674554.

Stalley, Phillip, and Dongning Yang. "An Emerging Environmental Movement in China?" *China Quarterly* 186 (2006): 333–56. https://doi.org/10.1017/S030574100600018X.

Stockmann, Daniela, and Mary E. Gallagher. "Remote Control: How the Media Sustain Authoritarian Rule in China." *Comparative Political Studies* 44, no. 4 (April 1, 2011): 436–67. https://doi.org/10.1177/0010414010394773.

Stolle, Dietlind. "Bowling Together, Bowling Alone: The Development of Generalized Trust in Voluntary Associations." *Political Psychology* 19, no. 3 (1998): 497–525.

Teets, Jessica C. *Civil Society Under Authoritarianism: The China Model.* New York: Cambridge University Press, 2014.

——. "Post-Earthquake Relief and Reconstruction Efforts: The Emergence of Civil Society in China?" *China Quarterly* 198 (2009): 330–47. https://doi.org/10.1017/S0305741009000332.

Teets, Jessica C., Reza Hasmath, Timothy Hildebrandt, Carolyn L. Hsu, and Jennifer Y.J. Hsu. "Volunteerism and Democratic Learning in an Authoritarian State: The Case of China." *Democratization* 29, no. 5 (July 4, 2022): 879–98. https://doi.org/10.1080/1351 0347.2021.2015334.

Tian, Fengrui, and Julia Chuang. "Depoliticizing China's Grassroots NGOs: State and Civil Society as an Institutional Field of Power." *China Quarterly* 250 (2022): 509–30. https://doi.org/10.1017/S0305741022000157.

294

REFERENCES

Tocqueville, Alexis de. *Democracy in America*. Trans. George Lawrence. New York: Harper Perennial Modern Classics, 1988.

Torpe, Lars. "Democracy and Associations in Denmark: Changing Relationships Between Individuals and Associations?" *Nonprofit and Voluntary Sector Quarterly* 32, no. 3 (September 2003): 329–43. https://doi.org/10.1177/0899764003254594.

Tsai, Wen-Hsuan, and Xingmiu Liao. "Institutional Changes, Influences and Historical Junctures in the Communist Youth League of China." *China Quarterly* 248 (2021): 161–80. https://doi.org/10.1017/S0305741021000813.

Unger, Jonathan, ed. *Associations and the Chinese State: Contested Spaces*. Contemporary China Books/Australian National University. Armonk, NY: M.E. Sharpe, 2008.

——. "Bridges: Private Business, the Chinese Government and the Rise of New Associations." *China Quarterly* 147 (1996): 795–819. https://doi.org/10.1017/S0305741000051808.

Unger, Jonathan, and Anita Chan. "China, Corporatism, and the East Asian Model." *Australian Journal of Chinese Affairs* 33 (January 1, 1995): 29–53. https://doi.org/10.2307/2950087.

Unger, Jonathan, Anita Chan, and Him Chung. "Deliberative Democracy at China's Grassroots: Case Studies of a Hidden Phenomenon." *Politics and Society* 42, no. 4 (2014): 513–35. https://doi.org/10.1177/0032329214547344.

Verba, Sidney, Kay Lehman Schlozman, and Henry E. Brady. *Voice and Equality: Civic Voluntarism in American Politics*. Cambridge, MA: Harvard University Press, 1995.

Wakeman, Frederic, Jr. "The Civil Society and Public Sphere Debate: Western Reflections on Chinese Political Culture." *Modern China* 19, no. 2 (April 1, 1993): 108–38. https://doi.org/10.2307/189376.

Wan, Yinmei. "Expansion of Chinese Higher Education Since 1998: Its Causes and Outcomes." *Asia Pacific Education Review* 7, no. 1 (2006): 19–31.

Wang, Lamei, and Judi Mesman. "Child Development in the Face of Rural-to-Urban Migration in China: A Meta-Analytic Review." *Perspectives on Psychological Science* 10, no. 6 (November 2015): 813–31. https://doi.org/10.1177/1745691615600145.

Wang, Qinghua, and Gang Guo. "Yu Keping and Chinese Intellectual Discourse on Good Governance." *China Quarterly* 224 (December 2015): 985–1005. https://doi.org/10.1017/S0305741015000855.

Warren, Mark E. *Democracy and Association*. Princeton, NJ: Princeton University Press, 2001.

White, Gordon, Jude Howell, and Xiaoyuan Shang. *In Search of Civil Society: Market Reform and Social Change in Contemporary China*. Oxford: Clarendon Press, 1996.

Wu, Fengshi. "An Emerging Group Name 'Gongyi': Ideational Collectivity in China's Civil Society." *China Review* 17, no. 2 (June 2017): 123–50.

——. "Environmental Activism in Provincial China." *Journal of Environmental Policy and Planning* 15, no. 1 (March 2013): 89–108. https://doi.org/10.1080/1523908X.2013.763634.

——. "New Partners or Old Brothers? GONGOs in Transnational Environmental Advocacy in China." *China Environmental Series*, no. 5 (2002): 45–58.

Wu, Jingrong, ed. *Ying-Han Cidian* [A Chinese-English Dictionary]. Beijing: Shangwu Yishuguan, 1989.

Xi, Jinping. "Speech at the Beijing 2022 Winter Olympics and Paralympics Review and Awards Ceremony." April 8, 2022. http://jm.china-embassy.gov.cn/eng/zgxw/202204/t20220411_10666791.htm.

Xiao, Qiang. "Wang Qishan jiaoting jilin shuji: zhe bushi xingshi ma?" [Wang Qishan Tells the Jilin Provincial Party Secretary to Stop: Isn't this Formalism?] *China Digital Times*, March 11, 2014. http://chinadigitaltimes.net/chinese/2014/03.

Xin, Ge, and Jie Huang. "Party Building in an Unlikely Place? The Adaptive Presence of the Chinese Communist Party in the Non-Governmental Organizations (NGO)." *Journal of Contemporary China* 31, no. 135 (2022): 428–44. https://doi.org/10.1080/106 70564.2021.1966901.

Xu, Bin. "Consensus Crisis and Civil Society: The Sichuan Earthquake Response and State–Society Relations." *China Journal* 71 (January 2014): 91–108. https://doi.org /10.1086/674555.

——. *The Culture of Democracy: A Sociological Approach to Civil Society*. Cultural Sociology. Medford, MA: Polity, 2022.

——. *The Politics of Compassion: The Sichuan Earthquake and Civic Engagement in China*. Stanford, CA: Stanford University Press, 2017.

Xu, Junqian. "Volunteering Not Voluntary." *China Daily*, December 1, 2011. http://www .chinadaily.com.cn/2011-12/01/content_14192894.htm.

Xu, Ying. "Chinese Communist Youth League, Political Capital and the Legitimising of Volunteering in China." *International Journal of Adolescence and Youth* 17, nos. 2–3 (June 2012): 95–112. https://doi.org/10.1080/02673843.2012.656195.

Yan, Yunxiang. "The Chinese Path to Individualization." *British Journal of Sociology* 61, no. 3 (September 14, 2010): 489–512. https://doi.org/10.1111/j.1468-4446.2010.01323.x.

——. "The Good Samaritan's New Trouble: A Study of the Changing Moral Landscape in Contemporary China." *Social Anthropology* 17, no. 1 (February 18, 2009): 9–24. https:// doi.org/10.1111/j.1469-8676.2008.00055.x.

——. "Introduction: Understanding the Rise of the Individual in China." *European Journal of East Asian Studies* 7, no. 1 (April 1, 2008): 1–9. https://doi.org/10.1163/156805808X333893.

Yang, Guobin. "Achieving Emotions in Collective Action: Emotional Processes and Movement Mobilization in the 1989 Chinese Student Movement." *Sociological Quarterly* 41, no. 4 (2000): 593–614.

——. *The Power of the Internet in China: Citizen Activism Online*. Contemporary Asia in the World. New York: Columbia University Press, 2009.

Yang, Mayfair Mei-hui. *Gifts, Favors, and Banquets: The Art of Social Relationships in China*. The Wilder House Series in Politics, History and Culture. Ithaca, NY: Cornell University Press, 1994.

——. "The Resilience of Guanxi and Its New Deployments: A Critique of Some New Guanxi Scholarship." *China Quarterly* 170 (2002): 459–76. https://doi.org/10.1017 /S000944390200027X.

Ye, Jingzhong, and Lu Pan. "Differentiated Childhoods: Impacts of Rural Labor Migration on Left-Behind Children in China." *Journal of Peasant Studies* 38, no. 2 (March 2011): 355–77. https://doi.org/10.1080/03066150.2011.559012.

Yu, Keping. *Democracy Is a Good Thing: Essays on Politics, Society and Culture in contemporary China*. Washington, DC: Brookings Institution, 2009.

——. "Zhongguo gongmin shehui yanjiu de ruogan wenti." [Several Issues in the Study of Chinese Civil Society], *Journal of the Party School of the Central Committee of the Communist Party of China* 11, no. 6 (2007): 14–22.

Yuen, Samson. "Friend or Foe? The Diminishing Space of China's Civil Society." *China Perspectives* 3 (2015): 51–56.

———. "Negotiating Service Activism in China: The Impact of NGOs' Institutional Embeddedness in the Local State." *Journal of Contemporary China* 27, no. 111 (May 4, 2018): 406–22. https://doi.org/10.1080/10670564.2018.1410976.

Zang, Xiaowei, and Nabo Chen. "How Do Rural Elites Reproduce Privileges in Post-1978 China? Local Corporatism, Informal Bargaining and Opportunistic Parasitism." *Journal of Contemporary China* 24, no. 94 (July 4, 2015): 628–43. https://doi.org/10.1080/10670564.2014.975956.

Zhang, Li, and Aihwa Ong, eds. *Privatizing China: Socialism from Afar*. Ithaca, NY: Cornell University Press, 2008.

Zhang, Naihua. "Searching for 'Authentic' NGOs: The NGO Discourse and Women's Organizations in China." In *Chinese Women Organizing: Cadres, Feminists, Muslims, Queers*, ed. Ping-Chun Hsiung, Maria Jaschok, and Cecilia Milwert, 159–79. Oxford: Berg, 2001.

Zhang, Xin, and Richard Baum. "Civil Society and the Anatomy of a Rural NGO." *China Journal* 52 (July 2004): 97–107. https://doi.org/10.2307/4127886.

Zhang, Yongling, and Jing Lin. "Volunteerism in China (I): National Policies, Student Responses, and Two Case Studies of Self-Organized Volunteer Programs: Guest Editors' Introduction to Part I." *Chinese Education and Society* 41, no. 3 (May 1, 2008): 3–13. https://doi.org/10.2753/CED1061-1932410300.

Zhejiang Province People's Congress. "Zhejiang sheng zhiyuan fuwu tiaoli" [Zhejiang Province Volunteer Service Regulations]. 2008. http://hszh.tx.gov.cn/web/zcfg/20150108/093550.html.

Zhou, Benshun. "Zou Zhongguo tese shehui guanli chuangxin zhi lu." [Taking the Road of Social Management Innovation with Chinese Characteristics] *Qiushi* 10 (2011). http://www.qstheory.cn/zxdk/2011/2011010/201105/t20110513_80501.htm.

Zhu, Yan. "Being Student Leaders or 'Ordinary' Students: Children's Emotional Experiences of Relationships with Others in a Chinese School." *Emotion, Space and Society* 40 (August 1, 2021): 100810. https://doi.org/10.1016/j.emospa.2021.100810.

Zi, Jun. "Chenglong jingshi yanlun: Zhongguoren bixu bei guan" [Jackie Chan's Shocking Statement: Chinese People Must Be Controlled]. *Kan Zhongguo* [*Vision Times*], April 20, 2009. https://www.secretchina.com/news/b5/2009/04/20/289041.html.

INDEX

activism, 6–7, 159; for human rights, *see under* rights; in NGOs, 43, 68, 215; pathways to, 83, 240; repression of, 22, 41; scholarly, 17, 27, 86, 189, 258

authoritarianism, hegemonic, 7, 32, 61, 239, 245; contests within, 53–61, *see also* counterhegemony; definition, 40–42; further research into, 247–49; in organizational culture, 6, 9, 253; in schools, 45–46; *see also* autocracy; cadre; hierarchy

autocracy, cf. democracy, 38, 126–28, 135; as ideology (*zhuanzhi*), 3, 6, 18, 56, 61, 242, 245; in practice (*laoda*), 50, 56–61, 123

benefit, public. *See* charity

bottom-up groups; 4, 6, 31, 47–48, 51, 193, 215; as civil society vanguard, 130, 166, 215, 246; cf. top-down groups, 55, 86, 98, 102, 186, 256–57; *see also* NGO, grassroots; voluntary association

cadre, 45–46, 61, 192

charity, as public welfare (*gongyi*), 169–70, 222, 234, 236, 278n16; as virtue (*cishan*), 98, 106–7, 168–69

Charity Law (2016), 50, 99, 101, 277n5

Chinese Communist Party (CCP), 5, 6, 11, 114, 162, 247; history, 16–24, 116, 173; ideology, 40, 46, 51, 116–17, 145; membership, 105, 138, 225; opposition to, 241

civic engagement, 28, 157–159, 171, 239, 248

civil society, 3–8, 11, 22–24, 66; and state relations, 47–50, 244–45; and volunteering, 97–102; cf. the West, 17, 36, 97, 110, 171, 183, 211, 241; definition, 44–45; organizations, 34, 43, 45, 49, 117, *see also* NGO; voluntary association; participants, 8–10, 13, 50–53, 62–63, 159, 247, 252; theories of, 7, 18, 31–41

class, socioeconomic, 37–40, 68, 155, 164, 182–85, 187; *see also* inequality

communication, challenges in, 67–73, 152; democratic, 65–66, 70, 90; effective (*goutong*), 11–12, 118, 135–42; in fieldwork interviews, 253–56; as information exchange, 60–61, 69; skills in, 65, 134–35, 158–59, 162–67; *see also* consensus building; language; listening

Communist Youth League (CYL), 40, 46, 54, 81, 95–96, 99–100, 121, 246, 275n24, 281ch9n6

compassion (democratic value), 26, 128, 155, 173–80
consensus building, 11–12, 20, 66, 74–80, 89, 130–52; and communication (*goutong*), 69, 135–37; and equality, 66, 137–41; obstacles to, 59–61; cf. voting, 142–45; *see also* communication
confidentiality, 257–58
conflict, avoidance, 128, 134–35, 156; in civil society, 33, 207; cf. cooperation, 73, 86; in hierarchy, 118; resolution, 131, 137, 140–43, 146, 175, 188; unresolved, 67, 136; *see also* communication
Confucianism, 16, 17, 22, 247
connection, emotional, *see* emotional tie; transactional (*guanxi*), *see* relationships
counterhegemony, 6, 7, 11, 38–40, 51, 62, 91, 245, 249; *see also* hegemony
culture, democratic. *See* democratic culture

democracy (*minzhu*), 51–52, 206, 239; history in China, 16–22; as socialist value, 51–52; as taboo word, 51–52, 85, 246, without a choice (*bei minzhu*), 212–13; *see also* voting
democratic culture, 3–7, 13, 24, 31, 36, 246; definition, 242; in the West, 14–15, 35–36, 248; cf. political culture, 24–27; in voluntary associations, 85, 153–187, 233–34
democratic habits. *See* habits, democratic
democratic values. *See* values, democratic
Deng Xiaoping, 11, 16, 22, 47, 56, 116
dignity, 21, 42, 47, 57, 62, 83–84, 114, 116, 120, 165, 167, 194, 243, 245; *see also* respect; values
dissent, 4, 21–22, 41–42, 47–48, 65, 113; stifling of, 7, 11, 12, 31, 32, 34, 48, 52, 59–61, 98, 213, 245
diversity, of opinion, 119–20, 122, 135–41, 202; of people, 161, 167–70, 175, 220, 276n1; *see also* equality; respect

education, attainment among civil society participants, 25, 68, 86, 168, 183–84, 240; as hegemonic institution, 40,

45–46, 82, 115, 124, 145; as social good, 117, 179, 239; *see also* school
election. *See* voting
emotional tie (*ganqing*), 110, 128, 139, 143, 177–78; cf. networking relationship (*guanxi*), 161; *see also* trust
empathy, 155, 173, 177–78, 180
entrepreneurship, 47, 118, 240
equality, 12–13, 34, 243; cf. hierarchy, 55, 114–23, 167–70, 219, 223–24; as shared decision-making, 64–66, 123–29, 204; as socialist value (*pingdeng*), 51–53, 117; *see also* inequality; values
ethics, in voluntary associations, *see under* values; in research, 257–58

family, cf. civil society, 64, 170, 187; obligations/pressures, 25, 132, 194, 235; strengthened ties after volunteering, 155, 178–80, 186; voluntary association as surrogate, 107; 177–78
Fei Xiaotong, 115–20, 123, 126, 275n1
freedom, of action in voluntary associations, 78, 82, 122, 195–97, 216; cf. authoritarianism, 15, 17, 42, 109, 170, 243; as socialist value (*ziyou*), 7, 21, 51, 78, 198, 241; *see also* democracy
formalism (*xingshi zhuyi*) in volunteering, 95–97, 103, 121; definition, 104; and emotional alienation, 109–112, 143, 222–23; as government-led practice, 12, 103, 108; inducements to participate, 104–109; cf. meaningfulness (*yiyi*), 107–8; as predetermined process, 109, 111, 134, 190–93, 203
Foucault, Michel, 27, 46, 101, 111

ganqing. See emotional tie
gender, 39, 56–57, 73–74, 86, 116, 247
Glasius, Marlies, 42, 56
globalization, 25, 51, 246
Gold, Thomas, 22–23, 108
GONGO (government-organized nongovernmental organization), 4, 8, 23, 43–45, 96; and authoritarianism, 23, 90, 244–53; as hierarchy, 54–61, 129, 148, 163; as state–society mediator, 98–102; *see also* NGO

gongyi. See under charity
goutong. See under communication
Gramsci, Antonio, 7, 11, 27, 32, 37–41, 45,
  62, 243, 245; *see also* counterhegemony;
  hegemony
grassroots. *See under* NGO
Guangdong, 16, 71, 99, 237, 242
guanxi. See relationship

habits, democratic, 4, 5, 7, 13, 28, 44, 90,
  130, 153–54, 182; in Tocqueville, 24, 34,
  37, 245; of volunteers, 118, 135, 148, 166,
  171, 219; *see also* law; skills
Hall, Stuart, 38, 40
hegemonic authoritarianism. *See*
  authoritarianism, hegemonic
hegemony, 6, 7, 31, 37–41, 45, 62, 245; *see
  also* Gramsci
hierarchy, 45–47, and autocracy, 50, 56–59;
  aversion to, 120–23, 129, 147, 167,
  205, 223, 272n6; as decision-making
  structure, 53–56, 152; cf. equality, 55,
  116, 129, 163; *see also* inequality
Hong Kong, and counterhegemony,
  51, 131–32, 242; culture, 18, 101; cf.
  mainland, 68, 71–73, 86–87, 262n1
Hu Jintao, 21, 49, 213; *see also* Hu–Wen
  administration
human rights. *See* rights
humility (democratic value), 89, 153, 155,
  164, 176–77, 225, 228, 248; *see also*
  values, democratic
Hu–Wen administration, 48–49

individualism, and autonomy (*zizhu*),
  47–49, 198; cf. democracy, 23, 203;
  and difference, 137; for Tocqueville,
  64–65, 170–71; as Western ideal,
  116; 187
inequality, as hierarchy, 12, 66, 114–18, 129;
  as poverty, 117, 164, 187, 234
INGO (international nongovernmental
  organization), 49, 71, 242, 277n5
institution, political, 3, 27, 182, 233,
  242; social, 31, 39, 45–46, 193;
  see also Chinese Communist Party;
  Communist Youth League;
  formalism

labor, division of, 84, 122, 134, 155–56;
  rights, 52, 58, 85–90, 240, 251
language, barriers, 86, 181–82; dialects,
  144, 164, 181–82, 254–55; formality of,
  17–18, 75, 254–55; of hierarchy,
  53–54, 89–90, 120–21, 202, 205,
  209, 214
laoda. See autocracy; leadership
law, 37, *see also* habits; mechanisms, 159,
  277n5, *see also* Charity Law; rights
  protection, *see* rights; rule of, 21, 35;
  student, 75, 77, 137, 234
leadership (*lingdao*), 17, 56–59, 82, 125;
  absence of, 13, 90, 91, 121–22; autocratic
  (*laoda*), 18, 45–46, 56–61, 89, 123; and
  equality, 123–29; idealized, 58–59, 148;
  see also autocracy
LGBT, 48, 240, 247
listening, active (*lingting*), 140–41,
  248, 255, 278n13, 278n14; problems,
  12, 57, 59, 60–61, 69–74, 127; skills,
  164–167, 220; *see also* communication;
  consensus building; hierarchy

Mao Zedong, 21, 22, 56, 61–62, 116, 126
market economy, 47, 51, 117
meaningfulness (*yiyi*), 12, 51, 96, 106–8,
  110, 135, 177, 274n29
meeting. *See* communication; consensus
  building
minzhu. See democracy

NGO (nongovernmental organization),
  4, 8, 43; communication in, 67–74,
  238; democratic culture building
  in, 41, 50–53, 86–89, 158, 207–14,
  243–44; government-organized, *see*
  GONGO; grassroots, 8, 43, 47, 48, 57,
  86, 123; 162, 188, 237; history in China,
  23, 43, 48; international, *see* INGO;
  professionalization of, 44, 52–53,
  86, 151–52, 185, 188–89; cf. voluntary
  association, 5, 44, 118–19, 123–24, 138,
  153

openness (democratic value), 84, 127, 165,
  170–73, 197–207; *see also* trust; values,
  democratic

order, as command, 53, 57, 103, 123, 143, 278n13; as harmony, 21, 46, 155, 157; as social/political system, 13, 37, 39–40, 114; *see also* autocracy; formalism; hierarchy

organization, hegemonic, *see* authoritarianism; voluntary, *see* voluntary association; *see also* INGO; GONGO; NGO

participation (*canyu*) (democratic value), 84, 118–19, 121, 139, 148–50, 196, 276n5; *see also* values, democratic

patriarchy, 50, 56–57

personal growth (*geren chengzhang*), 128, 134, 154, 157, 185–87, 278n15; opportunity for, 193, 218–19, 221; *see also* self-efficacy

perspective, shift in (*huanwei sikao*), 140, 155, 173–75, 187; *see also* tolerance

political culture. *See* democratic culture

politics, constraints on, 7, *see also* authoritarianism, autocracy, democracy; disengaged from, 36, 111, 246; reform, 11, 16, 20–22, 41, 47–48; sensitivity/risk in, 4, 65, 96, 101, 211, 215, 253, 257; systems/structures, *see* institution

power relations, 6, 40, 45–47, 66, 68–69, 115–17, 183–84; *see also* Foucault, Michel

qualitative fieldwork, 256–57

queer, *see* LGBT

relationships (*guanxi*), 107, 161; *see also* emotional tie

respect, for authority, 57, 73, 147, 209–10, 280n9; and autonomy, 78, 146; for diversity, 35, 135, 154–55, 173–75, 220; mutual, 82–83, 117, 127, 137–42, 167–70, 221–23; lack of, 57, 72, 109; as listening, 67, 72, 91, 165–66

rights, 19, 27, 47–49, 203, 247; activism, 21–22, 41, 112; labor, *see under* labor; legal protection (*weiquan*) of, 49; restrictions, 21, 177; state-controlled,

62, 276n5; for women, 43, 48, 116, 277n7

school, 45, 184, 186–87, 198, 235–36; credit/ rewards for volunteering, 102–3, 104, 111, 222, *see also* formalism; and Communist Youth League (CYL), 100, 102; as hegemonic institution, 45–6, 53, 62, 82; volunteering organized by, 107, 112, 120; as volunteering site, 9, 74–84, 95, 132–33, 160, 240

self-efficacy, 35, 176, 180–82, 186, 239

skills, communication, 65, 134–35, 162–67; democratic, 155–167, 186–87; organizing, 156–161; teamwork, 133–35, 156; *see also* habits; values, democratic

social capital. *See* empathy

Soviet Union, 37, 41

Taiwan, 15, 20–21, 25, 243

Tiananmen Square protests, 47–48, 51

Tocqueville, Alexis de, 11, 13; on civil society, 24, 31–37, 182, 251–52; on empathy, 173, 177, 245, *see also under* habits; on equality, 64–66, 170–71; influence of, 7, 90, 130, 158, 183, 241, 251–52

tolerance (democratic value), 14, 20, 34, 140–41, 174–75, 186, 242

top-down (*zishang erxia*). *See* autocracy; GONGO; hierarchy

translation, 8, 10, 67, 253–54, 256, 271n6, 278n16, 280n11

trust (democratic value), 97, 109–11, 153, 155, 164, 170–73, 252–53, 272n80; *see also* openness; values, democratic

university, student club, 62, 102–3; student union, 46, 102, 105–8, 121, 165, 191–92, 239

values, 76, 81; democratic, 6, 13–14, 35, 84, 239; as practices, 139, 148, 237; socialist, 51–52, 101, 117; of voluntary associations, 14, 76, 78–81, 137, 217–30

virtues, democratic, 35, 89, 140–41, 155, 173–77

voluntary association, 4, 5, 248; cf.
government-led volunteering, 108–
109; cf. NGO, 5, 44–45, 153; ideals/
principles, 82, 83–85; as "schools" of
democracy, 3, 31, 34, 130, 154; shared
goals in, 141–42; state antipathy to, 162,
245, *see also* Charity Law
voting, unavailable or "fake," 20, 117,
212–13, 246; in voluntary associations,
85, 131, 141, 142–45, 196, 200–213

weiquan. See rights, legal protection
welfare, public. *See* charity
women, 43, 48, 56–67, 73–74, 88, 115–16;
see also gender; patriarchy; rights

Xi Jinping, 49, 56, 111, 171
xingshi zhuyi. See formalism
Xu, Bin, 28, 96

yiyi. See meaningfulness
youth-based group, 66, 74, 153, 216,
246-7
youth-led group, 9, 23, 51, 246–7;
cf. government-led youth group,
108–109; cf. NGO-led group, 118–19;
cf. university student group,
55, 106

zhuanzhi. See autocracy
ziyou. See freedom

GPSR Authorized Representative: Easy Access System Europe, Mustamäe tee 50, 10621 Tallinn, Estonia, gpsr.requests@easproject.com

www.ingramcontent.com/pod-product-compliance
Lightning Source LLC
Chambersburg PA
CBHW032116020426
42334CB00016B/977